IIRM

With compliments

From : Vepa Kamesam, Managing Director
Institute of Insurance and Risk Management
Plot No. 38 & 39, Financial District, APSFC Building,
Gachibowli,Hyderabad - 500032
Ph : +91-40-23000005, 23002042, Fax :+91-40-23000254
Email : email@iirmworld.org.in, Website : www.iirmworld.org.in

GLOBAL
CRISIS
RECESSION
AND UNEVEN
RECOVERY

GLOBAL
CRISIS
RECESSION
AND UNEVEN
RECOVERY

Y. V. Reddy

Orient BlackSwan

ORIENT BLACKSWAN PRIVATE LIMITED

Registered Office
3-6-752 Himayatnagar, Hyderabad 500 029 (A.P.), India
e-mail: centraloffice@orientblackswan.com

Other Offices
Bangalore, Bhopal, Bhubaneshwar, Chandigarh, Chennai,
Ernakulam, Guwahati, Hyderabad, Jaipur, Kolkata,
Lucknow, Mumbai, New Delhi, Noida, Patna

© Y. V. Reddy 2011
First Published 2011

ISBN 978 81 250 4185 6

Typeset by
Le Studio Graphique, Gurgaon 122 001
in Arno Pro 11.5/13.8

Printed at
Aegean Offset Printers
Greater Noida

Published by
Orient Blackswan Private Limited
1/24 Asaf Ali Road
New Delhi 110 002
e-mail: delhi@orientblackswan.com

Contents

III

Public Policy: Challenges and Responses

IV

Global Financial Architecture: The Debates

V

India: Performance and Prospects

23. India's Financial Sector in Current Times:
    Priorities for Reform   335
24. Macro Framework, External Sector
    and Financial Sector   344
25. Financial-Sector Regulation in India:
    Review and Proposals for Reform   364
26. India, Asia and the Global Economy:
    Resilience and Recovery   381
27. The Global Crisis and Exit Strategies:
    An Indian Perspective   394

Index   411

Foreword

$\mathscr{F}$ormer New York Fed President and current investment banker Jerry Corrigan used to say that central bankers may leave their jobs, but their hearts never leave central banking. The calling of central banking is perhaps one of the most exalted public appointments, as one is entrusted with the stewardship of a nation's money and finance.

Great central bankers understand that on their shoulders are thrust the fiduciary duty that requires the highest order of professionalism, judgement and integrity, which are routinely put to test. In order to do their job effectively, they have to act on matters of monetary discipline and financial stability, often in situations of grave uncertainty. Occasionally, as Federal Reserve System Chairman, William McChesney Martin Jr put it, they have to 'take away the punch bowl just when the party gets interesting'. It takes individuals of strong intellectual and moral fibre, who are humble enough to realise that they are mere mortals, and therefore have to shoulder their duties with the help of strong institutions.

All leaders have blind spots. However, central bankers tend to be different from other breeds of public servants because they are incharge of money, which is the lifeblood of all economic activity. Not only do they formulate and implement monetary policies, they must also have a finger on the pulse of financial markets in order to intervene in money and foreign exchange markets and manage public debt. Since they have an overview of financial stability, central bankers must understand the psychology of markets and therefore immerse themselves in the animal spirits of not just dealing rooms, but also the complex minutiae of back-office settlement and clearing. To be truly effective, they must also appreciate the power of politics and public opinion.

And that is a tall order.

Despite this, central bankers generally have the best understanding amongst public servants of how markets function. This is typically true in emerging markets, where the general understanding of financial markets is usually shallow, and strong institutions are still under formation and learning about the complexity of modern finance.

In addition, because of the global nature of money and finance, central bankers have to master not only domestic issues, but also their international ramifications. As the famous Chinese Qing Dynasty warrior/intellectual Zeng Guofan used to say, to achieve anything, you begin with the big picture, but act on the small details. That requires leadership of a high order, attainable only by a rare few. There are many who can command both macro and micro aspects of finance, but often times, exaggerated belief in their own brilliance and exalted egos blind them to the fact that all human institutions are ultimately flawed.

Each country can count itself lucky to have strong central bankers who put institution-building and national interests ahead of their own egos.

India is a land of many talents, but it was in the stars to have central bank governors of the calibre of Professor Y. V. Reddy, who was confident enough in his own judgement (stubborn and obsolete, according to his detractors) not to succumb to the temptations of opening Indian financial markets before they were ready for global volatility. Asians instinctively understand that in times of profound change, just as important as knowing what to do is to know what *not* to do.

Professor Reddy has given me the high honour, and immense pleasure, to write a Foreword to his monumental study of *Global Crisis, Recession and Uneven Recovery*. He asked me because he wanted an Asian and a developing country perspective on the current crisis.

Having grown up in the East, studied in the West, worked in the Bank Negara, Malaysia and the World Bank during the banking crises in the 1980s, having survived the Asian crisis of 1997–99, and being an ardent believer in free markets after working in Hong Kong, I must confess that I was shaken to the core by this crisis. The current crisis represents not just a seismic shift in global economic power from the West to the East, but has exposed fundamental weaknesses in the intellectual underpinnings of Western economic dominance. As Chinese Vice Premier Wang Qishan famously asked, 'what do we as students do, when our teachers go wrong?'

The crisis was also as much a shock to the financial system of the West as it was to the confidence of Asians in the probity of Wall Street, long admired and imitated by Asians as the icons of financial excellence, dynamic innovators and paragons of integrity. To the credit of the West, the disclosures of the Financial Crisis Inquiry Commission (www.fcic.gov) have transparently exposed many of these myths. Laid bare for all to see are the shameless greed and moral decadence of Wall Street bankers, some of whom claimed that they were doing God's work whilst collecting mammoth bonuses even as pension funds and retirement savings disappeared in billions. My personal belief in Wall Street was completely shattered when the Chief Financial Officer of the leading investment bank in the world confessed before the whole world that effectively, as market makers, their job was not necessarily to look after the interests of their clients.

It then dawned on me that what he was saying was that finance is no longer an agent of the real sector, as intermediary, trustee and fiduciary guardian of public savings. Finance is supposed to serve the real economy. Instead, it has become the master. In a classic reversal of the Principal-Agent Problem of finance, the agent has become the principal. After all, since finance has grown five times larger than the global GDP,[1] finance is not just 'too big to fail', it had become 'too powerful to fail'.

The problem is also concentration of power. Roughly fifteen to twenty-five large complex financial institutions not only control or dominate global financial assets (roughly half), but also half or more of trading in financial derivatives. Their individual sizes are now larger than nations, best illustrated by the Icelandic banks that were seven times larger than the GDP of Iceland.

How do financial engineers make five to ten times more salary than physical engineers year after year? Is there magic in the financial institutions' ability to create return on equity that is significantly higher than real-sector companies like automobiles or energy? The answer is that they create risks through leverage and interconnectivity which, every ten years or so, become realised losses that are fully underwritten by the public sector through tax bailouts. The financial sector is being subsidised by all the holders of financial paper through zero interest rate policies. Their liabilities are still guaranteed by central banks.

Finance has become the biggest free rider of all time.

Bank losses are ultimately quasi-fiscal deficits. By underwriting these losses during this crisis, the central bankers of the advanced countries have, through their guarantees and bailouts, transferred the losses to the public purse, morphing (but not creating) a banking crisis into a fiscal crisis. By one Financial Services Authority (FSA) estimate, the amount of bailout was US$13 trillion, equivalent to nearly one-quarter of the global GDP of US$61 trillion.[2] According to Bank of England (BoE) Executive Director Andrew Haldane's estimates, the losses may be more than US$100 billion, 1.6 times the annual global GDP.[3]

Never have so many been held hostage by so few. Will this situation be allowed to continue? Based on the current reforms thus far, the answer appears in the positive. Despite G-20, this is an issue that has become 'too hot to handle'. It needs cooler heads and steelier nerves.

Is Evil Local or Global?

Some Asians like myself feel somewhat peeved by what is happening. After all, not more than a decade ago, East Asians suffered huge losses during the Asian crisis of 1997–99. During that crisis, we were told that 'all evil was local', the victims being responsible for domestic mistakes in macroeconomic policy that allowed asset bubbles, bad financial regulation, poor corporate governance and crony capitalism.[4]

During the current crisis, we are told that 'all evil was global', and to our horror of horrors, Asians are to blamed for excess savings that gave rise to low interest rates that caused the bubbles in the West.[5] It is as if the depositors are being blamed for the mistakes of a bank's management, and then have to give the bank management higher bonuses because their deposit rates are now cut to zero.

Is there an Asian View of this Crisis?

I am wary of offering any Asian view of this crisis because Asia is a continent, and not a unity. Asia is so large and diverse that there can be no one view that can be representative of a continent that is home to 55 per cent of mankind with probably more than 80 per cent of distinct human dialects. Furthermore, it is on record that I am against the notion that Asian values are superior to Western values, because my personal belief is that values, both good and evil, are universal and not the monopoly of any geographical region or culture.[6]

Let me also put on record that although some Asians may engage in 'Schadenfreude' (pleasure in other's pain), as *Financial Times* columnist Martin Wolf suggests,[7] my view is that East Asian surplus nations stand to lose more than 5 per cent of their GDP in net foreign asset exposure for every 10 per cent revaluation of their currencies. Asians and the rest of the world are all in the same boat, so no one should be laughing except bankers with larger bonuses.

Nevertheless, if you carefully read through Professor Reddy's book, you can discern several common Asian perspectives, in contrast to the mainstream Western (Anglo-Saxon and European) perspectives.[8]

What is so different about Asian perspectives?

For what it is worth, I offer my personal perspective of six stylised and perhaps over-simplified differences, fully recognising that for every case I offer, counterfactual arguments about Asian mistakes can be given. These are offered as a comparative and tentative critique, so that we all learn something from this complex crisis.

- First, with Asians being less theoretical and more practical in their approach, there is an awareness (conscious or implicit) that policymaking, particularly central banking and financial regulation, remains an art, not a science.
- Second and related to the first, Asians tend to take a holistic and human view of markets, not a partial view.
- Third, because of a longer historical legacy, Asians are inclined towards a long-term view of policy, rather than short-term expediency.
- Fourth, being more rooted in the primary and secondary stages of development, Asians pay more attention to real-sector issues than financial or virtual developments. This is both a strength and also a weakness.
- Fifth, given huge social and cultural diversities, Asians are sceptical of one-size fit all solutions, especially with respect to human behaviour.
- Finally, there is greater self-awareness, best epitomised by the sixth century BC Chinese military strategist Sunzi's dictum that before you know your enemy, you should know yourself, because it is that failure where the mistakes are often made.

Policymaking as Science or Art?

The older generation of Asian policymakers, myself included, tend to be less well-trained in quantitative economics than their

Western counterparties. This, of course, is less true of younger Asian technocrats who gobble up Basle models like ducks take to water. For example, the current Chinese Political Bureau, the highest policy decision making body in China, comprises all engineers and no economists. Being practical and having risen mostly through administrative ranks, their hands-on experience makes them much more sceptical of economics as a science.

Post-crisis, the misgivings about economics as a science prompted a defence by Professor Ben Bernanke, Federal Reserve Bank Chairman and former Professor of Princeton University, in his September 2010 speech at the Princeton University.[9] He distinguished between the scientific, engineering and management aspects of economics. For the most part, he felt 'the financial crisis reflected problems in ... economic engineering and economic management', rather than in the science. In our email correspondences on the subject, Professor Reddy rightly pointed out that 'when individual machines fail the fault may be with engineering or management, but if all machines based on that theory failed, it is more likely that theory also failed'.

On virtually the same day, Professor Paul Volcker, former Federal Reserve Chairman, speaking at the Federal Reserve Bank of Chicago Conference, lamented the fact that the financial system is broken and that central bankers in charge of financial stability must make some very difficult judgements. I commend his speech because here is someone who is not dazzled by brilliance, but who is wise. He understands that markets are human institutions, because 'market developments are the creatures of very clever people trained in the physical sciences, applying techniques of physical sciences to financial markets, which are not physical things, but human institutions which are prone to excesses ... and simply not well managed under the assumption that everybody follows the normal distribution curve which does not exist'.[10]

Even Professor Bernanke has urged economists to study more about human behaviour in a situation of 'unknown unknowns' or Knightian uncertainty. Perhaps through their long experience with uncertainty, Asians instinctively react to a crisis situation by not moving, which partially explains the Chinese decision to halt the flexibility of the RMB when the crisis broke out.

Silos Versus System-wide Views

The second difference is the failure of Western intellectuals to recognise that economics and other disciplines had become so specialised and government agencies so fragmented that the world has become one market, but is being viewed and governed in silos. *Mea culpa*. As a Western-trained technocrat, I made the same analytical mistake. But the Asian dialectic side of me forced me to look for interconnectivity and take a network or system-wide view of the crisis, which surely has causes outside the financial sector, including climate change and real-sector imbalances.[11]

Indeed, any analysis of the crisis must take a system-wide view, covering not just the macro, but also the micro aspects of human and institutional behaviour. Asians understand that silo-based fallacies of composition do not add up, as Mahatma Gandhi rightly said, 'we have enough for our needs, but not for our greed'. Chinese Taoism would recognise that short-term benefits do not necessarily mean long-term benefits, and that the world is constantly changing through interaction between dualistic forces. Human behaviour is simply not linear, and is in fact highly interactive. The world is constantly in the process of interactive change, so that any static or partial analysis is fundamentally flawed.

This point is best illustrated by a definitional translation. Neo-classical economic models are based on key assumptions, including some which are not articulated or specified well in the theory or model. The danger, as we have found, is that assumptions may often be wrong and lead to wrong conclusions that become disastrous policy recommendations. The Chinese definition of 'assumption' comprises two contradictory words—'false certainty'—illustrating the dialectics of Chinese thinking.

The Long View

The third difference arises from the historical fact that Asians have experienced centuries of cycles of famine and disaster, over-population and natural resource stress. Asian policymakers understand that human development is a marathon, not a sprint. The willingness to take a historical perspective is epitomised in Henry Kissinger's question to Chinese Premier Zhou Enlai in the 1970s on what were the implications of the French Revolution. Premier Zhou Enlai answered, 'it was too early to tell'.

This requires development to begin with the fundamentals, such as education and infrastructure, before moving on to more complex steps. Patience is seen as a virtue, rather than an obstacle to development.

Stick with the Real Sector

The fourth perspective is that Asian policymakers tend to pay more attention to the real sector than finance. In terms of a choice between real-sector policy reform versus financial-sector policy reforms, Asian policymakers are more likely to choose the former. In contrast to advanced country regulators, who are more sanguine about financial engineering, Asian regulators learnt bitter lessons from the power of financial derivatives in speculating against Asian currencies, plus speculative losses from the Sumitomo copper futures (1995) and China Aviation Oil from speculation in oil futures in 2004. This is perhaps why Asians are more likely to shun what they do not understand.

Although recent Asian growth was initially funded from high leverage (notably Japanese and Korean companies), Asian policy-makers have generally been bold on the real-sector investments and cautious or prudent on the financial front. For example, domestic fiscal investments have generally been funded from domestic savings. The Asian crisis of 1997–98 put paid to any doubts about the dangers of the double mismatch, namely borrowing short to invest long and borrowing foreign currency to invest in domestic assets.

The lack of attention to finance has resulted in an imbalanced development in Asia, since it is precisely the cautious approach to financial risk that has impeded the growth of Asian capital markets. This is a contradiction in policy that Asia must solve sooner or later.

Monoculture is Dangerous

Chinese Taoism which influences certainly North Asian bureaucratic behaviour, compares and contrasts action (*wei*) with inaction (*wu wei*). The dialectical analysis explains that too much of a good thing is bad, exactly what Minsky called 'stability breeds instability'. The dominance of one type of risk management model or one source of market information that seems to suggest that risks or market trends are unidirectional clearly generate their own momentum, and hence add to volatility or risks.

Surely, when everyone believed that the market is always right and even accounting standards are premised on that assumption, accounting standards themselves became procyclical in application and therefore one of the factors in the instability of the system.

As Professor Amartya Sen has convincingly argued, the history of heterodoxy and argumentative debate in India has contributed not only to the development and survival of democracy in India, but also to its social stability.[12]

The conclusion is that there can be no 'one-size-fits-all' solution for global problems, because the world is too diverse and heterogenic. This also implies that we can only at best agree on major principles at the global level, with implementation differences for different countries.

Self-Awareness

There is a distinctive trait in the analysis of the role of incentives in the current financial reforms. Regulators and policymakers have offered the combination of excessive management compensation schemes and moral hazard as the two most important incentives that led to excess risk building up in the system. As far as this author is aware, other than lone voices such as Professor Richard Posner and Paul Volcker, few Western opinion-makers are willing to discuss why there is no reform of incentives for policymakers or regulators to take unpopular action against the madness of crowds. The matter is conveniently put under the menu for action by the creation of financial systemic risk councils. But those who are wise need incentives to act or to persuade society to act against disaster myopia in the face of growing evidence of rising risks. Society must recognise that timely ruthless truth-telling,[13] despite it being highly unpopular, is vital in moments of impending disaster.

Furthermore, there is an unspoken assumption, stemming mostly from Newtonian physics, that the observer can be independent from the observed. This is not true. Ancient Asian wisdom suggests that it always pays to be self-reflective and understand not just others, but how our personal behaviour affects those around us. Interpersonal behaviour is always interactive, so the outcome is not always predictable. Sunzi famously called this 'know your enemy, and know yourself, and a hundred battles will not be at peril'. We must have the humility to understand that it is our own weaknesses and failure to act or discipline ourselves which may be at the root of many of the problems we confront.

Finally, there is a trait in Professor Reddy's book that is different even from other Asian policymakers. South Asian leaders tend to pay more attention to the small man or the poor in their reflections on policy. I commend this thoughtfulness on financial inclusiveness as in the run-up to the current bubbles, there was too much attention paid to how to become rich, with an inclination to forget the underprivileged in our midst.

TENTATIVE CONCLUSIONS

Professor Reddy has asked me to venture forth in deep inter-cultural areas that are quagmires of controversial debate. I have responded because we need to have alternative explanations of the current global crisis, which has not been satisfactorily answered in the on-going enquiries.

The current crisis is both a crisis of human governance and a crisis of human thought, including how man interacts with nature. We need the humility to appreciate that East Asia made basically similar mistakes as the West only twelve years ago under less sophisticated circumstances. It is arguable that the fundamental roots of the Asian crisis were never fully resolved, since the Fed took rapid action to increase United States' consumption, which pulled Asia out of recession. For that, credit must be given where credit is due.

The tragedy was to assume that 'this time it's different', or 'we have little to learn from the Asian crisis'.

However, the relative decline of the West, even if that is true, does not necessarily mean the rise of the East. The East is still far too backward in areas of science and technology, development, military might, and even social institutions to contemplate true competition. But debate and discourse improves knowledge and understanding for all of us. Both Mahatma Gandhi and the Confucian Analects acknowledge that all men are brothers and that through debate and discourse, our world is improved in harmony rather than in conflict.

For these reasons, I thoroughly commend Professor Reddy's book on *Global Crisis, Recession and Uneven Recovery* as an important contribution to the debate on how we should deal with the great financial crisis of our time.

24 September 2010   ANDREW SHENG
Former Chairman of Hong Kong Securities
and Futures Commission,
Adjunct Professor, Tsinghua University and
University of Malaya

NOTES

1. Advanced country (the EU, North America and Japan) financial assets (bonds, equities and bank assets, excluding derivatives) are US$173.8 trillion or 5.59 times the combined GDP of US$37.9 trillion (International Monetary Fund, *Global Financial Stability Report: Meeting New Challenges to Stability and Building a Safer System*, Washington DC: International Monetary Fund, April 2010, Statistical Appendix, Table 3).

2. Richard Sutcliffe, 'Regulatory Reform', Financial Services Authority (FSA), 10 June 2010, available at http://www.fsa.gov.uk/pages/Library/Communication/Speeches/2010/0610_rs.shtml, accessed 17 September 2010.

3. Andrew Haldane, 'The $100 Billion Question', Bank of England, March 2010, available at www.bankofengland.co.uk/publications/speeches/2010/speech433.pdf, accessed 17 September 2010.

4. Marcel Fratzcher, 'The Reform of the IMS: Getting the Policy Mix Right', paper presented at the Indian Council for Research on International Economic Relations (ICRIER) conference entitled International Cooperation in Times of Global Crisis: Views from G-20 Countries, New Delhi, 16–17 September 2010.

5. Ben Bernanke, 'The Global Saving Glut and the US Current Account Deficit', 10 March 2005, available at http://www.federalreserve.gov/boarddocs/speeches/2005/200503102/default.htm, accessed 17 September 2010.

6. Andrew Sheng, *From Asian to Global Financial Crisis: An Asian Regulator's View of Uneffected Finance in the 1990s and 2000s*, New York: Cambridge University Press, 2009.

7. Martin Wolf, 'Financial Reform: An Emerging Market Perspective', available at blogs.ft.com/martin-wolf-exchange/2010/09/07/what-should-emerging-countries-take-from-the-crisis, accessed 17 September 2010.

8. There are Western thinkers like Paul Volcker, Joseph Stiglitz and others who share these perspectives, but their views are at present not considered as mainstream.

9. Ben Bernanke, 'Implications of the Financial Crisis for Economics', speech delivered at the conference organised by the Center for Economic Policy Studies and the Bendheim Center for Finance, Princeton University, 24 September 2010, available at http://www.

federalreserve.gov/newsevents/speech/bernanke20100924a.htm, accessed 17 September 2010.

10. My transcription of the recorded speech is available under http://insider.thomsonreuters.com/link.html?ctype=groupchannel&chid=3&cid=146696&shareToken=Mzo5NTI2NzE2ZS1kYTU5LTQ0Z GQtYjU0Ny1mOTIyZDdmNDdhYmQ%3D, accessed 17 September 2010.

11. Andrew Sheng, 'Financial Crisis and Global Governance: A Network Analysis', in *Globalization and Growth: Implications for a Post-Crisis World*, ed. Michael Spence and Danny Leipziger, Washington DC: Commission on Growth and Development, The World Bank, 2010.

12. Amartya Sen, *The Argumentative Indian: Writings on Indian History, Culture and Identity*, New York: Penguin Books, 2005.

13. The phrase was attributed by Mervyn King to John Maynard Keynes' inaugural speech to the IMF in 1946, 'The Reform of the International Monetary Fund', speech delivered at the ICRIER, 20 February 2006, available at http://www.bis.org/review/r060222a.pdf, accessed 17 September 2010.

Acknowledgements

$\mathscr{I}$am grateful to Professors Seyed E. Hasnain, V. Kannan, P. C. Sarangi, G. Nancharaiah and J. V. M. Sarma of the University of Hyderabad; Professors K. L. Krishna, Ch. Hanumantha Rao and Dr Manoj Panda of the Centre for Economic and Social Studies (CESS), Hyderabad; Sir Howard Davies, Lord Nicholas Stern and Dr Ruth Kattumuri of London School of Economics and Political Science, for the institutional support in my academic pursuits.

I owe a deep debt of gratitude to Dr Andrew Sheng, a brilliant and affectionate friend, who consented to write a Foreword to this book. Though I have acknowledged in later sections, a special word of deep appreciation is due at the outset to the eminent persons who graciously gave endorsements to my book: Professor Jagdish Bhagwati, Sir Howard Davies, Professor Jose Antonio Ocampo, Dr Guillermo Ortiz, Professor Paul Volcker and Dr Yongding Yu.

I remain grateful to Professor Jagdish Bhagwati, who encouraged and inspired me in my academic pursuits. I have gained significantly in my academic interactions with Professor Arvind Panagariya, Dr Arvind Subramanian and Professor Eswar Prasad, on some aspects of global crisis, especially in relation to India.

I owe a debt of gratitude to Professor Joseph E. Stiglitz whose energy, enthusiasm and commitment to the welfare of all peoples of the world, especially the underprivileged is laudable. Others with similar attributes and from whom I gained immensely are Dr Yongding Yu, Professors Jomo Kwame Sundaram, Stephany-Griffith Jones, Deepak Nayyar, Jose Antonio Ocampo, Dr Martin Khor and Dr Yilmaz Akyuz. Ms Heidemarie Wiec Zorek-Zeul, Mr Avinash Persaud, Professors Charles A. Goodhart, Jean-Paul Fitoussi, C. P. Chandrasekhar, Jayati Ghosh, Ashima Goyal, Dr Pedro Paez, Dr Andrew Cornford and Dr Benu Schneider are among those from whose works and words I gained in my understanding of the subject.

The central banking community (which includes former central bank governors) has been particularly indulgent towards me in inviting me to several conferences and in exchanging views. These include Dr Mervyn King, Dr Heng Swee Keat, Dr Zeti Akhtar Aziz, Dr Tito Mbowemi, Dr Guillermo Ortiz, Professor Paul Volcker, Dr Tommaso Padoa-Schioppa and Mr M. M. Hamad Al Sayari. I am thankful to Dr C. Rangarajan, Dr Bimal Jalan and my successor Dr D. Subbarao in the Reserve Bank of India, for their continued advise though I suspect that they would have preferred me to write something better.

I am grateful to Dr Rajiv Ranjan, who has commented on many of the chapters included in this book and has been a source of encouragement and advice. Dr Rahul A. Shastri, Mr Narayan Valluri, Dr C. Rammanohar Reddy, and Mr S. Narayanan have also gone through some of the chapters and gave me the benefit of their advice. Dr A. Prasad, Dr Partha Ray, Mr K. Damodaran, Mr A. K. Misra and Mr Chaturvedi Vaibhav, provided me valuable inputs on a few chapters, while Dr Alok Sheel and Dr Arjun Jayadev commented on a chapter each, Dr Alpana Killawala and Dr Sandip Ghosh have enthusiastically extended their support to me in this venture.

Dr Rakesh Mohan, Mr V. Leeladhar, Dr Shyamala Gopinath, Dr Usha Thorat, Mr C. R. Murlidharan and Mr Anand Sinha have given me insights into several critical aspects of global crisis and India, and to them I remain indebted. Mr B. P. R. Vithal, my guru, had enthused me into this, though he would have preferred me to write more about the way I did my job as Governor, Reserve Bank of India.

Dr Y. R. K. Reddy, my brother, provided unhesitating support and guidance along with great affection. As always, Mr A. Premchand, my friend, philosopher and guide, has been a source of inspiration. Dr Shankar Acharya, Mr S. S. Tarapore and Mr Kanagasabapathy, extended their unbound intellectual support and personal affection to me during this period. Among the friends who gave me huge emotional support were Mr G. P. Rao, Mr R. Rajamani, Mr T. L. Sankar, the late Mr S. R. Sankaran, Mr C. Anjaneya Reddy, Mr Veernarayana Reddy, Mr K. Krishna Murthy, Mr C. S. Rao, Dr S. K. Rao and Dr D. Chakrapani.

The team that accepted the responsibility of publishing this book under the leadership of Dr Nandini Rao, ably assisted by her team, including Mimi Choudhury, Osamazaid Rahman and Mr B. M. Mohammed Ali, deserve my deep appreciation.

I have been fortunate in having Mr Sunil Nagpal as a one man officer-in-charge cum research assistant. He has distinguished himself with proficiency, professionalism, and pride in his work, and dignity in his conduct. When the pressure in the work mounted as the deadline for publication approached, Mr Chandrasekhar Reddy chipped in with commendable commitment to being prompt and efficient.

Each one in my intimate family—Geetha, Kavitha, Hari, Adithya and Swetha, in his or her way made sure that every facet of my life and work is full of purpose and happiness, and to them I dedicate this book.

Introduction

$\mathscr{T}$here have been a large number of books published on the current global financial crisis. Hence, it is necessary to justify publishing another book on the subject. Though central banks have been in the thick of crisis management, central bankers, holding official positions, are constrained in expressing their views on the crisis. What they say generally reflects the official position. Central bankers with expertise and experience in the subject, but currently not holding official positions are in a better position to express their views freely on the subject; however, there have been very few writings by former central bankers on the issue. The most notable book by a former central banker is that of Alan Greenspan, but that was before the full dimensions of the crisis became evident. This book provides a former central banker's assessment of the crisis and its impact.

Emerging markets have shown remarkable resilience during the crisis and are poised for respectable growth. Since the crisis originated in advanced economies, the view of the emerging markets which had to bear its brunt needs to be articulated. However, most of the existing literature on the crisis reflects the point of view of scholars and practitioners from advanced economies. The author has the advantage of expressing his opinion without a formal official position in government and without any close association with the private sector. However, he had the advantage of interacting closely with the academia, which gave him an opportunity to take a broader and longer term view of the issues. Since he had the benefit of being closely associated with several international initiatives to understand the crisis and identify the measures to be taken in response to a unique globally emerged perspective. The book also devotes considerable attention to the Indian experience.

This book is somewhat different from the available literature on the subject since it is a collection of lectures and comments of the author in conferences, most of which have not been in the public domain. Arranged in chronological order in each part, they capture the evolving debate on the crisis, since its onset in September 2008. For the most part, the edited versions of the speeches and the comments are non-technical, and presented as opinions and observations with an analytical underpinning rather than advocating any particular integrated theory or package of policy actions. The purpose of each chapter is to inform and provoke discussion on several complex issues facing the global economy, and in particular, policymakers. Most of the chapters are self-contained and can be read on a stand-alone basis, though the themes are closely linked. Hence, there may be some repetitions in a few chapters and some of the observations may be dated in view of rapid changes, but on balance of considerations it was decided to keep them as close to the original versions as possible in order to retain the thinking and expression in the given context.

India has been less affected by the crisis than many other economies, but there is a critical need for it to be fully aware of the historic events that are taking place in matters of public policy in the global economy. There is a fundamental shift in the understanding of economics and the conduct of public policies on several fronts, which need to be adequately appreciated and debated in India. The book is meant to aid the process of informed debate on the global crisis and enhance sensitivity to the implications for India.

This book is, in a way, a sequel to the one published in 2009 titled *India and the Global Financial Crisis: Managing Money and*

Finance. The earlier volume was a collection of speeches delivered by the author in his official capacity as Governor of the Reserve Bank of India (RBI). It explained his perceptions about the impending financial in stability at the global level, and the active precautionary measures taken in India to ensure growth with stability. While the 'Introduction' explained the background in which the policies were designed and implemented, the 'Epilogue' provided an exhaustive account of the causes of the crisis, and the manner in which India was affected.

This book devotes itself to developments since the eruption of the crisis into serious proportions after the fall of Lehman Brothers in September 2008 and focuses on global dimensions of the crisis and perspectives of developing countries, especially in Asia. It is addressed to the general reader as well as people across disciplines. The book is comprehensive and covers several aspects of the crisis. It should help fill in the gaps in understanding of those who have not been following all the dimensions of the crisis. Policymakers will find in the book many such dilemmas that are part of the global discussion on the subject. Market participants and academia seeking a reasonably well-informed, objective and pragmatic account of the ongoing debates and initiatives on the crisis and its aftermath will find it useful.

LOOKING BACK: CAUSES OF THE CRISIS

Many historic events are influenced by ideas, institutions, interests, individuals and integrity. The global crisis can be traced to the influence of all the five factors, though there could be legitimate disagreement about their relative contributions. There is a general recognition that several ideas governing economic policy and the conduct of the financial sector have influenced the direction of the events that led to the crisis. One set of scholars believes that this is a failure of economics as a discipline. There are others who feel that the crisis is not so much a failure of economics as a discipline, but a failure of a particular theory or ideology within the broad discipline of economics. There was a strong belief in a particular idea, i.e., the self-correcting feature of free or unfettered markets. It was held that one should expect optimal results through operation of market forces and regulation should be minimal. There is also a view that the crisis is not a failure of economic theory as such, but only a failure in its actual application. According to this view, it is economic engineering or economic management that has failed, and not economic theory. As against this, it can be argued that the failure of some mechanisms and not others can be attributed to engineering or management, but if there is a generalised failure, then it is more likely that there has been a failure of theory. Irrespective of nuances, it is undeniable that the application of a dominant economic idea in policy has certainly contributed to a lack of understanding of forces that were building up the crisis. A few economists and policymakers expressed discomfort, and in some cases dismay, but the dominant view dismissed such concerns. In any case, it is clear that several aspects of policy such as institutional dynamics, ethical dimensions, behavioural aspects, and the network nature of economic activities due to technological developments were ignored by the prevailing dominant economic ideas.

The capacity of the financial sector to bring about efficiency with appropriate stability in markets around the world was taken for granted, with the result that the commodity markets themselves became a platform for use of financial resources depending on the liquidity conditions in the financial sector. Regulation of the financial sector was considered to be, on the whole, inefficient going by the experience of the past evils of financial repression. The least regulation was considered to be the best regulation, and self-regulation was equated with optimal regulation. While integrated financial markets were considered to be vehicles of efficiency, regulation continued to be segmented, and regulatory approaches were characterised by what may be termed as 'silo thinking'. Regulators seem to have failed to appreciate the network nature or interconnected nature of the financial markets.

Institutions that were established over a period to ensure efficient and stable economic and financial activity globally, could not, by and large, anticipate the crisis. At the global level, the International Monetary Fund (IMF), which is responsible for surveillance of economic and financial policies of countries, did not predict the crisis. While it referred to economic imbalances, it expressed itself strongly in favour of the strengths, resilience and positive contribution of the financial sector. The Financial Stability Forum (FSF) which was created after the Asian crisis of 1997 did not issue an alert about the threat to stability. The Bank for International Settlement (BIS) could not identify the onset of the crisis, though some research publications alluded to the evolving risks. Reports of the United Nations Department of Economic and Social Affairs (UNDESA) and United Nations Conference on Trade and Development (UNCTAD) did indicate the evolving risks in their publications, but they had no operational significance. The most influential group of the global economy, the G-7/G-8 consisting of advanced economies, made occasional references to economic imbalances, but the financial crisis which was to originate from some members of this group was not perceived at all. The G-20, yet another group of twenty systemically important nations including emerging economies like China and India, created as a consequence of the Asian crisis of 1997, had not diagnosed the emerging risks in the financial sector. The international monetary system was described by some analysts to be a non-system prone to crisis, but the consequences of the state of affairs were not analysed in terms of their potential for a global crisis.

At the national level, some governments, particularly in advanced economies, could have contributed to the crisis by a pursuit of relentless deregulation in the financial sector and competing for financial sector activities in a globalised financial market as a means towards higher growth. Most national governments did not see the impending crisis on the horizon. The central banks in most countries believed that there could be evolving economic imbalances or risks in the financial markets, but that these were best managed by market forces themselves. There are exceptions to this approach of benign neglect of booms by monetary and regulatory authorities. The European Central Bank (ECB) had expressed its concerns about possible vulnerabilities in the evolving global economies and financial markets. Some countries including India had highlighted the issue of potential financial instability and had also taken precautionary measures to minimise the impact of the crisis through preventive monetary and regulatory measures.

It is noteworthy that the failure was not only in policy in the public sector, but also in the behaviour of the private sector. Participants in financial markets, including large financial institutions, had not anticipated the crisis. In fact, there is a perception that they prevented authorities in public policy from taking action to prevent a crisis and moderate adverse consequences if a crisis was to occur. The dominant market participants in the financial sector were the beneficiaries of the boom preceding the crisis and fervently resisted interventions to stem the boom. Professional bodies, such as accounting standing boards and credit rating agencies, had also contributed to the crisis by not pointing out the practices that enabled and encouraged excesses in the financial sector. There are several layers prescribed under law and regulations to ensure sound governance practices, and these include the independent directors on boards, audit committees, internal risk management committees, etc. There was obviously a failure in the governance of all these bodies designed precisely to avoid excesses that would impinge on society as a whole. It is thus clear that there was across-the-board failure of governance in public and private institutions, in global and national institutions, in academic bodies and professional institutions.

Powerful and vested interests also contributed to the crisis as is evident from several anecdotes and incidents. Professor Jagdish Bhagwati warned more than a decade ago of the existing nexus between Wall Street (financial markets) and Washington (government) in the United States (US), reflecting the cosy relationship between the financial sector and political activity. This has been particularly evident in some of the advanced economies where deregulation of the financial sector was initiated and reinforced through legislative changes, followed by regulatory policies consistent with the philosophy of deregulation. Some of the advanced economies were losing comparative advantage in agriculture, manufacturing and services to developing and emerging market economies (EMEs), while they continued to have huge competitive advantage in the financial sector. Hence, some of these countries, in particular the US and the United Kingdom (UK), perhaps felt that national interest lies in their dominating financial sector activity, and hence development of the financial sector was coterminous with their national interests. This approach could have led to a race to the bottom in financial sector regulation within their jurisdictions. The cross-border financial arrangements could be particularly conducive to the influential interests since it was possible for them to take advantage of differences in tax regimes and regulations in the financial sector. These cross-border operations could be undertaken by and through the globalised financial sector, especially international banks and their associates.

Individuals also make a difference to events as they unfold. There are many who attribute the deregulation in the US to President Reagan, who was followed by President Bush (Sr), President Clinton and President Bush (Jr). Chairman Alan Greenspan had served as Chief of Federal Reserve of the US for most of these years. Greenspan's diagnosis of increased productivity in the US and his attitude to financial innovations such as derivatives and asset bubbles had a strong influence on the thinking in policy circles across the world. The UK showed a similar pattern during the prime ministerships of Margaret Thatcher and Tony Blair.

A recent documentary movie, written and directed by Charles Ferguson, titled *Inside Job*, argues that the global economic crisis arose from a few thousand individual acts of craven self-interest, supported by regulation or lack of regulation. It argues that in many of these acts, there was a thin line between legality and outright fraud.

The failure of multiple institutions and individuals to prevent a catastrophe leads one to explore the possibility of intangibles such as integrity defined in a very broad sense. Perhaps, tolerance for unethical behaviour has been high and respect for material achievements has been equally high. Despite the fact that huge fines were imposed by regulators in several countries on large international banks, it is interesting that they prospered with no dent on their reputations. It is held that the pursuit of short-term gains and happiness prevailed over traditional values since there was a sense of impermanence of institutions. Companies could be brought into existence and could get merged or closed at very short notice. The argument is that the crisis was a consequence of the emergence of the cult of 'greed is good'. However, it may be difficult to make generalisations of this nature when the financial crisis originated in select countries and many others are perhaps innocent victims.

The retrospective analysis will be incomplete without the views of the dominant market participants in the financial sector. The financial markets still believe that the basic ideas that governed global economic and financial management have served the global economy well. The global economy has seen unprecedented growth rates and unparalleled uplift of the poor in recent years which they attribute to the growth of the financial sector. Cycles, according to them, are part of history and they are inevitable, and this is one such crisis. It would, in their view, be inappropriate to question the fundamental market mechanism, though incremental changes may be appropriate in its application.

As regards institutions, the market participants in the financial sector hold that the failures that caused the crisis were essentially those of public policy and not of financial markets. Monetary policy indulged in excess liquidity, causing market participants to search for yields involving risky activities. Public sector institutions failed to devise mechanisms that would enhance the skills of regulators in identifying risks, and to put in place appropriate regulatory frameworks. The major issue, according to them, was not lack of regulation, but quality of regulation, which happened to be poor. With regard to the housing markets in the US, the financial sector believes that the fault lies with those who borrowed more than what they could service and lenders cannot be blamed for such behaviour of borrowers. They hold that their relationship with the political management and customers of financial services is no different from that of other industries. The compensations that they received are, in their view, justified by the wealth that has been created by them. No doubt these contentions are not made with equal vehemence and, in any case, they do not go uncontested.

Looking back, it is undeniable that the crisis reflects a massive multi-dimensional failure in a synchronised fashion. It may be a long time before the causes of the crisis are fully understood. The failures were concentrated in a few countries and these happen to be systemically important for the global economy. Other countries were affected through their interlinkages, but undeniably they too benefited from the boom that preceded the crisis. The tasks ahead for policymakers, therefore, relate to designing systems that allow growth of prosperity and welfare but avoid the danger of a crisis, while protecting the weak and poor from the risks that may be inherent or inevitable.

CURRENT SITUATION: RECESSION AND UNEVEN RECOVERY

There is a sense of relief that a collapse of the financial markets and deep depression have been avoided through determined and timely actions at national levels which were coordinated globally. There is also recognition that almost all countries experienced recession and almost all of them are in a state of recovery. While the financial crisis is behind us, there are some voices which express fears of another crisis in the financial sector, especially in the US. The dominant view is that recurrence of a financial crisis is most unlikely. Recovery, however, is uneven, with some countries firmly on the path of sustainable recovery while in some others, the recovery is fragile and weak. There is a differential pace of recovery—what may be termed as multi-speed recovery—among different countries, characterised by fragility in advanced economies, especially in the US, where the financial sector faced deep crisis, and impressive growth in many EMEs, especially in Asia. Although there are signs of normality, and in some cases exuberance, in financial markets, and of resumption of growth, economic distress continues in some countries. For instance, in the US, the situation has been described as jobless growth, unsold houses, and empty offices amidst thriving financial markets.

The divergence between policy challenges of EMEs and advanced economies has become stark. Some of the EMEs are facing inflationary pressures while some of the advanced economies are still trying to counter deflationary tendencies. There are signs of boom in the equity and real estate markets in some EMEs while the housing markets in many advanced economies are yet to recover from their lows. The significant liquidity injected in advanced economies continues to find its way to EMEs and to trade in commodity markets rather than stimulating the advanced economies, which it was meant to.

There is some divergence in policy responses among countries, with some pursuing stimulus, some in a state of pause and others in a state of withdrawal. Such a divergence in policy responses essentially reflects the uneven recovery and varying degrees of fragility among economies. However, global coordination of economic policies is conspicuous by its absence, despite the rhetoric to the contrary, including in the G-20 forum.

The dissonance between the non-financial and financial sectors in advanced economies makes for a complex diagnosis of the state of their economies. The divergence in recovery and the dissonance between the financial and non-financial sectors have also complicated coordination of policies at the national level.

Deleveraging of the financial sector has taken place, but it is doubtful whether the process is complete in advanced economies. There is uncertainty about the implication of total withdrawal of government support to the financial sector in most affected advanced economies. While there have been efforts to solve the problem of financial institutions that are considered to be too bi. to be allowed to fail, the bailout of some large financial entities has created even bigger entities than before. The debt markets have overcome panic over the fate of government securities issued by countries in the Euro area, but are still fragile. Interestingly, the yields on government securities in debt markets do not seem to factor in serious possibilities of high inflation in the medium term.

Currency markets continue to exhibit signs of nervousness. There are conflicting pressures on the value of the US Dollar with preference for depreciation over the medium- to long-term, though it continues to be attractive as a safe haven in the short run. There is greater uncertainty about the actions of China in regard to its currency. While there are some who argue that allowing further appreciation of its currency by China is critical for rebalancing global economy; others hold that it will not solve the problem of global imbalances as a whole, but will only create problems for the Chinese economy. Intervention in forex markets is no longer confined to EMEs, while interventions in forex markets and imposition of capital controls in EMEs have been intensified.

There are serious differences in policy prescriptions for the most affected advanced economies. Some argue in favour of continuing monetary stimulus while others are convinced that monetary policy has reached the limits of effectiveness, and the threat of a liquidity trap is real. The scope for further fiscal stimulus is limited by the uncomfortably high level of public debt in the affected countries and a growing recognition of increasing structural components of fiscal deficits in these countries. The policy tools that are available to them appear to be getting blunted and choices are at best between more costly and less costly options in the immediate future.

The spillover effects of the current financial crisis into economic crisis in many advanced economies are raising the risks of social and political unrest. In contrast, many EMEs are experiencing growth rates close to pre-crisis levels. Even though their weight in global economic activity is growing, it cannot equal that of the advanced economies. The complex issue for the global economy is how coupling and contagion will operate between the divergent trends in groups of countries and dissonance between the financial and non-financial sectors in an environment of active but somewhat less effective options in public policy.

How do financial markets perceive the situation? The financial sector is generally confident that growth, especially in EMEs, is likely to be strong and sustained, and that it is a matter of time before the real economy picks up momentum. The stimulus is percolating and if premature withdrawal of monetary stimulus is avoided in advanced economies, adequate pickup in credit in those countries is likely. They are uncomfortable with current efforts to significantly enhance capital adequacy of banks, which they expect would adversely affect credit growth in an environment that is not conducive to expansion in economic activity. In their view, credit expansion is the immediate need and this objective will be defeated by reactive enhancement of capital needs. They would prefer focus on enhancing regulatory skills. There are uncertainties and discomforts mainly in currency and debt markets, but according to them, these are manageable. Over the medium- to long-term, growing sovereign debt of advanced economies could be a problem warranting credible assurances and policies to manage public debt and fiscal stabilisation.

THINKING AHEAD: HEIGHTENED UNCERTAINTIES AND VOLATILITY

A lasting impact of the crisis has been on the analytical framework governing economic management. The framework that governed policymaking in most countries during the recent years has proved to be less than adequate. While some countries followed the framework enthusiastically, others were moving in the same direction but with safeguards and caution. Recent events questioned the framework's foundations, but it has not been possible to arrive at a consensus on an appropriate alternative. This vacuum, which inevitably leads to uncertainties, could be illustrated with some examples. First, in macroeconomic policy, inflation targeting was the norm, be it explicit or implicit, and low and stable inflation was considered a desirable goal. There is a view now that a countercyclical policy is essential and this may warrant a not-too-low level of inflation. Second, fiscal policy was focused on maintaining budgetary balance and high public debt was viewed with serious concern. Currently, the issue is managing high public debt rather than targeting a low public debt in the medium-term. It was also assumed that there is virtually no default risk for government securities of advanced economies, but such an assurance no longer exists after the crisis in Greece. Third, in the external sector, it was felt that maintaining forex reserves is a costly option. It was also felt that free capital flows are optimal and capital controls result in distortions. These assumptions are being reviewed. Finally, the empirical evidence is increasingly contradicting some of the fundamental economic relationships that formed the basis for economic policy in the past. This discarding of old beliefs and current search for new beliefs is likely to result in uncertainties in public policy and consequently, volatility in financial markets.

The growth prospects for countries such as the US, Euro area and Japan, which were the drivers of global economic growth, are not encouraging. They still have a large weight in the global economy. There are EMEs such as China, India and others, which are expected to grow rapidly, but they also have large populations that could prove to be both a resource and a challenge. The issue is whether the good contagion of growth impulse from EMEs to advanced economies will happen, and if so, in what manner, and to what extent. The EMEs have to generate domestic growth impulses to compensate for loss of traction from developed countries and additionally give momentum to growth in developed economies.

It is not clear how the macroeconomic imbalances, in particular those relating to China and the US, will be resolved. Contentious issues will relate to burden-sharing between China and the US, as also between the two and the rest of the world. Further, fiscal and monetary stimulus to avoid collapse in financial markets and recession, has exacerbated some of the medium- to long-term challenges of macroeconomic adjustments, particularly in the US and China. These relate to restoring fiscal and current account balance in the US and enhancing domestic demand in China, particularly private consumption demand. The sovereign debt problems in Europe have brought to the fore some of the structural issues in the Euro area and these involve burden-sharing between countries in the Euro area and also instituting greater fiscal discipline in some countries in the future. Japan continues to suffer from a liquidity trap and stagnation in output.

There is considerable debate and some progress on regulation of the financial sector. It is unclear whether the process of deleveraging in the financial sector is complete and satisfactory in the US, UK and Europe. Some regulatory changes have been brought about to add stability to the system. There are differences among countries in the progress of reform of the financial sector. The US, UK, Euro area and Switzerland have embarked upon significant reforms in regulatory structures and policies. While most of them address issues of regulatory scope, regulatory coordination, regulatory capital, customer protection and systemically important financial institutions, there are ongoing debates on further steps to be taken. However, there are no significant changes in the regulatory structure in many other advanced economies and EMEs. Undeniably, the regulatory regimes are in a state of transition in systemically important advanced economies. There is still discomfort about the stretched timetable for implementation (up to 2019), which could add to uncertainties in the meantime and about the treatment of systemically important financial institutions. Admittedly, maximum attention has been paid to issues of regulation in global coordination and national action in most affected countries. The regulatory regimes governing international banks and cross-border banking are still to be clarified. In brief, the search for a desirable model of regulation of the financial sector is actively under way, and the immediate tasks are clear, namely, curbing excess freedom of financial markets in advanced economies and correcting patent over regulation or inappropriate regulation in developing countries. It is necessary to avoid the danger of making more demands on regulation and control in all countries in the belief that global coordination would require movement in the same direction in all countries.

A fourth pillar has been formally added to the Global Financial Architecture (GFA), namely the G-20, the other three being the IMF, World Bank and World Trade Organization (WTO). The G-20 was constituted in 1999 but has become an important forum for exchange of views and coordination among systemically important economies. It is a reflection of shifting balances across regions and countries in the global economy. There is a fervent hope that G-20 will evolve into a force that will bring about essential changes in the global economic order. The governance arrangement of the IMF and World Bank are sought to be improved with initiatives from the G-20; while the direction is clear, progress is painfully slow. In the meantime, resources at their disposal have been enhanced. There is an attempt to reorient their policies and improve global safety nets. The Financial Stability Board (FSB) was established in April 2009 after the recent financial crisis as an enlarged and more purposive version of Financial Stability Forum (FSF), which was established after the Asian crisis. A report of the UN Commission on the crisis has not received serious attention in any of these policymaking bodies, despite its objectivity, though many of the reforms that have happened are in the direction indicated by the Commission. Despite the severity of the crisis and the need for global coordination, the institutional changes in global architecture have been marginal, incremental and mostly informal. Above all, there is a concern about the implications of the international monetary system and the role of the US Dollar as an international currency. While the current state is described as a non-system, there are no serious initiatives to find alternatives except the launching of global safety nets to reduce demand for forex reserves by countries.

The most challenging issue for policy ahead relates to the balance between policy-autonomy for nations, which are accountable to their peoples, and global coordination or global agencies that are accountable to nations with unequal economic and global significance. The crisis was on account of globalisation of financial flows and financial markets ahead of a viable international monetary system as well as a globally binding regulation of financial markets. The extent of globalisation of finance, to be efficient and stable, should ideally be synchronised with the extent of global coordination of monetary policy and regulation. Further, experience in the Euro area has shown that transnational monetary union is bound to face stress unless there is a central fiscal authority. It is ideal to have such comprehensive global arrangements for coordination in economic policies across countries in a synchronised fashion. However, modest attempts at global coordination of exit policies in the context of the current crisis are facing difficulties. In brief, while globalised finance is desirable, the accompanying global coordination arrangements for efficiency and stability are yet to be agreed upon. The financial crisis has triggered realisation of this fundamental truth, namely, globalisation of finance has to be in sync with accompanying global arrangements, especially in monetary management and regulatory regimes. The uncertainties ahead for the global economy are a reflection of non-resolution of the issue of rebalancing between autonomy of public policy at the national level and coordination at the global level. Developments in technology, however, are operating in favour of globalisation of all activities, indicating a secular trend towards global arrangements for coordination of all economic policies.

Policymakers in EMEs, however, are currently concerned over the uncertainties in policy frameworks, growth prospects and volatility in financial markets. It is clear that they cannot assume that markets will adjust themselves smoothly, and hence precautionary measures will have to be taken by the authorities to avoid the adverse impact of volatility on output and employment while pursuing the goal of growth with equity. These challenges will have to be met at the national level, but keeping in view the increasing importance of global coordination.

A BRIGHT PROSPECT FOR INDIA

India has, undoubtedly, emerged stronger and more resilient after the crisis. Perhaps it is good that the crisis happened before India went irrevocably in the direction of excesses in the financial sector. The macro-balances that were judiciously maintained and pragmatic policies that were adopted, have earned appreciation globally. The potential output growth is clearly in the range of 8.5 to 9 per cent per annum with a scope for improvement, depending on trends in productivity. However, the critical policy challenges remain and these relate to the real sector deficiencies, especially in physical and social infrastructure and skills in the labour force, quality of fiscal management and standards of governance. These may be overlooked when the world is awash with liquidity and India happens to be one of the few islands of stability in the sea of turbulence. However, it must be recognised that most of the other EMEs that have shown resilience to the crisis and are growing rapidly have a strong fiscal position and current account surpluses.

The financial sector has served the country well so far, but there is scope for improvement. It shows signs of stability essentially due to the strength of the banking sector which is predominantly owned and dominated by the government. There are some weaknesses in the rest of the financial sector which are somewhat unique to India, and warrant attention. Other major reforms in the financial sector must be considered as and when there is a better understanding in global policy circles of the desirable regulatory framework.

In view of the heightened uncertainties and greater volatility in the global economy, this is an opportune time to focus on remedying domestic distortions and removing handicaps of the domestic economy. At the same time, precautionary measures must be considered on a proactive basis to protect against the serious adverse impact of global volatilities on domestic output and employment, while discharging the country's growing obligations to global governance in a responsible manner. Addressing the weaknesses and building on its strengths in domestic economic fundamentals,

India should continue to be among the very top, and conceivably the top performing economies in the world. In this background, global integration for India, as for most other countries, is intended to benefit the masses, especially the poor and the underprivileged, and not merely to enhance the nation's pride.

SECTION I

The Global Financial Crisis and its Aftermath

One

Central Banks, Financial Crisis and Rebalancing*

*T*his chapter initially examines the role of central banks in the evolution of the global financial crisis. This is followed by a brief account of the distinguishing role played by central banks in developing countries. Some aspects of the functioning of central banks in crisis management are also mentioned. The chapter concludes with an examination of the potential for a fundamental rebalancing in economic and financial management in the future, in light of the crisis and its management by central banks.

CENTRAL BANKS AND THE CRISIS

Central banks were fully aware of the build-up of excessive risks in the financial sector, and this awareness had been apparent since 2005. The central bankers articulated their concerns and expressed fears that financial markets were under-pricing risks. In response,

* This chapter is an edited version of the Keynote Address to the Multi-Year Expert Meeting on Services, Development and Trade: The Regulatory and Institutional Dimension, UNCTAD, Geneva, 17 March 2009.

financial markets questioned the competence of central banks to sit in judgement over the pricing of financial products, and in any case they strongly felt that it was up to the markets themselves to re-price the risks. In fact, some market participants warned that a crisis, if it did occur, was more likely to be triggered by policy mistakes than by the natural process of market corrections of an under-priced risk that might arguably have existed.

Instead of acting on their fears and apprehensions, it is evident that by and large, the central banks, including financial regulators (especially in some advanced economies), believed that the financial markets would ensure a smooth correction of mis-pricing of risks by themselves. In retrospect, such trust placed by central banks in financial markets seems to have been misplaced.

Many central banks noted that even if risks were under-priced, risks in the financial sector were widely dispersed due to the evolution of new intermediaries such as hedge funds and new instruments such as credit derivatives. Some central banks were uncomfortable with the fact that they were unable to locate where the risks lay, while accepting that the risks were dispersed but not banished. Most central banks, particularly in advanced economies, were confident that commercial banks were generally well-regulated, and hence unlikely to be vulnerable in the event of sharp corrections in financial markets. However, some central banks did feel that some pension funds or insurance companies could be vulnerable if they were less closely regulated and had large exposures to unregulated financial entities. In retrospect, it would seem that the assessments of most central banks or regulators of banks as to where risks resided and on the intensity of the regulation of banks' exposures were overly optimistic.

These facts raise the question of whether there was a 'regulatory capture' (that is, the regulated exercising of undue influence over the regulatory bodies), which could have led to wrong assessments by central banks and regulators. A close examination of various events in the years immediately preceding the crisis, such as legal changes, regulatory actions, policy analysis and even media focus in most economies, especially advanced economies, may point to the possibility of a 'regulatory capture', perhaps of a more comprehensive type than is usual. The regulated were able to influence not only regulators, but also the overall regulatory framework, including legal provisions, regulatory institutions and the conduct of the regulators.

The 'regulatory capture', as normally understood, means a capture of the regulator by the regulated, essentially based on an information asymmetry (the regulated have more and better information on relevant aspects than regulators). However, the capture in the context of the current crisis was more widespread and deeper. Financial markets had developed in size, wealth, income and influence far more rapidly than the non-financial sector. They exercised a strong influence on opinion-making, including through the media. Many high-profile economic analysts tended to be overly optimistic about the benefits of deregulation of the financial sector. There was a lurking suspicion in some quarters that the performance of central banks and regulators was in fact being significantly judged by the financial markets themselves. In retrospect, were there significant political economy factors driving the actions of central banks? Further, does such a phenomenon explain both the excessively accommodative monetary policy and soft regulation in some advanced economies?

It has been mentioned that many central banks were mandated to achieve price stability and that consequently, there was a vacuum with regard to the mandate for financial stability, which could have caused the crisis. It is also argued that the central banks were focused on inflation and not on the movement of asset prices (such as the prices of houses, real estate, equities) due to the inflation targeting framework. But the fact remains that central banks are *de facto* responsible for financial stability, either by mandate or by default. It is not possible to envisage any other public institution as being responsible for the overall stability of money and finance. Why did the central banks miss this?

Sometimes it is argued that regulatory arbitrage due to multiple regulators was responsible for the crisis. However, the crisis hit both countries that had multiple regulators and those that had single regulators. Experience shows that despite differences in regulatory structures, the financial crisis occurred in many countries. Obviously there was something more fundamental in the conduct of policy or availability of skills that made some of the central banks overlook some issues, or held them back from acting appropriately. Would this be comprehensive regulatory capture?

Further, the growth in the financial sector, especially in important global financial centres, was disproportionately higher than the growth in the real sector, both at the national and global levels. This raises questions about the role of central banks and financial regulators in the excess supply of financial services with high leverage, especially in systemically important financial centres. Were they mandated by public policy to adopt a loose monetary policy and soft regulation in order to attract financial services to their jurisdiction, and did that prompt the regulator's greater reliance on self-regulation by markets?

CENTRAL BANKS OF DEVELOPING ECONOMIES AND THE CRISIS

What has been the role of central banks in developing economies in the crisis? Barring those that have a high level of financial integration with global economies, most developing economies have in their financial sectors a domination of the banking system, relative to non-banks, with a large dependence on retail banking and minimal recourse to credit derivatives. Thus, the banking system by itself was not excessively leveraged in many developing countries, although in many countries it had been exposed to rapid growth in credit, especially to consumers and real estate.

Some central banks in developing countries took recourse to countercyclical regulatory policies (policies that restrain excessive credit growth in boom years and encourage credit growth in slack periods, in select sectors or across all sectors), making their banking system less vulnerable to the crisis. With regard to monetary policy, however, many of them were denied adequate policy space to adopt countercyclical policies due to an open capital account. When an economy has an open capital account, there are constraints on the effectiveness of monetary policy, depending on exchange rate regimes.

Furthermore, an excessive financialisation of commodity markets (using instruments of trading in commodities as a financial instrument, purely for financial returns), caused both by excess global liquidity and a deregulation of trading in futures in commodity markets, resulted in a huge volatility in commodity prices. This added to the complexities of monetary management in some developing economies, especially those heavily dependent on the export of commodities. The common challenge before many developing economies was managing volatility in both current (mainly export-import trade) and capital accounts (mainly inflow and outflow of foreign capital), with no visible assurances of support from global financial institutions (in case of serious economic dislocations).

A few analysts contend that some policies of developing economies also contributed to the global financial crisis. It is argued that an excessive build-up of foreign exchange (forex) reserves in some developing countries led to global economic imbalances. It is noteworthy that developing countries had to contend with excessive volatility in current and capital accounts with little assurance of a safety net from global financial institutions. Hence, they had to seek self-insurance in the form of forex reserves. In any case, it is unfair to apportion the responsibility for serious imbalances on to developing countries only. The responsibility for such international macroeconomic imbalances should normally be shared between large surplus and large deficit economies. In fact, it can be argued that greater blame should accrue to the rich who consumed more, than to the poor who worked harder and saved more.

It is sometimes argued that a lack of domestic financial markets in developing countries such as China was responsible for excessive savings. There is inadequate empirical evidence to affirm a link between the level of development of financial markets and the level of savings. For example, how does one explain the low level of savings in the US in relation to the sophistication of its financial sector?

It is also argued that the crisis is due to excess savings in the global economy, in which developing countries played a dominant part. Since the global economy is a closed economy and all savings have to be absorbed, there cannot be an excess of savings for the world as a whole.

The current financial crisis is coping with excessive leverage in financial institutions, insolvency and a lack of trust among the largest globally, systemically important financial institutions. The crisis is in fact characterised by a breakdown in the functioning of financial markets in international financial centres in advanced economies. Hence the contention that developing countries are innocent victims of a crisis caused by advanced economies.

CENTRAL BANKS AND CRISIS MANAGEMENT

Central banks are at the forefront of the management of any financial crisis since the relevant instruments—especially liquidity (quantity of money) and interest rates (price of money)—are at the disposal of a central bank. However, in a crisis situation the problem of distinguishing between solvency (the value of assets that could cover the value of liabilities in the market) and liquidity (timely prevalence of normal price for assets that could be realised) arise. If a central bank were to take the initiative to provide liquidity against assets whose solvency is in doubt at the time of crisis, such a central bank would be bearing a solvency risk. Solvency risk in times of crisis implies a possible drawing on resources of the government, and hence involves substantial or extraordinary quasi-fiscal impact. In these circumstances, a central bank needs some form of approval from the fiscal authority, namely, the government. In other words, the actions of central banks that may result in serious losses would require the approval of the government. Hence, though central banks are the first line of defence in crisis, they have to depend on government approval for any large-scale discretionary intervention to manage the crisis.

Furthermore, intensive coordination among several regulators and other related authorities is essential to influence sentiment as well as substance, warranting a demonstrable support of the public policy expressed by the government. Further, if the judgement of a central bank and that of a government differs in a crisis situation, it is understandable if the central bank, as a technical arm, ultimately abides by the judgement of the government in a crisis, in view of the overall governance arrangements relating to the ultimate accountability of an elected body, namely the government, to the people at large.

Initial cross-border cooperation among central banks has to be at the initiative of the respective central banks. However, if the crisis happens to be deep or lasting or has quasi-fiscal implications with a huge expansion in the balance sheets of central banks and possible dilution of the quality of assets on the balance sheets, the central banks need either the explicit or, at the very least, the implicit support of the respective governments. Hence, cooperation among governments is also critical in times of crisis. These situations may not be entirely devoid of diplomatic or geopolitical considerations.

The fact that the crisis warranted a meeting of the heads of government of G-20 (a group of twenty systemically important countries) to chalk out a globally coordinated response has significant implications. First, the management of an intense global crisis and real decision-making is driven by not merely a central bank or Ministry of Finance, but the overall public policy of governments as a whole. Hence, the accountability in regard to the management of the crisis will have to be shared between the central bank, the Ministry of Finance and, to some extent, the government as a whole. Second, there is the question of whether the exit from the current balances in decision-making between the central bank, the Ministry of Finance and the government will lead to a status quo ante or to new balances. How will the possible new balance, in light of the experience with the crisis and its management, impact central banks at the national and global levels in the post-crisis situation? It seems likely that the changes will be fundamental: incremental changes will not be enough, and they will be in terms of rebalancing competing considerations in several areas.

REBALANCING IN ECONOMIC AND FINANCIAL MANAGEMENT

The rebalancing that is likely to ensue in the wake of the current global crisis will involve multi-layered considerations and many dimensions. First, the balance between the state and markets may be reconsidered in view of the observed market failures and the net burden of such failure on society, after accounting for the gains that accrued in the past due to market efficiency. In recent years, there has been an almost irrefutable presumption in favour of markets, and this may be replaced with a refutable presumption in favour of markets. Possibly the burden of proof of delivering efficiency along with reasonable stability will be more evenly distributed between the state and the market than before.

Second, the balance between the real and financial sectors may change in favour of the real sector. This may be pervasive to cover not only public policy, but also the disposition of human capital, financial capital and corporate activity.

Third, the benefits of globalisation may not be taken for granted any longer, and this may prompt an exploration of the concomitants of good globalisation, especially of policies and institutions at the national level. Globalisation is a process that has to be managed well at the national level as long as national governments are responsible for the welfare of their respective citizens. Recent empirical evidence of the medium and long-term performance of economies points to the success of public policies that had undertaken globalisation in a calibrated fashion—success not only in terms of growth, price stability and financial stability, but also in terms of the large number of people who were moved out of abject poverty. On the whole, a more calibrated approach to globalisation may be expected, keeping in view the realities of progress in global governance arrangements.

Fourth, a review of the pace and sequencing of financial integration relative to trade integration in the global economy may be warranted. The potential for excess leverage and prevalence of huge externalities in the financial sector has been demonstrated by recent events. Above all, global financial markets treat advanced and developing economies differently, even if the fundamentals are similar. So long as such an asymmetrical treatment of economies persists, it will be inappropriate to urge authorities in advanced and developing economies to adopt exactly similar policies in their treatment of global markets. A more nuanced approach to the liberalisation of the financial sector and its global integration may be anticipated.

Fifth, the severity of the financial crisis in international financial centres, perhaps due to soft regulation, is already evident, and in this context the adverse consequences of offshore centres and tax havens are also being brought to the fore. Similarly, bilateral agreements resulting in preferred tax treatment to non-resident investors are encouraging the round tripping of investments by residents. Some of the practices that undermine the integrity of global financial markets may now be subject to a pragmatic review.

Sixth, in the context of regulation of the financial sector, one should expect a comprehensive review of the scope and intensity of regulation, while redefining the boundaries between banks, bank-like institutions and non-bank financial intermediaries. The stress on deregulation in the recent past may be replaced with redesigned regulations of the financial sector, focusing on comprehensiveness, transparency coupled with simplicity, countercyclicality, macro-prudential aspects, liquidity management and financial inclusion. It is clear that such developments will impact the role played by central banks in regulation of the financial sector. Some changes in the traditional wisdom regarding goals, independence, accountability and governance of central banks at the national level, and their interactions with global financial institutions at the international level, appear inevitable.

Seventh, the relative roles of national authorities and global institutions in the regulation of the financial sector may be reviewed. There are weighty arguments in favour of strengthening the policy space for national-level financial regulation, while demanding greater attention to the policies of systemically important countries and globally significant financial institutions in the market. Since the crisis arose mainly out of inadequate regulation at the national level, it would be appropriate to assign priority to strengthening national regulations. At the same time, since contagion to developing countries has occurred substantially through volatility in capital flows, an active management of the capital account by developing economies should gain acceptability.

Finally, consequent to the ongoing crisis, there has been a serious erosion of public trust in the financial sectors of some economies— and indeed of trust in each other—among leading global financial institutions within the financial sector. Rebuilding trust would demand many fundamental changes in the financial sector and beyond. The financial crisis has spilled over into the economic, social, and potentially the political arena. One should therefore expect changes in the thinking of economists, in institutional frameworks, in global socio-political balances and, above all, even in the philosophical outlook of individuals in their multiple economic identities—as consumers, investors and citizens.

Two

Ethics and the World of Globalised Finance[*]

$\mathcal{T}$his chapter initially lists the multiple explanations offered with regard to the causes of the global crisis. These include the failure of the state, market, governance, intellect and morality. This is followed by an account of the distinguishing features of the world of finance. There is a brief account of what values, morals and ethics mean. Against this background, the unique features of the world of globalised finance, as distinct from the world of finance in different countries, are explained. The concluding part contends that the issue of ethics in general and the world of finances in particular are relevant to the crisis; but that an important reason for the crisis is globalised finance.

The 'global financial crisis' and its aftermath, the 'global economic crisis' followed by 'global recession', has resulted in a review of theory and practice in several areas. A narrowly technical view of the events considers the problem to be essentially one of serious flaws in the financial sector, encompassing the regulators and financial markets mainly in select countries. A very broad view of the events considers

* This chapter is an edited version of the lecture delivered at the Satya Sai University, Puttaparthi, 28 August 2009.

the problem as one of unethical behaviour by several participants in the financial sector as a whole. Considerable attention has been paid to explanations relating to infirmities in markets as well as regulation in the financial sector, while there have only been some general observations on ethics and its role in the world of finance.

It is now generally conceded that the crisis was caused by failures on multiple fronts, and that the crisis in the financial sector, albeit a very important element, was only one of these. The crisis in the financial sector includes moral failure, which is itself an aspect of the failure of the economic system as a whole. Ethics is one of several fundamental issues relating to the crisis that are now being reviewed. In this regard, a critical issue is whether there are some distinguishing characteristics of finance that are especially relevant to ethics. In this light, the role played by values, morals and ethics in causing the crisis could be explored.

Multiple Explanations

There are several explanations for the crisis, which point to a failure on multiple fronts. First, the crisis is considered to indicate the failure of capitalism. While some argue that this could be the end of capitalism, most analysts believe that capitalism has demonstrated its capacity to reinvent itself and is likely to do so on this occasion as well. Second, the growing productivity of labour generated by capitalism in its relentless search for profits curtailed the demand for labour, reduced its bargaining power, and aggravated inequalities and the potential for demand deficiencies. It is argued that these problems were sought to be partially compensated for by the excessive development of the financial sector and its globalisation. In this view, the crisis is only one element of the correction in the financial sector, but it may not be able to solve the fundamental problems of capitalism. Third, the world has always seen a constant rebalancing of several forces, of ideas or influences, and such rebalancing occurs in several ways, including through the geographical redistribution of global economic activity. Such rebalancing has seldom been smooth. It is argued that the recent crisis is only the beginning of the process of rebalancing economic power from the Western world to Asia. Fourth, the crisis is explained as one of the failures of the Western liberal approach to market-based capitalism, as practised in its near pure form by advanced industrialised economies. The global crisis represents a failure of that specific model of capitalism marked by a near excusive faith in markets. The crisis is only one aspect of this failure, while environmental damage is another.

FAILURE OF THE MARKET AND THE STATE

In discussions in the context of policy responses to the crisis, the main focus has been on market failures that were not anticipated by the regulator, which in a way represents a failure of the state. Much of the current debate is on how countries should invoke greater intervention by public policy to moderate market failures. It is often argued that the ongoing financial crisis resulted from the excessive faith public policy placed in the efficiency and self-correcting mechanisms of markets. It is therefore argued that the state should be empowered, so that the balance between the state and the market can be restored with appropriate roles given to each. Various initiatives are being considered for strengthening financial regulation, establishing a new global economic order and reforming, as appropriate, international financial institutions that could provide public goods conducive to global growth, welfare and stability. Most of the proposals are essentially in the nature of strengthening the role of the state, broadly defined to include intervention by public policy in the functioning of markets.

However, it is possible to argue that the recent financial crisis represents the failure of the state as well as markets both within and across nation-states. The apparatus of the state, in particular the independent central banks and regulators in the financial sector, seems to have failed to discharge the duties assigned and deliver the outcomes they had assured. There are sufficient grounds to believe that the crisis is a result of a regulatory capture of the government by market forces, especially financial institutions and financial markets. In other words, it can be argued that the crisis was not caused by a mere failure of regulators, but by a capture of the regulators and the governments by financial markets. This plausible explanation for the crisis imparts an entirely different dimension to the traditional debate on state versus market. Consequently, the debate will have to concentrate a lot more on the relationship between the state or politics and the market or business in each country on the one hand, and the relationship between the nation-states, national markets and international markets on the other.

The narration of events that led to the current financial crisis provides some evidence of close cooperation between financial conglomerates and the ruling elite; of competition for resources between these constituents within each country; and shows that the action of these forces ensured contagion in different degrees to different countries. Thus, as the world was led into the crisis, there were different strategic elements of cooperation, competition and coordination between the state and the market, nations and supra-nations, financial and non-financial corporates.

The critical issue is not merely the dominance of the state or corporate or a bank, but of the quality of governance in them. Governance standards are obviously products of several factors: cultural, institutional, technological and social. It is variously recognised that while the behaviour of economic agents is influenced by a cultural matrix, markets themselves also tend to influence cultural factors, which in turn affect the functioning of markets and their relationship with the state.

Failure of Governance

The financial sector is dominated by corporate forms of organisation. Corporate behaviour is controlled by layers of boards, audit committees and shareholders. In addition, corporates are expected to have internal control and risk management practices. Each one of these is in some sense a check or a balance or a layer of control over the other. It now appears that each layer had failed in discharging its functions. Something seems to have happened, whereby not one of these multi-tiered layers in the leading institutions of the advanced economies was able to prevent the simultaneous emanation of crisis in so many organisations. It is also clear that many of these institutions comprise of the most educated persons, who command respect in society and have strong professional backgrounds.

The infrastructure for the financial sector has several institutional mechanisms to ensure efficiency and stability, which also seems to have failed to prevent the crisis. For example, audit boards and credit rating agencies, which have several layers of expertise, experience and regulatory regimes and are duly recognised and universally accepted by regulators and market participants, rarely pointed out the potential risks. The plethora of analysts and advisors also went along with the events without questioning them. Self-regulatory organisations preferred to remain the industry's lobbies, protecting their members rather than disciplining errant members of the profession who indulged in questionable practices.

It is possible, therefore, to argue that the failure of such a multitude of organisations in public, private and non-governmental sectors cannot but be reflective of something more fundamental than a mere failure of individual organisations. Does this broad-based failure have something to do with ethics?

INTELLECTUAL FAILURE

Many economists have failed to diagnose the impending crisis. It could be the failure of a particular ideology, but the interesting issue is the frequent neglect of the mounting empirical evidence undermining that particular ideology or the particular version of economics. Some attribute the popularity of a particular point of view in favour of unfettered markets to the funding that many academic institutions received from market-based organisations in the financial sector. The funding was made available to academic institutions as well as to individual economists who popularised a particular ideology. The media was also less than even-handed in its analysis. While the achievements of the financial sector were glorified, the penalties imposed on the financial sector by the regulators were underplayed. The advertisement revenue for the media from the financial sector was increasing at a high rate, reflecting an excessive financialisation of the institution.

Even those not wedded to a particular ideology could not comprehend the external risks to other sectors and the global economy that emanated from the network nature of the financial sector. In other words, the interconnectivity and complexity of relationships between different financial institutions, financial instruments and financial markets, spread among different countries, have not been fully appreciated by either the regulators or the intellectuals. As a result, little attention was paid to the idea of establishing 'circuit breakers' in the global and national economies, which could confine the damage to the source of a possible failure and limit the possibility of a wider crisis.

MORAL FAILURES

A common theme in the account of the failure of the market or the state or the overall governance or intellect is the element of money: huge sums of money involved in interactions among financial intermediaries and between financial intermediaries and the rest. It is therefore held that a moral failure arose because of the high respectability granted to greed by society at large in recent years. The slogan seemed to be that 'Greed was good'. All actions were viewed with reference to the benefits accruing to the individual in the very short run. In terms of dominant values, the recent decades saw historically unprecedented heights of respectability accorded to unfettered market forces.

Historically, trade and finance in general have been viewed with suspicion, even though their usefulness, and indeed their attractiveness, were not in doubt in most cultures, particularly in societies that valued material success. The heightening respectability of free markets in recent decades, which was followed by the recent crisis, has also resulted in—among other things—two sets of realisations. The first is that economists and policy-analysts had underestimated the ramifications of untrammelled greed in human character. The second realisation is that there has been a fundamental change in human values globally, which, in a manner, elevated markets to the status of God, replacing traditional religion.

THE WORLD OF FINANCE

Within the corporate world, the financial sector has emerged as a force by itself, and has begun to acquire the character of an end unto itself rather than a means. Historically, finance was critical to both political matters and economic life, but was viewed as a powerful ally of politics for the most part. In recent decades, the financial sector has acquired a life of its own, with a greater capacity to influence politics not only at a national level, but even internationally. Further, finance increased its hold over the real sector.

What appear to be the distinguishing features of the world of finance relative to that of non-finance? First, the world of finance has always been an important subject for religious prescriptions in almost all religions, and this amounts to an implicit recognition of the externalities inherent in the world of finance.

Second, the world of finance is characterised by intangibles. For instance, if a vegetable is purchased, one can see the vegetable, feel it, and relate it to immediate use. The feedback on the use of vegetables is almost immediately available. On the contrary, finance is intangible. The predominance of intangibility frequently handicaps markets when it comes to adequately negotiating risks and real-sector needs. As a result, risk is sometimes substantially underestimated, leading sooner or later to individual failures; and when an institution is large or there are many simultaneous individual failures, they precipitate a wider crisis, given the networking nature of the financial sector.

Intangibility has importance consequences: (i) the attractiveness of a financial instrument is based on trust; (ii) finance is a means and its usefulness is often in the future, and the future is uncertain; (iii) the vagueness of financial products and the capacity to manipulate them creates scope for financial innovations, while individual calculation and greed supply the incentive; (iv) in the real sector or non-financial sector, creative destruction enables economic development. In the financial sector, the development of financial innovations themselves became the instruments of destructive creation. Professor Paul Volcker has challenged protagonists of the financial sector to provide even one instance of a financial innovation that has demonstrably added to economic development or welfare. Although financial innovations are meant to ensure risk sharing and pricing of risk, they were often used to avoid regulatory burden, save capital, and above all, to redistribute wealth to those who managed the finances of others.

Third, since the income of dealers in finance is linked to the value of and income from transactions, they naturally concentrated on products that promised significant profits and extensive trade. The computer and Internet revolution increased these volumes to gargantuan levels by drastically reducing the time taken on these operations. Thus, the incentive system in finance, coupled with modern technology, has given financial activity an inherent bias towards excessive trading, churning and volatility.

Finally, as a business, finance has a potential for high returns. In agriculture, people have to work hard, take all the risks, and only then could there be some profit. Similarly, in the manufacturing industry a product has to be innovated or produced, and marketed before profits can be made. Relative to agriculture or manufacturing, the incomes and profits in the financial sector are potentially huge though risky, and may bear no relation to timely assessments of product quality by the consumers of financial products. Since finance is characterised by huge short-run rewards and complex and challenging products, it attracts the most intelligent, the most ambitious, and sometimes the most unscrupulous people to its fold. Do these unique special characteristics make the world of finance vulnerable to an erosion in ethical behaviour?

ROLE OF VALUES, MORALS AND ETHICS

In common parlance, the words values, morals and ethics are used interchangeably. But in many ways, they are also different in meaning, despite being closely interrelated. Values are broad understandings or non-formal rules by which decisions are made. They usually relate to what is right or wrong; what is good or bad; and above all, to what is more or less important. In many ways, values arise in the context of trade-offs between competing considerations. Values have both an individual and a social dimension to an extent, since individual values often reflect the predominant values in a society.

Morals have more of a social than an individual element, and generally convey a broad acceptance in a specific community or society. They are often judgemental. For instance, there is such a word as 'immoral', while there is no such word for values. Morals are often related to behavioural patterns. What is moral or immoral is generally contextual to the society at large, and is often predominantly influenced by religion.

Ethics tend to be codified into a set of rules or systems that are often explicitly adopted by a group of people. Generally, values may be derived from several sources, particularly from the family, relatives, friends, one's education, and the community in which one lives. Ethics are contextual to a specific group and a specific activity.

Thus, there are business ethics or medical ethics. In considering the role of ethics in the world of finance, it is necessary to recognise the interaction between ethics, morals, values, markets and finance.

ETHICS, THE WORLD OF FINANCE AND GLOBALISED FINANCE

There are many common characteristics of the world of finance, while there are also different models of financial markets. One can refer to the unique Anglo-Saxon model of financial markets, which is dominated by capital markets. The European model is generally considered to be dominated by financial institutions. The East Asian model has lent considerable emphasis to the role of government and of identifiable family connections. The Chinese model consists of predominantly public-sector oriented banking. In India, there is a dynamic mix of public and private sectors. The Scandinavian model is said to refer to states where the market economy is dominated by an underlying philosophy of welfare provided by the state. In recent times, one has noticed the growing popularity of Islamic finance, which technically does not permit the payment of interest or debt finance. Given this diversity of models, it could be argued that there is possibly a diversity of ethics in finance. On the other hand, global networking and the mobility of finance increase the pressure for broad similarities in acceptable ethical behaviour. In this context, it will be useful to recall some characteristics of globalised finance, and explore their links with the ethics of globalised finance.

The global crisis revealed that there are several countries whose financial sectors were less affected than those of others, both among emerging markets and in advanced economies. Serious problems arose mainly in centres of globalised finance and the contagion to others was through institutions, especially through financial conglomerates with strong cross-border activities. In brief, the world of finance consists of two somewhat overlapping segments. One is the world of finance that consists of the financial sector operating predominantly in the domestic arena with some characteristics unique to each country. The second is the world of globalised finance, which refers to financial institutions and the activities focused on cross-border and global-level financial operations. It is possible to identify some common characteristics of the segment of globalised finance and explore the relationship between ethics and globalised finance.

A major part of financial intermediation occurs within domestic economies (with the exception of very small economies or international financial centres). Cross-border finance, however, plays a critical role in the financial markets in many countries, and the world of globalised finance represents the operations of cross-border finance in which international financial conglomerates play a significant part.

Many financial conglomerates, especially international banks, played a crucial role in devising complex financial instruments. They were generally operated from international financial centres which had softer regulations than others. International financial conglomerates are in a privileged position for several reasons. They arbitrage between different sets of regulations in different jurisdictions. They operate between different sectors of the financial market. They conduct their operations across tax regimes. They operate at different levels of formal legality in different jurisdictions: large bank balances in some jurisdictions reach jurisdictions or places with inadequate transparency or tax havens, etc. They can facilitate the cross-border management of the political economy. They are in a better position with regard to domestic regulators in several jurisdictions, in terms of assuming risk and exercising their clout. They have huge financial resources that enable them to employ the best talent and provide, especially in the international centres, bonuses based on the generation of profits.

These international financial centres have left their stamp on the nature and ethics of globalised finance. From the epicentres of the crisis, they served as sources of contagion to other countries. Their ethics were also contagious. While the role of the ethics of business, including the financial sector, should be considered in its national context, there may be merit in drawing a distinction between the ethics of the financial sector and those of the world of globalised finance.

In spite of its national location, the world of globalised finance has no national roots in terms of sources of capital, assets or liabilities. The distinction between commercial banks and other financial institutions is often blurred because of the globalised, interconnected operations of the multiple constituents of the conglomerate. The distinction between hedge funds and banks is also blurred in this world of global finance. Globalised finance is able to make itself appear an attractive proposition to even the best and the brightest among the professionals to join them. It attracts influential people, especially those with links to regulators, by virtue of its huge profitability. The people working in these institutions develop a set of values, morals and ethics unique to them. Effectively, this world is dominated by a set of professionals who manage finance in a way that is divorced from the culture, institutions, values, morals and ethics rooted in any one community, or a group, or a country. Instead, their ethics tends to be dictated by the logic of free markets and untrammelled mobility.

Ethics in globalised finance thus tended to comply with the formality of transparency, but attached no value to the fairness of transactions between the contracting parties. Morals in globalised finance were dictated by the emphasis being technically on the right side of the law. In cases where there were violations of the law, penalties were miniscule, and there was no evidence of risks to reputation that mattered. Plea bargaining was easy and the rewards very attractive, relative to the costs of non-compliance with regulations. The level of interest charged, the level of profits made, or the level of remunerations to individuals were not required to be justified as morally right or wrong, because it was left to the markets to determine the appropriateness of compensations.

The ethics of globalised finance described above have been called into question by the global crisis. The crisis revealed the full extent to which the values of globalised finance could damage a world otherwise characterised by a considerable national diversity of models of finance and ethics. Given the enormity of the distress in the world, the ethics of globalised finance should be revisited with some care and concern in the ongoing process of rebalancing global finance.

In Conclusion

There are several factors that explain the crisis, and one of them relates to ethics in a narrow sense and to values in a broader sense. Several forces appear to have undermined the propriety expected from both public and private institutions. One of them may be the fact that large sections of society favoured individualism, narrowly emphasising value for money as consumers and returns on money as investors over other aspects of social behaviour, such as being a good citizen or extending corporate loyalty to an institution. These tendencies had an influence on the world of finance.

The world of finance has some characteristics that make it more vulnerable to greed. However, the most important source of the global financial crisis was the world of globalised finance with its unclear ethical foundations, dominated by what may be termed global financial conglomerates and facilitated by considerations of political economy, especially in the international financial centres.

Three

The Global Financial Crisis and Asia*

*T*his chapter postulates that the consequences of the global financial crisis would have historic significance, and one such result could be a shift in the balance of economic power in favour of Asia. The causes of the crisis are explained in detail and labelled as synchronised extensive excesses. There is an account of the way the crisis is being managed and the inevitability of rebalancing in several areas as part of reaching a new normality. The concluding part holds that Asia is likely to emerge as a region of immense economic significance and possibly of financial activity, provided public policies play a facilitating role.

The current global financial crisis is being compared to the Great Depression of 1930, and so it is natural to expect the consequences to be similarly important. The Great Depression changed the intellectual framework of managing economies with the onset of Keynesianism, which underscored the importance of public policy in avoiding such crises or minimising their impact. Several new multilateral institutions, especially the World Bank and the IMF,

* This chapter is an edited version of the Justice Konda Madhava Reddy Memorial Lecture, Hyderabad, 30 October 2009.

came into existence. Above all, the Great Depression shifted the geopolitical and economic balance from the UK and Europe to North America. Will the current crisis result in a similar shift of balance from America to Asia?

There are several reasons for taking such a prospect seriously. First, this crisis, unlike many others in the recent past, originated in the centres of global economic activity, especially the US and the UK, and not in the peripheries like Latin America, Asia or Eastern Europe. Second, the near collapse of markets began in the financial sectors of centres that were considered models for emulation by the peripheries. Third, the crisis calls into question the policies and procedures of regulators of the financial sectors of these countries in the centre, which were hitherto considered the best. Multilateral bodies, especially the IMF, pointed to the existence of some broad economic imbalances, but were unable to anticipate, prevent or moderate the crisis that erupted. Fourth, the crisis undermined the confidence in the leading global financial institutions based in the centre. Fifteen of these institutions, accounting for over 70 per cent of cross-border finance, suddenly ceased to do business with each other, in spite of having the best mathematical models for risk management and being 'too big to fail'. Fifth, the crisis exposed the vulnerability of the US economy, which has been depending consistently on a flow of resources from the rest of the world to finance its trade deficits. It also raised concerns over the ability of the US Dollar to efficiently fulfil its role as the global reserve currency. In sum, the crisis has called into question the pre-eminence of the US economy, and the economic policies, models and regulatory techniques followed by the current centres of the global economic system like the US and UK.

When the financial crisis erupted in the US, UK and Europe, Asia suffered due to linkages in trade and private capital flows. Asia depends upon the US for its exports and for investing its financial surpluses in the form of forex reserves of central banks and the sovereign wealth funds set up by its governments. At the same time, Asia also receives significant in-flows of capital on private account. Given this nature of global integration, some disruption was inevitable.

However, Asia suffered significantly less from the crisis than the rest of the global economy. It also appears to be recovering sooner than the rest and maintaining a high growth, which has been especially impressive in China and India. Above all, Asia has its own unique features of macroeconomic management that are now being assessed favourably in the current crisis.

Asian economies are dominated by banking systems that concentrate on traditional retail banking. They are not dominated by derivatives markets, which were partially responsible for the current crisis. Asia accumulated considerable forex reserves as an insurance against global shocks in the real sector through commodity prices, or in the financial sector through capital flows. Many Asian countries had a positive trade balance, although a few, like India, had modest deficits.

The relative success of the Asian model of macroeconomic management in the context of the failures of policies stemming from centres of the global economy is leading to a churning of ideas and a new search for policies and practices that would be appropriate for the global economy.

Given the depth of the crisis and the performance of the Asian economies, the global economy cannot return to normality in the form of the old world order. Instead, a new normality with a rebalanced world order is more likely. And in this new normality, Asia may play a more prominent role.

CAUSES OF THE CRISIS: SYNCHRONISED EXTENSIVE EXCESSES

The current global crisis originated in multiple causes that reinforced each other. Extensive excesses on several fronts, which occurred in a synchronised fashion, precipitated the crisis. These excesses were observed in liquidity, macroeconomic imbalances, focus on inflation, inequalities, financialisation, leverage, risk-taking, deregulation, financial innovation, networking, greed, globalisation and concentration. These factors are briefly discussed below.

Many central banks, especially in the US and UK, permitted an abundant supply of money at relatively low interest rates. This led to asset bubbles (in real estate, housing, equity markets, etc.) that ultimately burst, causing financial instability. Cheap money encouraged speculation in assets and even commodities, and promoted the taking of undue risks. Even when asset bubbles were noticed, central bankers, for reasons of ideology or convenience, felt that markets would correct themselves efficiently, if not smoothly. Thus, bubbles were built and excess volatility was injected into several markets.

Some countries, notably the US, had large current account deficits. Other countries, notably China and Japan, had large current account surpluses. Thus, in the global economy, one set of countries was consuming too much and saving less, while another set was saving too much and consuming too little. That these excessive imbalances existed was known, and concern had been expressed by many, but no policy action was taken to correct them, either at the national or the global level.

Governments and central bankers were focused on maintaining price stability; however, in some cases they narrowly defined price stability in terms of core inflation, thereby excluding price increases in food and fuel. In many cases there was a policy of inflation targeting, and this measure of inflation did not include asset prices—the prices of real estate or equity, for example. The growth in prices of financial assets was unrealistically higher than growth in the nominal Gross Domestic Product, leading to a growth of a paper asset economy and a relative neglect of the real asset economy.

Inequalities increased in many economies, especially the US, and labour's share in growth was less than the share of capital. This accentuated the potential instability in the aggregate demand for goods and services.

The financial sector grew far more rapidly than the real economy on the assumption that finance could lead to growth and improve growth with a more efficient distribution or allocation of resources, rewards and risks. In reality, the efficiencies assumed did not fully materialise, and the financial sector cornered a lion's share of the gains while spreading the risks to other agents, sectors or governments. Further, many participants in the financial sector multiplied transactions, since their incomes increased with the number and size of transactions. This too contributed to excessive financialisation.

The practice of doing business with a disproportionately high proportion of borrowed money became widespread. In some cases, regulators did not insist on adequate capitalisation in the regulated institutions as appropriate to the risks that they were taking. Non-banking institutions, such as hedge funds and private equity, remained unregulated. This resulted in excessive leveraging since the incentives for managers favoured excessive risk-taking and short-term gains. For instance, it was standard practice for fund managers to receive 2 per cent of the fund as management fee and 20 per cent of the profit as bonus, without sharing the losses.

There was a belief that the costs of the regulation of financial markets are often high relative to the benefits, and that mechanisms such as self-regulation and principle-based regulation are often more efficient. This belief led to a process of deregulation that commenced with Thatcher and Reagan, and was taken too far. Several legislative and policy initiatives were taken to deregulate financial systems, consistent with these beliefs.

There was a spate of financial innovations and new products like derivatives. These were expected to help disperse risks, although they did not dissipate the underlying risks of real transactions. Unfortunately, whether risks were dispersed or concentrated depended upon the intent and nature of the innovations, the magnitudes involved, and where the risks ultimately resided. The packaging of sub-prime housing loans and their financial marketing is a case in point. There was an explosive growth in derivative markets, which became a huge multiple of underlying transactions. There is a view that states that complexity was deliberately injected into these products and that trading was multiplied by the traders, while regulators allowed this process due to either ideology or a lack of skill or will. In the end, the crisis showed that the dispersal of risks from mainstream financial institutions was only apparent and not real.

Enabled by technological developments, financial markets entered a complex network encompassing countries, institutions and complex products. However, unlike the telecom or energy networks, no circuit breakers or sands under the wheel were considered, either by self-regulatory bodies or regulators.

There is a view that for some reason, the conduct of many participants in the financial sector was characterised by excessive greed. It is not clear whether such conduct was characteristic of the financial sector or of Anglo-Saxon values, or whether it was universal. In any case, the cult of financial markets led to a neglect of economic fundamentals and institutional incentives.

The financial sector was regulated by national authorities, while financial markets and the operation of financial institutions became increasingly global with a strong cross-border presence. Thus, while the regulatory framework that remained essentially national was deregulated prematurely or excessively, finance was globalised with support from multilateral institutions without an appropriate and effective GFA. The cross-border movement of finance was also stimulated by the desire to take advantage of the differences in the regulatory regimes of different countries.

It seems surprising that such extensive excesses developed synchronically over a prolonged period. It cannot have been an accident.

Why did such Extensive Excesses Occur?

Several explanations can be offered, each carrying a grain of truth.

First, the financial sector took full advantage of technological developments to innovate complex financial products, and utilised them to redistribute wealth in its favour. The process went overboard as there were no regulations in place to serve as checks and balances.

Second, the ideological preference for unfettered markets was particularly unsuitable for the financial sector in view of its huge externalities, since what happens in the financial sector affects other sectors significantly and disproportionately. Further, although a globalisation of trade in goods was beneficial in some ways and burdensome in others, the ideology of unfettered markets was particularly inappropriate for globalised finance, in view of the differences in the levels of institutional development between countries and the criticality of institutions for the financial sector.

Third, there was a convergence between the political leadership that looks for short-term gains and financial markets, which also have a short time horizon. For example, this resulted in the emergence of the Washington-Wall Street linkage in the US and similar linkages in other countries.

Fourth, there was a 'race to the bottom' in financial regulation, particularly among countries such as the US and UK, which wanted to be international financial centres. The nature of the financial sector, often described as footloose, is such that it gravitates with ease to centres that have less rigorous regulation. However, when problems arise due to soft regulation in such international centres in one country, globalised finance and trade transmit the problems to others, and many countries become innocent victims of such a contagion.

Fifth, competitive advantage in sectors like agriculture, manu-facturing and services shifted to the developing world, while the developed world retained competitive advantage in the financial sector. Consequently, there was a pressure from financial markets in developed economies to globalise finance without due regard for overall financial stability.

Sixth, global watchdogs like the IMF were influenced by the ideology and voting power of the developed world, and as a result they could not guide or assist the global economy towards stability.

Finally, most people saw themselves as consumers and investors, focusing on the price and quality of goods that they could buy and the returns that they could get on their investments, ignoring their identity as citizens or members of the community and long-term stakeholders in corporations. Democratic pressures were thus in favour of short-term gains rather than overall stability. All these factors added to the strength of the short-term horizon that financial markets favoured.

It must be recognised that the problem was not only with the financial sector or markets or liquidity per se, but was a result of synchronic excesses on several fronts.

CRISIS MANAGEMENT AND REBALANCING: TOWARDS A NEW NORMALITY

The immediate issue at the onset of the crisis was to manage it in a way that ensured it did not lead to a collapse. However, it was generally agreed that there were excesses in many areas of economic and financial management in many countries, and that there was a need to rebalance the systems in the long run for a return to normality. Since restoring the pre-crisis order seems inappropriate in view of the experience, such rebalancing would have to lead towards a new normality. The critical issue is deciding on the content of a new normality. The crisis has also left public policy with very difficult choices to make with regard to (i) measures for crisis-management, (ii) withdrawal of such extraordinary measures, and (iii) defining the parameters of a new normality through a process of rebalancing.

It is noteworthy that although the crisis was global, all policy interventions for crisis management had to be at the national level. Fortunately, the response of national policies to the crisis was prompt. Leading economies of the world cooperated, and central banks and governments took extraordinary as well as unconventional measures. As a result, it would seem that the goal of avoiding global recession and deflation has been achieved. Financial markets are functioning normally. The declining trends in real output and employment have been arrested, although the economic distress precipitated by the crisis still remains. In brief, there is no panic or despair, but uncertainties remain.

One way of managing the crisis was to supply a stimulus to the economy. Such a stimulus cannot but be temporary. In fact, a successful exit from the stimulus is the best evidence of having successfully managed the crisis. Mobilising consensus for and coordinating exit policies among countries and policy wings within each country will be complex and critical. It is possible that political leadership and financial markets may want to avoid the risk of premature withdrawal, and in the process embrace the risk of a delayed course correction. The pace and sequencing of the withdrawal of stimulus has to be specific to the problems of each country, and the bigger the original stimulus, the more complex the exit. The quality of the original stimulus is also important in its design.

More importantly, there may be difficulties and disagreements in the destination of exit, namely the new normality that should emerge. It is possible at this stage to indicate that the extent of rebalancing would depend on the extent and nature of the excesses that underlay the crisis. Since these excesses varied between countries, rebalancing would also vary similarly. On the other hand, since the contagion of crisis was a cross-border issue, the rebalancing of excesses relevant to contagion will have both national and multilateral dimensions.

Balances have to be recalibrated in at least four major areas in order to move towards a new normality. First, the balance between state or government and markets must be reassessed. It is clear now that the crisis was not merely a failure of markets but also that of the state, especially in the areas of money and finance. Hence, rebalancing should address the issue of governance in both the state and markets.

Second, the links between the real and financial sectors and the regulation of the financial sector need revisiting. Finance plays a critical role in the efficient allocation of resources among users, nations and over time; however, the crisis showed what can happen if the means become an end unto themselves. In order to avoid this, a process of de-leveraging and recapitalising financial institutions might be necessary. Unfortunately, it is difficult to reach a consensus on this. New balances may have to be struck between regulation, self-regulation and free markets in the financial sector. In particular, the scope of and limits to separating traditional banking activities and treating them as public utilities will have to be reassessed. The optimal framework for bank regulation may be more complex than the status quo ante.

Third, the overall approach to rebalancing in the global context has to take account of not only the excesses and experiences of some leading economies such as the US and UK that were hard hit, but also the experiences of those economies that were able to avoid serious problems in their jurisdictions. In this regard, the experience of Asia is particularly instructive.

Fourth, crisis management has shown the importance of actions at the national level, and also of coordinating mechanisms at the global level. Mechanisms like the G-20 are more representative, but remain informal. The formal global financial institutions providing global public goods are the IMF and World Bank. However, their governance arrangements are skewed in favour of the US, UK and Europe. Further, these institutions are associated with a particular ideological disposition that is not necessarily shared by many. Major issues relating to the persistence of global economic imbalances are yet to be resolved. The important questions that need to be addressed are: how can we rebalance the considerations of national sovereignty and the need to strengthen global cooperation? Should it involve resetting the limits to global finance—say through the national management of cross-border capital flows? Should it result in greater global surveillance and stronger global institutions? What should be the role of regional arrangements and bilateral treaties? In this context, it is relevant to assess the possible position of Asia in the future rebalanced world.

THE CRISIS AND RE-EMERGING ASIA

It has been estimated by Angus Maddison that in AD 1700, India accounted for 24.4 per cent of the world's gross domestic product (GDP), while China had a similar share and Japan a fifth of India's share. Thus, at the outset of the eighteenth century, Asia dominated the world. There is now a view that Asia will re-emerge to dominate the world economy soon, given the trends in the growth and resilience of Asian economies.

Already by 2007, Asia (including Japan) accounted for 67 per cent of the world's official forex reserves, 55 per cent of the world's population, and 25 per cent of the world's GDP. In a publication in 2007, Angus Maddison has projected that by 2018, China would overtake the US as the world's largest economy with India following in the third position, and estimated that Asia would account for 53 per cent of the world's GDP. In other words, by 2018 Asia will return to its position of dominance in the global economy after 300 years.

Growth in Asia has been impressive in recent decades. In spite of the Asian crisis that hit many countries in 1997, high growth rates have returned to the region. The region has proved more resilient than others in the ongoing crisis. Asia continues to perform well, with China and India leading the world growth rates during the crisis, in spite of the global contagion. It is also noteworthy that exit from stimulus to manage the crisis has already commenced in parts of Asia. During the crisis, financial markets in most Asian countries faced temporary turbulences, but the financial institutions, banks included, did not generally need to be bailed out by the government or central banks.

The growing importance of Asia has been recognised in the ongoing dialogue on reform of the GFA. At the same time, Asia has taken several initiatives to strengthen cooperation within the region.

THE OUTLOOK FOR ASIA IN THE NEW NORMALITY

There is broad agreement that the crisis has reaffirmed the prospect of the re-emergence of Asia as a dominant region in the near future. In this context, it is critical for Asia to assess its problems, prospects, and its role in the process of rebalancing and designing the new normality in global economic management. It would seem that although there are opportunities and prospects, significant challenges remain to be addressed at the national and, to some extent, the regional levels before Asia can aspire to exceed or equal the dominance of Anglo-Saxon or Europe-American regions.

One reason for Asia's strong prospects in the emerging rebalancing will be the definitive and massive aggregate economic activity there. The annual additions to the workforce are likely to be huge and standards of living will keep improving. This will generate a huge demand supported by the growing new middle class of Asia, which will be met by a growing supply supported by the growth in the supply of both labour and capital that will flow from the culture of savings in Asia. Growing urbanisation and the concomitant infrastructural demands are likely to spur massive economic activity. Indonesia and Vietnam are developing in ways similar to China and India. The region has a great diversity in demographic cycles with Japan at one end and India or Indonesia at the other; China is at the intermediate state. This characteristic could lend considerable regional stability in the demand for and supply of labour, as well as goods and services.

With this home advantage, Asian multinationals could take centre-stage in the world. Intra-regional trade can be expected to grow very rapidly, reviving the old glories of the Silk Route and the Spice Route. The defining factor in the re-emergence of Asia as a force to reckon with in the global economy may be the magnitude of the trade balance and the quality of trade between China and India.

A major challenge for Asia will be the education and skill upgradation of the estimated annual addition of 40 million to the workforce. Handling the migration of people from rural to urban areas and the demands on public health and medical care will also be challenging. Water may prove a complex issue, while the problems posed by climate change will be daunting. Above all, the social consequences of growing inequalities and inadequate social security could be serious. Most of these challenges are in the domain of public policy, but the private sector cannot prosper if these issues are not resolved satisfactorily.

Asia has the potential to become a hub for global financial activity with a growing pool of capital and human skills in managing finance. Hitherto, domestic or regional financial markets in Asia have tended to follow rather than lead global finance, although recent initiatives in this regard, particularly by China, have been noteworthy. The major issue, however, relates to infrastructural services for financial activity, such as credit rating services, business news agencies, standard contracts and dispute resolution mechanisms. The dominant global financial conglomerates are still based out of the US, UK and Europe, but their ownership could over the years change in favour of Asia, reflecting the changing balances in economic activity between Asia and the rest of the world.

Leadership in the global economy has significant links with leadership in thought and innovation, as history shows. Asia as a region is yet to invest adequately and demonstrate its strengths in thought and innovations. Japan has demonstrated significant capabilities in technological advances, but the region as a whole has a long way to go before achieving excellence in research and technological innovation on par with the West. Both public policy and private-sector initiatives have to be geared towards this end.

The size of the economic and financial activities in a region or a country do indicate its immediate importance for the global economy, but standards of governance in governments, political stability, the assured existence of property rights, and the enforcement of contracts are more important for commanding the confidence and credibility of global markets in the long run.

Regional arrangements and initiatives in Asia could supplement its efforts to assert and advance its emerging role in the global economy and global multi-level institutions. Intra-regional cooperation is already taking place on several fronts and in various bodies. The most notable examples in this regard in the recent past have been the multilateral fund under the Chang Mai Initiative, and the agreement to have surveillance at a regional level. This initiative does not, as yet, include India. However, in order to be effective in the global context, Asian regional cooperation may have to rest on four pillars, namely Japan, China, India and the Association of South East Asian Nations (ASEAN).

History indicates that major shifts in the balance of political or economic power in the world take place over a period of decades, and may not necessarily be smooth. The transition from the UK and Europe to the North Atlantic was relatively smooth because of underlying common cultural features, and the post-war collapse of Europe. The shift in balance from the West to Asia may not have the same advantage, but it may be facilitated by the technological developments and globalisation that have already taken place. In spite of this, the transition will involve considerable policy initiatives within Asia and between Asia and the rest of the world. The shift will also be smoothened by its acceptance by other regions like Latin America and Africa.

Four

Life after the Global Financial Crisis*

*T*his chapter provides, as a background, an overview of the prolonged extensive excesses that acted synchronically to cause the global crisis, and lists the elements of global coordination and actions that were taken at the national level to manage this crisis. The implications of these actions and unconventional measures are described, since most have to be, by their very nature, withdrawn or unwound in due course. Unlike the relatively smooth coordination of policies to manage the crisis, the exit from unconventional measures that is beginning is likely to be characterised by pulls and pressures. Further, exit strategies need to reckon the destination of exit, which has to be a new normality and not the old one that had proved unsustainable. Several approaches towards a new normality are detailed, most of them involving a rebalancing of competing considerations.

The global financial crisis was a product of several prolonged extensive excesses that acted synchronically. There had been excess

---

* This chapter is an edited version of the S. Ranganathan Memorial Lecture, delivered at the India International Centre, New Delhi, 30 November 2009.

liquidity in the global economy for a prolonged period. Too much money was permitted in the system, especially in the US, the epicentre of the crisis. The excess liquidity was due to excessive financialisation of the economy, that is, the financial sector grew far more rapidly than was warranted by the growth of goods and other services, and the needs of the real sector. In a way, the financial sector managed to create an illusion of wealth, and consequently stimulated consumption beyond sustainable means.

The excess liquidity led to the building up of price bubbles of physical assets such as real estate and financial assets like share prices (equities), while monetary authorities were focused exclusively on targeting the general inflation. The excessive financialisation often resulted in the redistribution of wealth in favour of a few, more than the creation of wealth. In the process, the overall system generated excessive inequalities. In the US, for example, labour's share in growth was far less than that of capital. Excessive inequalities generally lead to a less stable aggregate demand in the long run.

The excessive financialisation was also accompanied by a multi-plication of transactions, excessive leverage and excessive risk-taking. Multiplication of transactions was justified by a claim to efficient price discovery. Its most evident effect, however, was to enhance the income of financial intermediaries, often without much relation to the growth of the real sector. Excessive leveraging was stimulated by the desire for higher profits, since it meant using more of others' money than their own, but it also extended the chain of vulnerability. Owing to the lax regulatory climate and excessive financialisa-tion, individuals and institutions developed a belief that they could obtain a share in the profits, while the burden of losses was diffused over larger numbers. This resulted in excessive risk-taking.

The excesses in the financial sector occurred under a benign public policy that believed the costs of regulation to be greater than its benefits. Even the existing regulation was stymied by excessive innovations in finance that aimed to avoid the prescribed regulatory capital, and injected complexity to undermine the rules of transparency prescribed by regulators.

There was also excessive networking within different segments of financial markets and across the borders of countries, which made it difficult for regulators to impose 'circuit breakers', akin to an electricity grid. This excess networking reinforced the strength of large conglomerates, which in turn became 'too big to fail'. More importantly, they were aware that they were too big to fail, and this could have tempted them to take undue risks. These multiple excesses were accompanied by an excessive globalisation of finance. While financial institutions and markets became global, regulation remained national.

It must be recognised that these synchronised extensive excesses were particularly prevalent in some countries like the US and UK, where the crisis originated. The crisis spread to other economies through several channels such as finance, trade and sentiment. In a way, other countries became, to different extents, innocent victims of these excesses in a few countries. The severity of the impact on each country depended both on the vulnerability of the macroeconomy and the financial sector of the country concerned, and the nature as well as extent of the country's integration with the global economy.

Why did these excesses occur? There are several explanations, and each is perhaps partially true. These include: (i) an ideological preference for unfettered markets; (ii) yawning international economic imbalances that witnessed persistent large current account deficits with some countries, especially the US (that is, depending on capital inflows from the rest of the world), enabled by the fact that the US Dollar is a global reserve currency, while other countries such as China developed large current account surpluses; (iii) a race to the bottom in the regulation of finance in order to attract financial activity, especially among those countries like the US and UK that wanted to be global financial centres; (iv) a capture of regulatory authorities by the powerful and increasingly wealthy lobby of the financial sector; and (v) the dominant influence of large systemically important countries such as the US and Europe over the ideology and operations of multilateral watchdogs such as the IMF.

There are some who attribute the excesses to the greed and incentive framework in financial markets, while a few blame the lack of will or skills on the part of regulators to contain the excesses. In many cases, there was undoubtedly a failure of arrangements for sound governance in both the private and public sectors.

It is clear that to the extent that some excesses had caused the crisis, a resolution of the crisis would warrant, at some stage, rolling back the excesses or moderating them towards an appropriate level or pace. It is understandable that such a process of moderation—or what may be termed de-excessing—may be difficult when crisis and abnormal conditions persist. However, de-excessing is inevitable if one has to move forward, and the challenge facing public policy is to ensure that such a process is non-disruptive and resilient.

MANAGING THE CRISIS: GLOBAL COORDINATION AND NATIONAL ACTIONS

As the crisis erupted, it disrupted the normal functioning of financial markets, especially in developed economies, and threatened the confidence in and solvency of many leading financial institutions in the world. The events that unfolded carried the potential for a prolonged recession and collapse of economic activity. Initially, the response of monetary authorities, followed by fiscal measures, was confined to the US, UK, Switzerland other European countries, and Japan, but it was soon realised that it was necessary to involve other countries as well in globally coordinated actions.

The initial responses could be described as 'fire-fighting' operations. All actions to avert a breakdown were at the national level, but they were broadly agreed upon at the strengthened forum of G-20 heads of governments. These extraordinary measures to avert a crisis imposed burdens on people at large, prompting a perception that in managing the crisis, profits were privatised and losses socialised.

By November 2009, financial markets and large institutions resumed functioning without disruption. In fact, there were some signs of euphoria in financial markets, despite the fact that the huge public funding of the financial sector in the Western world persisted, along with the bloated balance sheets of central banks. Further, the declining trends in output and employment were arrested, and growth restored in some countries. However, the adverse impact the crisis had on economic activity and employment remained evident in many countries.

In brief, there is no panic or despair and there are grounds for hope, but huge uncertainties remain with regard to the hidden vulnerabilities, the journey towards normality, and the exit from unconventional measures and stimuli.

IMPLICATIONS FOR THE FUTURE

It is necessary to explore the implications of these largely successful unconventional measures and stimuli for the future. First, the large amount of liquidity that has been injected has the potential to fuel inflationary expectations and possibly inflation, unless the appropriate magnitudes, manner and timing of withdrawals are devised.

Second, the fiscal stimuli often have the effect of increasing public debt, which has to be serviced in the future. This could increase the burden on future taxpayers unless there is a significant accelerated growth in the future, and/or substantial unutilised capacities with no supply-side bottlenecks.

Third, the nature of the stimulus is critical to the 'medium to long'term process of de-excessing or correcting imbalances. Some of the actions taken to mitigate the crisis may make the corrections of imbalances that are necessary for normality particularly burdensome. Some examples may be in order here. An admittedly fundamental long-term problem in the US is that of low savings. The stimulus in the US is aimed at boosting aggregate demand, possibly resulting in a further reduction in savings. Hence, the short-term compulsions and longer-term requirements of the economy could come into conflict.

Similarly, in China the problem is one of excessive investment relative to domestic consumption; however, the stimulus has increased public investment significantly, thereby increasing the burden of adjustment in the future.

Fourth, if there were to be an abrupt reduction in consumption on a large scale in, say, the US, it could seriously dampen export, and thus economic activity in China. It is recognised that stimulating private consumption demand may take time to fructify. The pace of adjustments in different countries may also need to be in harmony.

Fifth, if the fiscal stimulus had large elements of recurring entitlements or recurring expenditures, the withdrawal of such a stimulus would pose problems. For instance, if the wages of government servants are increased to stimulate expenditure when the economy is threatened by a crisis, such entitlements cannot be withdrawn easily.

Managing the crisis has been critical and largely successful, thus front-loading the benefits, but the costs are back-loaded. (If the costs or benefits of a process are concentrated in its early parts, it is said to be front-loaded. If the larger costs or benefits are concentrated towards the end of the period, it is said to be back-loaded.) The distribution of burden among different sections of people in the future may be contentious. Unless vigorous growth is restored in ample measure, the burden on the taxpayers, the stress on public services—including healthcare, and the pressures on prices may be onerous.

In brief, the crisis is global; actions are national; benefits could be selective or universal; but burdens in the future may have to be largely borne by the masses who bear no responsibility for the crisis, and those who did not benefit materially from the events that led to the crisis.

Exit Strategies: Beginnings, Pulls and Pressures

It is essential to exit from extraordinary measures and instruments to a more normal set of policies and instruments in a timely and non-disruptive manner. Exit becomes essential as the risks to growth abate and inflation risks emerge and intensify. The re-emergence of bubbles in asset prices due to excess liquidity becomes possible. Inflation risks arise due to a highly accommodative monetary policy, excess liquidity in the banking system, and scope for de-anchoring of inflationary expectations. Further, the process of exit itself may signal the policy perception of a return to normality, and add to positive sentiments in the markets.

The timing of exit is critical, since premature exit may derail recovery and growth while delayed exit may feed inflation and threaten growth over the medium term. These are genuine dilemmas, and the indicators generally used in the past to resolve such dilemmas may not be adequate in view of the prevailing extraordinary events. There are no ready precedents and hence no easy ways of assessing, ex-ante, the consequences of a withdrawal of stimulus from a crisis of this nature. In fact, by the end of November 2009 there were already disturbing signs of disconnect in many countries between indications of the health of the financial sector and the status of the real sector, that is, of output and employment.

Exit strategies are further complicated by the pulls and pressures that operate to resist the process. While avoiding a collapse of the financial sector at the time of crisis, the interests of central bank regulators, the political leadership and financial markets converged with a clear short-term horizon. The exit strategies, on the other hand, are meant to avoid longer-term adverse consequences, but involve the withdrawal of short-term props and comforts. Financial markets are typically fearful of the potentially uncertain consequences of exit. Further, the convergence of interests of all countries to avoid collapse will at the time of consideration of exit be replaced with an individual assessment of national macro-conditions, financial sectors and supply elasticity.

Each country will have to consider its exit tools. Depending on the pre-crisis as well as crisis frameworks of monetary, regulation and fiscal conditions, the tools available for use would vary. Needless to say, unconventional and ineffective measures, and measures that have already served their intended purpose will precede others in exit. It must be recognised that the transmission of conventional policy measures will be choked or distorted if the unconventional measures are not withdrawn.

The differences in the consequences of exit over time between different countries make the task of exit particularly onerous for many countries. The more seriously affected economies that led the way in crisis management may arguably tend to follow rather than lead the process of exit. The spillover of unabsorbed liquidity from some countries that exit later to others that attempt to exit earlier may intensify cross-border capital flows. On the way forward, therefore, excess volatility in capital flows, which has the potential to adversely impact the return to normality, should be of great concern to public policy.

More importantly, the communication of policies and intent becomes challenging if the interests of financial market participants and the intent of policy diverge. Fortunately, such a divergence has not been observed in recent years in most, though not all, economies.

In brief, the journey to exit from crisis management to normality is likely to be less than smooth, if not bumpy, for most economies. There is, however, hope for a smooth exit and transition to normality under some circumstances. Awareness of the complexities of exit strategies already in evidence is likely to moderate the potential for policy failures. The gains from the coordination of policies at the national level may favour a continued coordination of policies between monetary, regulatory and fiscal authorities. The benefits of an international harmonisation of policies, especially by the G-20, could spur continued harmonisation.

The major threat to a smooth exit to normality may be the continued and demonstrated short-term horizon of participants in financial markets, particularly in view of their current clout in decision-making in many systemically important countries.

ISSUES FOR A NEW NORMALITY: REBALANCING AND RETHINKING

The objective of exit strategies would normally be to restore normality. This normality could be taken to mean going back to the legal, institutional and policy framework that existed prior to the onset of crisis. This approach to normality holds that boom and bust are normal parts of any economic activity; and history has shown that they keep recurring, although every crisis has unique features. Further, while crisis may provoke some reactions and apparent correctives to weaknesses at the margin, the fundamental reality is the benign nature of free markets, and that has to remain unfettered. This is one extreme view that prefers normality to mean business as usual, as in the pre-crisis period.

At the other extreme is a view that holds that recent events signify the death of capitalism since the crisis erupted in the epicentres of capitalism, namely the US and UK. In this view, there will have to be a new world comprising of a socialist global economy and not simply a new normality. The middle ground, which is the mainstream view, holds that the exit cannot be to the old normality, since it has been proven to generate crisis; it has to be a new normality. What does a new normality signify?

There are, broadly speaking, two approaches to the new normality. One approach advocates a rethink: a rethink of the fundamental, ideological and theoretical foundations of a market economy. This rethinking was most poignantly reflected in an informal comment made by a Chinese official. He said that they used to look upon the US as their teacher, but now that they had realised that the teacher keeps making mistakes, they had decided to quit the class. There are some who express doubts about the validity of conventional wisdom after assessing the relative economic performance of the US and China. For example, China has shown that a stable and high growth in the real sector for a prolonged period was possible without any significant development of a modern, free market-based financial sector. On the other hand, it is also not clear how China is able to ward off inflationary pressures if their currency has systematically remained devalued for a prolonged period. At a minimum, the Chinese experience shows that developing countries need not necessarily generate a current account deficit to help development. Many transition economies and some in Latin America (or Turkey) whose policies were in greater alignment with conventional wisdom find it difficult to compare their performances favourably with Asia, in particular China.

At an analytical level, initiatives have recently been taken to develop new economic thinking (INET), which has an advisory board that includes two winners of the Nobel Prize in economics. It may be recalled that Keynesianism and multilateral institutions were consequences of the Great Depression. It is therefore argued that the current Great Recession, comparable to the Great Depression, may result in such a fundamental rethink of theory, practice and institutions. A rethink cannot be dismissed lightly, although in practical terms it is clear that some rebalancing of competing considerations will occur to arrive at a new normality. The alternate view is that while markets do benefit the society and economy significantly, some of the excesses or aberrations that took place and led to the crisis need to be rebalanced within a broader, existing framework. At this stage, it is reasonable to assume that the destination of exit strategies currently under consideration would be towards a new normality-based, but as yet ill-defined rebalancing. Such a rebalancing is likely to have several dimensions.

The State and Markets

The fact that financial markets did not correct the excesses without a large-scale intervention of the state lends credence to the view that market failures could be extensive and lead to great social costs. But a regulatory failure is also in evidence. It is argued that the failures have occurred in a sector that is under some form of regulation. The crisis warranted policy support to banks, which are the most intensely regulated within the financial sector. These are indicative of a failure of the state or government, rather than that of the market. There is a third view, which has considerable intellectual support—that the apparatus of the state was comprehensively captured by the special interests of the financial sector, and hence the rebalancing has to move beyond the state and market, or governance in the public versus the private sector.

There are reasons to believe that excessive greed and inappropriate incentives in both the public and private sectors could have caused the crisis. This explanation takes the subject beyond the realm of the conduct of narrow economic policy in the journey to a new normality.

On the whole, however, it is possible that while the rebalancing will be in favour of the state, the presumption will continue to be in favour of the relative efficiency of markets, but with a clear understanding that it is a presumption that could be rebutted when appropriate, with the state acquiring the policy space to intervene at its discretion.

The Financial and the Real Sector

It is recognised that there has been an excessive financialisation of the economy with a cognisable disconnect between developments in the real sector (that is, finally consumed goods and services) and that in the financial sector. The growth in the financial sector and the share of wealth and income claimed by the financial sector relative to the rest has been high, with no empirical evidence of its corresponding contribution to output in the real sector. Instead of being a facilitator, the financial sector became an end unto itself. Thus, recourse to large-scale financial transactions in the name of price discovery, and their grotesque disproportion to the underlying real economic activity was traced to the income-generating potential of multiple financial transactions in favour of the participants.

On the other hand, finance plays a critical role in mobilising resources and allocating them efficiently. Finance contributes to the well-being of people in a variety of ways. The real issue is determining the appropriate level, sophistication and regulation of financial sector development that could promote genuine innovation and curb excess speculation.

In any case, there is a consensus over the dangers of excessive leverage in the financial sector. Some curbs on the growth of the financial sector relative to the real sector thus seem to be part of the rebalancing that should occur. This may take several forms, which are already under consideration, namely, higher capital cushions; curbs on managerial remuneration; changes in the incentive framework; taxes on financial-sector transactions; measures for investor and consumer protection, including certification of the safety of financial products; restrictions on 'over the counter' trade; expanding the scope and intensity of regulation, etc.

Re-regulation and Innovation in the Financial Sector

There is a virtual consensus that the regime of financial sector regulation in major developed countries needs a thorough overhaul. Several reports (the G-30 report; Geneva report; Turner review; European Union report; Warwick Commission; G-20 working Group report; and above all, the report of the Stiglitz Commission) have taken this issue on board. The recommendations of all these reports is to: strengthen regulation; reverse the process of deregulation of recent years; increase the scope of regulation; make regulation countercyclical; emphasise macro-prudential regulations; take cognisance of liquidity risks; explore methods to tackle the 'too big to fail' institutions; alter the framework of managerial incentives; widen the range as well as scope of instruments of regulation consistent with the multiplicity of objectives and complexities in the market; enhance the scope for discretion of regulatory authorities while upgrading their skills; focus on structures and systems rather than only on mathematical models; and expand the obligation of financial instruments to be traded on exchanges. While there is acceptance of the possible contribution of financial innovations, it is proposed that they be subject to severe scrutiny. It is held that in the past, such innovations helped only to redistribute wealth in favour of the financial sector instead of creating wealth, and possibly encouraged irresponsible lending.

While at an analytical level there is considerable support for re-regulation, there are some who suspect that there has been a comprehensive capture of the state apparatus by financial markets, and that it will continue. Hence they anticipate only a marginal rebalancing in major financial centres of the world. The extent and nature of rebalancing will undoubtedly depend largely on the country context, especially on initial conditions and political economy considerations.

National Regulation and Global Finance

The crisis has strengthened the view that the globalisation of finance carries significant risks, unlike the globalisation of trade, which has been on the whole beneficial. The crisis has, in any case, highlighted that while financial markets became global, their regulation remained national. The rebalancing could happen through globalising regulation or recalibrating the globalisation of the financial sector, or a combination of both. Efforts have been made to develop globally acceptable standards of regulation at a technical level in a body set at the initiative of the G-20, the FSB. A recalibration of global finance may be indicated by the renewed interest in capital controls, the Tobin Tax (a tax on foreign currency trading), and strengthening of regulation by host countries. There are deep global concerns about tax havens, which is a recognition of the fact that harmonisation of financial regulation at a global level may not, by itself, address the relevant issues.

A more general and sticky problem is that of countercyclical regulation. Such regulation also affects the balance between the policy space available at the national level and the compulsions of global finance. National authorities have to decide on the weight to be given to national-level economic and global cycles, unless they happen to be synchronised. Further, countercyclical policies, in order to be effective, require a harmonisation of policies of financial regulation, monetary and fiscal authorities. All these are part of the larger policy space appropriate to the national level.

In brief, the rebalancing exercise in the regulation of the financial sector may have to address broader issues of policy space for national authorities and the governance of arrangements that oversee the globalisation of finance. The latter would encompass the reform of Brettonwoods institutions and the establishment of new multilateral institutions under the UN system, as proposed by the Stiglitz Commission.

Greed and Need

Mahatma Gandhi is reported to have said that there is enough on this earth to meet the needs of all, but not the greed of all. If greed, as has been argued by some, is the root of the crisis, then tackling it is a task beyond finance and indeed even economics as we understand these subjects today. Further, greed may not be unique to the financial sector or specific to some countries. One way of appreciating the trends may lie in the more popular attitudes in recent years. Most people seem to value being consumers or investors more than being workers or citizens. Perhaps the markets responded to that universal need amounting to greed, while catering to the greed of financial market participants themselves. There is thus a need to rebalance the roles of investor/consumer and citizen in the self-image and perception of the common man.

Five

The Future of Finance*

$\mathcal{T}$his chapter attempts to speculate on the future of the financial sector in light of the experience gained so far with the global crisis. The section on the background explains the context in which the future of the financial sector is being considered currently, with respect to central banks, commercial banks, non-banking financial companies (NBFCs), financial markets and globalised finance. This is followed by some general observations on the future of the financial sector.

BACKGROUND

There have been deep and wide-ranging global debates on the future of finance consequent to the global financial crisis. Theories governing economics and of public policy are being intensely reviewed. Some of the subjects under discussion and review are appropriate policies relating to the adequacy of institutions, the framework of incentives in institutions, governance arrangements in various institutions, the macroeconomy, financial sector, role of finance in the context

---

* This chapter is based on the Acceptance Speech of the Finance Man of the Decade 2000–10 Award, Bombay Management Association, Mumbai, 5 February 2010.

of economy, and the future of globalisation of finance. Sometimes the issue of sustainability of the global financial system is linked to overall global economic stability, sustainability of the climate and, in fact, the stability of the global social fabric as a whole. Apart from the review and reform of the financial sectors in the US, UK and Euro area through expert committees and legislative debates, there have been multinational initiatives to make recommendations for the future of the financial sector.

The global financial crisis has also resulted in unprecedented monetary and fiscal actions to avoid the collapse of the financial sector, prevent deflation, avoid depression and enable recovery. In the process, issues relating to the management of large public debt in the future have gained priority. Some proposals that were previously not acceptable, such as the Tobin Tax or Robin Hood Tax, or Tax on Bonuses, are now being discussed. Uncertainties remain with regard to the exit from stimulus and the possible course of economic recovery. Above all, although there is an agreement that status quo ante is not desirable, there is no consensus on what the new normality in the global economy should be. Despite these uncertainties, it will be instructive to speculate on the future of finance in light of the ongoing debates and developments. There are four broad areas relevant to finance that are under review, namely, macroeconomic policies, regulation of the financial sector, international financial institutions and the international monetary system. This chapter is confined to the most intensely debated area, and one in which considerable initiatives for reform have been noticed, namely, finance, and its future.

FUTURE OF CENTRAL BANKS

In the boom years preceding the crisis, central banks took credit for maintaining price stability. They also took credit for growth, basically on the ground that growth was supported by considerable productivity increases, which in turn were enabled by an appropriate monetary policy, deregulation of the financial sector and globalisation of finance. Central banks gained considerable independence. They commanded professional skills of a high order, and in systemically important countries, they were headed by economists of enviable reputation. Hence, when the crisis erupted, there was a sense of shock, dismay and anger directed at the central banks. However, central banks played a crucial role in averting financial collapse by taking prompt, effective and coordinated action. The crisis was followed by a global recession, with some hope for recovery. Simultaneously, and as part of overall debates on reforming the financial sector to make it less vulnerable to crisis in the future, the role of central banks came under review. It appeared inevitable that the experience with regard to the crisis and its management would have an impact on the future of central banks in terms of (i) their role in maintaining financial stability; (ii) their relationship with the regulation of commercial banking; (iii) the arrangements relating to their governance, independence and accountability; and (iv) the philosophy governing their operations.

Handing some institutions a formal mandate for maintaining financial stability has been considered appropriate. Such a mandate may be given to a single institution or to a body with which several institutions may be associated. In the event that a single institution was to be given the mandate, a central bank appears to be a natural choice, for several obvious reasons. A central bank has the capacity to create liquidity and has a better overview of the financial sector as a whole, relative to any other institutions. Further, whenever there is a threat to stability, monetary policy is the first line of defence. Above all, the adoption of countercyclical regulatory policies requires a view of the cycle, and will have to be coordinated closely with monetary policy. A view on the cycle is best taken by the monetary policy authority, which has a mandate for price stability and often growth. However, the operationalisation of financial stability, involving cooperation between monetary authorities, regulatory authorities and ideally fiscal authorities as well, would require arrangements for coordination among these three wings of the public sector. Such arrangements can be designed with the leadership of central banks, or that of the government. Irrespective of formal arrangements that may be evolved, it is inevitable that central banks will continue to play a crucial role in maintaining financial stability by virtue of the functions inherent in it.

To the extent that financial stability is likely to be added either formally or substantively to the mandate of central banks, it will play a crucial role in ensuring coordination among monetary, fiscal and regulatory policies. Normally financial regulators design, maintain and enforce the rules of the game within which participants in financial markets have to operate, while the central bank influences the relevant prices and, on occasion, participants in the market through intervention, whenever considered necessary. The central bank is in a unique position when it comes to ensuring coordination among the regulators, to the extent that it deals with the quantity and price of money, the pith and substance of the financial sector.

Since the critical role of commercial banking in ensuring stability has been recognised, it has been suggested that the regulation of commercial banking should ideally lie with the central banks. This suggestion seems to be prompted by the experience in Great Britain, where the regulation of banking vests with a single market regulator: the Financial Services Authority (FSA), and not the Bank of England (BoE). Experience shows that the crisis has hit some economies irrespective of variations in regulatory structures. While the issue is not fully settled, it is possible that regulation of banking will be more closely linked with monetary authority in the future, than it has been in the past. This may take place by merging financial-sector regulators with central banks or by transferring the regulation of banks to the central banks. It is quite possible that the function of regulating commercial banks will continue to remain with central banks in economies where central banks play a key regulatory role. In other economies, it should come as no surprise if the regulation of commercial banks is restored to the central banks.

Governance arrangements in central banks have come in for considerable criticism consequent to the crisis. Many central banks are owned by the government. There are some central banks owned by non-government entities, but governance arrangements are dictated by law and regulations relating to central banking. There are very few cases where ownership vests with institutions that the central bank regulates. However, there is discomfort with the fact that the governing boards of central banks are often almost wholly dominated by economists and financial experts. Insofar as the functioning of central banks has to take into account broader issues relating to society, it is quite possible that the governance arrangements will be reviewed to make them more representative of societal needs, and less representative of financial markets.

The issue of accountability and independence of central banks has gained attention in light of the crisis. There is a perception that the independence of central banks was promoted to the detriment of accountability, which could have facilitated the crisis. There will, therefore, be considerable pressure to emphasise accountability with regard to the actions taken to mitigate the effects of the crisis, and in the state of new normality after the crisis. While the operational autonomy of a central bank will continue to be respected, harmonisation in policies and accountability will gain priority.

The philosophy governing the operations of central banks may also be different in the future. The dangers of unfettered markets have been demonstrated, and the philosophy that markets will, when left to themselves, always correct themselves smoothly has been given up. Hence, the scope and depth of the intervention of central banks will increase. Further, they may be compelled to take up a more pragmatic view in choosing between rules and discretion in their operations. Perhaps in future recourse may be to a policy of flexible rules or constrained discretion. In view of the growing uncertainties, discretion is likely to play a greater role in monetary policy in the future.

In brief, while the prestige and importance of central banks may have been dented, the centrality of central banks in the financial sector as a whole will be reinforced, and the mandate to intervene in the functioning of markets also strengthened. At the same time, there will be greater emphasis on standards of governance and accountability for their actions.

THE FUTURE OF COMMERCIAL BANKS

During the boom years, the main thrust of policy in advanced economies with regard to banking was towards universal banking, so that banks were in a position to provide a wide range of financial services, including investment banking. In addition to the enabling of universal banking, the economic use of capital was given importance. Consequently, the interest of shareholders in increasing their net worth and the incentives to the management for take risks became paramount. Liquidity problems that the banks could face were neglected when principles-based regulation was emphasised. Capital adequacy calculated on the basis of similar mathematical models was adopted in major economies. Further, each bank focused on the strength of individual balance sheets and regulations governing the entities, in the process neglecting system stability.

Prior to the onset of the crisis, some analysts asserted that the totality of risks had increased during the period of low interest rate regimes; however, they held that the risks were dispersed widely. It was clear that among financial intermediaries, banks were closely regulated and, by implication, were assumed to be less vulnerable. In the US, the crisis hit investment banks, but what was shocking in this regard was that the banks themselves became vulnerable, and non-banks began performing bank-like functions, usually described as shadow banking.

The experience of the crisis has led to a considerable debate on restructuring the regulatory framework. Surprisingly, there has been little or no introspection or attempt to change the way commercial banks have been functioning internally. One of the main reasons for such inertia towards internally generated change may be that most of the shareholders and the management benefited from the bailout in most countries, leaving little incentive to change. It is not clear whether governance arrangements and internal processes in commercial banks can afford to remain unchanged.

Governments in the countries most affected, having paid a heavy price for the crisis, are under intense pressure to bring about a change in their regulatory framework. This would largely determine the future of commercial banking in such countries. It is likely that universal banking will be de-emphasised and narrow banking, in the sense of banks concentrating on core commercial banking or deposits and lending, will be emphasised. Alternately, in any universal bank the functions related to commercial banking will be kept distinct and subject to intense regulation. Restrictions on the amount of risk a bank will be permitted to undertake are also likely. This may be done by prohibiting bank financing of highly risky activities or severely restricting such exposures. Proprietary trading in financial markets, that is, trading in financial markets with owned funds rather than merely as an agent, would be restricted. Considerable constraints may be placed on the use of the originate to distribute model (a procedure by which lending by banks is securitised and sold in the financial market, thereby taking it out of the balance sheet). In brief, commercial banking is likely to be closer to a public utility than before, and hence subject to regulations akin to public utilities.

Capital adequacy requirements are likely to be strengthened. The aggregate capital required for a given set of assets may be enhanced. In addition, the quality of capital may be increased by severely restricting quasi-equity such as long-term bonds. Banks may be encouraged to pay greater attention to the funding aspects of assets, along with their liquidity aspects. In addition, financial inclusion may be emphasised and focus may revert somewhat to traditional lending to small and medium enterprises.

The rate of growth in the balance sheets of banks, especially credit, is likely to be monitored closely. There is recognition of the fact that risks are assumed by the bank as and when credit is extended, and not at a later stage when the asset actually becomes a non-performing asset. Further, the pricing of the risks of various activities can no longer be left entirely to individual institutions. The regulator will have to take a view on the assessment of the risks to which an individual bank is exposed as part of the process of supervisory review.

On the issue of ownership and governance, the general belief that public ownership should be avoided and that private ownership is the most desirable option is likely to be replaced by a more nuanced approach. The crisis forced some countries to nationalise, and exit from nationalised banks may not be that smooth or easy until trust and confidence are fully restored in the financial system. Hence, continued coexistence of government-owned and privately-owned banks will not be unusual. Both the government and private shareholders could have ownership in banks. The attitude of regulators to the shareholding of banks by sovereign wealth funds is not yet clear.

The applicability of laws relating to competition may also become more nuanced. Since there is a fear of allowing banks that are 'too big to fail', an imposition of limits on the size of banks may also be considered. Further, there may be additional capital requirements on larger banks. It is possible that the existing large banks may be forcibly split. There may be differential capital requirement depending on the size and nature of a bank. There may also be different types of deposit-taking institutions, each one subject to different degrees of regulation, including capital adequacy, depending on the nature of activities and the systemic importance of the relevant entity. The power of the banking regulator to enforce compulsory mergers—which had been given up in recent years in many countries—may be restored.

The incentive structure in the banking system is likely to be subjected to regulation. This may include the incentives available to the management; fit and proper criteria for the Board, the shareholders and the management; and a more rigorous enforcement of safeguards against the operation of conflicts of interests.

A major area of change in commercial banking will be with regard to cross-border banking. Regulation by the host country is likely to be intensified. A distinct preference for the cross-border presence of banking services through the incorporation of subsidiaries in host countries, rather than through branches, may be expected. An un-level playing field between domestic and foreign banks should not be ruled out. Banks with significant cross-border operations may also be subjected to relatively more stringent regulations.

FUTURE OF NON-BANKS IN THE FINANCIAL SECTOR

Financial intermediation by non-banks was permitted and, in some cases, encouragedin the past on two assumptions. First, savers and investors have different appetites for risks, and a variety of financial institutions and instruments should be made available to meet these preferences. Second, a multiplicity and diversity of institutions and instruments imparts stability to the overall financial system by spreading risks widely, and they add to enhanced competition in financial markets, resulting in efficiency as well. These assumptions were proved wrong in some respects in light of the experience gained with the crisis. In future, the regulatory regime will be extended to all deposit-taking institutions as well as to non-depositing institutions with systemic stability implications. The scope of regulation is likely to be extended to other institutions like hedge funds as well. Limits on the aggregate leverage of all non-banks in the financial sector should also be expected. The extent of regulatory rigour may vary, depending on the nature of the activity, the size of the institution, and the characteristics and liabilities of assets.

FUTURE OF FINANCIAL MARKETS

Before the crisis, regulatory policies with regard to financial markets were governed by the assumption that financial markets would ensure an efficient allocation of resources and simultaneously promote a dispersal of risks. The assumption was that both integrated and complete markets were the best means to achieve these objectives. They were also expected to be self-calibrating. Financial innovation was considered essential for achieving these objectives.

Under this approach, transparency was insisted upon as part of the regulation, so that contracting parties were fully aware of the financial products being transacted. Any regulation beyond the insistence on transparency was considered an undesirable intrusion into the functioning of the markets, and the burden of proof of the desirability of such intrusion was placed upon the regulator.

However, recent experience indicates that financial markets had not adequately met the expectations on which the above approach to regulation was based. This resulted in instability, since the objective of transparency was diluted by the injection of complexity. Integrated markets resulted in magnifying the risks. Financial innovations did not add to growth or economic welfare in a demonstrable manner. The freedom to trade freely resulted in over-the-counter trades, characterised by opacity and inadequate safeguards against the counter-party risks.

In view of the experience with the crisis, it can be expected that (i) the segmentation of markets may be induced by regulation; (ii) the use of taxation to discourage transactions or segmented instruments of markets should not be ruled out; (iii) the safety of the financial products may be insisted upon; (iv) over-the-counter trade may be prohibited or restricted and (v) infrastructure arrangements, including credit-rating agencies, will be subjected to rigorous public policy considerations.

FUTURE OF GLOBALISED FINANCE

Globalisation of finance grew by leaps and bounds in the decades preceding the crisis, based on new technology, a networking of institutions, new products and innovations, and, above all, on a growing emphasis on the free flow of capital. Any action to control or impede the free flow of capital in the global economy was considered to go against the interests of both the global economy and the country imposing such restrictions.

Globalisation of finance was expected to result in a flow of resources from rich developed countries to developing countries with a view to financing investments, and thereby redistribute global growth in favour of the developing countries. It was also expected to spread the risks over several segments of markets, institutions and countries. The voluntary adoption of international standards of disclosures and regulation were also expected to protect individual institutions from serious problems and also bring about systemic stability.

However, in practice, many of the stated objectives of globalised finance have not been achieved. Globalised financial markets moved resources from poor and developing countries to richer developed countries, especially to the US. A significant part of the capital flows financed consumption rather than investments. Short-term capital flows were dictated by carry-trade in currencies without any regard for economic fundamentals. These imparted considerable imbalances as well as excess volatility to capital flows and financial markets. Exchange rates tended to deviate significantly from the fundamentals for a prolonged period, with the resultant impact on the real economy. Regulatory prescriptions on individual institutions were either ineffective or unable to moderate cross-border contagion.

In spite of these unanticipated results of the globalisation of finance, it is difficult to reverse the process in any significant manner because of the easy mobility of goods and services across national boundaries, enabled by the continuous development in technologies. Further, the implications of the crisis are still under evaluation, and disappointment with such a process has not led to a new model. Yet, it is possible and worthwhile to outline some possible scenarios concerning the future of globalised finance.

In the first scenario, faith in globalised finance may intensify. The arguments in favour of reinforcing globalised finance are that issues of economic imbalance and instability arose because of incomplete globalisation. The argument is that full mobility of all factors of production in the global economy will make the world resemble a country, with the result that economic imbalances will cease to matter. In other words, as per this line of thinking, the benefits of the globalisation of finance can be enhanced and costs reduced by moving ahead with reforms supporting greater global integration. In this scenario, in order to reap the benefits of globalised finance, emphasis may be placed on globalising the regulation of finance, on the globalised coordination of the tax regimes and the globalised harmonisation of monetary policies. Countries with a dominant financial sector are likely to support this scenario. However, for this scenario to be realised, the prerequisite is virtual global governance arrangements that are binding on all national governments. This would mean a considerable erosion of space for public policy at the national level.

In the second scenario, there may be significant strengthening of the policy space in the countries. In other words, further globalisation of financial instruments, financial markets and financial institutions may be moderated by different countries. If successful, such an approach is likely to seriously undermine the importance of existing international financial centres. However, it may be difficult to effectively bring full segmentation into operation for several reasons. To a certain extent, globalisation of finance rides on the back of globalisation of trade, which has brought about some benefits. Technology enables the movement of goods and services, including finance, in a relatively easy, fast and economical manner. Hence, there are limits on the extent to which countries may impose restrictions on cross-border financial flows.

A third possibility is recalibration of the extent of the globalisation of finance and strengthening of the public policy of individual countries. In this scenario, the regulatory discretion available to national authorities may be increased. A variety of instruments may be used by individual countries at their discretion, and measures such as financial-sector taxation may be adopted with or without global agreements. In other words, there can be an ill-defined and constantly changing balance between national policy and globalised finance, and between regulation and financial markets. This somewhat unstable balance may continue for a considerable period.

FUTURE OF THE FINANCIAL SECTOR

In light of the experience gained, it may be possible to make a few general observations on the future of the financial sector. First, faith in the financial sector as a means to achieving efficiency and stability on its own momentum has been shaken. There is public anger at the functioning of the financial sector. Restoring the trust of people in the functioning of the financial sector may take considerable time. Second, links between the financial sector and political economy and, in particular, the observable capture of the public decision-making process by the financial sector has become evident. At best, this relationship may be unwound only over a prolonged period. There is a convergence between the financial sector and political economy, aimed at shoring up the performance of the financial sector in the hope that it will herald improvements in the real sector. Also, systemically important global financial centres like the US and UK have large stakes in the dominance of the financial sector, and they admittedly wield disproportionate influence over governance arrangements in the GFA. Third, at an analytical level, it has been recognised that the financial sector has grown excessively, and that a process of de-leveraging is inevitable. However, such de-leveraging is likely to be somewhat painful and prolonged. Fourth, the relationship with the real sector will be more closely observed; for instance, a closer link between financial transactions and corresponding real sector activities may be insisted upon in commodity markets. Finally, in the academia, theories and ideologies advocating largely unfettered markets as the optimal solution are under review. The ideology of free markets as applied to the financial sector seems to be under attack. It is not clear whether a review of ideologies is necessary for the management of economic policies as a whole, or whether such unfettered markets are inappropriate only with respect to financial markets. While simple theories and complex models relating to the financial sector and based on unrealistic assumptions stand discredited, there has as yet been no coherent, consistent model of thinking that could govern the future role of the financial sector.

The most challenging task for public policy is likely to be managing public debt, since the level of peace-time public debt is at an all-time high in many countries. Most of the debt of governments is held by financial intermediaries, and a significant part is traded among them. Financial markets play a critical role in the financing of public debt. A large part of the additional public debt was incurred to avoid financial collapse, to bailout institutions and normalise markets. Sometimes, the bailout of sovereigns has been to the advantage of financial intermediaries. However, public policy will have to depend heavily on the assessments and sentiments of the same financial institutions that it helped to bailout. In the absence of a nationalisation of banks and other intermediaries, the balance of power and influence between governments and financial markets will perhaps depend on the management of public debt, especially in advanced economies. In an environment of globalised finance, the dependence of national governments on global financial markets could be a matter of great concern for public policy.

Six

Global Economy 2010 and Beyond[*]

$\mathscr{T}$here is now relief the world over that financial collapse due to the crisis in 2008 has been avoided, and that although the world experienced recession in 2009, the prospects for 2010 appear to be better. However, there is some uncertainty about recovery and prospects for the future. This article (i) provides a brief account of the crisis of 2008, the policy response and its observable outcome; (ii) assesses the potential costs of having avoided the collapse; (iii) outlines the features of what may be described as the great recession of 2009; (iv) notes the signs of uneven recovery observed in many countries and the uncertainties on the path to normality and (v) highlights some of the implications of these developments for public policy in India.

[*] This chapter is an edited version of the lecture delivered at the Centenary Celebrations of Professor Malcom Adiseshiah, Madras Institute of Development Studies, Chennai, 30 April 2010.

THE CRISIS OF 2008: RESPONSE AND OUTCOME

The crisis had multiple causes that can for the sake of brevity be reduced to five factors. These are: (i) inappropriate macroeconomic policies; (ii) ineffective regulation of the financial sector; (iii) an inadequate GFA, especially the international financial institutions and international monetary systems; (iv) the inevitability of cycles in the market economy and (v) an extraordinary but synchronised failure of markets. While there is no agreement on the weight to be attached to each one of these explanations, public policy has responded to the crisis in a proactive manner in order to avoid serious adverse consequences.

The policy response was initiated in the US, where the crisis originated. Almost simultaneously, there was coordinated action among select advanced economies. Subsequently, a coordination of policies among several important countries was designed on a global scale, mainly among the countries of the G-20. It is useful to note that most actions with regard to the crisis were taken at the national level, although there was a degree of harmony and coordination.

The objective of the coordinated response was to prevent the collapse of financial markets, and simultaneously to explore methods of avoiding similar occurrences in the future. The instruments used at the national level were addressed to the immediate task of avoiding the persistence of the crisis in the financial sector and its serious spillover to the economic sector in the form of deflation, loss of economic activity and possible depression.

The instruments utilised by different countries varied, but there was an observable pattern. In countries where financial markets were seriously affected, monetary policy was utilised to assure liquidity and make it available to the markets. Open market operations were conducted on a massive scale. Extraordinary measures were taken, such as assuring liquidity for prolonged periods against collateral of doubtful value. Monetary policy became highly accommodative with low interest rates and ample liquidity. Individual financial institutions were bailed out with massive fiscal support. Coordination between monetary and fiscal policies became critical. Fiscal stimulus measures were undertaken in many countries to make up for the loss of economic activity in the private sector. These included increased public expenditures and relief on the tax burden. Administrative measures through directions and regulations in several areas, as appropriate, were taken in several countries.

The actual mix of the policies and instruments varied, depending on the country's context. For example, in countries where financial institutions were not seriously affected, bailouts were not necessary. In countries where the fiscal situation was already under stress, fiscal stimulus was somewhat constrained. Some of the countries that were severely affected approached the IMF and World Bank for support. Unlike in the recent past, even industrialised countries approached the IMF.

The immediate outcome of the policy responses has been to avoid a serious collapse of financial markets. While some financial institutions did go bankrupt, a number of large financial institutions that were considered vital for systemic stability and 'too big to fail' were bailed out. In some cases capital was infused into such institutions, while a few others were nationalised.

By and large, it was observed that the financial sectors in the US, UK and Western Europe were seriously affected, relative to other countries. There was contagion to other countries through several channels, namely, finance, trade, corporate and sentiment. The impact of the contagion was greatly moderated by virtue of the harmonised actions. However, economic distress persists, and so while financial collapse was avoided, economic distress could not be averted. In some countries, there are indications of the economic distresses having spilled over into political and social unrest.

COSTS OF AVOIDING COLLAPSE

It is possible to argue that the bailout was unnecessary, and that the most efficient way of correcting imbalances would have been to allow the markets to bear the costs of unwinding the excesses that had led to the crisis. At the other extreme is a view that the stimulus, particularly fiscal stimulus, has been inadequate and, therefore, the effort should be towards immediately intensifying the stimulus to make it effective and minimise the cost of the crisis. The dominant view appears to be that the fiscal and monetary policy responses have been, by and large, in the right direction and in the limited context of avoiding a collapse, although opinions may differ about the quality of fiscal stimulus and the transparency of some of the measures. There is merit in assessing the possible costs that may have to be incurred as a result of the actions already taken to avoid a collapse of the financial markets, and minimise the chances of depression in the global economy.

First, the mounting public debt incurred, particularly in advanced economies, on account of the stimulus measures is an area of considerable concern. The magnitude of public debt in major advanced economies is tending to be the highest in peace time history. Servicing such a public debt will have serious implications for medium-term growth and inflation.

Second, the highly accommodative monetary policy that has been adopted could, in some circumstances, lead to inflation, while in some others it can lead to a liquidity trap.

Third, the excess liquidity in some countries may encourage capital flows to other countries, and in view of the uncertainties involved, capital flows could become more volatile. Moreover, if different countries exit from the accommodative monetary policies at different times, the differences in monetary policies may trigger short-term flows, particularly through 'carry trade in currencies'.

Fourth, it is also suggested that the excessive leverage that led to the crisis has not been fully corrected. As a result, the process of de-leveraging will have to be continued in the private sector, with its corresponding burden on the economies.

Finally, in some important countries the short-term measures taken to manage the crisis may have a tendency to aggravate the problems of adjustments over the medium-term. For instance, in the US, measures were taken to augment private consumption in order to emerge from recession. But in the long run, this will aggravate the fundamental problem of excess consumption over savings that the US is facing now. Similarly, in China, the long-term problem is the imbalance between investment and consumption, with investment being very large relative to consumption. However, the stimulus policy was essentially based on increasing investment expenditure in the public sector. This short-term solution may make medium-term adjustments more difficult.

Thus, success in averting a collapse has obvious costs; however, these are likely to be experienced over the years. The distribution of these costs and burdens between countries and within each country will raise contentious issues. Each country will be tempted to minimise the costs of adjustment on its own citizens and shift the burden to the external world to the extent possible. There will also be the problem of distributing the burden of adjustment between sectors, and between various sections of the population within each country. In fact, some discussion is already taking place about making the financial sector bear a part of the burden through mechanisms such as taxes.

Further, international financial institutions that assist a number of countries have recently been extending assistance to advanced economies as well. This is raising issues of equity in the distribution of risks and burdens in extending such assistance. International financial institutions are already burdened by ideologies that are now widely perceived to have been partly responsible for the crisis. There are also issues of deficits in governance arrangements, which have been acknowledged and are still in the process of correction. Thus, as the global economy moves on to face the potentially significant costs of avoiding a collapse, it will have to take stock of the contentious issues in sharing the burden of consequences of actions already taken. These issues are likely to have considerable spillover effects beyond economic management into political management and social balance.

THE GREAT RECESSION OF 2009

It may be useful to clarify the of concepts depression, recession and slowdown. A slowdown is understood to be a clear fall in the growth rate of an economy or of the overall business activity. It is usually a short-term phenomenon lasting, say, a quarter or a year. In this chapter, it is defined as a drop in the growth rate by one percentage point, or a hundred basis points.

Recession refers to a sustained decline in the overall economic activity, but not solely reflected in the GDP. While there is no universally accepted definition of recession, a prolonged slowdown to the point of growth being negative is generally taken to mean recession. In the US, the word recession is used to describe the negative growth in GDP for two consecutive quarters. In this chapter, however, the term is used to denote one year of negative growth.

Depression, however, lasts longer than a recession and refers to a longer and larger decline in business activity, mainly reflected in a huge drop in output and employment. The Great Depression that had embraced the global economy started in 1929 and continued till the late 1930s, although the word was coined much after its commencement. Personal income, tax revenue, profits and prices dropped, and international trade plunged by a half to two-thirds. Unemployment in the US rose to 25 per cent, and in some countries rose as high as 33 per cent. Cities all around the world were hit hard, especially those dependent on heavy industry. Construction was virtually halted in many countries. Farming and rural areas suffered as crop prices fell by approximately 60 per cent.

After World War II, there have only been occasional depressions in specific countries, for instance, the recent depressions in Finland and Indonesia. Recessions and slowdowns, on the other hand, have been far more frequent and common.

The Associated Press style book formally recognised the term 'Great Recession' on 23 February 2010. The term refers to the downturn that began in December 2007 in the US. It is generally believed to have been first used by Paul Volcker, former Chairman of the US Federal Reserve.

The recession of 2009 qualifies, in any case, to be described as 'Great' because it embraced so many countries. The World Economic Outlook, published by the IMF in April 2010, reveals that all major advanced economies, namely, the US, Germany, France, Italy, Spain, Japan, UK and Canada had a negative growth rate in the year 2009. The advanced economies as a group had a negative growth rate in GDP of about −3 per cent p.a. The newly industrialised Asian economies also recorded a negative growth rate. Negative growth rate was also recorded in Central and Eastern European countries and the Commonwealth of Independent States (CIS). Recession embraced most of the western hemisphere, including Brazil and Mexico. Thus, in terms of its sheer sweep, the recession of 2009 deserves to be characterised as the 'Great Recession'.

A caveat may be in order here. Although the Great Recession was international and global, it was not universal, and many countries escaped it. As a group, emerging and developing economies had a positive growth rate. The geographical regions of developing Asia, the Middle East, North Africa and sub-Saharan Africa did not show negative growth rates, although individual countries within these broad groups did experience recession.

However, all the countries that escaped the Great Recession, with the prominent exception of China, did experience a slowdown. China's growth rate also declined in 2009, but the fall was less than one percentage point, thereby technically escaping a 'slowdown'.

The uneven spread of the Great Recession was generally due to differences between individual countries in terms of the (i) vulnerability of their financial sector; (ii) the existence of macroeconomic imbalances or vulnerabilities; (iii) the extent of stimulus employed and (iv) the nature and extent of the economy's integration with the global economy. Experience shows that broad generalisations such as coupling or decoupling nations with the global economy are oversimplifications of a reality that is significantly more complex. It may be useful to approach the subject of coupling with an examination of the nature and extent of coupling a nation's economy with others.

Uneven Recovery in 2010

If the Great Recession was uneven, so is the recovery.

The initiation of policies to exit from the extraordinary and stimulus measures undertaken to avoid or moderate depression, deflation and recession provide early signs that spread expectations of recovery. On the other hand, there is an opinion that stimulus should be intensified in some countries where it has so far been inadequate. There is thus recognition—in principle—that exit policies should be considered by each country, depending on its circumstances.

Some countries, including India, initiated the process of exit in the last quarter of 2009. However, many other countries are yet to formally initiate exit policies. It is also recognised that exit from extraordinary measures may be gradual, unlike the entry of the measures, which was prompt and synchronised. Moreover, the measures to exit may be undertaken over different periods of time in different countries. There is evidence of two important problems with regard to exit, namely, the problem of coordination of policies, especially fiscal and monetary, within each country, and the problem of coordination of exit policies between the countries. It is recognised that the risks of both premature and delayed withdrawal are very different for individual economies.

The recovery of countries could follow one of the five possible patterns. These may be signified as: **V, U, W, √, L**

V represents a rapid reduction in economic activity promptly followed by rapid recovery. This signifies a highly resilient economy.

U represents an economy that is less resilient and, therefore, one that would require a longer time for public policies and private-sector participants to adjust to the new realities and ensure full recovery.

W represents a double dip recession before recovery. In this scenario, there could be some recovery followed by another recession or slowdown before a sustainable recovery. This pattern may be witnessed more frequently in economies that are tracked on a quarterly basis.

√ shows economies that undertake structural measures over a prolonged period, reflecting slow but consistently positive recovery after recession.

L represents economies that register a low level of economic activity for a prolonged period, a level of activity that could be close to zero.

According to the IMF report, a multi-speed recovery may be expected in the year 2010 for the world as a whole, and for both advanced and developing economies. The turnaround in GDP between 2009 and 2010 is expected to be 5.5 per cent in the case of advanced economies, while it would be 3.9 per cent in developing economies. Asia, which did not experience recession, will experience a turnaround of only 2.1 per cent. The growth rate for 2012 is expected to be maintained at the same level as that in 2011. However, these estimates made by the IMF in April 2010 have to be viewed against the growing uncertainties of the prospects for growth.

A disaggregated view of the prospects for countries, on a judgemental basis, may add to an understanding of the prospects. Countries that are most resilient and experiencing fast recovery would naturally include China, India, Brazil and Korea. Countries hard hit by the crisis but firmly on the path to recovery would include Hong Kong, Singapore, Taiwan, Thailand, Russia, Argentina and Chile. There are some who would include the US in this category. Countries hard hit by the crisis but with uncertain prospects for recovery would include Germany, Japan, Italy, the UK, France, Greece, etc. This group would also include countries of East Europe and the CIS. In the developing world, Turkey, Mexico and Venezuela are prominent examples of hard hit countries with uncertain prospects.

Thus, recovery is bound to be uneven. This large divergence in the prospects for recovery between countries implies that policy space at the national level has to be given greater weight than policy coordination at the global level. Larger economies may be inclined to take policy actions at the national level that may appear to be a setback, perhaps a temporary one, to process of globalisation, in particular of finance.

POLICY CHALLENGES FOR INDIA

India has been less affected by the crisis than most other countries. Of the several reasons responsible for this, the most important have been the avoidance of macroeconomic imbalances; more active countercyclical policies in the monetary and financial sectors; and a moderate integration with the global economy. The policy response was also prompt and effective. A well-thought-out use of a range of policy instruments already put in place during the boom years helped to effectively manage the crisis.

The impact of the crisis on the slowdown in the Indian GDP in 2008 and 2009 has to be viewed against the background of domestic cycles and the performance of agriculture. Economic growth in the years immediately preceding the crisis was considered to be showing signs of overheating, and some correction was in any case due in India. Further, the poor performance of agriculture had its impact on the growth of GDP. It can be argued that the effect these factors had on the slowdown should be accounted for, and only the balance attributed to the effects of the global crisis. Thus, the impact of the global crisis was far less than what the slowdown in GDP growth rates indicates.

The policy responses to the crisis on the part of fiscal and monetary authorities were prompt and effective. It can be argued that the safety factor in the responses was fairly high, in the sense that the measures were undertaken on the principle that it is better to be safe than sorry. One evidence adduced by analysts in favour of this argument is the extent of liquidity that the RBI had to absorb on a day-to-day basis, and the extent of unutilised refinance facilities from the RBI. Against this background, the management of exit has to take account of the excesses, if any, of the stimulus undertaken.

It is noteworthy that India was one of the earliest and foremost countries to commence exit in the sphere of monetary policy. However, the process of gradual exit will necessarily have to take into account the management of expectations as well as some underlying vulnerabilities in the economy. Domestic supply rigidities continue in India unlike in many countries, where unutilised capacities may be found in the context of the slowdown or recession. The three important sources of external shock, relating to food, fuel and finance, are also mired in global uncertainty. Moreover, India is among the few countries that did not face the threat of deflation during the slowdown; instead, it actually faced significant inflationary pressures in Consumer Prices Indices. There has been notable evidence of mounting inflationary pressures in the country during this period.

Against this background, the emphasis on economic management will have to be less on the integration of India with the global economy and more on installing shock absorbers to moderate the impact of global uncertainties on the Indian economy, while focusing attention on the bottlenecks in the domestic economy that impede accelerated inclusive growth with stability.

Three areas of policy action deserve priority at this juncture. First, globally there has been increasing evidence of market failures in several activities, both in financial and commodities markets. Uncertainties mark many global markets. Public policy in India has to take a conscious decision to insulate the country from the transmission of excess volatilities of the global economy. Such commitment to avoid a contagion of excess volatility should be transparent and determined. The application of a precautionary principle to public policy is therefore called for at this juncture. In general, the precautionary principle involves acting to avoid serious or irreversible potential harm, in spite of the lack of scientific certainty as to the likelihood, magnitude, or causation of that harm. Although it is an established principle of environmental governance, such an approach may be desirable in the current state, where the outlook for the global economy is uncertain.

Second, uneven trends in recovery in different countries point to the possibility of a large degree of volatility in cross-country capital flows, and consequently to excessive volatility in foreign exchange markets globally. The US Dollar, which is the international reserve currency, is subjected to two equally strong and conflicting forces, namely, the longer-term requirement that it should depreciate given America's current account deficit, and the short-term use of the dollar as a safe haven given the uncertainties in competing currencies like the Euro, UK Pound Sterling and Yen. Hence, there is merit in an open commitment to manage the capital account actively, thereby discouraging financial markets from taking extreme positions. This precautionary approach will be more fruitful than engaging in a more active management of the capital account after serious problems arise in the currency markets.

Third, the sentiment with regard to public debt in general could turn negative in global financial markets. However, this might not immediately or directly impact India, since non-residents hold a very small fraction of Indian government securities. However, India's very success may lead to vulnerability in this area. The proven resilience of the Indian economy and the anticipated bright prospects for growth may whet the appetite for Indian government securities in international financial markets. This will increase the pressure on government by global financial markets for greater access to the public debt of India. If India gives in to such pressures, it would undermine an important policy source of stability in Indian debt markets. The lessons from Greece should not be ignored in haste. Further, in these uncertain times, the existing arrangement of public debt management by the RBI should continue to be a cornerstone in the successful management of the large government borrowing programme in India. Criticism with regard to current arrangements, which state that the RBI has been 'fixing' the government securities market to enable a smooth borrowing programme by the government, ignores the fact that it is an arrangement that is most suited to meet global uncertainties of the nature that we face now, and perhaps for several years ahead.

SECTION II

Financial Sector:
Retrospect and Prospects

Regulation of the Financial Sector in Developing Countries: Lessons from the Current Crisis*

$\mathcal{T}$his chapter is divided into five sections. The first section provides an overview of the considerations that are important in drawing lessons from the global crisis, especially from the point of view of developing economies. The second section addresses the major issues concerning the scope of and limits to countercyclicality in regulation, in view of the widely perceived need for such an approach to avoid similar crises in future. The third section addresses issues relating to comprehensiveness in the regulatory scope of the financial sector, which have recently found focus. The fourth section explores possible improvements in regulatory structures suggested by the recent crisis. The concluding section lists several broader

* This chapter is based on a paper presented at the Financial Regulation Conference held at the Columbia University, New York, 13 November 2008. A version of the paper has been published in Stephany Griffith-Jones, Jose Antonio Ocampo and Joseph E. Stiglitz (eds), *Time for a Visible Hand*, New York: Oxford University Press, 2010.

issues that need to be kept in mind while considering improvements in the future regulation of the financial sector.

The observations in this chapter are essentially from a practitioner's perspective. Further, several comments are based on experiences in the RBI. Consequently, while they have the advantage of pragmatism, they may not necessarily carry universal validity or acceptance.

Drawing Appropriate Lessons from the Crisis

There have been extensive analyses of the origin and evolution of the current financial crisis, and these are very valuable for drawing lessons. However, there is no agreement on several aspects of the crisis, and it is not yet clear how the consequences of the crisis will unfold. Hence, while all the lessons from the current crisis are valuable, they may be subject to possible modifications as greater insights into the events are gained.

Further, developing economies are very diverse and are at different stages vis-à-vis the development of their financial sectors and the extent of integration with the global economy. Thus, while some generalisations based on lessons from the crisis are possible, they have to be placed in the context of the particular economy under consideration.

It is equally important to recognise that financial sectors in various economies have been impacted with different degrees of intensity. For example, the extensive crisis in the US is in contrast to the relative stability of its immediate neighbour, Canada, which has a fairly developed financial system and is an open economy. In other words, lessons need to be drawn not only from the experiences of those countries that are seriously affected and are consequently under intense scrutiny, but also from those economies, both advanced and developing, that are less intensely affected.

It is noteworthy that in terms of the first-order effects of the crisis, financial institutions in developing countries have been less affected than those in advanced economies. This could partly be due to the fact that financial sectors in the former are dominated by traditional banks, and have not hosted complex financial products. The credit crunch and volatility in equity markets in advanced economies have certainly impacted institutions in developing countries, essentially by way of contagion, especially when such markets or institutions happened to be over-leveraged. The contagion is, in any case, being transmitted though a liquidity and credit crunch. To the extent that money and credit markets in the developed world squeeze the credit available for cross-border trade, the availability of trade credit to exporters and importers in developing countries also gets constrained. In addition, this puts greater pressure on the spot domestic money and forex markets, as importers seek to borrow domestic currencies to purchase foreign exchange in order to honour their obligations. Therefore, there are also issues in the opening letters of credit by banks.

The second-order effect of the crisis acts through volatility in capital flows, which seriously impacts the exchange rates. This aspect is currently high on the agenda of developing economies.

The third-order effect, which is already influencing sentiment in all economies, acts through linkages with the real sector, especially with trade. There is extraordinary volatility in several commodity prices at the same time, which has a severe impact on many developing economies. The consequential impact of linkages in the real sector on growth and profitability in developing economies has the potential to generate non-performing assets in the balance sheets of banks in developing economies.

The causes and cross-border transmission of the crisis may differ significantly between the advanced as well as between the developing economies. An appreciation of these differences is critical for drawing appropriate lessons from the crisis, both for advanced and developing economies.

The impact of volatility in capital flows may be particularly severe on developing countries due to the mere fact of their being developing economies, although the soundness of their regulatory structures, policies or economic fundamentals would still be relevant. There may be several reasons for this; for example, developing economies have limited access to international reserve currencies. Further, their scope for coordinated intervention, akin to that by the G-7 economies, is very limited. Moreover, international financial markets perceive the risks and rewards in developing economies as being qualitatively different from those in advanced economies.

There are several features common to all economies in their policy responses to the current crisis. These include a focus on the fiscal stimulus to growth, injection of liquidity and reduction in policy interest rates. But there are also differences between them. The most visible difference is in the magnitude of the injection of capital into banks and other financial intermediaries. The most affected among advanced economies took recourse to coordinated action by major central banks and their governments, while the seriously affected developing economies approached multilateral agencies, particularly the IMF, for support. This is in spite of the fact that some developing countries—other than those most seriously affected—command significant foreign exchange reserves. It is also significant that advanced economies had the freedom in policymaking to take recourse to measures that are somewhat unorthodox, even by self-set standards.

In order to draw appropriate lessons from the crisis for regulating the financial sector, it is essential to look beyond this sector, not only because the crisis, having become an economic crisis, is now no longer financial, but also because it itself reflects the prevalence of several macroeconomic imbalances and political economy considerations. In spite of these complexities, this chapter tries to focus on factors directly relevant to the financial sector while drawing lessons from the crisis.

The prevailing standards of capital regulations for financial intermediaries, that have some degree of acceptance at the global level, are Basel II standards. It has been argued that the crisis is in some ways a reflection of the inadequacy of the Basel II framework, even though it was developed by regulators of advanced economies working over several years. It is also noteworthy that the origin and initial intensity of the crisis in the financial sector have substantially been in the two leading international financial centres, which may have been guilty of soft regulation.

It can be held that an incentive for softer regulation may exist when there is competition between a few countries to attract the financial services industry. The emphasis on saving capital in the regulation of the financial sector and excessive dependence on self-regulation by market participants, instead of imposed regulation, may be considered signs of intense competition to attract the industry to the concerned jurisdiction. In this process, the regulators concerned may have underestimated the risks to the system and the costs of a bailout. In theory, over a long period, markets should be able to perceive the risks emanating from self-regulation in a particular country. However, in practice the incentives involved and the relevant time horizons may lead to an underestimation of such risks by market participants for a prolonged period. Financial market participants had short time horizons and large incentives to take undue risks. This may have led to a serious underestimation of risks for prolonged periods. The reliance on self-regulation by market participants, the principle-based approach to regulation involving a limited use of prescriptions or rules, the evolution of a shadow banking system as well as rapid innovations may have reflected the attitudes of regulators, incentives for the regulated and the inclinations of public policy. Associated entities such as credit rating agencies may also have an interest in such a framework, which is conducive to both their expansion and continued dominance.

In this context, it is essential to recognise that eagerness for a thriving international financial centre is often, explicitly or implicitly, a decision of a broader public policy, and not merely that of the regulators. In the normal course, the regulatory framework may have to align itself to such a public policy stance, thereby attracting several political economy considerations. In India, a committee was appointed by the government to recommend measures to develop

Mumbai (Bombay) into an international financial centre. The recommendations were far-reaching and involved the whole gamut of fiscal, monetary and prudential measures for the country as a whole. There was an implicit assumption that the financial centre in India would not only provide employment and generate output, but will also lead real-sector development in the entire country. In the view of this author, development of the financial sector plays a critical, but not necessarily a leading, role in facilitating growth with stability. Hence the need to persevere with reforms in the financial sector along sound lines to serve the main goals of the real economy. For this purpose, financial-sector reforms need to take into account progress in fiscal and institutional areas as well.

In this context, the recent experience of the financial crisis has generated debates on several fronts. This chapter draws attention to three important areas specific to the regulation of the financial sector: the relevance of countercyclical regulation, the need to make regulation more comprehensive and the scope to refashion the regulatory structures.

COUNTERCYCLICAL REGULATION

Several arguments have been advanced in favour of injecting elements of countercyclicality in regulation. In particular, scholars in the BIS have, in recent years, advocated greater attention to the rapid growth of credit, deterioration in the quality of credit and the steep acceleration in prices of assets. The RBI and a few others, such as the Central Bank of Spain, have taken recourse to various instruments of countercyclical prudential regulation. The RBI identified early signs of overheating in 2006, and had been tightening the monetary policy in an uninterrupted fashion since 2004 until a few months ago, using both direct and indirect instruments of monetary policy. It has also been using prudential measures relating to foreign currency exposures of all financial intermediaries under its jurisdiction as part of the management of the capital account. Further, a range of monetary, prudential and fiscal instruments have been used to influence the overall liquidity in the markets. On the basis of this limited experience, it can be held that it may be operationally feasible to design instruments for countercyclical regulations and to use them effectively, consistent with high growth in output, low inflation and the overall stability of the financial sector.

The case for countercyclical policies is stronger in developing economies in view of the greater weight that has to be accorded to stability in these economies. Growth is essential for the eradication of poverty in such economies, but the gains from growth typically trickle to the poor after a time lag. In contrast, the pains of high inflation as well as financial instability visit the poor instantly. Moreover, the poor have only marginal capabilities and resources with which to manage or mitigate risks, while most governments in developing economies have very few mechanisms for social security.

At the same time, designing and implementing a countercyclical policy is more complex in developing economies. The cycles are not easily identifiable, especially if a significant structural transformation is underway in the economy. In some countries with persistent fiscal deficits, the head room for an expansionary fiscal policy may be limited. The transmission of monetary policy is constrained by several factors, particularly by the level of development of financial markets. The environment of public policies, especially through administered interest rates and directed credit, make the transmission more complex. The effectiveness of prudential measures depends on the standards of governance in the financial institutions operating in the country. Above all, a relatively open capital account muffles the transmission of monetary policy. In developing countries, therefore, there is a special case for harmonised countercyclical policies in the three policy spheres, namely, monetary, prudential and fiscal.

The difficulty of identifying the building up of asset bubbles is well-recognised. But the issue for operational purposes is: where should the judgement tilt when there are doubts? Perhaps in all developing economies the tilt may have to be to protect, at a minimum, what may be considered critical financial institutions, namely banks, from the serious ill-effects of the bubble if it were to build and burst. Banks stand out as most critical since a common person, particularly in developing economies, seeks an institution, traditionally banks, to keep his meagre personal savings safe. It is essential for public policy to assure such a facility, and recent events have shown that governments would be obliged to make such a facility available even in the event of a crisis. In brief, there is a strong case, based on the experience of recent events, to ensure that bank depositors are protected from the ill-effects of volatile business cycles. The RBI's approach in response to the rapid growth of credit and asset prices was through temporary measures aimed to generally increase the risk weights, seek additional provisioning, impose quantitative limits and indulge in supervisory review of select banks to protect them, to the extent feasible, from a serious downturn in asset prices, if one were to occur. The quantitative limits on exposures and a few other prescriptions were flexible with reference to any specific institution, if it were able to establish its risk containment policies to the satisfaction of the regulator.

COMPREHENSIVENESS IN REGULATORY SCOPE

Recent events, particularly in the US, have triggered a debate on the need to expand the scope and coverage of financial regulation. There is a plea for greater comprehensiveness in institutions that are subject to regulation, and the reasoning is broadly as follows.

First, while regulators focused their attention on banks, the crisis stemmed essentially from non-banks, especially investment banks, and in some ways from hedge funds or private-equity funds. Second, the relationships between banks and non-banks were not adequately regulated, and as a result the assurance of liquidity support from banks, implicit in such relationships, was not monitored. The consequences of the 'originate and distribute' model partly reflected this weakness. Third, while regulating banks, their excessive dependence on resources other than deposits was not monitored. Fourth, large corporates emerged as big players in financial markets; however, financial regulators could not regulate them. Some of the players operated in such a way that their operations became 'too big to fail'. When a market player perceives itself to have become 'too big to be allowed to fail', it takes undue risks in anticipation of being bailed out by public policy, if it falls into difficulties. Fifth, the risk of individual financial institutions could have been assessed by each institution to the satisfaction of the regulator. But the exposures of institutions to each other within the financial sector might have been largely ignored. It may be noted that this phenomenon is different from the consolidated supervision of conglomerates, in the sense that it relates to the exposures of conglomerates to each other collectively. Sixth, financial innovations appeared to have spread the risk widely and often away from regulated entities, like banks and institutional companies. In reality, however, such innovations removed the risks from the regulator's radar, while substantively reverting to the banking system under stressful conditions. Correspondingly, the off-balance sheet obligations of financial institutions might have been seriously underestimated by the regulators.

There are several issues concerning the costs and benefits of more comprehensive regulation, but recent events have *de facto* enlarged the scope of central banking in terms of the institutions dealt with and instruments used. The frontiers of financial regulation already stand redefined in the context of the crisis. In a way, therefore, comprehensiveness in financial regulation has perhaps come to stay. But what is needed is a well-thought-out redrawing of the boundaries and intensity of financial regulation across financial institutions and their activities.

The RBI had attempted to address these issues in several ways, even as problems were building up in the global financial sector.

The RBI retained its jurisdiction to regulate about 30,000 NBFCs, although operationally it focused only on a few—the deposit-taking institutions and systemically important ones defined on the basis of the size of their balance sheets. Regular monitoring of systemically important NBFCs helped timely correctives, particularly in terms of enhancing capital requirements in 2006. Further, the extent of both direct and indirect exposures of the banking system to such NBFCs was also regulated. The NBFCs themselves were divided into several categories and regulatory regimes were fine-tuned to suit each category. Noticing the tendency of banks to hold each others' equities on their books, a limit of 5 per cent of the total equity was placed on any bank's holdings in any other single bank. The guidelines on securitisation issued in 2006 provide for a conservative treatment of securitisation, exposures for capital adequacy purposes (especially with regard to credit enhancement) and liquidity facilities. In order to reduce the extent of concentration of banks' liabilities, guidelines were issued placing prudential limits on the extent of the inter-bank liability of banks. Further, guidelines aiming to contain the risks arising out of banks' investment portfolio, in particular their holdings of non-government securities, were issued. Banks were specifically advised not to be guided solely by the ratings assigned to these securities by credit rating agencies. An articulation of issues relating to financial stability in the public domain, moral suasion, supervisory review of over-extended individual banks, and emphasis on regulatory comfort rather than mere regulatory compliance were the important instruments used with regard to several areas of regulatory concern. In brief, the experience of the RBI indicates that it is possible to dynamically define the boundaries of regulation, depending on evolving conditions in the financial sectors, provided that regulators have the mandate, the skills and, above all, real operational freedom. A comprehensive coverage in accordance with the mandate combined with operational freedom, executed in terms of exhaustive monitoring but with selectivity in prescriptions and intervention appear to add to the capacity of the regulator to dynamically redefine the boundaries of its activities.

REGULATORY STRUCTURES

There is a view that the current crisis is essentially on account of regulators' inability to cope with the pace of financial innovation, and partly on account of weaknesses in regulatory structures at the national and, to some extent, the international levels. In this regard, it is useful to note that the most seriously affected financial institutions are those that were reputed to have the best capabilities in risk assessment and risk management. Similarly, the reportedly high regulatory standards of the most seriously affected countries were not adequate to avert a crisis. Consequently, it is held that the fault may lie with the structures of regulation, and hence a plea is made for improvements in regulatory structures. At a very general level, it can be argued that there is no convincing evidence of serious shortcomings in the regulatory environment in developing economies as far as the current crisis is concerned, and hence the focus should be on issues of regulation in advanced economies and on global regulatory structures in view of the contribution of the globalisation of finance to the crisis.

Current debates on appropriate national-level regulatory parameters are of interest to developing economies too, both due to the globalisation of finance and their goal of aligning with internationally set standards. It is first suggested that a single regulator for the financial sector would avoid regulatory arbitrage and add to stability, while the central bank should be responsible for monetary policy and financial stability. Another view is that, ideally, the central bank itself could assume the responsibility of a single regulator, combining both monetary and regulatory functions. A third view, particularly relevant for developing economies, is that the regulation of banking should lie with the central bank and that of other financial institutions could lie with other regulators. The empirical evidence so far appears mixed, and hence it may not be appropriate to take a definite view on the issue of a single versus multiple regulators. However, whatever be the structures, close coordination between regulatory functions is undoubtedly critical, irrespective of whether they are located with a single or multiple authorities.

In India, the RBI, in addition to regulating banks, regulates the NBFCs, the money and government securities markets, and the payment system. Regulation of other activities in the financial sector is distributed between a capital-market regulator, an insurance regulator and a regulator of pension funds. However, there is a High Level Committee on Capital and Financial Markets presided over by the Governor of the RBI, and its members include the heads of the regulatory bodies in the financial sector mentioned earlier as well as the permanent secretary of the Ministry of Finance. This High Level Committee has in its turn constituted standing technical committees to ensure coordination on operational issues, and more generally to assist the Committee. In brief, the Indian experience points to the desirability of establishing standing mechanisms for a close and continuous coordination of regulation in the financial sector, irrespective of the fact that statutory compulsions do not exist for such mechanisms.

Another view states that the regulation of the financial sector has often been left to experts in finance, money or economics, and that such an approach encourages an inward-looking view in regulation, while possibly ignoring the implications for other stakeholders, including depositors or borrowers or consumers of financial services. As against this, there is the recognition that the regulation of the financial sector is highly specialised and technical in nature. In India, a Board for Financial Supervision (BFS) has been established within the RBI to make regulation and supervision somewhat autonomous within itself. The Board advises and guides the RBI in all matters relating to regulation and supervision of banks and NBFCs. The Board, which meets at least once a month, is presided over by the Governor, RBI, and in addition to the deputy governors has four non-official, part-time, independent members. They are eminent people, currently drawn from the fields of accounting, macroeconomics, corporates in the real sector, and those from civil society associated with non-government organisations. It is interesting to note that the BFS identifies any bank whose functioning gives rise to regulatory discomfort and subjects such a bank's functioning to a monthly monitoring. Yet another set of institutions is the technical advisory committees, which address issues relating to regulation. These consist of representatives from academics, self-regulatory organisations, industry associations and select representatives of the regulated entities. These committees meet less frequently than the BFS and have no statutory backing, unlike the BFS, which has been duly notified under law.

Finally, there is a view that a formal mandate to a central bank for financial stability is desirable. In India the RBI has no such formal mandate, but it has interpreted its mandate on monetary stability to include, for operational purposes, both price and financial stability, in addition to growth. The general approach has been to pursue multiple objectives with an explicit statement on relative priorities from time to time, depending on the circumstances evidenced by multiple indicators. In fact, regulation of banks is one of the multiple instruments used for operational purposes by the RBI in the pursuit of policy objectives.

SOME BROADER ISSUES

Several broader issues need to be kept in mind while considering changes in the regulatory structures of regimes of the developing economies, in light of the recent financial crisis. Most developing economies recognise the need for reforms in their financial sectors. However, recent developments raise doubts as to the efficacy of known and existing models of the financial sector in advanced economies. Hence, in future, reforms in the financial sector may have to take cognisance of the evolving wisdom on the subject, and this suggests the need for gradualism. Further, fundamental changes in regulatory regimes do require acceptance by political authorities and legislative actions. The prevailing uncertainties may inject elements of reaction into what should ideally be a well-thought-out action in public policy. However, changes in regulatory regimes that are considered essential to managing the crisis itself should receive priority. Changes in regulatory policies as distinct from structures may certainly be warranted to meet the challenges. In this context, the experience with sub-prime lending in the US seems to question the wisdom of financial inclusion as a goal of public policy, although such an inference is unfortunate. Financial inclusion should mean ensuring access to all relevant financial services to all sections of the populace, and should not be equated with aggressive lending or a simple provision of micro-credit driven by a profit motive.

Recent debates on the crisis have focused on the role of tax havens, and in this regard developing economies have a high stake in view of the large share of capital flows through such tax havens. In addition, the enforcement of financial regulation is made particularly difficult by the inadequate attention paid to 'Know Your Investor' in some jurisdictions, and tax regimes that encourage cross-border round tripping of funds by residents.

The role of credit-rating agencies has also come under considerable adverse attention. The relevant issues for regulators in developing economies are: the appropriate regulatory frameworks for rating agencies, use of credit ratings by the regulators and, more importantly, the desirability of encouraging domestic credit-rating agencies that could serve the growing needs of developing economies. Such domestic credit-rating agencies could have the potential to compete with the existing international agencies.

One of the most important lessons learnt from the crisis is the need to recognise linkages between the financial and the real sector. The recent experience with what may be termed the excessive financialisation of economies has brought to the fore several important questions. Should there be a review of the sequencing and pace of reforms in the financial sector relative to the fiscal and real sectors in developing economies? In view of the observed volatility in capital flows and also of commodity prices, how should policies relating to the financial sector in developing economies provide cushions against such shocks? Similarly, should there be a review of the sequencing of various elements in the development of domestic financial systems in developing economies and their integration with the global financial system? Finally, is it inevitable that relationships between the government, central banks and financial regulators be redrawn in view of the very serious consequences of the present crisis?

Eight

Countercyclical Policies in the Financial Sector: The Indian Experience*

$\mathcal{T}$his chapter is divided into six sections. The first section provides a background on the major features of the Indian economy that are relevant to the regulation of the financial sector. The second describes the dynamics of countercyclical policies in India to illustrate the interactions between the government and other public institutions on the one hand, and the central bank on the other, in the evolution and conduct of the regulation of the financial sector as a whole. The section illustrates the operation of the political economy in regulation. The third section discusses the countercyclical policies adopted by India, which could be contrasted with the dominant view before the crisis—that such policies are inadvisable and, in any case, ineffective. The fourth section provides a detailed account of the specific measures adopted to induce countercyclical elements at the time of boom. The fifth section explains the policy response

* This chapter is based on comments made by the author at several international conferences held in 2009. A version of this chapter has been published in the *Journal of Globalization and Development*, Vol. 1, No. 1, 2010.

to the crisis, and illustrates how the instruments used at the time of boom could be used to counter the dampening effects or shocks arising out of the global financial crisis. The last section draws a few broad conclusions from the Indian experience.

SALIENT FEATURES OF THE RECENT INDIAN ECONOMIC PERFORMANCE

The major features of the Indian economy that served as a background to countercyclical policies in recent years may be summarised as follows. The growth of output has been impressive, self-accelerating and less volatile over a prolonged period. It averaged at 6 per cent p.a. since 1980 and accelerated to an average of 8.6 per cent p.a. during the four years preceding the global crisis. This was enabled by acceleration in domestic savings and a generally stable current account deficit, which stood at around 1 per cent of the GDP, a surplus being an exception. Household savings were stable, while savings by corporates increased, and negative savings of the government sector were reduced. The investment demand increased while the consumption demand remained strong. The productivity of capital, as evidenced by capital output ratios, remained better than the rest of Asia, mainly due to the rapid growth of the capital-light services sector. While imports grew impressively from a low base, domestic demand continued to dominate most sectors in the economy. The strong and stable performance of export of services, mainly through information technology and remittances from non-residents, accounting for about 6 per cent of the GDP, helped to finance the huge deficit in the external trade in goods. All these indicators suggest a robust performance.

A few words on the policy backdrop of India's management of the external sector may be necessary. In India, while the current account was fully convertible, the capital account was managed. Management of the capital account consisted of restrictions on inflows through non-trade related short-term credit, external commercial borrowings and access to domestic bond markets. Restrictions on capital outflows were mainly on account of household and un-hedged exposures of financial intermediaries to foreign currencies. By the standards of the developing world, India maintained a reasonable degree of price stability, although at a higher level than the developed world, and the tolerance to volatility in prices was low. These features constituted the basic strengths of the economy.

There were some deficits in the economy that dominated public policy. The fiscal deficit was consistently high, with a dominant structural component. The persistent revenue deficit posed issues of quality vis-à-vis fiscal management, although there was some improvement in fiscal health during the boom period that preceded the crisis. A major part of the financial sector and monetary policies was devoted to ensuring a smooth financing of the large fiscal deficit. The infrastructural deficit, especially in areas of power, shipping, transport, etc., was acutely felt, imparting rigidities to the supply side of the economy. Institutional deficit was evident in bureaucratic delays, high transaction costs and less-than-clear enforceable property rights.

In view of the socio-economic factors, several policy interventions were put in place, such as price controls and public distribution mechanisms, especially of food, fuel and finance. These had a stabilising effect on the real economy, but also inhibited a smooth and effective transmission of market signals. Against these public policy constraints on markets, a vibrant democracy, political system stability and popularity of the media provided some countervailing forces.

The overarching objectives of public policy were accelerating growth, maintaining price stability and eliminating poverty. In recent years, the operational implications of these objectives has included a progressive increase in (i) the role of market forces, including the financial sector; (ii) integration of the Indian economy with the global economy, including the financial sector and (iii) a rapid transformation in structural elements of the economy, which often overlap with cyclical elements as well.

These salient features outline the country-specific context that is relevant to understanding the countercyclical policies in the financial sector.

DYNAMICS OF COUNTERCYCLICAL POLICIES IN INDIA

The term 'public policy' is used here to describe the full range of policies adopted by the government and all its public-sector constituents. The monetary- and financial-sector policies are a subset of public policy, but are exercised with some degree of independence enjoyed by monetary and regulatory authorities. Countercyclical policy is an important, but only one, element of the conduct of public policy in general, and of policy for the financial sector in particular. The alignment of such policies in the financial sector with policies in other sectors, especially with fiscal and monetary policies, is important.

As already mentioned, the structural nature of the persistent high fiscal deficits over several years in the past had dominated the conduct of monetary policies, the progress of reforms in the financial sector and the pace of liberalisation of the capital account. The financing of fiscal deficits did not pose serious problems in the boom period due to large capital inflows. However, public policy, both at central and state levels, recognised the need for fiscal consolidation, and took advantage of the boom to reduce the level of revenue and fiscal deficits, subject to the compulsions of political processes. Legislation to limit fiscal deficits was approved, although that did not fully capture the need for countercyclical policies. In the context of the boom that preceded the global crisis, policies attuned to reducing fiscal deficits in compliance with the thrust of legislation on fiscal responsibility acted somewhat countercyclically, providing some headroom for fiscal stimulus when the crisis broke out. However, it must be noted that fiscal policy was in a mode of consolidation as part of the process of economic reform, and there was no explicit recognition of the need for countercyclicality.

The dynamics of the conduct of monetary policy, however, were far more complex.

First, public policy was pleased with having achieved the long-cherished goal of high growth in output. It was averse to any action in the monetary arena that could impede or even moderate the momentum in growth. Both global and domestic forces contributed to price stability, although there were steep increases in the prices of two commodities, food and fuel, during the period. Since these price increases were considered to be shocks, any action on the monetary front was considered inappropriate by public policy. In addition, in view of the level of integration of India with the global economy and finance that had been achieved and was being sought further, public policy felt that monetary conditions, especially interest rates, should move in tandem with the global trend, which was mostly towards easing of monetary conditions. It was felt that the tendency to indulge in 'carry trade in currency' (that is, trade in foreign exchange aimed at taking advantage of the differences in interest rates between countries by selling the low interest currency and buying the high interest currency) could be curbed by monetary policy if it was aligned with other major economies. Further, there was a strong disinclination to accept proposals to curb capital inflows on the ground that such curbs would be ineffective. In particular, access to external commercial borrowings was very attractive, and was perceived to be economical for large corporates with huge financial needs. There was a fear in public policy circles that imposing restrictions on capital inflows would annoy the financial markets, in particular the global financial players. Finally, there was also a fear of erosion in the reform credentials of public policy if monetary policy intervened actively in the functioning of markets.

As against these reservations, however, there were conflicting views from those in the real sector—especially those with large import requirements due to their investment plans who preferred appreciating the rupee—and those in the export sector. The profitability of the export sector was threatened by the tendency of the external value of the rupee to appreciate. These pressures necessitated containing the extent of appreciation in the real external value of the rupee by a combination of some intervention in forex markets and some sterilisation.

These competing considerations defined the policy space for national authorities. Although corner solutions (when only one of the several alternatives available is exclusively chosen) were eschewed and a balanced policy mix chosen, the preference of public policy was towards alignment with globally popular trends with regard to monetary stance and openness of the capital account. The only exception to this approach was a response to the sudden spurt in headline inflation in mid-2008. In fact, two committees were appointed: one to develop Mumbai as a regional financial centre and another to fundamentally overhaul monetary- and financial-sector regimes. The recommendations of both committees were broadly consistent with the orthodoxy prevailing then, essentially based on the much sought after Anglo-Saxon model of the financial sector.

Second, there was considerable convergence between the preferences of financial markets and some reform-oriented elements in public policy with regard to the stance of monetary policy and openness of the capital account. Understandably, the need for a countercyclical policy was not an important element of their main thrust. In the conduct of monetary- and financial-sector policies, as also in the design of reform for the future, the countercyclical approach was considered conservative and backward-looking by financial markets and a segment within the public policycircle.

Third, the RBI had a broad legal mandate, described in terms of 'securing monetary stability and generally to operate the currency and credit system of the country to its advantage' (the RBI Act). The RBI interpreted this to mean the dual objectives of growth and price stability, the relative emphasis being dependent on the context. Since 2004, the RBI has added financial stability to this mix in its articulation of the policies, since the financial sector was growing too fast for its comfort. It may be useful to recognise that monetary stability generally related to the value of money, interest rates and exchange rates, and the stability of the financial sector as a distinct goal is a product of the development of financial markets. Monetary stability and financial stability are undoubtedly closely linked. In view of the fact that large segments of the Indian population have no hedges or social security, the RBI laid greater store by stability. In its stated view, while the benefits of growth accrue to the poor with a time lag, instability impacts the poor almost instantly.

Operationally, the RBI pursued multiple objectives; adopted multiple indicators, including growth in credit and money, to track the economy; and used multiple instruments to implement its policy. It concentrated on analysing trends in inflation in general instead of focusing on targeting exclusively on one indicator. The RBI avoided sending signals to financial markets about the likely future path of interest rates. It shared its analysis fully and placed it in the public domain, but did not offer forward guidance since it did not want to assume to know the future path better than what markets could assess. Moreover, it was felt that markets should be allowed to have diverse views on such matters to the extent possible. Further, the contention of the RBI in deviating from globally popular monetary policy practices was that domestic factors dominated the economy— although global factors were increasing in importance—and that alignment with all global practices could not be an end in itself.

The RBI sought policy space by insisting on managing the capital account, to the extent feasible, to avoid excess volatility in forex markets. Above all, it highlighted the importance of developments in the real sector and held that the rigidities in supply conditions were critical in identifying 'early signs of overheating'. In brief, countercyclical elements of monetary policies were emphasised by the RBI, and it could earn an autonomous policy space to act accordingly, even though public policy in general did not assign a central role to such a formalised countercyclical policy.

It must be admitted, however, that public policy allowed the RBI to pursue a countercyclical policy. For instance, the RBI devised a set of instruments to moderate the impact of volatility in capital flows, which included the government's agreement to transparently bear the fiscal cost of sterilisation up to the limits specified by it. In other words, managing a messy 'impossible trinity' became the joint responsibility of the RBI and the government, and this helped to harmonise the objectives of growth and stability. It is held that it is impossible to have a fixed exchange rate, an independent interest rate and free movement of capital at the same time. This is called the 'impossible trinity' or a trilemma. If the central bank attempts to stabilise the exchange rate when interest rates are different, the continuing movement of capital will put pressure on the domestic interest rates. Thus, if we have free capital movement, there is a conflict between an independent interest rate and a stable exchange rate. One or the other of the latter two has to be dropped to resolve the conflict, or the conflict has to be monitored and managed on a continual basis. The RBI indicated to the government that a combination of measures would be required on a dynamic basis to manage this impossible trinity, which would entail possible fiscal costs. The RBI sought the government's agreement to bear an agreed part of the cost, which it did.

Briefly stated, there was an implicit, informally agreed upon, approach in public policy in favour of policy activism on the part of the RBI in discharging its functions to enable growth while ensuring overall conditions of stability, both in prices and in the financial system as a whole. The informally agreed approach influenced the conduct of day-to-day policy as well as the pace of economic reforms, particularly in external and financial sectors. Differences always surface vis-à-vis sequencing or emphasis on specific actions; however, the shared goals have helped to resolve the differences.

COUNTERCYCLICAL POLICIES IN THE FINANCIAL SECTOR

The regulation of the banking sector, NBFCs, and money forex and government securities markets are vested with the RBI. There are separate regulators for stock exchanges and capital markets, insurance and pension funds. Coordination is ensured through inter-regulatory bodies with a high-level committee chaired by the Governor, RBI, and with representation to the Ministry of Finance.

The overall approach to the regulation of the financial sector, particularly in relation to countercyclical elements, takes account of priorities in public policy and the responses of financial markets and regulated institutions.

The financial system in India is dominated by commercial banks, and these are regulated by the RBI. A major part of the banking sector, accounting for about 70 per cent of banking assets, liabilities and activities, is operated by commercial banks that have a government majority in ownership and control. Further, direct interaction between the government and management of banks is normal, although boards do function as per legal and regulatory prescriptions. Among the market participants, the branches of foreign banks and large, locally incorporated private-sector banks are more inclined to adopt global practices, and consequently expect the regulatory framework of India to follow the leads of the US and UK. As already mentioned, public policy has a legitimate concern not to disrupt momentum in growth. The net impact of these various factors on the approach to countercyclical regulation was for public policy to (i) seek 'proof' that there were indeed signs of boom and asset bubbles and (ii) to ensure a broad alignment with global best practices, for obvious reasons.

The RBI articulated its approach to countercyclicality in its policies by indicating the criticality of the banking system for large segments of the population and for the economy as a whole. Hence, the RBI adopted a precautionary approach to essentially protect the banking system from a 'bust', were it to occur for any reason. The possibility—and not absolute proof—of bubbles was explored in terms of broad indicators and possible threats. Whenever the price of an asset rises steeply above that which can be explained by the 'fundamentals' of the asset, it is called a bubble, because it can collapse when pricked by chance. The 'fundamentals' may refer to the real factors associated with the asset—for instance, the income that it yields. In any case, the major thrust of countercyclical policy was to ensure that highly risky activities were adequately backed by additional capital, while monitoring possible mechanisms for circumventing the intent of such regulations put in place by banks themselves, or through other related entities. The implicit, informally agreed approach between public policy and the RBI in this regard was to enable the RBI to exercise its regulatory jurisdiction, keeping in view the imperative of smooth, economical and easy flow of credit to productive sectors like agriculture, small and medium industry, and affordable housing. Some explanations regarding the approach of the RBI to financial innovations may be in order. Financial innovations generally refer to creating and marketing new types of securities. One example of financial innovations is interest rate swaps, which are one kind of financial derivatives. These are agreements that enable one party to exchange a stream of interest payments with a 'counterparty' for a different type of cash flow on some future date. For instance, fixed interest rates can be exchanged for floating interest rates in the same or different currencies, or fixed interest rates in one currency can be exchanged for fixed interest rates in different currencies. In this manner, counterparty can reduce its exposure to one type of payment, at a price. Financial intermediaries can arrange the swap and benefit from the spread between the bids of the two counterparties. Swapping, like other derivatives, can be used to reduce risks of exposure (hedge) or to speculate on future changes. Some types of swaps can be traded in the futures markets. Since financial derivatives are based on the future, which has a somewhat speculative existence, their valuation can depart drastically from the conditions of the underlying transactions. The RBI took a precautionary view and banned or discouraged them, or provided safeguards depending on the extent of the awareness of risks and rewards.

The RBI was concerned with the activities of large, systemically important NBFCs, particularly activities that it viewed with disfavour. Banks were a significant source of funds for these non-banks and the latter could therefore be used as conduits to carry out bank-like functions that regulations do not permit banks to undertake—often described as shadow banking. Public policy was supportive of the RBI's initiatives to curb such shadow banking. With regard to the development of derivatives markets, the RBI adopted a cautionary approach given the preference of public policy, and disfavoured large-scale participation of individual banks in such derivatives. In general, participants in financial markets wanted banks to be actively involved in mutual funds, the functioning of derivatives markets, venture capital funds or private equity, etc. The RBI was averse to permitting an extensive use of banks' resources for such risky activities or for complex financial products.

COUNTERCYCLICAL MEASURES

The countercyclical elements in the regulation of the financial sector were designed in this context, and the specific measures implemented by the RBI are briefly described here.

First, in the year 2000, the RBI conducted a stress test of banks' investment portfolio in an increasing interest rate scenario, when the general trend was of decreasing interest rates. In order to meet the adverse impact of interest rate risk, banks were advised in January 2002 to build up an Investment Fluctuation Reserve (IFR) within a period of five years. This countercyclical prudential requirement enabled banks to absorb some of the adverse impact when interest rates began moving in the opposite direction in late 2004.

Second, regulatory guidelines in India were revised to allow for countercyclicality. These guidelines require banks to classify their investments as per international standards. While the earlier pre-scription for a category was relatively more conservative, the revised guidelines of September 2004 recognised the dynamic interface of investments with interest rate cycles, and were countercyclical.

Third, risk weights were increased whenever the build-up of bubbles was suspected. In order to calculate the capital that is adequate to support banking operations, exposures to different areas are assigned different weights in order to reflect the difference in the risks of operating in them. Thus, the more risky exposures are given a greater weight and require more capital to support them. Under international practice, the standard risk weight categories were 0 per cent for short-term government bonds, 20 per cent for exposures to

Organization for Economic Cooperation and Development (OECD) banks, 50 per cent for residential mortgages and 100 per cent weighting on unsecured commercial loans. The highest weight of 150 per cent was recommended for borrowers with poor credit ratings. The percentage of risk-weighted assets to be held as capital was 8 per cent. In India, the risk weights are generally more conservative, and in fact the minimum capital adequacy was prescribed at 9 per cent, above the global norm. Even so, noticing the steep increase in the prices of real estate, the risk weight on banks' exposure to commercial estate was increased from 100 per cent to 125 per cent in July 2005, and further to 150 per cent in April 2006. The risk weights on housing loans extended by banks to individuals were increased from 50 to 75 per cent in December 2004, with some relief for housing loans to individuals up to US$75,000. When there was a boom in consumer credit and equities, risk weights for consumer credit and capital market exposures were increased from 100 per cent to 125 per cent.

Fourth, the provisions for standard assets were revised upwards progressively in November 2005, May 2006 and January 2007, in view of the continued high credit growth in the real estate sector, personal loans, credit card receivables, and loan and advances qualifying as capital market exposure. The provisioning requirement for all other loans and advances, classified as standard assets, namely, direct advances to the agricultural and small and medium enterprise sectors and all other loans and advances were kept unchanged.

Fifth, a revised framework to address issues pertaining to the overall regulation of systemically important NBFCs and the relationship between banks and NBFCs was put in place in December 2006.

Sixth, the RBI issued guidelines on the securitisation of standard assets in February 2006. A unique feature of these guidelines, which may be at variance with accounting standards, is that any profits on the sale of assets to the Special Purpose Vehicle (SPV) are not allowed to be recognised immediately on sale, but over the life of the pass-through certificates issued by the SPV. It should be noted that SPVs are created to fulfill narrow, specific or temporary objectives, for instance to own and handle a single asset. They are typically used and created by companies wanting to isolate themselves from the financial risk associated with the operation. They are also commonly used in complex financings to separate different layers of equity infusion. The RBI exercised vigilance to discourage the use of SPVs to circumvent regulatory prescriptions.

Seventh, moral suasion and the public articulation of concerns helped in achieving a desired rebalancing of suspected excesses in risk-taking among banks. Some of the areas where moral suasion was used were: the need for banks to monitor un-hedged foreign currency exposures of their corporate clients; adoption of appropriate incentive mechanisms by banks to encourage disclosures of derivative exposures by their corporate clients; banks' reliance on non-deposit resources to finance assets; their excessive reliance on wholesale deposits and uncomfortable loan-to-value (LTV) ratios with respect to housing loans, etc.

A review of the functioning of select banks was initiated, a process generally described as a Supervisory Review Process (SRP). It involved the identification of select banks that had a significant exposure to the sectors or activities defined as sensitive in terms of risk to the banks. This included real estate, consumer credit, reliance on call money market, etc. The SRP was undertaken so as to ensure that effective risk mitigation and sound internal control systems were in place in banks that had been identified for the purpose. In the first round, a framework was developed to monitor the systemically important individual banks. The second round of SRP was directed towards analysing banks' exposure to sensitive sectors and identifying corrective actions.

POLICY RESPONSES TO THE GLOBAL FINANCIAL CRISIS

India's policy responses to the global financial crisis were governed by several objectives, namely, ensuring orderly functioning of markets; preserving financial stability; countering dampening effects on growth through fiscal and monetary measures; and countercyclical prudential measures as well as unconventional measures to ease the flow of credit.

First, to address liquidity concerns, rupee liquidity, which had been impounded in the pre-crisis years through the Liquidity Adjustment Facility, Market Stabilisation Scheme and cash reserve ratio (CRR), was released into the market. Similarly, foreign currency liquidity was provided by drawing from the forex reserves built up during the period of excess capital inflows. Operationally, the measures also involved a reduction in the policy interest rates, a lowering of the quantum of bank reserves that had been increased in the earlier boom period, and expanded refinance facilities to banks from the RBI to finance exports. A rupee-dollar swap facility for banks was also announced to provide comfort to banks that needed sudden or large forex for short periods, in view of the disruption in trade finance among globally active banks. These were meant to supplement open market operations in money and forex markets.

Second, among the financial institutions, mutual funds and NBFCs experienced some stress on liquidity for some time. To meet this problem, the RBI had to design special liquidity facilities, primarily through the banking system. The actual utilisation was only a part of the assured amounts of liquidity.

Third, the dampening effects on growth were sought to be addressed both by stimulating aggregate demand and actions aimed for select sectors, especially sectors dependent on exports. While there were some tax cuts and attempts to enhance investment expenditures, the major stimulus was through enhanced government consumption expenditures. A substantial part of the latter came in the form of upward revisions in the pay of public-sector employees, and rural employment guarantee schemes. Although such measures had a counter-crisis effect, they are not strictly countercyclical since they have no exit components and create entitlements of a permanent nature. As such, they can be carried over into recovery and boom, creating inflationary pressures.

Fourth, as already mentioned, monetary measures were also broadly countercyclical in terms of easing liquidity conditions and reduction in policy rates. The RBI was also active in open market operations in money markets, government securities markets and forex markets. However, it is noteworthy that the RBI consciously avoided exposing its balance sheet to the risks arising from dealing with entities other than banks and with uncertain collaterals while implementing unconventional measures.

Fifth, as already mentioned, in order to ensure that asset quality was maintained in light of the high credit growth, risk weights and provisioning requirements on standard advances for banks' exposures to sectors showing higher than average growth had been progressively raised during the four years preceding the global crisis, as a countercyclical measure. However, with the global financial crisis starting to affect the Indian economy from September 2008 onwards, the RBI reduced the enhanced risk weights and provisioning requirements to the normal level. In view of the growing concern about the possible increase in stress in the Indian banking system, certain modifications were made to the guidelines on restructuring of advances in August 2008 as a one-time measure and for a limited period of time.

It may be noted that countercyclical prudential regulation has so far focused on unwinding the more rigorous prudential measures at the time of boom, and has not indicated any noticeable softening in the standards of such regulations meant for normal times. However, as a measure of support to ensuring credit flow to productive sectors, the RBI provided special refinance facilities for established national-level open institutions disbursing credit to small industry, housing and exports-imports. These were in addition to the special refinance facilities offered to banks to provide liquidity to mutual funds and NBFCs.

SOME BROAD CONCLUSIONS FROM THE INDIAN EXPERIENCE

First, the effectiveness of macro-prudential financial regulation is enhanced when the desirable countercyclical policy is pursued by monetary authorities. The challenge is to ensure the coordination of monetary and regulatory policies in recognising asset bubbles and synchronising measures over time, and in terms of the extent of policy intervention. The view that policymakers or regulators have no means of recognising asset bubbles and consequently should not be expected to act finds far less support now after the global crisis. The problem, however, is the extent to which such countercyclical policies should be rule-based or discretionary. If discretionary elements dominate—which is not unlikely—policy coordination becomes more complex.

Second, with the increasing importance of international trade, migration of labour and a relatively open capital account, economic or trade cycles of countries impact each other. The policy space available for each country thus depends on the nature and extent of its integration with the rest of the world, as also on the state of the institutional and financial markets within the country. As such, policies relating to the external sector have a bearing on the financial sector and its stability—for example, the implications of persistent large current account deficits or a fully open capital account, especially in developing countries, for financial stability are better appreciated now, although the inherent dilemmas, or trilemmas, remain.

Third, countercyclical policies in the financial sector are facilitated if significant automatic stabilisers exist in the fiscal regime. Further, such policies are more effective in the financial sector when they are accompanied by a similar action in the fiscal arena.

Fourth, the dangers of allowing the growth of the financial sector as an end in itself, without developing its contribution to what may be termed the 'real' or non-financial sector, have to be appreciated. Hence, the design, timing and sequencing of countercyclical measures should take account of the structural transformations underway in the real sector, and their impact on development and welfare. For this purpose, disaggregated or sector-specific approaches to countercyclical policies may be essential in the case of developing economies. For instance, countercyclical measures may be addressed to specific areas where bubbles are noticeable.

Fifth, the support of public policy and financial markets for countercyclical policies is likely to be less during the building of boom, while it could be significantly more when the markets are in distress. However, the process of exit from stimulus as and when warranted may witness differences between the preferences of public policy and regulators of the financial sector. In sum, countercyclical policies in financial regulation need to (i) recognise the importance of coherence between various components of public policy as a whole in view of developmental and welfare implications; and (ii) continue to reckon the short-time horizons of both public policy and financial markets relative to the necessarily longer horizon warranted by evolving macroeconomic conditions.

Nine

Emerging Issues in Financial Sector Regulation*

$\mathcal{T}$his chapter draws attention to the major issues relating to the regulation of the financial sector that are being debated consequent to the global crisis. The first section explores the links between macro-policies and the regulation of the financial sector. The second analyses the changes being contemplated in the regulatory structures. The third section provides a detailed account of the relationship between competition, regulation, ownership and governance. The fourth section merely poses questions relating to financial innovation in the context of regulation. This is followed by an account of the issues relating to the regulation of institutions and markets, including infrastructural services. The concluding section is devoted to the broader issues of national regulation and global finance.

* This chapter is based on comments made on papers circulated in several international conferences during 2009. An earlier version of this chapter has been published in T. S. Ninan et al. (eds), *Business Standards India 2010*, New Delhi: Business Standard Books, 2010.

MACRO POLICIES AND REGULATION

The importance of links between the regulatory framework and other macroeconomic policies—monetary, external, fiscal and, to an extent, those governing the 'real' sectors—has now been recognised. However, the question is: how do we devise an operational regulatory framework that balances the need for growth in the 'real' economy with that of the financial sector?

First, the objectives of monetary policy are no longer confined to maintaining price stability and, where applicable, maintaining the growth of output and employment. Its objectives extend to the maintenance of financial stability. The fact that both monetary policy and the regulatory framework have multiple objectives warrants a consideration of multiple instruments. The effectiveness of macro-prudential financial regulation is also enhanced when the desirable countercyclical policy is pursued by monetary authorities. Hence, both monetary and regulatory authorities should be able to share similar perceptions regarding the existence of asset bubbles or deflationary pressures, and coordinate their countercyclical measures. To this end, it is necessary to establish some rules that should form the basis of their independent actions with regard to countercyclical approaches. At the same time, significant subjective elements are involved in assessing the cycles and appropriate policies from time to time, warranting considerable room for discretion without excessive restrictions on either the monetary authority or the regulator.

Second, the level of economic activity and consequently the stage of the cycle is determined by both domestic and global factors. However, it is not necessary that domestic and global factors should always point in the same direction of the cycle. Thus, it is possible that both monetary and regulatory policy would face the challenge of addressing domestic concerns, which could be different from a globally transmitted concern. The magnitude and complexity of such challenges will depend on the linkages in the current account, including through workers' remittances, and in the capital account, between the domestic and global economy. The varying perceptions of coupling and decoupling theories between EMEs and advanced economies since 2008 are a reflection of the complexity of these challenges. In turn, these complexities require an appreciation of the policy space available to national authorities to address them.

Third, the fiscalisation of the financial sector is very apparent, as evident in the fiscal implications of bailout packages for financial markets and institutions. The most telling illustration of the new reality is the serious consideration given to the levy of the Tobin tax on financial transactions—even between banks in the domestic economy—as a measure to reduce the scope for excess volatility due to multiple transactions by participants in the financial sector. Heavyweight support—Paul Volcker, former Chairman of the United States' Federal Reserve, and Lord Turner, currently Chairman of the Financial Services Authority of the UK—in favour of this tax have added to the seriousness of the debate. More generally, countercyclical policies in the financial sector are facilitated if significant automatic stabilisers exist in the fiscal regime. Further, countercyclical policies are more effective in the financial sector when accompanied by a similar action in the fiscal arena, as evidenced by the management of the global financial crisis.

Fourth, the belief that growth of the financial sector leads to economic development, and hence greater financialisation would necessarily add to efficiency and stability, stands discredited. Greater attention is being paid to assessing the contribution the financial sector could make to the growth of employment and output in the economy as a whole, and to the real sector in particular. The tendency of the financial sector to redistribute wealth in its own favour rather than create wealth, and its potential to distort commodity prices from genuine supply-demand factors indicate the need for an assessment of the optimal financial activity in any system.

REGULATORY STRUCTURES

There has been an active exploration of appropriate regulatory structures in view of the experience of the crisis. This crisis has affected countries with a variety of regulatory structures, and dissatisfaction with prevailing structures is apparent in almost all developed economies.

Although there are some concerns about the role played by central banks in contributing to the crisis, there have been several serious proposals to expand and strengthen their authority. This is because a central bank's mandate is no longer restricted to price stability or monetary policy; it now also plays a critical role in maintaining financial stability. In terms of detail, one view accords primary responsibility to central banks, while another view would rather that it be the responsibility of the government. A third view is to have a council, or collegiums of financial regulators, with variations among the relative roles of the government and central banks. Restoring the functions of regulation and supervision of commercial banks to central banks is also being considered in view of how critical commercial banks are for financial stability.

There is a plea for making central banks more accountable, but it has to be balanced with the issue of preserving their independence from political forces. This debate notwithstanding, there is a demand for an association of broader social interests and disciplines in the governance of central banks, rather than limiting it only to professionals drawn from economics, finance and business. This is despite the fact that the concentration of professional skills and the tradition of a longer-term and macroeconomic view in central banks (relative to others in the financial sector) is better appreciated now.

The debate also extends to unified regulation versus the two-pillar approach. Under the former model, all regulatory and supervisory functions are to be vested in a single regulator, which would be part of the central bank. In the two-pillar approach, the central bank itself would be responsible for regulating financial institutions while a separate agency would constitute the other pillar, with the remit of protecting the interests of investors and consumers of financial services and products. A more modest change, as proposed by the United Nations' Commission of Experts of the President of the General Assembly on Reforms of the International Monetary and Financial System—also known as the Stiglitz Commission after its Chairman, Joseph Stiglitz—is to have a Financial Products Safety Commission along the lines of the Food and Drug Administration's certification of the safety of drugs. In any case, the function of the lender of last resort may continue to remain with central banks, making it de facto in charge of financial stability.

There is virtual unanimity on the view that the legal framework of the regulatory structure should provide for effective regulation and supervision of non-bank financial intermediaries and all deposit-taking institutions. Further, additional powers to regulate and supervise systemically important financial institutions are considered essential, and there is some preference for having central banks discharge this responsibility.

COMPETITION, REGULATION, OWNERSHIP AND GOVERNANCE

The underlying philosophy behind financial regulation has been to promote efficiency through competition, while protecting the interests of investors and perhaps avoiding serious threats to stability. In practice, however, there are severe entry barriers to a major part of organised financial activity, especially in banking. Further, the burden and complexities of compliance with regulatory requirements, borne by the regulated, tend to favour a large size in financial services, especially for operations across differing regulatory jurisdictions in countries and across regulators. In some cases, public policy encouraged consolidation, merger and acquisition on the assumption that such a process enhances efficiency. The recent experience with the crisis calls this assumption into question: the emergence of institutions that were conscious of their being too big to fail encouraged them to take excessive risks in the pursuit of higher profits and bonuses. This realisation has engendered the following debate: how can the emergence of such institutions be halted? Would it be desirable to enforce splitting the existing large conglomerates into smaller units? Should there be more rigorous regulation, including an insistence on higher capital adequacy, for the systemically important financial institutions?

In the context of the legal difficulties faced recently by some central banks in ordering the compulsory mergers of banks under stressful conditions, consideration is being given to the restoration of such powers to central banks. These developments warrant a review of competition laws insofar as they relate to banks.

In terms of public ownership, the more immediate issue relates to governance arrangements that should be put in place in cases of a bailout by either central banks or the government—as in the US and UK. A related issue is the manner of exit of public ownership from financial institutions. At one stage, sovereign wealth funds held significant stakes in banks, provoking the question: should such ownership be treated as public ownership, or not?

In many jurisdictions, there have been 'fit and proper' tests for private ownership as part of the financial sector's regulatory structure. However, in the context of managing the crisis and to assure the recapitalisation of banks, there has been a deliberate dilution of such standards of ownership and governance, especially with regard to private equity. The importance of enforcing 'fit and proper' criteria for ownership and board-level appointees has since been recognised, as has the need to improve governance arrangements in financial institutions, especially banks.

Financial Innovation and Regulation

An important contributory factor to the global financial crisis has admittedly been the unbridled expansion of financial innovation. Several issues are being addressed on the appropriate balance between the freedom of financial markets to innovate and regulation to moderate the risks arising out of such innovations. First, what constitutes financial innovation, in contrast to technological innovations such as automated teller machines? Second, what is the primary objective of any innovation and what are the possible consequences? Is the main purpose only to dilute capital adequacy stipulations or to increase leverage or to circumvent the intent of regulation? Is it the intent of an innovation—as has been observed in the past in some cases—to merely redistribute wealth in favour of the financial sector, with no creation of wealth? What are the limits or constraints on the regulator's skills to approve or disapprove such innovations? Does a process of regulatory approval constitute an endorsement of such products? Is it possible to control the spread or magnitude of such innovations after they have been launched? How do we ensure that complexity is not deliberately injected into such products by market participants to undermine transparency? What are the mechanisms for safeguarding against downside risks?

REGULATION OF INSTITUTIONS

A major area of concern is the emergence of what has been described as the shadow banking system, whereby institutions other than banks undertake activities that were considered difficult by banks, but often with resources or guarantees from banks. As a consequence, there has been an attempt to expand and intensify the regulation of non-banks in the financial sector. This expands the scope of financial-sector regulation to include non-banks, but the intensity of regulation may vary, depending on the nature of the institutions and the activities they undertake. For example, there are proposals to expand the scope to include private pools of capital, such as private equity and hedge funds. There are also proposals to identify systemically important financial intermediaries, say by size, interconnectedness and nature of operations, with a view to intensifying regulation, say by seeking additional capital. Admittedly the variety of financial institutions, the diverse activities they undertake and complex inter-relationships make the prescription of a regulatory framework for non-banks very complex, and hence large elements of discretion to the regulators may become inevitable.

The traditional functions of banking are now more or less considered a public utility. The issue now is how to ring-fence banks and banking functions from riskier activities. The proposals in this regard include regulating all deposit-taking institutions on par with banks, and treating banks as special for purposes of financial regulation. The special treatment meted out to banks would involve restrictions on their undertaking riskier activities, and on those that could provide opportunities for conflicts of interests. The benefits of the 'originate to distribute' model of bank lending (through securitisation of loans made by banks) are considered suspect, and the costs proved to be high.

There is virtual unanimity on reassessing the requirements of capital with regard to banks, in particular providing adequately for the trading book. There are also proposals to prescribe maximum gross leverage ratios to avoid excess leverage. The off-balance sheet items are also coming under scrutiny to ensure that they are covered by an appropriate capital buffer. Finally, the scope of financial-sector regulation is sought to be extended to the structure of compensation for executives, and other incentives that have a bearing on the tendency to take excessive risks.

The regulation of micro-finance institutions has not come to the fore in the current debate since they have not posed systemic risks. A review would, however, be inevitable to the extent that they focus on lending to the poor, and more importantly perform functions akin to deposit-taking institutions and constitute a form of shadow banking. In fact, Nobel Laureate Mohammed Yunus maintains that for-profit micro-finance institutions are no different from traditional money-lending, and they should be subject to laws either relating to money-lending, usurious conduct, etc., or treated on par with any other financial intermediary performing similar functions.

REGULATION OF MARKETS AND INFRASTRUCTURAL SERVICES

A major issue concerns the costs and benefits of short-selling and derivatives, especially in their efficiency in price discovery relative to injecting excessive volatility. With respect to derivatives, at one extreme are proposals to ban them altogether, while the other view merely proposes to educate regulators on these aspects. There is a growing consensus on insisting upon exchange-traded derivatives while providing for a limited use of over-the-counter trades to facilitate some innovations.

Improvements in the regulation of money markets are being attempted, with a focus on ensuring appropriate liquidity. More generally, there is a plea for regulatory focus not only on the quality of assets, but also on liabilities or funding of the assets.

In view of the proclivities of participants in financial markets for multiplicity in transactions, introducing the Tobin tax for both domestic and cross-border transactions is under consideration. One should expect greater momentum to such ideas even as efforts are on to examine the complexities in operationalising such a tax, especially if over-the-counter transactions dominate. The proposal to have an authority to certify the safety of financial products, or introducing mechanisms within the existing regulatory processes to serve the same purpose continues to be an active item on the agenda of the reform of the regulatory structure.

Finally, the use of regulatory regimes to influence or direct the flow of resources in the financial sector, especially in the form of private-sector lending or even selective credit controls, has found its way into the agenda for reform. Countercyclical policies do involve the use of tools (such as changes in provisions, assigning risk weights, prescribing margins and imposing limits on exposure) based on the nature of activities, and these are inherently in the nature of selective credit controls. Similarly, predatory and irresponsible lending have become serious concerns. Although we have established that operations in lending and other financial transactions should ideally not be left entirely to unfettered markets in the future, defining the scope of and limits to justifiable restrictions by regulators remains highly complex.

The crisis has revealed the systemic importance of infrastructural services for financial stability. These include custodial services, payment, clearing and settlement systems, accounting standards, credit ratings, and above all, conflicts of interests between the providers of these services as also between them and other participants in financial markets. While several issues are being debated, concrete proposals to address these are yet to emerge. A major issue remains the possible politicisation of changes in accounting standards if flexibilities or countercyclical approaches are adopted.

NATIONAL REGULATION AND GLOBAL FINANCE

According to Mervyn King, Governor of the BoE, the recent experience has shown that while banks are global in life, they are national in death. The implication of the statement is that the globalisation of finance has happened ahead of the globalisation of regulation. The current challenge is to harmonise regulation at the national level with the globalisation of the financial sector. It should be possible to achieve such coordination following the examples of civil aviation and telecom, where there are globally agreed-upon mechanisms. However, there are complexities in evolving a global framework for finance since the financial sector has significantly greater externalities and is not entirely on par with the global trade in goods either. Keeping in view these issues, several initiatives have been taken to improve the framework for cooperation in financial regulation at the global level.

First, the body setting standards for financial stability has been expanded to include countries such as India. Some recommendations, broadly in the direction of what may be termed regulation, have been made in the context of capital adequacy and compensation packages for executives. The G-20 group had also constituted a Working Group on Financial Regulation, whose recommendations provide some basic guidelines. Second, at an academic/policy level, the Geneva Report (chaired by Professor Charles Goodhart) provides a roadmap. The most comprehensive, objective and representative set of recommendations is available from the UN Commission (the Stiglitz Commission). Third, at the country level, there have also been several reports on financial-sector regulation, and these include the Report of G-30 (chaired by Paul Volcker) in the US; the Report of Lord Turner in the UK; and the Report of Jacques de Lorosiere for Europe. Fourth, there are intense policy debates on the proposals made, in particular in the UK and the US.

There is as yet no concrete agreement on the reform of the financial sector at the national level among various segments of the government, namely the executive, regulators, central banks and legislatures. Hence, agreement on the parameters of ideal regulation at the global level would be somewhat difficult, and the enforcement of an agreed framework may be very complex.

TOWARDS A GLOBAL FRAMEWORK

The emerging issues in developing a global framework for regulation are worth noting. First, the country context is very important; different countries are at different stages in the development of their financial markets and integration with global finance. The new global framework should provide for flexibility in meeting these diverse needs.

Second, since major problems arose in the financial sectors of the US, the UK and Europe, reform in regulation ought to take place in these jurisdictions on a priority basis. These economies are also important from the point of view of the global economy. It is also noteworthy that policy reviews and the reform agenda have been kept on hold in almost all developing countries, pending clarity on the evolving reforms in major centres of global finance.

Third, it is recognised that excessive deregulation, particularly in the US and the UK, was the main reason for the crisis, while globalised finance and open capital accounts were the main reasons for contagion. Hence, it can be argued that prescribing minimum standards of regulation to be adopted by all national authorities would be appropriate. Such a prescription gives policymakers at the national level the freedom to design their own standards, provided of course they meet the minimum requirements. This approach may have to be accompanied by freedom granted to each country to manage their capital accounts.

Fourth, a countercyclical policy at the national level would normally respond to trade cycles in the country concerned. Globalisation of finance would restrict the policy scope for such actions.

Fifth, international financial markets treat developing countries differently even if the fundamentals are similar to developed countries. The examples of Mexico and Korea, which experienced the crisis even after becoming members of the OECD, are illustrative. Hence, there is a compulsion for greater policy scope for developing countries.

Finally, cross-border activities of the financial sector are influenced not only by market participants taking advantage of the differences in regulatory standards between countries, but also by differences in the tax regimes between countries. In addition, cross-border activities of the financial sector have a relationship with conditions in the real economy, such as differences in wages as between countries. It may be recalled that some time ago, Mervin King, Governor of the BoE, remarked that inflation in the UK is influenced not only by monetary policy, but also by policies relating to immigration, which influence the wage level in the UK, and consequently the price level.

CONCLUSION

The emergence of the global financial crisis and consequent review of the regulatory structure reveal that the most critical tasks relate to rebalancing the competing considerations that govern regulation.

The importance of the financial sector has to be better balanced with the real sector, and it should be recognised that the former is a means and not an end. Financial markets play a critical role, but they cannot be unfettered. They require an active public policy, but with the recognition that the apparatus of the state is also vulnerable to capture.

It is not speculation or volatility per se, but excessive speculation and high volatility that cause serious problems. No doubt what is excess is often contextual and judgemental. Further, public policy can ill-afford the dominance of speculation over fundamentals. The adequacy of the policy space for national authorities has to be reconciled with the compulsions of global trade and technological developments.

Ten

Proposals for Financial-Sector Regulatory Reforms: Perspectives of Developing Countries*

*T*his chapter presents the perspective of developing economies on reforms in the regulation of the financial sector, which are under consideration globally in response to the global financial crisis. The first section indicates the context and relevance of the reforms proposals, followed in the second section by a more detailed consideration of some of the proposals for reform under discussion globally. The third section highlights some of the missing elements in the agenda for reform, while the fourth section poses some broader issues for consideration. The fifth section mentions a few issues concerning the role of the G-20.

* This chapter is an edited version of the lecture delivered at the second session of the UNCTAD Multi-year Expert Meeting on Services, Development and Trade: The Regulatory and Institutional Dimension, UNCTAD, Geneva, 18 March 2010.

CONTEXT AND RELEVANCE OF THE PROPOSAL FOR REFORMS

It is useful to note that while developing countries have been seriously affected by the crisis, especially through the trade channel, cross-border finance channel and the sentiment channel, their domestic financial sectors were far less affected. The fiscal support extended by governments of developing economies to their financial sectors is negligible. There may be several reasons as to why financial sectors in developing countries were less severely affected. First, the financial sectors in these countries were dominated by the banking system and banks concentrated on retail banking. Second, the financial markets did not have sophisticated instruments. Third, there was inadequate scope for high leverage for households or financial intermediaries. Fourth, deregulation of the financial sector was not carried forward to the extent that it was in the US and UK. In other words, the ideology of market fundamentalism was less prevalent in many, if not all, developing economies. Finally, in spite of sporadic efforts, no developing economy accorded high priority to developing itself as an international financial centre.

The reform proposals under discussion in the context of the crisis naturally address the problems of instability induced mainly by excessive deregulation. It is therefore necessary for developing countries to recognise that much of the reforms is a reaction to what happened in select developed countries, and hence its applicability to the developing world will depend on the extent of deregulation that had already been undertaken in their economies. In brief, it may not be appropriate to adopt, without due consideration, all the solutions offered through the reform proposals, since many of those problems may not exist in the developing country concerned. At the same time, it is necessary to identify sound principles behind the solutions offered as part of the reforms, and adopt them if they have universal validity, as warranted by the circumstances.

The overhaul of national, international and financial-sector regulations now on the policy agenda at the global level comprises stronger surveillance, a clearer mandate for regulators, strengthening the macro-prudential framework, strengthening risk mitigation structures, improved data management, stress test, enhancing transparency, improving cross-border cooperation, reform of accounting standards, etc. It is implicit that the strengthening and improvement will have to be considered with reference to the current state of affairs in each of the countries.

One broad lesson the global financial crisis has taught is that there should be synchronisation between regulators' skills and sophistication in the financial markets. One of the proposals in the reform agenda is improving the skills of the regulators themselves, in order to enable them to regulate the financial sector better. As against this, it can be argued that sophistication in the financial sector should be permitted only to the extent that regulatory skills are able to manage. In other words, it is preferable to restrict sophistication in financial markets to match the skills of the regulators, recognising that such skills are difficult to build in developing countries in the short run. It may not be desirable to allow sophistication in financial markets to occur before improving the skills of regulators.

The crisis is also indicative of the fact that globalisation of finance preceded globalisation of regulation. Hence, an effort is being made to introduce mechanisms for coordination in financial regulation among countries. Currently severe problems and difficulties are being faced in agreeing on the appropriate regulatory structures and standards within countries such as the US, UK and Euro area. The globalisation of regulation may be more complicated and an agreement may have to be very broad to gain acceptance—but then it may prove too broad to be effective. Further, global governance arrangements to enforce a global financial regulatory regime are inadequate. There are serious dangers in imposing a common regulatory standard since there is admittedly no single regulatory system that is right for all times and for all countries. Countries with different levels of development and regulatory capacities will have to adopt different regulatory approaches. Under these circumstances, matching the globalisation of regulation with the globalisation of finance could be a complex task for global bodies.

PROPOSALS FOR REFORMS

There are wide-ranging proposals for reforms in the regulation of the financial sector. For analytical purposes, these are discussed in terms of reforms relating to the objectives of regulations; scope of regulation; structure of regulatory bodies and the regulation of institutions; regulation of instruments and markets; regulation of incentives and regulatory approaches, including issues relating to cross-border regulation and 'too big to fail' institutions.

The basic objectives of regulation in the past were to ensure a level playing field in the market and the solvency of individual institutions—including, in some cases, the protection of depositors. Consumer protection was also provided for, either within the framework of the regulator in the financial sector or outside. The objectives of regulation are now sought to be redefined to include financial stability. This includes an element of countercyclicality, taking cognisance of asset prices movements, and some focus on the interests of depositors. From the perspective of a developing country, expanding the objectives of regulation and orienting them towards stability should be welcome. The Indian experience indicates that these proposed changes in the objectives of regulation are appropriate.

In some countries, the scope of regulation was restricted to commercial banks, and regulatory regimes were somewhat soft on NBFCs such as investment banks. Some entities such as hedge funds were kept outside the scope of regulation. Currently, the proposed reforms intend to expand the scope of regulation to include non-banks. This expanded scope takes into account the importance of deposit-taking activity, the capacity to create liquidity, and the criticality of the institution for systemic stability. It is also proposed to link the intensity of regulation with the nature of functions being performed by the institutions in relation to their relevance to stability. From a developing country point of view, this should be welcomed in principle. The Indian experience indicates that such an expanded scope of regulation adds to stability; in particular, it demonstrates the importance of regulating the nature of transactions between banks and non-banks. It also illustrates the advantage of restricting the exposure of banks to risky businesses and to non-traditional retail lending businesses.

The reform proposals with regard to the structure of regulation address the issue of a mandate for financial stability and ensuring accountability. It should be noted that there is no empirical evidence showing—in the context of the current crisis—that a particular regulatory structure has contributed to greater stability. There is as yet no agreement on the need for creating a new institutional structure. At the same time, there is no agreement on giving the mandate entirely to the central bank either. Where new institutional arrangements are proposed, it is not clear whether it is the government or the central bank that will play a leading role. There is, however, a broad agreement that these arrangements should (i) ensure a better focus on financial stability by the monetary authority, both by the regulators and by the government; (ii) ensure a greater degree of coordination among them; (iii) strive for greater accountability; and (iv) not dilute the operational autonomy of the regulators concerned.

In developing countries, it is possible to apply these general principles, but with a full understanding of the institutional capabilities and nature of arrangements of governance in public policy. Central banks in developing countries generally command greater credibility than other newly created institutions for regulation. They usually have a command over technical expertise that the others do not. In view of the importance of traditional commercial banking, the banking regulator will play a critical role. With respect to developing countries, there is therefore considerable merit in formalising a mandate for financial stability to a central bank, which should also be responsible for the regulation of banks and payment systems.

It can be argued that a central bank should be a natural choice for according a mandate for financial stability. The central bank as a monetary authority inevitably bears responsibility for liquidity, and is also the lender of last resort. Hence, its centrality in maintaining stability is inevitable, whether formally stated or not. In developing countries, it will be ideal to vest the responsibility for stability with the central bank and put in place arrangements for the exchange of information and coordination, both at the technical level and at the levels of heads of regulators with appropriate participation by the government. These arrangements should provide for coordination, but the autonomy and accountability of individual institutions would remain. The Indian experience has shown that such arrangements have functioned well.

An appropriate framework for the regulation of financial innovations is on the agenda, although it is still contentious. There are several contrasting views regarding their role. These are: (i) they contribute nothing to economic development or welfare; (ii) they enhance efficiency and stability by diversifying risks and saving on capital, provided the regulators know how to regulate them; and (iii) they may contribute to increased efficiency of use of capital, but have a tendency to enable the appropriation of all gains by the select few while adding to instability. Empirical evidence about the benefits of many of these instruments is not very positive, although financial market participants in developed countries insist on their beneficial role. There is a reasonable consensus, even as proposals for reform are being considered, that the beneficial effects of these innovations should be demonstrable before they are permitted. From the perspective of developing countries, there is merit in strengthening the regulation of such innovations and, in fact, in assessing the benefits over a considerable period before permitting them in their jurisdictions. Wherever such innovations are considered, developing countries may assess both market and regulatory capabilities in obtaining benefits from such instruments and avoiding risks. The Indian experience of waiting for the benefits of such instruments to be proven and prescribing necessary safeguards before permitting them—and, in any case, restraining the banks from involving themselves excessively in these instruments—has proved to be workable and beneficial.

A related area is the extent to which over-the-counter trading (OTC) should be permitted with respect to financial instruments. Over-the-counter trading is trade in financial instruments such as stocks, bonds, commodities or derivatives directly between two parties, unlike trading through stock exchanges or futures exchanges, etc. Often, it is directly between an investment bank and its clients. There is a general agreement that OTC is favoured by market participants for promoting innovations, but that their overall desirability cannot be assessed in advance. Hence, the proposals are two-fold, namely (i) to restrict OTC to the extent possible and make it an exception to the general rule of exchange trading; and (ii) have safeguard mechanisms such as Products Safety Commissions akin to the pharmaceutical industry. There is merit in developing countries exercising greater restrictions than developed countries in permitting banks to indulge in over-the-counter activities.

A proposal has also been made for a Financial Products Safety Commission or Authority to avoid 'bad' innovations and permit only 'good' ones. In principle, the regulatory regime should take into account the safety of the financial products for the health of the financial sector, but it is possible to argue that the function of assessing safety could be built into the processes of the existing institutions of regulation. It is important to ensure the application of the principle of safety of the financial product in the regulatory regime. Whether it is done through a separate agency, or through a separate wing in the existing agency, or through appropriate formal mechanisms is a matter of detail and related to the context of the country. In view of the institutional capabilities and scope for such innovations, there is merit in incorporating the processes for certifying safety in the existing regulator. Further, for developing countries, tried and tested innovations with abundant safeguards would be consistent with a precautionary approach. It may, however, be noted that the work relating to safety in the financial sector may be different from health or environmental standards.

Incentive structures that deter excessive risk-taking, particularly with regard to compensation, are proposed to be introduced through regulations. The industry, however, has been resisting such changes by arguing that such restrictions will have an adverse effect on competitive efficiency. Developing countries will have an additional reason to take serious note of these developments, since inequalities in income and wealth may be exaggerated, with adverse consequences. The Indian experience has so far been positive with a system of formal approval of compensation packages for the Chief Executives, although compensations to other functionaries are not yet subject to the approval of the central bank.

The reform proposals include fundamental changes in the approach to prudential regulation, and those most significant for developing countries relate to increasing the quantity and quality of bank capital, increasing trade book capital, emphasising countercyclical capital buffers, containing liquidity risks, and a cross-leverage ratio backstop. It is essential for developing countries to analyse the underlying logic and relevance of these prescriptions to local conditions, and consider adopting them with suitable modifications and at an appropriate pace.

In the past, the regulatory approach in India had been broadly in the directions under contemplation as part of the current regulatory reform. However, the approach in India made a clear distinction between three sets of banks, with some variations with regard to the rigour of regulation. One set was applicable to the branches of foreign bank in India and Indian banks with a cross-border presence. The second was applicable to those operating entirely within the country. The third set of banks essentially catered to local needs, either through a corporate or a cooperative structure. Further, in many respects the safeguards and precautionary approaches adopted were stronger than global standards. A more flexible timetable vis-à-vis the pace of implementation was adopted to enable adequate preparedness. However, this three-pronged approach could generate problems of synchronisation of regulatory regimes if the financial sector of a developing country is closely integrated with a developed or a global economy.

The approach to cross-border regulation is now occupying centre-stage. There is increasing emphasis on host country regulation. It is thought that regulators in countries hosting global financial institutions and banks should be able to dictate the laws under which those subsidiaries and branches operated, instead of depending on the regulation of parent companies in their country of origin. This would necessitate policy space for the host regulator in relation to the common standards of regulation that are sought to be prescribed. Developing countries have a disadvantage when it comes to regulating complex products and institutions that operate within their jurisdiction. A complex, commonly agreed-upon regulatory framework puts regulators of developing countries at a disadvantage. Perhaps this is an area where more work has to be done, and developing countries do have a stake in these issues, particularly with regard to the activities of the branches or subsidiaries of foreign banks in these jurisdictions.

There is an intense debate on managing institutions that are considered 'too big to fail'. The prevalent view seems to be that breaking up existing large institutions will not be possible without serious disruption. Hence, there is a preference for prescribing more intrusive regulation, higher capital and even a tax on such institutions. There are several complexities in this regard. As experience has shown in India and some other countries, for example Germany in 2008, a bank may be systemically important without being too big. Moreover, what is too big to fail in one country may not be so in a large international financial centre, and vice versa. However, large-sized financial institutions are very likely to be systemically important. The major issue is whether an institution or a bank considers itself too big to fail. Once a market participant perceives that it is too big to fail, there is a temptation to take extreme risks. It is doubtful whether prescribing additional capital provides enough incentive to avoid excessive risks if they perceive that they will not be allowed to fail. Therefore, for developing countries, there is considerable advantage in prescribing a limit on the extent of an institution's share in the financial sector. It may also be necessary to consider prescribing a limit on the share of a foreign bank. It is often the case that specific institutions have a disproportionate share of specific markets. For instance, in India, a few foreign banks account for about half the forex market and a quarter of the secondary market in government securities.

MISSING AGENDA FOR REFORMS

From a developing country's perspective, stability has to be given great importance because social security mechanisms are generally absent or weak. Instability inflicts suffering on a large number of underprivileged people. Further, structural transformation and the faith of the people in the economic reform of the real sector would be seriously hampered if there was financial instability. At the same time, it is important to recognise that the financial sector should also be an instrument of public policy for facilitating development. Simply put, if public intervention is necessary and justified in the interest of correcting market imperfections to assure stability, there is no reason why public policy should not use regulation for developmental purposes. Further, if regulation is justified for containing possible asset bubbles in a free market system, there is no reason why that regulation should not be used for the creation of assets, especially more productive assets. Some prescriptions with regard to the allocation or pricing of credit should be considered less unfavourably than before.

The proposals under consideration are yet to analyse the adverse impact of excessive deregulation on both development and growth. Among developing countries, China and India have been directing and regulating the financial sector with a view to encouraging the financing of directly productive activities in the real sector. Empirical evidence shows that their policies have resulted in positive outcomes for growth and stability relative to other EMEs with significant deregulation of the financial sector.

It is essential to recognise the importance of public policy in ensuring that the financial sector, particularly the banking sector, covers a large part of the population. In many developed countries, the poor are excluded from the organised financial sector by virtue of low personal credit ratings or for having dropped out of the banking system due to defaults, etc. In most developing economies, there is a significant exclusion of people from organised banking services. Policy initiatives for financial inclusion appear appropriate, and the gains from such inclusions for commercial banking are evident in India. There is merit in incorporating incentives for financial inclusion in the regulatory regimes of developing countries.

A large part of the regulatory reforms proceed on the assumption of efficiency of what may be termed integrated markets. In other words, there is an assumption of the superiority of integrated financial markets reinforcing each other domestically as well as globally. Since developing countries have bank-dominated systems, it is quite possible that a continuance of bank-dominated regimes with distinct and special roles for traditional banking would be appropriate. Experience shows that reliance on more advanced institutions and instruments has resulted in risks in even advanced financial markets, and the efficacy of the improvements under contemplation has not yet been established. It is possible to conceive of a regulatory regime that is more appropriate for bank-dominated systems, as prevalent in developing countries.

In the past, a large part of the discussion on regulatory regimes was directed at maintaining a level playing field as essential for competitive efficiency. Recently, there have been debates about banks that may be too big to fail and the need for enhanced capital requirements. In some ways, this is an acceptance of the desirability of an unlevelled playing field. It is possible to extend the basic logic to an unlevelled playing field based on (i) the size (large or small) of institutions; (ii) the nature of financial institutions (commercial banks, investment banks, hedge funds); (iii) the complexity of financial activity or the nature of the activity of the institutions; and finally (iv) the type of country (developed, developing, emerging markets, etc.). Further, financial markets tend to view developed countries differently from developing countries even when the fundamentals are similar. The public policies of different countries cannot afford to ignore these realities and assume that there is a level playing field in global finance. In light of the observations of the Warwick Commission Report, the scope for and desirability of an 'unlevelled' playing field as an instrument of financial-sector regulation ought to be explored.

There is some recognition of the problems in the infrastructure relating to financial markets, particularly credit-rating agencies and news agencies. Genuine competition in these areas is perhaps conspicuous by its absence. Serious correctives to this situation as an enforceable part of the package of the reform of regulations may be warranted, particularly for developing countries. If correctives are not assured, alternative frameworks may be needed.

The imposition of the Tobin tax has been brought on the agenda, but the implications of providing options to levy the Tobin tax as part of regulatory regimes have not been assessed in the reform agenda. In other words, the proposals for reforms could debate and consider whether the Tobin tax should be an option available to public policy, both with regard to financial transactions within the country and cross-border transactions. More importantly, complementarities between the tax on banks and regulation of banks, which have the effect of a tax burden, cannot be ignored.

ISSUES AND ROLE OF THE G-20

It is noteworthy that the agenda for financial-sector reform in the G-20 and the Financial Stability Forum is concentrating on the appropriate reforms in the regulation of the financial sector, taking into account essentially the experience of the US, UK and Europe. However, there is a larger dimension to the issue, pointed out by the Stiglitz Commission and to some extent by the Warwick Commission. It is possible that the experience of countries where the financial sector was less affected, such as Canada and Australia, may have important lessons to offer. Similarly, recent developments question fundamental assumptions regarding the advantages of globalising sovereign debt or utilising sophisticated instruments in government debt markets. The experience of Asian countries, especially China and India, could be contrasted with some others, particularly in Eastern Europe and Latin America or Africa to draw lessons. While it is true that reform proposals have to accord highest priority to those countries that are systemically important for global finance, it is wise to derive lessons from the experiences of other countries in the global economy while considering regulatory regimes for global finance. There are a few instances where lessons have been learnt— as shown in some recent IMF publications—but they appear to be reluctant modifications of pre-existing ideologies and lay claim to the discovery of new truths rather than acknowledging the lessons learnt from the experiences in many developing countries. However, UNCTAD has been wisely capturing diverse experiences in its publications.

It is clear that by and large, developing countries have not been seriously affected by policies related to the financial sector within the economy; however, they have been affected mainly through the linkages that their financial sectors had with developed countries. In other words, the problem for developing countries during the crisis was one of contagion through cross-border flows of capital and the cross-border presence of financial intermediaries. The agenda for reform is proceeding on the assumption that adverse contagion can be reduced and the beneficial impact of globalised finance enhanced through (i) the adoption of the proposed regulatory framework for countries, and (ii) the coordination of regulation on a global scale. One is not sure, however, whether these basic assumptions are valid. There has been a welcome change in the attitude to capital controls or capital account management. It is not very clear whether the proposals for a review of the financial sector are taking into account the possible impact of a wider acceptance of capital account management by developing countries. The Indian experience shows that capital account management is more effective when it is supplemented significantly with prudential prescriptions on financial intermediaries, especially on banks. Once the desirability and effectiveness of capital account management has been accepted (either temporary or not so temporary), the link with the regulatory regime may have to be recognised.

The linkage between macroeconomic policies and financial-sector regulation is receiving greater attention in discussions on the reform of the financial sector. There have been instances of countries that are facing a crisis because of serious interaction between the macro and financial sectors; these include developed countries like Spain, Iceland and Ireland, and the developing economies that have approached the IMF for relief. A closer examination of the interaction between the macro and financial sectors may warrant a greater policy space for national authorities in both sectors in an inter-related fashion. This may call for an entirely new paradigm— on the relationship between the macro and financial sectors on the one hand, and national and global financial markets on the other. The close link between macro policies and financial markets has been recognised in the proposals for regulatory reforms under discussion, as evidenced by the emphasis on macro-prudential regulation and countercyclical policies. However, it is quite possible that different countries experience different economic or trade cycles. Policymakers may find it difficult to harmonise monetary policy and a financial-sector policy that simultaneously addresses the domestic trade cycle and the global economic cycle, if they tend to diverge.

The current crisis has raised doubts as to whether serious problems could arise for developing countries in the future. Perhaps the growing public debt in developed economies to manage the crisis could precipitate unprecedented and serious situations, and a set of totally new challenges. The increasing public debt to GDP ratios in developed economies would imply a manifold global increase in the global public debt, which has to be financed by the somewhat integrated global financial markets. Public policy has incurred huge debts to bailout large financial institutions, and ironically in the future, governments would have to rely heavily on, if not be at the mercy of, the same financial markets. It is possible that the resultant crowding out of the resources available for the private sector may impact developing countries significantly, given the excessive preference of financial markets for developed economies. This is illustrated by the history of ratings given in the recent past to India, Korea, China, Greece, Ireland, Spain, etc. Developing countries that are members of the G-20 should urge a serious consideration of the impact of the high public debt incurred by advanced economies in the context of the crisis concerning the management of public debt in developing economies. From a developmental perspective, there is a need for considerable public investment in developing economies, which could play a critical role in improving the potential output. In analysing the impact of high public debt on developing economies in the context of the crisis, it may be necessary to note that advanced economies have relatively low domestic savings; hence their capacity to service public debt may be constrained, resulting in a larger absorption of global savings by them.

It has been suggested that India and China, along with some other developing countries, should take the initiative to convey the perspectives of all developing countries. Such an effort should convey the following concerns. First, developing countries that closely followed the models prescribed by the IMF perceive that they are paying a heavy price, and that the IMF should be held accountable and be subject to scrutiny. It is gratifying to see some signs of rethinking on the part of the IMF vis-à-vis some desirable policies. Second, many of the new regulatory standards being developed do not appear to be equally relevant to developing countries. A case could be made for a separate subset of standards of bank regulation, applicable to the needs of developing countries, and the G-20 should also be considering them. Third, there are several areas of difference on the agenda for the reform of the financial sector between the US, UK and Europe. While these are discussed in the G-20 and the FSB, the position of important countries in the G-20—like China and India—on these is not clear, and may go unnoticed or unheard. Finally, countries like India and China should legitimately be among the leaders within the G-20 in championing the concerns and causes of developing countries as a whole, and should not appear to only be following the lead of others in the G-20.

CONCLUSION: THE WAY FORWARD

Developing countries have to cover three broad policy areas related to the future of financial-sector regulation on their way forward. The first relates to macroeconomic management on which several lessons have to be drawn, many of them relevant to the financial sector. The second concerns the policy related to the future of their domestic financial systems, on which the recent debates on financial-sector reforms aim to provide some guidance. The third relates to the management of the integration of their financial systems within the international financial system, particularly the international regulatory architecture. This is indeed a very complex territory.

Eleven

Redefined Approach to Globalisation of Finance and Regulation*

$\mathscr{T}$his chapter highlights the importance of redefined approaches to the GFA, with special reference to the regulation and globalisation of the financial sector. The first section advocates a multi-level approach to globalised financial architecture. The second section describes the process of rebalancing and the importance of decentralisation and diversity. The third section makes a distinction between multinational and international banks in the design of the globalised regulation of the financial sector. The fourth section proposes a possible redefined approach while the concluding section endorses, with some caveats, Professor Stiglitz's analytical framework for such a redefined approach.

* This chapter is an edited version of the paper presented at the Institute for New Economic Thinking (INET), Annual Conference, King's College, Cambridge, 8–11 April 2010.

NEED FOR AN INTEGRATED APPROACH

The issues relating to the GFA have to be positioned within the overall approach to globalisation, while specifically relating it to the financial sector. The recent events have shown that the challenges facing the globalisation of finance could be different from those relating to the process of the globalisation of trade. The GFA should also be viewed in the context of the totality of several inter-related layers. These are: (i) national-level public-policy institutions (government, central bank, financial sector regulator); (ii) national-level financial markets and financial institutions; (iii) supra-national level but sub-global level public policy institutions (such as Euro area; Asian regional initiatives); (iv) global-level public-policy institutions, in particular the IMF, World Bank and the United Nations at a formal level, and G-7, G-20 or FSB at an informal level; and (v) financial institutions operating predominantly in global or cross-border financial markets. An appropriate GFA should take cognisance of the various levels and elements of the system and their interrelationship, rather than focus mainly on global-level institutions.

PROCESS OF REBALANCING: IMPORTANCE OF
DECENTRALISATION AND DIVERSITY

It is possible to consider the reform of the globalisation of finance and globalisation of regulation under consideration as part of a process of rebalancing, consequent upon the experience gained with the global crisis. Such a process has several dimensions. There is a need to rebalance the relationship between financial-sector regulation, monetary policy and fiscal policy by formally recognising the inter-dependencies at the national level. In principle, this rebalancing in favour of a harmonised approach is evidenced in the emphasis on countercyclical regulations in the financial sector. The redefining of the relationship between governments and regulatory agencies is under consideration at the national level in several jurisdictions. The relationship between regulators is also being rebalanced in some countries to ensure coordination in the interest of stability. There is a rebalancing of relationships between governments within the supra-national but sub-global levels, such as in Asia and the Euro area. Finally, there have been global attempts to strengthen the GFA, which should ensure stability. Conspicuously absent in the debates is the developmental dimension to the financial sector. In brief, the design of the GFA has to recognise the changing balances between different arms of public policy at the national level; the state and market in different jurisdictions; and national and regional as well as global levels.

The current reform proposals with regard to the GFA are based on an assumption that creating new institutions is more complex and time-consuming. While structural elements of the reform of institutions such as the IMF are considered time-consuming by their very nature, there is considerable discussion on strengthening the institutions in their existing forms of governance in order to meet the emerging problems in global finance. In a way, this approach amounts to strengthening institutions that are admittedly suffering from a governance deficit, credibility deficit, and arguably an effectiveness deficit. However, it is possible to consider an alternate approach based on developing counter-balancing institutions that could be devised either at the global or at the decentralised level. For instance, it is possible to recognise and encourage several regional-level arrangements for the financial sector, including its regulation. It is possible for the IMF to play a facilitating role in developing the counter-balancing institutional arrangements—to the extent acceptable to the concerned countries—as regional-level bodies.

More generally, all the arrangements under consideration are indicative of centralisation in the management of the global financial sector. It will be interesting to imagine what would have happened if such a binding centralised framework had existed, say, five years ago. It would not have permitted the diversity in policies in the financial sector and in monetary policy that had been adopted by India and China, for instance. Hence, to ensure stability in the future, there may be merit in enabling some diversity in public policies in different parts of the world in matters relating to economic issues, on which there is far less certainty than in matters such as electricity and telecommunications. In other words, in dealing with human behaviour and human institutions—in contrast to physical sciences—full integration and centralisation may be risky, even when accompanied by what has been described as circuit breakers. In fact, it is possible to argue that the centralised approach implicit in the current proposals for reforms in regulation may either require or promote a synchronised global boom and bust, which could be even more difficult to manage than diversity.

STRENGTHENING REGULATION OF INTERNATIONAL BANKS

The approaches to reforms in the GFA, insofar as they relate to the regulation of the financial sector, focus on a globally acceptable regulatory framework that reduces the risks of financial instability while facilitating the globalisation of finance. The mismatch between global financial integration and its regulation is sought to be bridged through the various proposals for reform. The global financial crisis originated in countries with a national-level regulation that was particularly soft, and in the financial conglomerates that concentrated on cross-border finance and thus facilitated contagion. These financial conglomerates are generally based out of jurisdictions that have soft regulations. It will be useful to make a distinction between multinational banks and international banks for analytical purposes. Multinational banks may be defined as those that operate sizable foreign branches and subsidiaries in multiple jurisdictions, and in their pure form, fund their positions locally in the host countries. In other words, they do not undertake significant cross-border financial transactions. During the crisis, such banks showed better resilience. A second set may be defined as international banks, which may operate out of one home country or from a major financial centre, but under the umbrella of a conglomerate. The main characteristic of such international banks and their associates is the dominance of cross-border business on their balance sheets.

It is possible to argue that the global financial crisis arose out of the unique position of the international banks in conducting cross-border business with significant benefits to themselves, high risks to the system, and questionable gains to the cause of economic development. Empirical data may be necessary to establish this fact, but a quick assessment of the major institutions that suffered during the crisis is indicative of the fact that even within developed countries, it was mainly international banks or banks with large cross-border exposures that were significantly involved.

It is useful to consider empirical evidence on whether international banks were responsible for devising financial instruments that specialised in injecting complexity into financial products in the name of innovation with two objectives, namely, (i) satisfy the regulator that there is transparency, but defeat the purpose of transparency; and (ii) take advantage of cross-border operations to spread the risks to other financial institutions, including those that are otherwise confined to domestic financial markets.

It is possible that international banks, as part of financial conglomerates, are in a privileged position for several reasons. First, they arbitrage between different sets of regulations in different jurisdictions. Second, they simultaneously operate between different sectors of the financial market. Third, they conduct their operations across tax regimes. Fourth, they are able to operate at different levels of formal legality in different jurisdictions. In other words, if there is a concern of public policy with regard to large bank balances in some jurisdictions with inadequate transparency, the money could not reach such jurisdictions or such places without the active involvement of international banks. Finally, it can also be argued that cross-border activities gives them a special advantage in a non-tangible way. For example, they can induce a race to the bottom in regulation. They can foster and facilitate the cross-border management of the political economy. They are in a better position in relation to domestic regulators in several jurisdictions, in terms of assuming risk and exercising their clout.

If the empirical evidence is indicative of the fact that international banks, or banks that were active in cross-border transactions operating essentially from international financial centers, have been the main sources of the financial crisis, then the attention of the reform of the globalised regulation of the financial sector and the GFA should be on the activities of such international banks.

POSSIBLE REDEFINED APPROACH

In light of the approaches described, the focus in the debate on the regulation of the financial sector could be on the following lines:

(i) The regulation of the financial sector should essentially be the responsibility of the national authorities, and every effort should be made to ensure that they serve the national interest, in the process ensuring that there are no serious risks for the rest of the global finance. International coordination is thus required only to manage the systemic risks and serious spillovers to other countries.

(ii) In order to avoid the risks of soft regulation on the global economy, minimum standards of regulation could be prescribed for all countries, more particularly with respect to institutions or markets of the countries that have significance for the global economy.

(iii) A degree of diversity consistent with the institutional as well as socio-economic contexts of different countries and different regions should be consciously encouraged.

(iv) Scope for counter-balancing and decentralisation of global-level institutions to bring about a better balance between stability and efficiency could be explored in parallel with reforming the existing global-level institutions.

(v) While focusing on improvements in the global monetary system, the regulation of the financial sector at a global level should concentrate on those institutions that are in the nature of international banks, mainly concentrating on cross-border financial transactions. The focus of globally enforceable regulatory requirements should be most intense with regard to these institutions. This could be viewed as globally, systemically important financial institutions being subject to global-level regulation to supplement the rigour of national-level regulation.

PROFESSOR STIGLITZ'S ANALYTICAL FRAMEWORK FOR A REDEFINED APPROACH

An analytical framework for a redefined approach to the issue of global financial integration with special reference to the regulation of the financial sector is available in a paper by Professor Joseph E. Stiglitz, 'Risk and Global Economic Architecture: Why Full Financial Integration may be Undesirable'. The paper provides a general analytic framework within which the optimal degree and form of financial integration could be analysed. It indicates that full integration is not, in general, optimal. In this regard, the paper identifies the problem relating to risks and one relating to contagion, which should be contained through well-designed circuit breakers in networks, such as the imposition of capital controls. 'Restrictions on capital flows in times of crises act as circuit breakers'.[1] However, it can be argued that ideally circuit breakers are mounted not after the event, but are built into the system. Further, the financial sector has a considerable element of behavioural dynamics relative to the networks in an electric grid or telecommunications. Hence, there is a greater justification for the continuous presence of such circuit breakers, whose design and magnitude should be calibrated depending on the behavioural dynamics in financial markets.

Professor Stiglitz also refers to the fact that the world is rife with non-convexities, and hence global integration based on the assumption of convexity may not be desirable. He notes, 'The intuition behind why integration should be desirable was based on "convexity": with convex technologies and concave utility functions, risk sharing is always beneficial. The more globally integrated the world economy, the better risks are "dispersed". But if technologies are not convex, then risk sharing can lower expected utility' (pp. 5–6). In this regard, he refers to externalities such as bankruptcy and information costs. However, it can be argued in this regard that international banks and financial conglomerates may have the capacity to inject information cost and complexity.

Professor Stiglitz adds that 'simulations within a variant of our model show that an appropriately designed circuit programme can be welfare enhancing' (p. 9). However, it may be more useful to examine whether the appropriate mechanism for the financial market should be a circuit breaker or a voltage stabiliser, or a combination of both.

In conclusion, the debate on approaches to GFA should include a questioning of the fundamental assumptions behind the risks and benefits of not only the deregulation of the financial sector, but also the globalisation of the financial sector, which has been the foundation of our economic thinking in recent years. In questioning the assumptions of risks and benefits of the globalised financial sector, two realities have not been fully appreciated. First, despite the enthusiasm for and benefits of globalisation that have been observed so far, the welfare of the people is the primary responsibility of national governments. The national governments are accountable to the people. Further, labour as a factor of production is not as mobile as goods or finance. Labour is mostly confined to a nation while goods and capital are mobile, thus reducing the bargaining power of labour in its relation with capital. Limits to the globalisation of economies may not ignore the restrictions on the cross-border movement of labour.

Notes

1. Joseph E. Stiglitz, 'Risk and Global Economic Architecture: Why Full Financial Integration may be Undesirable', NBER Working Paper 157, 18 February 2010, p. 4.

Twelve

Reforms in Regulation of the Financial Sector: An Outlook*

$\mathcal{T}$he global financial crisis has led to a reconsideration of the benefits and risks of liberalising the financial sector. The first section of this chapter describes the agenda for assessment and reform of the financial sector in response to the lessons learnt from the crisis. The second section lists the balancing of critical considerations for assessment and reform. The third section provides a summary of the globally coordinated approaches to the reform, and also discusses the impact of Basel III proposals. The fourth section narrates the reforms undertaken or proposed (or under consideration) in select countries. The fifth section considers some select issues, urges for a development orientation to the reforms, and makes a brief mention of the outlook for the reforms.

Agenda for Assessment and Reform

An assessment of regulatory system in the financial sector should ideally take into account the purpose of the financial system, in view

* This chapter incorporates comments made in the Global Economic Governance Conference, sponsored by the Institute for Policy Dialogue, Columbia University and Foundation for European Progressive Studies, Brookings Institution, Washington DC, 8 October 2010.

of its facilitating role for economic well-being and the broader goals of economic policy. To serve this purpose, the regulatory system should be consistent with economic objectives and the financial system. The regulatory system should have well-understood objectives and a given perimeter or scope of operations. There should a structure, a philosophy and a set of tools for the regulators to operate. These are discernable from both external and internal features of regulatory bodies, such as the legal framework (an external feature) or the governance approach and skill (an internal feature). The financial system has three broad overlapping segments, namely, financial institutions, markets and instruments. The regulatory system will have components directed at each of these segments, but it is extremely complex to compartmentalise them, thus making coordination—formal and informal—critical. It is possible to argue that in the pre-crisis years, some of the regulatory regimes had a somewhat over simplified view of achieving economic efficiency and stability through an essentially market-driven self-regulatory system, while the financial systems were growing rapidly and adding to complexity. Experience with the crisis, both in countries severely affected and those less affected, enables a list of general principles for assessment of the adequacy of regulatory regimes. In considering the general principles, it is necessary to recognise that the objectives of the financial and regulatory systems should legitimately be country specific. In view of the systemic risks generated by the individual and collective behaviour of firms coming into sharp focus, the critical role of macro-prudential regulation in complementing micro-prudential regulation became evident. Macro-prudential framework should be so designed that there is adequate capital with the financial institutions to absorb a variety of risks both in normal and abnormal times. Hence, the regulators have to prescribe a quantity of capital that is adequate to absorb these risks. In computing the requirements of capital, an assessment and quantification of risk is critical. In assessing capital requirements of individual institutions, there is a need for a countercyclical approach. In other words during good times capital should be set aside so that in bad times it will be able to take care of the risks. In aggregate, the bank's balance sheet should not be excessively leveraged, and hence the ratio between owned resources and borrowed resources in the conduct of business should be reasonable. The quality of capital is also important. In other words, the practice of treating borrowed capital also as risk capital may have to be restrained. The regulatory framework should also take into account systemic risks and not merely the risks of individual institutions. It is quite possible that individual institutions considered separately may be healthy, but as a part of the system they may become vulnerable in terms of the capacity to take risks of interconnections in their operations. Hence, the regulatory framework should take a view of the systemic risks and in that context stricter norms for systemically important financial institutions (SIFIs) and an effective regulation mechanism for such institutions should come into prominence.

The perimeter of financial sector regulation has to be well designed. If one segment, say banking, is subjected to rigorous regulations, and the non-banking segments are not subjected to such regulations, than those institutions may find ways of performing prohibited banking functions through some innovative mechanisms taking advantage of the regulatory gaps. Further, banks themselves may finance banking activities outside their own pools. In addition, private pools of capital such as hedge funds or private equity funds could be large and may have systemic implications. Such pools of capital may also have to be regulated, but the extent of regulation cannot be at par with banks. In brief, different segments of the financial sector will have to be subjected to different types of regulations, to ensure that regulatory arbitrage is minimised. In other words, the same type of activity undertaken by different types of financial institutions should be subjected to the same type of regulation. Furthermore, improving transparency and regulatory oversight of hedge funds, credit rating agencies and over-the-counter (OTC) derivatives should become a priority in the light of the experience from the crisis.

The recent financial crisis witnessed the collapse of large investment banks in the US, which rekindled a discussion of optimal banking models. There are three views about the structure of banking institutions. One view is that the economies of scope and efficiencies of scale can be captured by the financial sector if banks are able to perform a range of financial services of which retail banking is one. These are described as universal banks and are recommended on grounds of efficiency. A second view is that universal banking incorporates within itself significant conflicts of interests between different businesses and they may tend to take excessive risks. Further, this institutional structure may neglect retail banking which is of interest for a large section of the population. The traditional banking function includes the payments system, which is of considerable significance and therefore, should be treated as a public utility. Hence, some commend banks to devote exclusively to retail banking and this is sometimes described as narrow banking. An intermediate view is that a bank should predominantly continue with the traditional retail or commercial banking functions, while the other riskier activities should be either prohibited or permitted only under stringent restrictions, depending on the nature of financial activities.

The financial intermediaries often have mismatches in regard to maturity between assets and liabilities. It is necessary to ensure that the mismatches are within limits, and the financial intermediaries are not excessively dependent on money markets, i.e., very short-term lending and borrowing. The regulation should, therefore, take into account the liquidity requirements.

With the improvement in technology, financial services industry has brought about several innovations. These financial innovations, which are in the nature of complex instruments, are expected to spread the risk widely and help in efficient price discovery. In practice, however many of the innovations have tended to circumvent regulations and, in any case, they often inject complexity in financial products. It is, therefore, necessary to ensure that only good innovations are permitted by the regulator and bad innovations are discouraged or even prohibited. No doubt, it is difficult to distinguish between good and bad prior to their actual working. Moreover, the complexity with regard to some of the innovations warrants protection of consumers of such products from undertaking excessive risks. Transparency by itself may not help if the complexities merely become transparent, but the innovations are not simple enough to understand. To the extent the innovations are new and uniquely designed, it is difficult to subject them to standard trading practices such as on exchanges. While OTC transactions enable innovations, they also have embedded risks. Hence, appropriate regulatory framework that ensures good innovations and sound trading practices should be considered.

Although accounting conventions were not the causes of the financial crisis, certain accounting measures, such as the use of fair value accounting for illiquid financial instruments and the important model for loans and debt securities, have been viewed as weak areas that exacerbated the problems. In order to operationalise the principles in a clear and non-discriminatory manner, accounting standards should be of a quality that are sufficiently standardised, well understood and subject to common interpretation. The accounting standards, to the extent they depend on market prices for valuation, can be pro-cyclical, thus adding to the problem. Hence, they should be stable as also be able to capture the impact of cycles on the financial intermediaries.

The incentive structures to the management and staff in each financial institution should be such that they are not encouraged to take excessive risks. In particular, the remuneration for senior executives when linked to the short-term profitability may have the potential to increase risk taking by the institutions. Mechanisms should, therefore, be designed that provide incentives for good performance, but disincentives for excessive risk taking. A major area requiring regulatory intervention is the complex task of avoiding conflict of interests. The erection of firewalls within an organisation between functions involving conflict of interests may not necessarily serve the purpose, since firewalls in financial transactions have a tendency to be porous and almost invisible.

The legal and institutional arrangements governing the regulatory framework should provide regulators with adequate authority, coupled with accountability. Where multiple regulators exist, arrangements are required for formal and informal coordination. Similarly, in the case of large or systemically important financial institutions, special coordinating arrangements would be required among the regulators. In addition to the structures, the regulators should have a mechanism for capacity building, and to keep pace with innovations in financial markets.

The credit rating agencies play a vital role in the financial sector since they are also used by regulators for specific purposes. However, the rating agencies also have inherent conflict of interests as they are hired by the rated, giving significant scope for conflict of interests. The rating agencies inadvertently contributed to the build-up of systemic risk during recent times by issuing unrealistically high ratings.[1] It is therefore necessary to reduce the dependence of regulators on rating agencies and, at the same time, ensure that the quality of rating is appropriate.

Above all, it is the quality of supervision that is important since it has been found that even though the regulations did exist, their compliance was poor and supervision inadequate or ineffective. In brief, there is a realisation about the criticality of equal emphasis on what may be termed as sound principles for regulating and effectively supervising the financial sector. An assessment of the financial sector with reference to these sound principles is the first step towards the reform of the financial sector in any country. However, in considering the general principles, each country has to take account of the objectives of regulation as part of a broader public policy.

BALANCING OF CRITICAL CONSIDERATIONS

There is a broad agreement on most of the general principles of regulation and supervision of the financial sector, in the light of the crisis. However, conflicting considerations in the actual framing of regulations and their implementation need to be explicitly assessed and balanced. It is extremely difficult to weigh the benefits and risks with regard to these conflicting considerations. The financial crisis has shown that, in the past, in the absence of a good balance between conflicting considerations, private interests have prevailed over public interests, resulting in considerable social costs.

First, it is generally assumed that market forces and competition will have a tendency to impart efficiency. In the financial sector, however, short-term efficiency may often threaten longer-term stability.

Second, the interests of shareholders who have to contribute to the capital of the financial intermediaries should be weighed against the benefits of giving higher priority to social goals such as development or stability.

Third, assurances of support in times of difficulties would enable the financial intermediaries to assume risks that could add to overall efficiency in normal times, but there is a moral hazard since assurance of support may encourage excessive risk taking. Assurances of support should be minimal and only to the extent of not creating a moral hazard. However, it is very difficult, in practice, to say what is an ex ante minimal support.

Fourth, it is well-known that higher the risks (measured in terms of price), higher is the returns in a risk-return frontier. The accumulation of higher risk by several financial intermediaries in the system may threaten systemic stability, especially if the risk is being taken with borrowed resources. An issue is whether the consumer of the product is provided with full information to assess risks and returns.

Fifth, there is need for market participants to be fully aware of the rules that they should follow. But, it is not possible to envisage all circumstances and lay down rigid rules in advance. However, giving excessive discretion to the regulations may add a premium for uncertainty, thus adding to the cost of intermediation. It is also possible that the regulators are captured by the regulated. One approach is to depend on rules in normal times while permitting discretion under extraordinary circumstances; though it may be difficult to define extraordinary circumstances in advance.

Sixth, an intrusive regulation may not be commensurate with the costs of the regulation and the costs of its compliance. On the other hand, soft regulation especially self-regulation is less costly since the regulator can state principles that should be complied by the regulated, and leave details to the regulated. Experience has shown that excessive reliance on self regulation has a tendency to become weak regulation, thus defeating the objectives of the regulation. Where standards of governance are high, self regulation could be preferred to external regulation and hence the regulatory framework could focus on standards of governance more than external regulation. Defining appropriate governance standards and ensuring their implementation, however, is a complex task and may involve subjectivity.

Seventh, the regulators have a fiduciary responsibility in as much as the banks are licensed to conduct businesses that are highly leveraged and take deposits without colaterals. Hence, some regulatory prescriptions are essential, but beyond a point they restrain market operations that are essential for promoting efficiency and constrain competition.

Eighth, because of the changing circumstances, particularly fast changing technologies, the regulatory framework should be dynamic enough to be able to cope with changes in the market's products and practices. At the same time, some stability in the regulatory regime is essential for market participants to conduct their operations without imposing a high uncertainty premium.

Ninth, consumers of financial services, in particular retail depositors, need to be protected from sale of low quality or toxic products. However, undermining basic principle that buyers should be vigilant about their products is not conducive to efficiency or choice.

Finally, the regulatory framework will have to take into consideration the relevant trade-offs in the context of a particular country. However, to the extent, finance is increasingly globalised, these trade-offs will have to be built into a globally applicable framework for financial sector regulation. The financial sector may be increasingly globalised, but its regulation continues to be national, since the regulatory system of a country should fit into the financial system prevalent in that country and subserve the objectives set for regulations in public policy. At the same time, regulation and supervision of cross border financial institutions and activities are inevitable and hence some arrangements for coordination among the national level regulations would be essential.

COORDINATED APPROACHES TO THE REFORMS

In the light of the crisis, there are attempts to design best practices in financial sector regulation, encourage countries to adopt them and monitor the progress. A reform agenda for the financial sector has been set by the G-20 for the medium-term with a timetable for action. Accordingly, international norms of capital, leverage and liquidity are to be finalised by end 2010 and implemented by 2012. Reforms in OTC derivatives, their exchange trading and clearance through central counter-parties (CCPs), and trade reporting requirements are to be completed by 2012. A single set of high quality accounting standards should be in place by end 2011. The compensation reforms and prudential rules for the systemically important financial institutions and finalisation of the architecture of cross border resolution are expected to be completed by end 2010. In a meeting of the G20 to be held in November 2010, the G20 is expected to review implementation of reforms in the financial sector in member countries and consider 'Basel III' proposals, described later in this chapter. There is however no agreement within the G-20 on levy of taxes on the financial sector—banks to finance public expenditure relating to the crisis or on the regulation of pools of private capital such as hedge funds, though both are under consideration in several countries. The G-20 recognises the need for some emerging economies to develop their financial sector to provide depth and breadth to financial services required to promote high rates of economic growth. Financial inclusion has been identified as a priority item for emerging markets.

It is clear that financial sector reforms will be based at the national level and will take into consideration the circumstances of the country concerned, but broadly the reforms will take shape according to the deliberations in the G-20. The pace of reforms will also depend on the assessment of the current situation in respective countries. A peer review put in place by the G-20 mechanism imposes some pressure on individual countries to honour the agreed global standards.

The Basel Committee on Banking Supervision (BCBS) in close association with the BIS has developed, what may be described as, minimum standards or guidelines on capital of banks. The prevailing standards, described as Basel II, were exposed to several inadequacies in the light of the recent financial crisis. Hence, the BCBS decided to update their guidelines on capital and liquidity reform proposals. Collectively, the revised Basel II capital framework and the new global standards announced in July and September 2010 have come to be commonly referred as 'Basel III'. The Basel III guidelines includes tighter definition of Tier-I and Tier-II capital; minimum norms for common equity component and Tier I, and the introduction of leverage ratio; a capital conservation buffer and a framework for countercyclical capital buffers; enhanced measures of counter-party credit risk; and short-as well as medium-term quantitative liquidity ratios. Some explanation of the improvements suggested, though somewhat technical, may be useful.

Basel III proposals emphasise that the capital base of banks should be characterised by full loss absorption capacity. Base III has, therefore, proposed that common equity will be the predominant form of capital. The minimum common equity ratio (as a percentage of risk weighted assets) would be increased from the current 2.0 per cent to 4.5 per cent. The Tier-I capital ratio would be increased from 4.0 per cent to 6.0 per cent. The total capital adequacy requirement will continue at the existing 8.0 per cent. A new criteria on certain capital elements would be introduced to make them stronger. There will be no sub-categories of Tier-2 capital such as upper Tier-2 and lower Tier-2. There will be only one form of Tier-2 capital with minimum maturity of five years. Basel III has also proposed measures to reckon counterparty credit risk for derivatives repos, and securities financing along with capital. The Systemically Important Banks (SIBs) or Systemically Important Financial Institutions (SIFIs) will be subjected to additional capital and liquidity measures (the exact quantum yet to be decided), in addition to exposure limits and intensive supervision.

The Basel Committee is proposing to test a minimum Tier-1 leverage of 3 per cent during the parallel run period covering January 2013 to January 2017. Specific steps have been proposed to ensure that the banking sector is able to maintain the flow of credit to the real economy during times of stress. A capital conservation buffer i.e. a buffer of 2.5 per cent composed of common equity only and established above the common equity requirement is contemplated along with constraint on distribution of earnings as dividends and bonus payments when capital levels fall below this limit. Introduction of contingent capital in the regulatory capital framework is being explored for SIFIs. Contingent capital would be debt or debt like instruments, which would convert into capital on some pre-specified trigger events such as capital adequacy falling below the specified threshold or on the event of a catastrophe. The use of contingent capital in meeting countercyclical buffer requirements and additional surcharges for SIFIs and introduction of two ratios, namely liquidity coverage ratio and net stable funding ratio have also been proposed.

Impact of Basel III

It is thought that implementation of Basel III proposals may have some macroeconomic impact on growth through the cost of capital channel and impact on lending. If banks have to retain more capital (a more costly source of finance), then that will have impact on the final lending rates which may have its impact on the growth of the economy particularly at a time when slackness in credit growth is a matter of concern. The other channel could be the overall lending. Since the norms are ratios between capital and risk weighted assets, in the absence of raising of capital or inability to raise capital, the ratios can still be met by contracting the assets such as lending. This in turn could have adverse impact on the economy when overall credit supply cannot grow to the requirements of the economy.

There is much agreement on the view that there are clear net long-term economic benefits derived out of the increased safety and soundness of the global system from higher minimum capital and liquidity requirements under Basel III. The benefits of higher capital and liquidity requirements accrue from reduction in the probability of financial crisis and the output losses associated with such crises. The benefits substantially outweigh the potential output costs for a range of higher capital and liquidity requirements. The transition to stronger capital and liquidity standards is likely to have a modest impact on aggregate output as higher requirements are phased in over a medium term time horizon (four years). Further, the burden of mobilising additional capital will be on those who happen to be severely under-capitalised and sooner the de-leveraging is achieved the better it will be to regain trust in the financial sector.

In view of the criticality of the time-frame in implementing the Basel III norms, attempts have been made to compute the possible impact of adoption of Basel III on aggregate output, depending on the pace of implementation of new standards. According to the BIS, if higher requirements are phased within a period of four years, each 1 percentage point increase in banks' actual ratio of tangible common equity to risk-weighted asset may lead to a decline in the level of GDP relative to its baseline path by about 0.20 per cent after implementation is completed. In terms of growth rates, this means that the annual growth rates would be reduced by an average of 0.04 percentage points over a four and a half year period, with a range of results. A 25 per cent increase in liquid asset holdings is found to have an output effect of less than half that associated with a 1 percentage point increase in capital ratios. No doubt, there are differences between the official estimates of BCSB and that of the banking industry lobby (the latter estimates higher costs in terms of loss of output).

There is hope for reducing the risks of instability in the financial sector since there is agreement on major issues such as leverage, liquidity, countercyclicality and attention to systemically important financial institutions. Agreement on parameters of capital adequacy is also welcomed. The fears of possible adverse impact on growth are possibly exaggerated. The real issue is therefore the challenge ahead of some of the advanced economies that have to deleverage and reach the standards prescribed by Basel III. Notably, many emerging markets already meet these norms. There are apprehensions that Basel III in its present form may not meet the concerns of global community in view of the time table that appears stretched till 2017 with the scope for dilution as time passes and the potential for instability in the interim period. It is also feared that the principles set forth appear adequate, but they may be diluted in practice. More importantly, there is a widespread discomfort with the manner in which the 'too big to fail' issue is being addressed by the reform proposals.

Reforms in Select Countries

In the US, a comprehensive legislation was enacted on 21 July 2010. An independent consumer financial protection bureau, with jurisdiction over firms that sell consumer financial services, has been created at the Federal Reserve. The private pools of capital, namely, private equity and fund managers have to register with the Securities and Exchange Commission (SEC) as investment advisors, who may be required to observe disclosures and investor protection. Large hedge funds or private equity funds, which are considered systematically important, are subjected to the jurisdiction of a council of regulators. Large banks are barred from owning significant stakes in leveraged buyout funds or hedge funds. With regard to derivatives, there is a requirement that over the counter derivatives be registered with clearing houses, who may put some safeguards, but there are several exceptions to this stipulation. The pay packages and remuneration for senior executives and directors under certain categories are subjected to regulation. A Systemic Risk Council has been created with broad powers to regulate systemically significant institutions. The Federal Reserve is charged with conducting annual stress tests of systemically significant institutions. The proposed Systemic Risk Council has authority to place bank holding companies and other systemically important institutions into a resolution process—a process whereby equity capital may be eliminated, bondholders may be forced to take cuts and management replaced.

In Europe, a pan-European financial regulatory architecture has been approved to help develop common European rules for national regulators to follow. Three pan-European supervisory authorities have been created for banking, insurance and pensions, and for securities and markets. While the European Systemic Risk Council (ESRC) has been set up for macro-prudential regulation, the European System of Financial Supervisors (ESFS) corresponds to a micro-prudential approach. Extraordinary regulatory processes have been acquired by the European Parliament when emergency is declared for regulatory purposes. In brief, the regulatory coordination in the EU area has been the major focus of reform. However, with regard to several other areas, such as regulation of hedge funds, private equity funds and policy in regard to 'too big to fail' institutins, lack of progress is conspicuous. There are two factors for the reform-process to be different from that of the US, namely, the reluctance of UK in some matters which are critical for the Euro area; and the difficulties of negotiating agreement with member states since they have financial systems with different characteristics.

In the UK, an overhaul of the financial structure has been announced. The FSA, the single regulator and supervisor for all financial services providers in the UK will cease to exist. The tripartite structure consisting of the treasury, the BoE and the FSA gets dismantled. The key role in financial structure is now assigned to the BoE; which becomes the institution in charge of the monetary policy, lender of last resort, special resolution regime, macro-prudential supervision, and oversight of micro-prudential supervision. A new prudential regulatory authority as a subsidiary of the BoE and a financial policy committee within the BoE, have been proposed and both will be chaired by the Governor of BoE. There will also be a new Consumer Protection and Markets Authority and an Economic Crime Agency. An independent commission on competition in banking industry has also been announced. Switzerland, which was also severely affected by the crisis, has a financial system dominated by very few and very large entities. The reforms focused on several relatively stringent regulatory prescriptions to ensure stability. These relate to capital buffers, leverage ratios and safeguards in regard to their systemically important financial institutions.

Some generalisations on reforms in the financial sector in these select countries may be made. First, noticeable reforms have been implemented, in those countries which experienced excesses. That is a matter of comfort. Second, the underlying logic is essentially towards greater weight to stability than before. There is some discomfort about the time path given in some reforms which appears stretched. There could be pressures to dilute the standards over time and in detailing the measures for application. Third, the design, content and pace of reforms are clearly country-specific or Euro area specific. Fourth, major areas of cross border regulation, and sources of contagion have not been addressed adequately, presumably on the assumption that strengthening regulation at the national level would serve the purpose for the present. Fifth, there have been no cognisable reform initiatives in other advanced economies like Australia, Canada and Japan. Almost all EMEs have not considered it appropriate to attempt reforms at this stage. However, many of them are addressing issues relating to volatility in capital flows by using regulation in the financial sector as one of the instruments. Korea provides a good illustration of this approach.

Developing Countries Perspective

In countries that experienced the financial crisis in acute form, some reforms took place, while in others, especially in developing countries where the impact was not as severe, they are still waiting to the overhaul of the international financial regulatory architecture, so they can adapt appropriately their national regulatory framework.

The developing countries may view the reform proposals in Basel III and the G-20 with a mixed feeling. Measures to strengthen the financial system in advanced economies should be welcomed. Since many of the developing countries satisfy most of the stringent criteria on banks, there may not to be an additional regulatory burden on them. They are not over exposed to sophisticated financial products requiring actions stipulated by Basel III in this regard. In fact they may gain by better safeguards in the regulatory framework governing financial innovations. Lesser dependence on credit rating may also be to their advantage. The emphasis on financial inclusion in the G-20 is also appropriate though it is not clear how it is being operationalised in the reform proposals. Further, financial inclusion should not be an excuse for pushing credit or irresponsible lending as it happened in sub-prime lending. It should not be an excuse for circumventing regulatory rigour. There is a recognition that regulatory intervention is desirable for stability, but a similar dispensation to achieve objectives of growth with equity through influencing direction and price of credit is not observed. In particular, issues relating to long-term financing needs of development and significance of small and medium enterprises for employment are not recognised. Adequate weight has not been given to the comfort of relationship lending and collateralised lending prevalent in developing economies.

Impact of Basel III proposals on EMEs may be illustrated with the Indian case. The effect of proposed Basel III is expected to be minimal on the capital requirements of Indian banks. For example Tier-I capital in banks at 9 per cent is above the stipulation of 6 per cent. Deductions in capital proposed are already in force in India. Counter parity credit risk framework may impact a few private sector or foreign banks which have significant exposures to trading book. The banks are not excessively leveraged and hence stipulations on leverage ratios will have little or no impact. On countercyclical policies, India follows a sectoral approach. For a rapidly growing economy, credit to GDP ratio in the short run may be too aggregative to reflect building of systemic risks. Indian banks have not faced the type of stress that advanced financial markets did. Assessment of liquidity stress scenarios is a new task for Indian banks. The banks in India are strong for two important reasons namely dependence on more stable retail business and the regulatory requirements, that banks should hold a significant part of assets in the form of government securities.

SOME SELECT ISSUES

It is necessary to set-out the purpose of developing the financial system in order to assess the appropriateness of the regulatory regimes and design suitable agenda for reforms. The objective is no doubt to maximise output, employment and broader social objectives. Financial sector should facilitate real economic activity, at a minimum cost and on an assured basis. To achieve these objectives, the financial sector has to match savings, investment and liquidity in an optimal manner. Further, in view of the nature of externalities in the financial sector regulation become inevitable. But, there is a need to look at expectations from the common person, particularly in developing countries, in setting out the objectives of the financial system. These are: (i) consumption smoothing, since income stream and expenditure stream may not converge; (ii) payment transfers in an efficient and economical manner; (iii) safe custody of deposits without serious loss of value of their earnings through enabling supply of at least one instrument of safety and (iv) making available a choice of institutions and instruments for savings and investments and not merely enable lending or extending credit. Public policy should, therefore, address two sets of issues, namely,

(i) meeting the needs of the common man, and providing financial services with sensitivity to price and quality and (ii) facilitating growth by enhancing efficiency, imparting stability taking account of externalities that characterise the financial sector.

The financial sector reform debate now is essentially a response to the crisis and the focus is on correcting the excesses of the past; especially excessive deregulation which caused the crisis. Almost all proposals involve tradeoffs, at least in the short run. Tradeoffs are often contextual, to the society, to the economy and to the institutional needs. But minimum and common standards are necessary in view of linkages between the financial sectors of different countries. Currently, there are two sets of reform-ideas under debate, namely, reforms in individual countries especially the US, UK and Europe, and minimum standards as per G-20 reform agenda and Basel III proposals. Some advanced economies have brought about changes in regulatory regimes in the light of their experience and these are of systemic importance to the global economy. Emphasis on stability in their reform agenda is inevitable since the reform is in reaction to the crisis, but a development orientation is equally relevant for the global economy since there is a paradigm shift in the role of regulation of the financial sector. If intervention of the state in markets is necessary for ensuring stability, there is a valid reason for intervention by the state to ensure economic development.

There is a case for the design and policies of regulation of the financial sector, but the sceptics argue that regulation is not the best instrument and in any case it may be difficult to operationalise such a policy. First, the mandate for regulators should include utilising the regulatory tools to achieve objectives of not only stability but also development as allocation of credit to different uses prescribing differential margins. Second, where subsidies from government are warranted, as in the case of development financial institutions, the regulations should also be aligned to achieve objectives of development. Similarly, a longer term view may be taken in regard to risks assigned to longer term direct finance of infrastructure. Third, the budget of regulators should be used for promoting use of technology or extending financial services to backward areas or remote areas or poorer sections which may not be profitable in the short to medium term. Fourth, with regard to policies such as licensing of branches of banks, incentives and disincentives could be considered in favour of under-served areas. Fifth, access to payment and settlement facilities should be ensured at an affordable price and acceptable quality in favour of the poor. Exploitative practices in certain activities such as credit cards should be curbed. Sixth, financial and technological innovations that are likely to favour the poor should be encouraged and, if need be, subsidised by the regulators. Financial institutions devoted to retail operations and without serious systemic implications should be nurtured. Finally, the weight for financial stability should be higher in developing economies where social safety nets do not exist. For example, the practices and products that are innovative, whose risks are indeterminate, should ideally be tested in advanced economies before the regulators allow them to be used in developing economies unless the regulators are aware of and comfortable with implications of innovations.

The experience of China and India with public sector banks and financial institutions in successfully using them as instruments of public policy is relevant in this regard. The trust that people have placed in public ownership under stressful conditions in advanced economies is also relevant. In fact, the presence of some public sector units in the financial sector along with the private sector helps reduce information asymmetry between the regulator and the regulated, since incentives in the public sector are conducive to transparency. Further, as experience with the crisis has shown, in times of stress on public policy, existence of some public sector enterprises improves effectiveness of public policy.

In the agenda for reform of the financial sector consequent upon the crisis, taxation of the financial sector has been prominent, although no agreement could be reached. As a broad generalisation taxation of the financial sector should be consistent with the regulatory objectives, and burdens or benefits of both should be assessed in a comprehensive manner. Differences in tax burdens and regulatory burdens across countries may not be viewed in isolation. Financial sector taxation as debated in the context of the crisis, may have several objectives, namely, to share the burden of bailout expense (which is indeterminate so far); to build a buffer for the future crisis (which should ideally be designed as an insurance fund); to raise resources for budget (similar to any other tax); to discourage excessive speculation or unnecessary multiplication of financial transactions (which exist in some advanced economies also, like stamp duty or securities transaction); and to raise resources for global public goods. In the current context, the use of financial sector taxation has been advocated mainly by advanced economies to pay the bailout costs and to build a buffer for any future crisis.

In respect of developing economies, the bailout is not relevant and cost of funding of future crisis is not a priority. However, taxation of financial sector for resource-raising, discouraging excessive financialisation and possible funding of global public goods are relevant objectives. The taxation of the financial sector as compared to the non-financial sector, and different institutions or different instruments in the financial sector would have consequences for both development and regulation. The financial sector could potentially be an instrument of development policies and these may impose regulatory burdens, say on banks in the short run. Any discussion on financial sector taxation should therefore include an assessment of regulatory burden due to development objectives. Hence, taxation of the financial sector should remain as a national imperative. However, international agreement on levy of Tobin Tax would be in the interest of developing countries since it would moderate excess volatility in currency markets.

On the basis of the Indian experience it can be argued that regulation of the financial sector could be used as a tool for macroeconomic management. For example, in India the cost of sterilised intervention in forex markets is shared by the banking sector through the imposition of unremunerated CRR, as needed. More important, the large borrowing programme of the Indian government is facilitated by a stipulation that deposit taking institutions in the financial sector are required to invest stipulated amounts as a proportion of balance sheets in government securities. These stipulations provide reasonable stability to banks and assured support for the borrowing program of the government, as these securities are relatively less risky. The effect of such mechanisms is similar to domestic financial sector taxation.

Prudential regulation may also be used as an instrument of capital account management. For example, limits are set on foreign currency exposures of financial intermediaries, including a limit on their external debt. These stipulations have the effect of tax, but serve the purpose of moderating volatility in capital flows. The use of financial sector for macro-management has elements of tax burden.

An Outlook for the Reforms

The outlook for a globally coordinated and sustained regulatory reform appears to be uncertain. First, there is no clarity on what is a right model for regulation of the financial sector, though there is a recognition of some general principles. Second, there are several tradeoffs involved that are more often than not country specific. Third, the immediate compulsions for urgent reforms appear to be for a few countries which were significantly affected by the crisis as a result of excessive deregulation. Fourth, regulation of the financial sector cannot be divorced from other aspects of macroeconomic policy, such as monetary and fiscal policies, especially with regard to countercyclical approaches. Fourth, the capacity of countries and societies to bear risks varies, with developing countries being at a disadvantage. Hence, several policies in the nature of self-insurance are inevitable, and such policies may include financial regulation. For example, prudential measures may be used for capital account management in developing countries. Fifth, experience has shown that regulatory capture in a comprehensive manner, and inadequate or ineffective supervision were often sources of fragility, and not necessarily the regulatory framework. Sixth, there may be merit in recognising that financial sector regulation would be essentially at the national level. Search should therefore, be to identify regulatory standards and practices in each country that are likely to have negative externalities to the global economy.

A possible approach to reconcile the need for policy space for national authorities and the need for global coordination may consist of three sets of actions. They may consist of reaching agreement on (i) basic principles of national regulations that could address national level activities of the financial sector (ii) standards of regulation for systemically important financial intermediaries at the global level and (iii) minimum standards for systemically important financial centres in the global economy. The basic principles of national regulation may have to identify the 'bad' practices and create mechanisms to persuade countries not to adopt them while continuing a search for the 'good' that is equally good for all countries in a global economy where only nation states are accountable to their people. The regulations at the national level are most appropriate for institutions and markets that are predominantly national. To supplement these minimal national standards, focused globalised regulation should be evolved in respect of large financial intermediaries whose activities are predominantly cross-border. A distinction could be made between national and multi-national banks whose main activities are within a country's jurisdiction and international banks that are large institutions and operate across financial markets, regulatory jurisdictions and tax regimes. International banks are the main sources of diluting policy autonomy including regulation at the national level. They should be subjected to global stringent regulations.

These centres which have the privilege of being international financial centres have a responsibility to subject themselves to globalised regulation. Such a focused approach to regulation of the financial sector in financial centres and banks of international significance will be consistent with differentiated regulatory regimes that have been accepted now for systemically important financial institutions.

There are two views on the way forward with regard to sustained regulatory reforms in the financial sector. One view is that regulators have been excessively defensive in view of the crisis and political pressure has been brought on the proposed framework due to public outcry. This view questions the wisdom of many initiatives for enhanced role for external regulations. The alternate view is that the financial sector lobby continues to exercise influence over decision making processes and hence the framework is possibly weak and in any case will be diluted in practice. The developing economies have been innocent victims of the global financial crisis and they have every reason to guard against facing adversities in the post-crisis management of the financial sector in the global economy. Much of the debate and action so far has bypassed concerns of developing economies despite their recently acquired importance in the G-20, FSB and BSCB. This is evident from the reforms that are missing in the agenda, namely, the basic purposes of the financial system, the legitimate expectations of the common people, development orientation and finance as a possible supplement to macroeconomic management including capital account management, and possibly in supporting the very large borrowing programmes of some governments.

NOTE

1. Bank for International Settlements, *79th Annual Report, 1 April 2008–31 March 2009*, Switzerland: Bank for International Settlements, 2009.

SECTION III

Public Policy:
Challenges and Responses

Thirteen

Desirability and Feasibility
of Tobin Tax*

$\mathcal{T}$he first section of the chapter briefly mentions a revival of interest in a tax popularly known as the Tobin Tax. The objectives of the Tobin Tax, the case for such a tax and the case against such a tax are then listed. Since one of the main arguments against such a levy is feasibility, the next section explains how such a tax is feasible. This is followed by a brief review of the experience with such taxes in financial-sector transactions. The concluding section commends such a tax at the national level and encourages the consideration of globally coordinated action.

BACKGROUND

The Financial Transaction Tax or the Tobin Tax deserves more attention than it has received so far, and is likely to gain greater support as the underlying causes of the global financial crisis are fully appreciated. When, five years ago, the author as the Governor

---

* This chapter is an edited version of a lecture delivered at the seminar on Europeans for Financial Reform, organised by the Global Progressive Forum, Brussels, 15 March 2010.

of the RBI had in the course of a speech mentioned that 'price-based measures such as taxes could be examined, though their effectiveness is arguable' in the context of the management of capital accounts, there was a strong and adverse reaction from participants in financial markets in India. The Finance Minister had to soothe the markets with an assurance that no such proposal for taxes was under consideration in the government. This had to be supplemented by a clarification by the RBI on the undesirability of the Tobin Tax. The atmosphere governing the thinking on Tobin Tax seems to have changed since then, although there is no evidence that the sentiments of financial markets on the subject have altered.

THE OBJECTIVES OF THE TOBIN TAX

An American economist, James Tobin, first made the suggestion for a tax on currency transactions to dissuade shorter currency speculation in the 1970s. He made the suggestion with two main objectives, namely, to make exchange rates reflect to a larger degree the long-run fundamentals relative to short-run expectations and risks; and to preserve and promote the autonomy of national macro-economic and monetary policies. It is essential to constantly revisit the relevance of the objectives in considering both the desirability and the feasibility of the Tobin Tax. In fact, the underlying approach of taxing transactions has the potential to be applicable to not only currency markets, but also other markets, particularly after the experience with regard to the global financial crisis.

THE CASE FOR TOBIN TAX

The levy of the Tobin Tax has been the subject of policy debates amongst politicians, economists and participants in financial markets since it was mooted. During the debate, Professor Tobin seems to have agreed with some of the arguments relating to the difficulties of implementing such a tax. At the international level, however, Tobin Tax had gained some popularity prior to the current global crisis in view of its potential for funding global public goods. There has been notable support, particularly in the UK and Euro area and also among civil society organisations, for such a levy to fund global public goods addressing climate change and poverty issues.

After the global financial crisis, the approach to the Tobin Tax has acquired a different focus, greater urgency and some policy relevance. First, such a tax is considered necessary to recover the bailout cost incurred by the governments to avoid collapse in the financial sector. Second, the ill-effects of excessive financialisation have been realised now. The volume of Foreign Exchange transactions is $2,000,000,000 ($2 trillion) a day, while only 5 per cent of this is necessary for financing trade in goods and services. Third, the impact of excess volatility in financial markets on the rest of the economy is better appreciated now. It is also realised that the ill-effects and risks of volatility are inherent in all financial markets and are not confined to currency markets. There is apprehension that several elements of financial-sector growth are in excess of socially desirable levels. Fourth, some developing countries have found it necessary to moderate capital flows through the use of several instruments, of which the Tobin Tax is just one. In view of the emerging uncertainties, developing economies find greater appeal in such options.

Finally, this issue was formally placed on the table of the global agenda in a meeting of the G-20 in November 2009. It was mooted as part of 'a better economic and social contract between financial institutions and public'. Four possible reforms were proposed as part of such a contract, one of them being the financial transactions tax. Several economists, including some Nobel Prize winners, have become active proponents of a tax on financial transactions, including the tax on currency transactions.

The Case Against Tobin Tax

The desirability of the Tobin Tax has, however, been questioned on several grounds:

(i)   it is not possible to differentiate between the 'real variables' driving exchange rates, such as the GDP, employment and output, and 'unreal ones' that create speculative bubbles;

(ii) the Tobin Tax distorts market mechanisms;

(iii) it is better to improve the underlying policies and environment that generate volatility in financial markets instead of imposing a tax;

(iv) the Tobin tax increases transaction costs, but the increase may be small relative to the expected profits from market activity. Hence, volatility may not be curtailed by such a tax, and it is possible that volatility may even be enhanced.

(v)   All short-term capital movements may not be bad, and some of them may be good for efficiency in markets;

(vi) The revenue yield from such a tax is highly uncertain.

It is important to look at the assumptions underlying some of the arguments against the desirability of the Tobin Tax. Their implicit assumption is that financial markets always play a useful role in reflecting the fundamentals and should always be left to do it with minimum friction. Hence, any attempt to interfere with market mechanisms is likely to be inefficient and ineffective. Moreover, there is the belief that in any case, it is difficult for non-market authorities, including public policies, to make a judgement on speculative and non-speculative factors, as also on the existence of excess volatility.

Clearly, the experience of the global financial crisis makes it difficult to continue with such strong beliefs in the efficiency of financial markets, especially after the massive intervention of public policy to save them. Under these circumstances, the most credible arguments of those who oppose the Tobin Tax are that it is non-feasible, or that it could serve purely as a temporary measure to get over the crisis.

The argument of non-feasibility rests on the following propositions:

(i) It is difficult to get international consensus on such a tax;
(ii) It is difficult to estimate the revenue from such a tax and to agree on the distribution of the proceeds between sectors and countries;
(iii) Enforcement of such a tax is difficult;
(iv) There may be an incentive for some countries to opt out of the regime and attract financial-sector activities to its territory;
(v) Financial markets are fully integrated, and hence it is possible for them to avoid the burden of tax through financial innovation.

FEASIBILITY OF THE TOBIN TAX

On the other hand, those who argue that such a tax is feasible advance several reasons.

(i) The statement that the underlying policies that generate volatility should be addressed assumes that there are other instruments which can by themselves moderate excess volatility. No convincing set of such measures have been identified.
(ii) Eighty-four per cent of gross currency transactions take place in only nine countries, and hence agreement is not too complex.
(iii) Settlement in currency markets is centralised or centrally overseen. Hence, tracking of the trades is feasible.
(iv) The information technology (IT) infrastructure enables an effective imposition as well as monitoring of such transactions.
(v) There are international agreements on very complex matters relating to finance. For example money laundering, which is also a cross-country phenomenon, is extremely difficult to implement or monitor, but there is a determination and effort to deal with money-laundering issues on a global basis.
(vi) The G-20 has already initiated concerted action over the last year on tax havens and non-compliant jurisdictions. Hence

it should be possible to work on a Tobin Tax through an international agreement backed by national legislation. The agreement could cover transactions where the deal is made and where transactions occur.

A close examination of the arguments about the feasibility of the Tobin tax would indicate that they reflect difficulties of cross-border cooperation in matters of currency markets. However, it is interesting that cross-country coordination of public policy was achieved at short notice to avoid a collapse in financial markets. These included broad monetary measures, market intervention and the bailout of institutions. If cross-country cooperation in public policy is feasible when it suits the financial markets, it should be possible, if there is political will, to continue with such cooperation in the larger public interest.

If desirability is established, then feasibility has to be explored with a view to implementing it. It may be recalled that when the imposition of tax on income was being considered initially, the main argument against it related to difficulties in implementation. In fact, it may be argued that some countries might consider the imposition of taxes similar to the Tobin Tax unilaterally. It is difficult to deny that the incentive to multiply short-term financial transactions is reduced by such a tax. The profitability for those engaged in such transactions is also reduced by the imposition of such taxes.

It is sometimes argued that measures such as the Tobin Tax are not effective over the long run, but may be useful in the context of a crisis. The objective of the Tobin Tax is clearly to prevent the eruption of volatility, and therefore to argue that it should not be taken up before the occurrence of a crisis is somewhat surprising.

REVIEW OF EXPERIENCE

It will be useful to briefly review the experience with regard to such taxes or measures that have the effect of such a tax. A quick review of the literature available on the subject leads to some very general observations.

(i) The experience of Thailand has not been very positive in terms of realising the objectives. However, it may be argued that adequate determination of public policy to implement measures to curtail inflows, including tax, was not evident. In any case, the possible volatility in the absence of such measures is difficult to assess.

(ii) In Columbia, the capital controls reduced external borrowings, but the overall impact is not clear.

(iii) In Chile, there was a reduction in short-term flows and some injection of stability, and to that extent the taxes may be considered to have been partially effective. However, quasi-fiscal losses, lower investment and growth cannot be ruled out.

(iv) In Malaysia, the intended results were obtained on all fronts. It is noteworthy that there was a display of the determination of public policy in the intervention and coordination of several policies.

(v) In Brazil, it is still early to draw conclusions, but the tax appears to have achieved some of its intended results according to the Institute of International Finance.

(vi) Both China and India have taken recourse to several measures that have had the effect of Tobin Tax in some ways. The empirical evidence in terms of stability and longer-term growth is noteworthy.

While it is difficult to generalise, the cross-country analysis made so far seems to indicate that capital account management, in particular measures like the Tobin Tax, has the effect of dampening short-term flows. There is some change in the composition of flows towards the longer term. Non-financial direct investment is relatively unaffected. The longer-term implications for growth are not easy to assess. Often, these measures had been undertaken in the context of a crisis, and it is difficult to judge what the position would have been had these actions had not been taken. At any rate, there is no evidence of serious downside risks of capital account management and recourse to the Tobin Tax.

In this context, it will be useful to review the variety of existing taxes on transactions in the financial sector. These taxes vary between different countries. An examination of these taxes would show that serious distortions or adverse effects of such taxes on the efficiency or profitability of the financial sector should not be assumed. Stamp duties are out-dated, but not inconceivable. In many countries, there are financial transaction taxes (including on repos, swaps, etc.), and there are also turnover taxes on financial institutions. There are value-added taxes on the financial sector. Taxes on bank debits and credits are not uncommon. In brief, such taxes, similar to the Tobin Tax, are in vogue in a wide variety of national jurisdictions, including China, Philippines, Argentina and Israel. There are also proposals for 'withholding' taxes of all private capital inflows.

CONCLUSION

To conclude, it is essential to address the issue of excessive reliance on market mechanisms, in particular the excessive growth of the financial sector. Hence, there is considerable merit in countries insisting on keeping open the option of levying taxes on all financial transactions as a matter of public policy. Such a tax may ideally cover several financial markets, in particular currency markets. Keeping a tax regime in position, even at nominal rates, would be advisable so that financial markets remain aware of the instrument at the command of public policy and its willingness to use it. The experience with regard to the benign neglect of asset bubbles in the recent crisis and preference for countercyclical policies provides the logic for putting mechanisms similar to the Tobin Tax in place on a continuous basis.

The measurable downside of such taxes appears to be negligible. While it is held that the Tobin Tax may be ineffective, it has never been the case that it has toxic potential, like some financial innovations. It is true that revenue is uncertain, and it is also true that international agreement on such taxes and distribution of such revenues are difficult; however, difficulties have not deterred cooperation in many initiatives.

The case for the Tobin Tax to meet the objectives set by Professor Tobin is now well-established and revenue is only an additional attraction. It cannot be the case that the Tobin Tax would be effective by itself, but it has immense potential when used along with complementary policies, in particular countercyclical and macro-prudential measures, which are being currently recommended for adoption. A review of the existing taxes at the national level in some jurisdictions would point to the feasibility of such taxes at the national level. International coordination for the levy of such taxes must be pursued vigorously, but national-level initiatives for the Tobin Tax, as part of measures to achieve financial stability by individual countries, also have much to commend for themselves. It is undeniable that globally coordinated action will enhance the effectiveness of policies at the national level.

Fourteen

Developmental Dimension to the Financial Sector*

$\mathscr{T}$he global financial crisis has resulted in a dramatic review of the role of the financial sector in economic management. One of the most significant developments in this regard has been a review of the policy of deregulation of the past, with emphasis on maintaining financial stability. This chapter argues that a rebalanced regulatory regime for the financial sector, which is currently under consideration globally, should address issues of both stability and development.

The chapter initially explains the benefits that might have accrued due to deregulation of the financial sector in the past. This is followed in the second section by a narration of excessive deregulation and its possible adverse consequences. The third section explains the measures under consideration for a rebalanced regulation while making out a case for development finance in such an approach to rebalanced regulation. The concluding section emphasizes the need to avoid extremes in the new balance being contemplated. With regard to India, a case is made out for domestic orientation in the search for new balance in the regulation of the financial sector.

---

* This chapter is an edited version of the lecture delivered at The Sixth M. R. Pai Memorial Award Function, Mumbai, 6 May 2010.

FINANCIAL REPRESSION AND BENEFITS OF DEREGULATION

In the post-colonial era, developing countries used the financial sector as an instrument of public policy, in particular for development. In some countries, banks were nationalised. The policy framework governing the financial sector was oriented towards promoting economic development. Even in advanced economies, the use of the financial sector for reconstruction was not uncommon. In India, banks were nationalised in 1969 in order to ensure that they achieved development and welfare objectives.

However, there was a convincing body of literature which argued that these measures amounted to financial repression, and that such repression of market mechanisms resulted in serious inefficiency in the allocation of resources, thereby retarding growth in the real economy. In brief, it was felt that financial repression, which includes the policy framework within which the financial sector operates and the excessive regulation of the financial sector, does not aid development, but often undermines it. Hence, it was argued that the thrust of the financial-sector reforms should be to remove such financial repression and allow market forces to determine the allocation of financial resources through deregulated financial markets. The movement against financial repression coincided with a growing popularity of theories decrying the inefficiencies of the state or governmental intervention, and emphasising the benefits of allowing market forces to allocate resources. This philosophy, as applied to the financial sector, held that the development finance as it was being practised was tantamount to financial repression. This approach was also popularised in the developing world, and became a staple element of financial-sector reforms. In this approach, deregulation of the financial sector was itself an instrument of development.

The process of deregulation of the financial sector was initiated in many countries, and had several dimensions. First, the overall policy constraints on banks' ability to perform their core functions were removed. Second, 'universal' banking was encouraged, in the sense that banks were increasingly permitted to undertake activities other than the core banking functions of accepting deposits and extending loans to households and enterprises. Third, entities other than banks were also encouraged to undertake financial intermediation so that the different risk appetites of savers and investors were matched. Such diversified financial intermediaries were expected to lend stability to the financial system, in addition to adding to the overall efficiency. Fourth, the role of financial markets in allocating resources was emphasised, and these included equity, debt and forex markets. Fifth, it was considered necessary and useful to integrate the different financial markets within the country into what is sometimes described as the bond-currency-derivatives nexus. Finally, there was increasing globalisation of finance, which reinforced the integration of different financial markets within the countries.

It is essential to note that the process of deregulation unfolded over three decades after 1980, commencing at different points of time in different countries. It was rapid in some cases, while it was gradual in others. Deregulation did not mean an absence of regulation, but a marked preference for minimising regulation. Market efficiency was assumed and the case for regulation had to be proven; thus putting the onus of the proof of market failures on the regulator. The twin objectives of financial regulation in this policy framework of trust in market efficiency were protection of consumers and depositors, and solvency of individual financial institutions.

Perceptible benefits in terms of accelerated development did accrue as a result of deregulation, although there were banking and currency crises after the process was initiated in many developing countries, and in some advanced economies as well. The overall impact of the persistent and continuing deregulation was assessed as undeniably positive until the global financial crisis erupted in 2008. The process of deregulation did eliminate or reduce costly distortions or tardiness, and enhanced efficiency in several dimensions.

EXCESSIVE DEREGULATION AND ITS CONSEQUENCES

The extent of deregulation varied significantly between different countries. This gives some leeway in suspecting a broad pattern in the softness of regulation and its consequences. It was particularly countries with a desire to develop into international financial centres—the US and UK, for instance—that adopted relatively soft regulation. Larger economies in Latin America and other economies of Eastern Europe and the CIS countries, like Russia, also considerably deregulated their financial sectors. Most of these economies were severely affected during the financial crisis. On the other hand, there were other countries, particularly in Asia, where deregulation was slower and lower, and most of these were less affected by the financial crisis. It is also interesting to note that in those economies that were less affected, traditional banking was dominant, and there was less extensive use of financial innovations such as credit derivatives. Among the large economies whose real economy performed relatively well in the global crisis but in which the degree of deregulation in the financial sector was modest are China and India. However, this broad pattern is not universal, as evident from instances of countries such as Canada and Australia where, in spite of considerable deregulation, the financial sector was not severely affected.

As a preliminary generalisation of the global experience with deregulation, it may be offered that deregulation was desirable and added to efficiency in those economies that were suffering from financial repression, but that if deregulation crossed a limit, it became excessive and imbued with a potential for causing more harm than good.

In assessing the benefits of deregulation, it is necessary to distinguish between the benefits that accrued from (i) a widespread use of technology, especially the spread of computerisation, at about the same time as the process of deregulation was underway; and (ii) the enhanced competition that was made possible due to deregulation. The interaction of these developments is two-sided and causality is ambiguous. In this context, it may be useful to make a distinction between deregulation of the domestic financial sector and liberalisation in terms of the cross-border exposures of the financial sector. It is possible to generalise that an excessive liberalisation of the financial sector thus constituted a conduit for the contagion of stress and crisis from economies with soft regulation to others during the recent crisis, although it could have contributed to good contagion of efficiency and good practices during the pre-crisis period.

The crisis unveiled several unintended consequences of excessive deregulation. It is widely thought that it enabled the development of large institutions that were 'too big to fail'. This perception provided such institutions with the incentive to take excessive risks. Being large, these institutions were also capable of influencing the political economy of the regulators. This may have stimulated irresponsible behaviour on the part of many such institutions.

Another unintended consequence of excessive deregulation was irresponsible lending, particularly exemplified by housing finance in the US. In some other countries, where banking shifted focus to activities in financial markets from the credit needs of large sections of the population, micro-finance emerged. In many cases, micro-finance institutions also tended to indulge in predatory lending. In many developing economies, foreign banks tended to concentrate on participation in equity, debt and forex markets, rather than on traditional deposit-taking and lending. On the whole, a highly deregulated atmosphere led to excessive leverage, recourse to high risk activities, concentration on a fee-based income and experimentation with innovations, while their social or economic benefits were suspect. All these consequences cumulated into the crisis. As a result of the crisis and a broad appreciation of the consequences of deregulation, there is now a general global consensus towards revisiting the totality of the regulatory framework.

It is possible to locate some illustrations of the consequences of a highly deregulated atmosphere in India as well. For several years, Urban Cooperative Banks were subjected to softer regulation relative to commercial banks. Many of them deteriorated rapidly. Some private-sector banks that were recently licensed took undue advantage of the deregulated atmosphere, resulting in the mergers and acquisitions of a substantial number of newly licensed private-sector banks. There were several scams, some of which could be attributable to inadequate regulation. There is considerable evidence of the hollowing of traditional bank lending, particularly to agriculture and SMEs. The deregulated atmosphere also seems to have encouraged a large expansion of consumer and real estate credit, although some timely correctives were taken by the regulators. Finally, the use of banks' resources in risky activities such as private equity funds and venture capital funds also expanded. Fortunately, none of these problems led to serious systemic instability in India. However, they do provide some pointers to the possible negative fallouts of excessive deregulation.

Towards a Rebalanced Regulation and Un-level Playing Field

Globally, there is recognition that the excessive deregulation that had taken place needs some undoing and that financial regulation requires rebalancing. The measures of rebalancing being considered fall within two sets: (i) those measures that relate to the regulatory structures, boundaries and jurisdictions in the financial sector, which are mostly determined by legal frameworks; and (ii) those measures that relate to the regulatory philosophy, standards and measures to be adopted by the regulators.

In this context, the balance in the emphasis on principle-based vs. rule-based regulation is also being reviewed. Traditional regulation prescribes how firms should operate their business and resorts to supervisory actions. In contrast, principle-based regulation specifies the desirable regulatory outcomes and rules which serve as 'principles' for firms' behaviour. Thus, principle-based regulation tries to leave the responsibility of deciding how best to align their business objectives and processes with the regulatory outcomes specified by the regulator to the firms themselves. Given the complexities of economic life and behaviour, regulators should use both methods and choose an appropriate balance between the two, instead of relying excessively on principle-based regulation.

The rebalancing of regulation simultaneously addresses several constituencies, namely regulatory institutions, regulatory entities, functioning of markets, financial instruments, and infrastructure such as clearing and settlement mechanisms, in addition to credit-rating agencies.

While a rebalancing of regulation is being attempted in several areas in different countries, there has been a simultaneous effort to bring about globally acceptable standards of regulation. For this purpose, a FSB has been constituted, in which both developed and developing countries are represented. Almost all the deliberations (in the FSB) so far have been focused on achieving financial stability in the functioning of the financial sector without sacrificing the benefits of market mechanisms, including financial innovations, to serve the goal of efficiency in the allocation of resources. The most important of the measures suggested include the adoption of countercyclical regulation, emphasis on macro-prudential regulation, treating banks or banking activities as special, ensuring the safety of financial products, expanding the scope of regulation to the shadow banking system, modifying incentives to excessive risk-taking, and intensifying the regulation of infrastructure agencies, such as credit-rating and clearing systems.

It is necessary to recognise that there has been a fundamental change in the philosophy underlying regulation. The assumption that the financial sector will have self-correcting mechanisms to bring about stability has been questioned and diluted. It is recognised that public policy has to go beyond consumer protection and solvency of individual institutions and intervene in the market in order to avert financial instability. The regulator too has to take a view on the price of assets in order to adopt countercyclical policies. A distinction between highly risky and less risky activities has to be drawn by the regulator. This would include both the nature of the sector and the appropriate financial activity. The extent and pattern of regulation has to be based on the size of a financial institution. Those that are considered large or systemically important may be subjected to a different regulatory regime through measures such as higher capital prescriptions. In other words, the rebalanced regulation increases the overall magnitude of regulation and introduces or creates an 'un-level' playing field between financial institutions, the nature of financial products, the end use of funds, etc. Since the main instrument of the rebalanced regulation under consideration is the creation of an 'un-level' playing field, this raises another fundamental issue: should such an un-level playing field be entirely rule-based or predominantly discretionary? The current consensus is in favour of a rule-based approach, although the details remain unresolved.

REBALANCED REGULATION AND THE CASE FOR DEVELOPMENT FINANCE

While the measures currently under consideration for a rebalanced regulation address only stability issues, the basic implication of the suggested approach to inject an un-level playing field is significant. The un-level playing field can become the basis for introducing developmental objectives in regulation, as argued below.

First, it is generally agreed now that the proposed rebalanced regulatory regime should avoid pro-cyclical tendencies and prefer countercyclical measures. However, it is very difficult to distinguish *ex-ante* between the cyclical and structural elements in the economy. This is particularly true in developing economies, where significant and rapid structural transformations are taking place. Further, if the financial system requires to be regulated in order to avoid cyclical fluctuations, there is no particular reason to oppose the use of public policy to strengthen the financing of structural changes in the economy.

Second, the proposed regulatory framework is expected to moderate the generation of large asset bubbles. If regulation is expected to moderate asset bubbles, then it is possible to argue that regulation should legitimately promote the financing of productive assets.

Third, if sector-specific capital provision or the prescription of an appropriate ratio of loan to value is considered a legitimate instrument for directing credit to avoid instability, the use of similar instruments in favour of productive investments or longer-term goals such as financial inclusion cannot be ruled out.

Fourth, presuming that systemically important institutions could be subjected to high capital requirements, there is no reason why systemically less important institutions that operate primarily within the country or within smaller jurisdictions should not be subjected to a softer type of regulatory framework.

Finally, if intervention by public policy is required in the normal functioning of the financial sector in order to achieve stability, it will be very difficult to insist that the achievement of developmental objectives be left only to the market forces, with a minimal or no role given to public policy.

REBALANCING: NEED TO AVOID EXTREMES IN THE NEW BALANCE

The current debates and proposals with regard to rebalancing the financial sector are focused essentially on correcting the risks that arise due to excessive deregulation. However, it may be simplistic to assume that the correction of excessive deregulation will be a simple re-regulation, or a simple reverting to an era where there was significant regulation. In other words, rebalanced regulation will have to focus on the effectiveness of regulation, and hence will have to be different from excessive deregulation as well as from the excessive regulation of the past. The rebalancing should therefore strive for what may be described as a new balance. This new balance should be able to moderate excessive deregulation, and in the process should not be dogmatic but pragmatic. A new balance will have to take into account first, the technological developments that have already taken place, and second, the growing globalisation of trade, which requires funding and consequently a noticeable element of the globalisation of finance.

The current discussions on the regulatory reforms warranted by the experience of the crisis unveil the danger of extremes, namely, of over-regulation and under-regulation. The danger of over-regulation arises from several sources. First, there is a huge reaction in intellectual debates to the costs of market failures in the financial sector, which seeks a significantly larger role for public policy. Second, there is strong political pressure from citizens in seriously affected countries due to the economic distress, and particularly due to high unemployment. Increase in public debt, particularly to bailout the financial sector, is indicative of the burden tax payers would face in the future, and this fear is causing resentment. The insistence on huge bonuses by the financial sector during this critical period has invited the fury of large sections of the population. In some countries where IMF programmes had to be put in place, the austerity required is generating social tensions. Hence, the legislative framework for rebalancing regulation may yield to popular pressure. Third, the governments could be tempted to use the crisis as an excuse to extend their reach and control over the financial sector.

There are several countervailing forces operating against large-scale changes in the current deregulated financial sector, and if they prevail, there is a danger of under-regulation rather than over-regulation. First, it is evident that the financial sector enjoys enormous influence over the decision-making processes in many countries. Many parts of financial markets and institutions are resentful of significant changes. They advocate that it would suffice if regulators improved their operational skills, and argue against significant change in the overall regulatory framework. Second, tightening of the regulatory framework may expose several existing weaknesses of both governments and regulators and may add to the loss of confidence in the entire financial system. Therefore, both the government and the financial sector may consider not disturbing the status quo beyond a point to be in the larger public interest. Third, free market ideology still dominates several economic policies, and the financial crisis is considered only an aberration or a part of the cycle. In this view, public policy is only needed to smooth over the sharp edges of the crisis, but the system does not warrant any expanded role for public institutions. Fourth, the financial sector is dominated by the international financial centres of New York and London, both of which have believed in soft regulation. There is a strong incentive for them to retain this advantage of soft regulation so that economic and financial activity continues to be dominated by these centres. Finally, developing countries may find it difficult not to follow the globally coordinated views on these issues.

In brief, it is very difficult to state at this stage how these opposing forces in favour of and against significant changes will operate, and where exactly the rebalanced regulation would ultimately settle. This has important policy implications for developing economies. In view of the huge uncertainties, it is better for developing countries to avoid extreme solutions. It is also necessary to wait and see the global developments before undertaking any radical reform based on the unsustainable models of regulatory framework advocated in the past, or the as yet unclear regulatory framework for the future.

INDIA: NEED FOR DOMESTIC ORIENTATION

In the 1970s and 1980s, India experienced the adverse consequences of financial repression. Considerable progress has since been made in terms of dismantling financial repression.

Since the reforms of the early 1990s, deregulation has imparted significant benefits to the Indian economy. Increases in efficiency, quality, resilience and diversity of financial intermediation have been evident in India after the commencement of the gradual and calibrated deregulation of the financial sector. The savings rate, as a percentage of GDP, has increased substantially.

At the same time, there have been instances where the economic system had to pay a price for premature or excessive deregulation. Thus, the Urban Cooperative Banks that had spread under a softer regulatory regime had developed weaknesses, and a number of banks went into bankruptcy. More than half of the new private-sector banks disappeared due to mergers and acquisitions. Some banks have also paid a price for their excessive participation in equity. Some financial scams also accrued during the period of reform. In brief, therefore, while there was no systemic instability, the adverse consequences of premature or excessive deregulation—where they existed—have been witnessed in India.

With regard to the liberalisation and opening up of India's financial sector, the benefits of a gradual liberalisation of the capital account have been recognised globally. In brief, India has experienced both successful deregulation and cautious liberalisation with some lessons that are particularly relevant in the context of the global financial crisis.

Unfortunately, in this period of deregulation in India, which was by and large beneficial, the role of public policy in utilising the financial system for reaching out to large sections of people as also serving agricultural and small industry has not been up to expectations. Hence, the lesson for India is clear, namely, that it will not be appropriate to increase or expand the regulatory regime, although there can be considerable scope for enhancing the effectiveness of regulation with a developmental orientation.

India must therefore concentrate on rebalancing the regulatory framework, drawing lessons from its own experience with the regulatory framework and with liberalisation. While domestic factors will have to dominate the reform of regulatory regimes, India will have to keep careful watch on developments in global bodies and other countries, so that lessons from the global experience can also be taken into account as some clarity emerges on a new balance in global regulatory standards. It is important for India to recognise that some assertions associated with the benefits of a deregulated financial sector are no longer valid, and there is as yet no clear emergence of a new balanced regulation or a new balanced deregulation.

REBALANCING AND DEPOSITORS' INTEREST

In the days of financial repression, depositors had the comfort of safety, but service was poor and the options available to depositors were limited. Deregulation has helped to promote genuine competition. Several new financial products were developed. However, the benefits that accrued to retail depositors were far less than those that accrued to others, such as the large, institutional, wholesale players in the financial markets.

Excessive deregulation resulted in a situation where the focus of all institutions, including banks, was on financial markets. Banks themselves were emphasising income from fees, thereby undermining traditional banking activities. Banks also started taking recourse to non-transparent practices. Traditional banking was almost neglected. While credit cards became a large source of income for financial intermediaries, a number of institutions took recourse to the injection of complexity in financial products to confuse the depositors. Finally, efficiency gains due to technology, innovation and competition in the financial sector were appropriated almost wholly by the management, and to some extent by equity holders, thereby ensuring that there was little or no percolation of gains to the depositors.

During the crisis, the importance of depositors became evident from the fact that in some countries, the blanket guarantee on the safety of depositors was extended. Many of the reform proposals under consideration globally are oriented towards ensuring the safety of deposits in banks by insisting on the Volcker rule. The Volcker rule emphasises that banks should concentrate on traditional banking activities and should be subjected to more intensive regulation, and that they should not be exposed to excessively risky activities. Proposals also include appropriate regulation for all deposit-taking institutions, and not merely for banks, as narrowly defined. There is also a focus on ensuring the safety of financial products and making them as simple as possible, which should be helpful to depositors.

In brief, the interests of depositors, particularly retail depositors, are gaining attention, and banking itself is being treated as a public utility. However, this shift in emphasis is largely incidental to the goals of financial stability, rather than being due to a heightened consciousness regarding the interests of depositors. If the financial sector is also imparted a developmental dimension, depositors' interests may not necessarily be protected—as shown by the experience of the period of financial repression in India—unless special attention is paid to depositors' interests. Hence, while evolving the new balance in the regulatory framework, stability and developmental issues should be taken into account along with depositors' interests. It should be recognised that there will be no banks if there are no depositors.

Fifteen

Financial-Sector Taxation: New Approaches[*]

$\mathcal{T}$he context in which the taxation of the financial sector is being intensively examined now, consequent upon the global financial crisis, is explained in the first section of the chapter. The second section summarises the new approaches under active consideration for taxing the financial sector. The third section comments on general issues, while the fourth section comments on the Indian context.

THE CONTEXT

Taxing the financial sector has gained significance in the context of the crisis. There are several arguments in favour of redesigning taxation of the financial sector at this juncture. First, several governments had to incur debt to bailout some financial institutions and stimulate their economies, and it is therefore necessary for the financial sector

* This chapter is an elaborated version of the comments made in the Seminar on Taxing Financial Markets: Alternate Mechanisms and Reserve Application, Fundacion IDEAS, Madrid, 28 April 2010.

to bear at least a part of the burden. Second, it may be necessary to tax the financial sector so that the cost of bailout or other costs related to failures of the financial sector in the future are borne by the financial sector itself. Third, irrespective of the crisis, there is a need for funding economic development globally and funding global public goods. The revenue application (the utilisation of tax collections) for funding global public goods has been active on the agenda since 2005, but has been activated in the light of the crisis. Some of the proposals for taxation under consideration globally seek a combination of all three objectives.

As a result of the analysis of events leading to the crisis, fundamental issues relating to the taxation of the financial sector have also come to the fore. First, there has been a huge increase in trade in foreign currency, often fuelled by short-term flows and excessive speculation. Hence, there is merit in putting sand in the wheel in the form of tax on such transactions, broadly on the lines of the Tobin Tax. Second, there has been excessive financialisation, which requires to be curbed. For instance, in 2007, the financial activity in terms of turnover of spot and derivatives market in financial markets was seventy times that of the world GDP in 2007. A combination of the regulation and low or under-taxation has resulted in excessive speculation. This could be curbed by appropriate corrections to the tax regime. Third, in many countries financial transactions are often outside the indirect taxation system, partly for historical reasons, but partly due to international tax competition for investment flows or financial-sector activity. Fourth, financial activities are amenable to creating entities in such a way that they could avoid tax liability in any jurisdiction. These loopholes in taxing financial institutions have to be plugged through new levies. Fifth, there is a need to curb illegal activities and those activities often operated through tax havens, and in some advanced economies under bank secrecy laws. Sixth, there are significant financial transactions outside the stock exchanges and through unorganised markets. It is necessary to capture information on their activities and tax them through new levies.

New Approaches

Several tax proposals have been put forth consequent upon the experience of the crisis. Some of them have been advocated earlier as well, while a few of them have already been levied in some jurisdictions. First, Currency Transactions Levy (CTL) is a levy on wholesale inter-bank transactions or transactions between financial intermediaries in foreign exchange markets. The classic example of currency transaction levy is called Tobin Tax. The objective of such a tax is to curb excessive speculation in foreign exchange markets by making short-term trading more expensive. A Tobin Tax has not been tried yet, although there is greater interest in the subject now than before the crisis.

Second, Robin Hood Tax is one type of financial transactions levy. The Robin Hood Tax is on various categories of transactions, such as stocks, bonds and currency. The purpose of the Robin Hood Tax is to pay for global public goods as against the Tobin Tax version, which is meant to reduce speculative activity. Non-governmental organisations and some countries in Europe, the UK, as well as Japan have been showing interest in this type of tax.

Third, Financial Transactions (FTT) is a tax on transactions in any of the financial instruments, while the currency transactions levy is confined to foreign exchange transactions. Among the financial transaction taxes currently in operation in some parts of the world are the Value Added Tax on financial activity, sales tax, stamp duty and securities transactions tax. A bank debit tax on transactions of customers with banks is also in vogue.

Fourth, there can be a tax on bonuses paid to senior management. Alternatively, the bonuses paid to senior management may not be allowed as legitimate expenditure for tax purposes, since the bonuses are over and above the wages and hence are in the nature of distribution of profits. In other words, a bonus is a claim on profits after all expenses and hence should be treated on par with profit, and not on par with debt obligations or other legitimate expenses for business operations like wages (the counter-argument is that bonus is a deferred wage).

Fifth, there may be direct taxes on financial institutions apart from the financial transactions tax, which may include currency transactions. To the extent that a financial institution is a corporate entity, it is liable to corporate tax, as in the case of any financial or non-financial corporate. However, there are difficulties in computing income and locating the jurisdiction of the generation of income and setting an appropriate rate based on accounting valuations with regard to corporate tax; however, these difficulties are far more complex with respect to financial entities. In this regard, a distinction is often made between banks, and corporates. Sixth, interest payment on debt is treated as a business expense, and there may be merit in disallowing such treatment to reduce the incentive for excess leverage (it is also argued that tax treatment of interest on debt should be similar to dividend on equity).

In brief, there is a consensus in favour of a review of the totality of taxes on the financial sector, encompassing institutions, markets, instruments and trades, to reflect the experience gained from the crisis with respect to different countries. The main political and social compulsion for levies on the financial sector is the popular resentment at placing a burden on tax payers on account of the failures that brought about the financial crisis. These pressures are mostly in advanced economies, which had to bailout financial institutions and incur debt for fiscal stimulus. The developing countries and advanced economies that did not have serious problems with the financial sector are not enthusiastic for globally binding tax measures. Taxes aimed at paying for the bailout as well as insurance for the future have national significance. At the same time, the pressures against such taxes, both at national and global levels, arise from the financial institutions in advanced economies that are active in cross-border financial activities. There is reason to believe that going forward, the subject will continue to be of significant interest.

COMMENTS

An assessment of the impact of taxation on activity in the financial sector is critical for any policy action. Depending on the design of taxes and rates, a tax could make financial activity very illiquid at one extreme, and could totally fail to curb excessive speculation if the gains from transactions are relatively large. Similarly, its impact on the overall economic activity will depend on the incidence of the tax. It is not clear whether incidence of a tax on the financial sector will be on the financial sector or on the final consumers of financial services, in particular depositors. Further, each tax on the financial sector cannot be viewed in isolation, because the cumulative effect of all taxes on the financial sector is appropriate. In brief, a review of the existing tax regimes on the financial sector is called for, but the design and implementation of taxes are critical.

The impact on the economic activity of taxes on the financial sector is country-specific, and is critical to any packaging of taxes on the financial sector. The financial sector needs to facilitate allocative efficiency, but it also operates as an instrument of public policies, particularly among developing economies. In advanced economies financial institutions need to de-leverage as a consequence of this crisis, and hence they need additional capital in the future. Thus, it is often agreed that an additional burden of taxes will be overdue at a time when the development process is underway. In developing countries, the links between the real sector and financial sector are critical, and in most developing economies banks play a dominant role in the dispensation of credit. Any additional burden of taxes could make credit expensive in such economies, which were not responsible for the crisis. However, a review of the existing systems of taxation on the financial sector, keeping in view the lessons learnt from the crisis, is warranted.

It may not be appropriate to link the tax on institutions in the future with the expenditure of the past on bank bailouts. The issue of bank bailouts and the exact cost of such bailouts are somewhat difficult to quantify. There may be merit in each country deciding whether such a link is desirable, and whether such a link could provide respectability to the bailout process of the past.

A tax on financial institutions may not be related to the funding of future problems, since the latter is essentially in the nature of insurance. If insurance is considered necessary, a separate fund should be created for the purpose, and amounts separately collected. The amounts to be collected as compulsory insurance may be fixed depending on the nature of institutions and activities. It is presumed that this is in addition to the possible compulsory deposit insurance with regard to retail deposits up to a particular level. For instance, in India, all bank deposits up to Rs 100,000 are compulsorily insured by a deposit guarantee institution. This institution is a subsidiary of the central bank.

With regard to taxes on financial transactions, it is ideal to have a tax regime which covers all the instruments and all the markets, including derivatives. That should be applicable for instruments traded on exchange or over-the-counter. While a universal transaction tax would be ideal, it is possible to differentiate the rates with a provision for surcharge relating to volatility. In other words, there could be built-in transparent surcharges when the transactions exceed a particular magnitude, or in the event of excess volatility. This is in the nature of 'voltage' stabilisers to supplement the circuit breakers on trading available now. The existence of these powers in the public policy domain will act as a disincentive for participants in the financial market, whose focus is often on short-term gains from uncertainty and volatility.

There are several reasons why every country should consider taxing the financial sector without necessarily waiting for global coordination, although such global coordination may be useful. First, the global financial crisis warrants a review of all aspects of the financial sector, and tax treatment is an important source of incentives and disincentives for agents and activities in all countries. A variety of taxes on the financial sector already exists, and these do vary across jurisdictions. Second, any effort to link revenues from such global coordination with the end use of such revenues will become contentious and take away the focus on the tax regimes that are important for the improvement of the financial sector. Third, it is extremely difficult to obtain a global consensus on levies with regard to specific taxes in the financial sector. However, global cooperation should focus on arrangements that undermine the effectiveness of taxation at the national level. These relate to bank secrecy laws, tax havens, some extraordinary bilateral tax treaties, etc. Hence, a code of bad practices in tax regimes relevant to the financial sector needs to be drawn up and avoided. In fact, some of the existing treaties need to be revisited.

Fourth, empirical evidence shows that many countries (including the UK, Brazil and India) currently have different types of taxes on the financial sector. There is no empirical evidence to show that national-level taxes seriously divert economic activity. Fifth, we have a situation where there are some very rich individuals who are residents of no country for purposes of taxation of their personal wealth and incomes. This is a serious loophole which should be addressed by national-level authorities.

Taxation as an instrument influencing financial activity, including excessive speculation, should be viewed as a complement and not on a stand-alone basis. The extent and nature of financial activity through institutions, instruments and trade are also influenced by the regime of regulations in the country concerned. The rigour and cost of regulation on categories of institutions, say banks vis-à-vis non-banks, and on categories of instruments, say debt vis-à-vis equity mutual fund units, may vary. While contextually the reform of the tax regime may appear necessary to counter the excessive deregulation that caused the crisis, future tax regimes should take account of regulatory regimes of the future. It appears that such a complementarity between regulation and taxation is best brought about at the national level.

It is also essential to recognise that there are difficulties in the design and implementation of taxes on the financial sector. First, there is huge diversity in financial institutions such as banks, insurance companies, mutual funds, pension funds, etc. There is also diversity in terms of products such as equity and debt, in addition to hybrids and derivatives. Second, the scale and pace of innovation in the financial sector puts a strain on traditional concepts and definitions. This provides scope for the avoidance of taxes. Third, the form of a financial transaction can be manipulated without altering its economic substance far more easily than in the case of non-financial transactions. Fourth, valuations of financial products are not straight-forward. The valuation of a large number of transactions is not cash flow-based but valuation-based, and hence there is scope for tax avoidance.

The incidence of taxes on the financial sector should be an important consideration in the design of a tax. The design of a tax system should ensure that its intent in terms of the relative burden on sections of the population, social or economic activities, retail or wholesale customers is realised. These are difficult challenges, but ignoring them due to complexities could defeat the objectives of taxation. These complications are mentioned not to undermine the importance of an appropriate tax regime, but to emphasise the need for (i) close collaboration between regulations and tax authorities; and (ii) the importance of discretion to both regulators in the financial sector and tax authorities.

COMMENTS ON INDIA

There are several reasons to believe that policies in India have a bias in favour of the financial sector relative to the non-financial sector. In India, capital gains from equity instruments attract a considerably lower level of tax for short-term, and virtually no tax on long-term, capital gains. With respect to shares traded on the exchange or on which securities transaction tax (STT) is paid, short-term capital gains are taxed at a low rate while there is no tax on long-term capital gains. Long-term is defined as more than one year. Since bulk deals (which are essentially privately negotiated although subject to Securities and Exchange Board of India (SEBI) regulations on pricing) can also be put through outside the exchange and merely reported on the exchange by mere payment of STT, tax exemptions become available on these bulk deals. Security transactions (equity) are subject to STT, but some derivatives such as currency derivatives presently traded on exchanges, and where the volumes traded are large, are not subject to STT. Hence, it may be useful to consider establishing a general principle that capital gains from all financial assets should not be taxed less than non-financial assets.

Second, there are no taxes on dividend in the hands of the recipient. There is no ceiling on the amount available for this exemption. The argument is that the company pays the income tax and, therefore, dividend income should not be taxed. This argument is not entirely valid when the company enjoys tax exemptions (the effective tax rate is lower than the nominal). Moreover, given the large holdings by promoters in India, huge benefits accrue to a few. One option would be to replace the dividend tax with Tax Deduction at Source, and subject the dividends to normal taxes in the hands of the recipient. Overall, the current tax regime in India favours non-wage income and, in particular, the richer segments of the population.

Third, the general principle could be that all taxes on income or wealth with regard to financial assets should not be less than what they are on non-financial assets. Fourth, a higher tax on short-term capital gains with regard to financial assets relative to the long-term capital gains is likely to have a stabilising influence on financial markets. Fifth, double taxation treaties, such as the one between India and Mauritius, may negate the impact of some of the taxes on the financial sector. Hence, such arrangements may need to be reviewed.

Where there are differences in the tax treatment of financial institutions for tax purposes, the possibility of transactions among these institutions, amounting to round tripping, should not be ruled out. For example, Mutual Funds enjoy differential tax treatment in India. Sizable investments by banks and corporates are made in Mutual Funds. In fact, banks invest large sums in Mutual Funds and the Mutual Funds in turn invest these amounts in Certificates of Deposits of Banks. Every quarter the funds are redeemed to book income, and then the amounts are reinvested. Since a number of Mutual Funds are floated by corporates, there are a large number of related transactions.

In India, Participatory Notes (PN) is one such instrument that is traded outside the country. While the STT is paid with respect to shares traded or exchanged, or reported to the exchange in India, no such tax is paid with respect to trades that occur through Participatory Notes outside India. The Participatory Notes are issued by Foreign Institutional Investors registered with the securities regulator. There is a proposal to insist that, in order to be eligible for settlement, all trades in Participatory Notes should be registered within the jurisdiction (India) and securities transactions tax should be paid on them on par with equities traded in India. The proposal has not yet been implemented, but it shows that it is possible to devise mechanisms of taxing transactions that may take place outside the jurisdiction as long as there is a link with domestically issued or traded assets.

Sixteen

Fiscal Implications of the Global Financial Crisis*

*T*his chapter is divided into five sections. The first section explores the extent to which fiscal policies were the cause of the crisis and the direct impact of the crisis on the fiscal position. The second section explains the fiscal response to the crisis, including the composition, extent and quality of the stimulus. The third section elaborates on the limits to the stimulus; exit from the stimulus and the consequences of the fiscal stimulus. The fourth section narrates the challenges of management of public debt as a consequence of the fiscal stimulus. The concluding section relates to the way forward with regard to fiscal management globally.

FISCAL POLICIES AND THE CRISIS

It is widely recognised that the crisis is a result of multiple failures, public policy being one of them. Monetary policy and policies relating to regulation of the financial sector are considered to be the crucial elements of public policy that were directly responsible for

---

* This chapter is an edited version of the lecture delivered in the University of Hyderabad, 28 July 2010.

the global financial crisis. However, large and persistent fiscal deficit in the US, co-existing with persistent current account deficit, is considered to be an indirect cause for global economic imbalances, which enabled the crisis. While the fiscal position in the US is not considered to be a cause of the global crisis, many considered it to have facilitated the crisis. It is useful to note that Japan among the advanced economies and India among the EMEs have large fiscal deficits in a persistent fashion, and have high public debt to GDP ratios, and yet they cannot be considered to have contributed to the global financial crisis. Hence, there is no conclusive empirical evidence that fiscal weaknesses have caused the crisis in any significant manner. However, the stress due to the global financial crisis seems to have triggered sovereign debt crisis, notably in some advanced economies.

The impact of the financial crisis on fiscal position was universal, but in different degrees and in different ways across countries. The impact was adverse on revenues due to slowdown in the growth of incomes, in world trade and in prices of many commodities. The impact on expenditure was due to the automatic stabilizers such as unemployment benefits that increased the expenditures, the uncertainties due to exchange rate and increased costs of debt servicing where the crisis impacted on the debt markets. The deterioration in fiscal position may be in all levels of government, but often the increase in fiscal deficits of sub-national governments are not apparent or transparent.

In some cases, particularly in global markets the cost of raising debt increased. However, the US, as the issuer of pre-eminent reserve currency, faced little difficulty, while other major issuers of dominant currencies of advanced economies such as Euro, and UK British Pound and Sterling faced some difficulties in terms of cost of fiscal resources. Those countries which were in a position to raise debt from non-residents in their own currency, faced less difficulties. Those countries which had significant forex reserves did not have to depend on the volatile global financial markets for raising sovereign debt. Countries with low level of forex reserves, but were not in a position to raise foreign currency loans, in the face of a current account deficit or those with large fiscal deficits, were generally affected by the crisis.

FISCAL RESPONSE TO THE CRISIS

Fiscal response is a part of the overall response of public policy to the crisis. In terms of sequencing, monetary policy has been the first line of defence, particularly in dealing with the crisis in financial markets and, to some extent, financial institutions that were 'too big to fail'. Simultaneously, policy relating to financial sector regulations and in some cases external sector management, became critical in the early phases of the response of public policy. The administrative and other control measures also formed part of the public policy response. However, coordination of these policies was essential within each country and also across countries.

Between fiscal and monetary policy, the latter is the first line of defence, but its effectiveness depends on the transmission mechanisms. Further, monetary policy cannot assume solvency risks of the institutions, and monetary policy may be inadequate for addressing issues relating to specific institutions and markets. Hence, fiscal policies also have to play a critical role in responding to the crisis.

There are two important objectives of recourse to the fiscal policy in the context of the global crisis. Firstly, it has to avoid collapse of the functioning of the financial sector and the markets. Secondly, it has to avoid depression as it happened eighty years ago which could result from precipitous drop in economic activity in the private sector on account of the crisis in the financial sector. An important measure to avoid collapse was either a direct bailout of institutions, or indirect assistance through the central bank's assurance of guarantees. Maximum recourse was taken in the critical phase to inject liquidity into the market in the US and UK. The injection of liquidity into the market by the central bank involves the assuming of price of an asset acquired by the central bank in a highly illiquid market. Hence, there is often a significant quasi-fiscal contingent impact of these operations. Similarly, explicit and sometimes not so explicit, financial support or guarantees are extended by the government to financial institutions either directly or through the central bank. There are difficulties in quantifying the aggregate fiscal impact of some of the open market operations and guarantees by the central banks.

The fiscal stimulus which may be differentiated from bailout by fiscal authorities is meant to moderate the deflationary impact of the crisis and avoid recession and unemployment. The instruments used by fiscal authorities are aimed at avoiding recession, unemployment, deflation, etc., by making up for loss of aggregate demand in the private sector due to stress in the financial sector. One set of instruments relating to increasing the public consumption relates to transfer payments from the government to enable increased private consumption. The available evidence shows that India was one of the countries which took maximum recourse to increasing public consumption as part of the stimulus. The second set of instruments relate to enhancing public investment. China and South Africa are examples of taking a significant recourse to these instruments. Tax cuts on consumption is yet another instrument for stimulating private consumption and this was administered by the UK. Tax cut on capital to enhance investment are also possible, just as tax cuts on earnings of labour, but recourse to these have been somewhat marginal.

The extent of stimulus is generally measured as a percentage of GDP for the relevant year. The advanced economies, as a whole, are estimated to have stimulated their economies to the extent of 6 to 7 per cent of GDP with the US, UK, Russia and Saudi Arabia utilising more than 9 per cent of GDP in 2009. This is a very steep increase compared to the relatively low level of fiscal deficit in the pre-crisis period. For 2010, advanced economies, as a whole, were in the same range, but there was a reduction in the case of the US and Saudi Arabia. Emerging market economies, as a whole were estimated to have a fiscal stimulus program of over 5 per cent in 2009. It is expected to have been reduced to a little over 4 per cent in 2010. Essentially, the advanced economies had to take care of support to the financial sector and in addition stimulate the real economy. In most emerging economies, the support to financial sector was not essential. Asia in particular adopted fiscal stimulus promptly, but in terms of the magnitude, it was less than in many other regions.

It is not merely the quantity of stimulus, but also the quality of stimulus that matters for achieving the objectives. There are several issues in this regard. First, what is the multiplier effect of the fiscal stimulus? For example, it is observed that fiscal stimulus that encourages consumption is likely to have greater multiplier effect than bailout of the financial sector. Second, how much of the stimulus is cyclical or discretionary, and how much is structural? In other words, if the fiscal stimulus is such that it results in entitlement of the future or it cannot be withdrawn easily, the stimulus which is expected to be cyclical could turn out to be structural. Once it becomes structural, it ceases to be a temporary stimulus. Third, how much is investment relative to consumption in the stimulus package? Expenditure on investments is likely to add to the potential of output of the economy or the productive capacity of the economy. Fourth, what is the scope for cross border spill-over of the stimulus? For example, increase in consumption of an advanced economy like the US may not necessarily imply additional demand only for the goods produced in the US, but it may result in additional demand for goods imported from China, and hence additional demand in China. Fifth, the nature of trade-off between immediate impact and medium term implications with regard to fiscal stimulus is important. For example, in China stimulus concentrated on boosting investment demand, but the medium-term rebalancing may warrant movement away from investment demand towards consumption demand. Similarly in the US, the stimulus may aim at increasing private consumption, whereas the medium to longer term effort should be to reducing consumption and increasing savings. Finally, the fiscal stimulus is most effective when it is directed to activities that result in increasing the demand for those goods and services that happen to be suffering from deficiency in demand as a result of the crisis. The export-demand from advanced economies for exports from developing economies could be an illustration. But the limits to success of stimulating export demand would be set, among other things, by the scope for substituting it with local demand and the similar stimulus by other countries which compete for the same segments of global markets.

LIMITS, EXIT AND CONSEQUENCES

Fiscal stimulus cannot be unlimited. This is partly because the effectiveness may be in question; the returns from the stimulus may be diminishing; and any stimulus usually involves addition to the public debt of the government. With regard to each country, the limits to fiscal stimulus depend on several factors. First, the head-room available for cyclical fiscal stimulus will depend on the initial fiscal position. In other words, if a country does not have structural fiscal deficit, or has only a modest structural fiscal deficit, there would be a head-room for undertaking cyclical measures to stimulate the economy. Second, the limits will have to take into account an estimation of slackness in the aggregate demand so that the extent of the stimulus is calibrated with the needs. The timing of initiating withdrawal of the stimulus will have to coincide with the evolving conditions of slack in and revival of private sector demand, respectively. Third, the perceptions of financial markets and their sensitivity to the levels of sustainable public debt are important. It is well-known that financial markets and rating agencies take account of several factors, including geopolitical ones, in addition to economic fundamentals, while assessing the credit-worthiness of a sovereign nation. Fourth, the possible inflationary consequences of the fiscal stimulus could vary among countries and these may partly depend on the flexibilities in the economy, and in particular, supply elasticity. Finally, the fiscal policy has to supplement and complement the stimulus in monetary policy and policy in regard to financial markets regulation. In other words, if transmission of monetary policy were effective, the burden on the fiscal policy is moderated, and vice-versa.

The exit from the stimulus involves critical trade-offs. The exit, unlike the launch of the stimulus measures for which the provocation is often fairly clear, may have to be gradual, depending on the developments in the aggregate demand of the private sector. It is natural that the first stage of the exit will be stopping further stimulus, and the second stage will be withdrawing the stimulus. It may, however, be noted that it is possible that fiscal policies may continue with the stimulus, while monetary policies may commence withdrawing the stimulus. Similarly, withdrawal of fiscal policy may succeed monetary tightening. Further, the various components of the fiscal stimulus and monetary policy will have to be assessed individually, and then sequenced, taking into account the magnitudes that are appropriate, from time to time. As a general rule, exit from unconventional measures should precede a calibrated exit from conventional measures, since in the latter, exit from the stimulus is through direction and magnitude only.

In this regard, there are two sets of considerations involving trade-offs. There is a risk of depression or continued stagnation or double dip recession if the stimulus happens to be delayed, inadequate, or is inappropriately packaged or sequenced. It is also possible that monetary instruments might have been totally used up, leaving greater burden on the fiscal situation. On the other hand, fiscal policy also might end up being ineffective, if it were to add excessively to future debt burden or result in unacceptable inflation, since uncertain future creates the effect of depressing the sentiment to spend among all economic agents. These are trade-offs which involve considerable elements of judgment and are unlikely to be rule-based at the shorter end of the policymaking.

There are two types of coordination issues in designing strategies for exit from the stimulus: (i) coordination of policies among institutions within a country, in particular, fiscal authority, monetary authority and regulators; and (ii) coordination of policies across countries. With regard to coordination across countries, a major issue arises when the response of aggregate private demand is uneven across countries, resulting in divergence in the state of the economic cyclicals among countries. In other words, while convergence for avoiding collapse of financial markets during the crisis was commendable, it has now been replaced by divergence due to different conditions of economic revival in countries, particularly between advanced economies and EMEs. Advanced economies are battling with serious problems relating to the financial sector, and those relating to the deficiency in aggregate demand, while the EMEs are generally addressing the issues of containing signs of asset bubbles, if not, possible excesses in aggregate demand. The advanced economies are battling deflationary pressures, while the EMEs are addressing issues relating to inflationary pressures. In designing monetary and fiscal policies, conflicts between what domestic factors demand and what global factors warrant are evident now since uncertain future has the effect of depressing the sentiment to spend among all economic agents. In this situation, the excess volatility in cross-border capital flows has acquired significance for public policy, since movements in capital across policy regimes could undermine effectives of monetary policy at the national level with consequent implications for fiscal policy also.

The consequences of fiscal stimulus are not easy to assess. On a counter factual basis, it may be held that in the absence of massive fiscal stimulus that was undertaken, there could have been a collapse of financial markets. Serious disruption in the working of financial institutions has been avoided. The threat of depression has been eliminated. Great recession has occurred in some countries, while recession has been faced by many countries. Overall, however, the global economy is on the recovery path, though differences persist on whether the recovery in a country is fragile or solid. It must be recognised that the credit for avoiding the serious adverse consequences of the crisis cannot be appropriated in its entirety by the fiscal policy. Further, to the extent the fiscal policy is discretionary, it is possible that non-economic factors and considerable discretion, if not patronage, was exercised by the fiscal authorities in undertaking the stimulus and the consequences may not be transparent. It is, therefore, difficult to assess the technical efficiency of the fiscal stimulus.

There are several positive consequences of the fiscal stimulus, but there are several negative consequences also. The negative consequences will have to be faced over a period of time. The most important is that public debt has increased, particularly in advanced economies. The guarantees that have been extended in some form or the other constitute hidden public debt, and it may take time for them to crystallise. The net cost of central bank operations in the financial sector in advanced economies are still uncertain and, therefore, the quasi-fiscal implications of the unprecedented expansion of the balance sheets of central banks are almost indeterminate. There is nervousness in financial markets about financing of the increased debts. The debt to GDP ratios increased in most advanced economies to unprecedented levels in peace-time. It is widely believed that about one decade of austerity would be needed in some large advanced economies of the world to restore complete normality in their fiscal situation. With regard to EMEs, however, there has been only a marginal increase in the debt to GDP ratio. No doubt, the sustainable level of public debt for developing economies and EMEs, as a percentage of GDP, is usually far lower than in advanced economies with similar economic fundamentals in terms of current assessment by financial markets. This position could change rapidly in the future. There is virtual unanimity that managing large public debt especially by the advanced economies is a major challenge in the post-crisis situation.

MANAGEMENT OF PUBLIC DEBT

There are two types of challenges with regard to management of public debt, namely, challenges of managing operational aspects of public debt, and secondly challenges of reducing public debt to sustainable levels. The complexities in managing operational aspects of public debt depend on several factors. First, a high growth rate provides scope for managing public debt comfortably. Second, a higher level of domestic savings usually provides a cushion for the government to mobilise savings domestically. Third, if the maturity profile is essentially longer term, the gross borrowing requirements on a yearly basis will be less, and hence the task of mobilising resources will be less onerous. Fourth, if the stock of public debt is essentially on a fixed interest rate, there is a greater freedom for monetary policy actions that would not impact the fiscal position. In other words, if the debt is at fixed interest rate, the government's debt burden is fixed and the impact of any changes in the interest rates will be absorbed by the holders of the government debt. Fifth, the currency in which the stock of public debt is denominated will also be relevant. If most of the stock of public debt is denominated in the domestic currency, the fiscal authorities do not bear exchange risk directly. If, however, a large part is denominated in foreign currency, and if much of the government's budgetary transactions are in domestic currency, the mismatch can prove to be a burden. Sixth, if the holders of government debt are residents, there is likely to be less volatility in the government securities markets, in view of domestic bias of many households and some other savers. However, if a large part of the debt is held by non-residents (who are in most part financial intermediaries), in times of stress the volatility in debt markets may be excessive. Seventh, the importance of the national balance sheet should not be under estimated. In other words, the aggregate external assets held by the residents and external liabilities of the residents would be critical to the confidence of international markets on the credit worthiness of the countries concerned. A national balance sheet, therefore, would take into account both the private sector balance sheets and the public sector balance sheets, in terms of external assets and liabilities.

The second set of measures relate to the reduction of public debt to a sustainable level which is related to macroeconomic policies. Reduction may be facilitated by a number of factors. First, a high growth would facilitate a reduction in public debt as a proportion of GDP, thus enhancing the capacity of the economy to service the debt, but history is indicative of the fact that high public debt puts a downward pressure on growth over longer term. Second, demography plays an important role in the burden imposed on a generation to service public debt. In this regard, the concept of fiscal gap has gained importance. Fiscal gap is computed on the basis of difference between expected stream of revenues over two or three decades and the expected expenditures over the same period. During this period, there is a positive impact on revenues if the working population is large, while expenditures increase if the older population prevails, if provision has to be made for health and social security. Third, austerity measures by the government in a medium-term on a credible basis should help reduction in burden of public debt. Fourth, allowing some increase in inflation to reduce the real burden of public debt is not uncommon. Fifth, debt restructuring, including debt default, cannot be treated as an option, but history is full of examples when this option was exercised to reduce the burden of public debt on the resident citizens of a country. Sixth, if the debt is denominated in foreign currency, devaluation of a currency will have the effect of increasing the burden. Seventh, using the financial sector or financial repression, particularly impacting the banking sector, is not unknown. This can take several forms, and in particular, in the form of statutory requirement that banks hold a stipulated amount of government securities. These stipulations could be extended to all regulated entities such as insurance companies and pension funds. Just as monetary policies sometimes use a part of the package to reduce public debt by allowing over inflation or devaluation, regulatory policies may indulge in financial repression. Finally, no doubt, credible assurance of fiscal management with binding medium-term framework for fiscal consolidation would improve the confidence of the financial market and provide greater manoeuvrability for fiscal authorities in reducing public debt.

Huge public debt could dampen growth, and more important, could dampen the perception of growth prospects and comfort of bond holders. There are significant differences in the sustainable level of public debt between advanced countries and EMEs. Overall, the sustainable levels of public debt would depend on the perceptions of bond markets. It is generally expected that for the global economy as a whole, at least one decade of adjustment would be required to bring the public debt to sustainable levels.

WAY FORWARD

The outlook for public finance in the medium term is highly uncertain and overall pessimistic at a global level. While the advanced economies are facing the most difficult problems of managing public finance for the next decade, the EMEs, and in particular Asia, are less vulnerable. The difficult public finances of advanced economies may not leave the public finances of EMEs unaffected. India is unique among the major EMEs in having a high public debt to GDP ratio and persistent fiscal deficit, as contrasted with most of the Asian economies.

Globally, magnitudes of public debt have increased to unprecedented levels in peace times. Fiscal solvency may be at stake in several cases, in the years to the come. Such issues may arise with regard to advanced economies with low savings and aging population, which need health and social security. In other words, in the global market for sovereign bonds, it is likely that in future there would be a risk shift from EMEs to advanced economies. It is difficult to speculate how the advanced economies would manage their finances out of the current situation. While sovereign default is most unlikely, debt restructuring in some form is not impossible in a few cases. Painful fiscal adjustment may be inevitable and this may be combined with small doses of inflation. It is useful to note that high public debt may not necessarily result in higher inflation, as the example of Japan illustrates. Further, the response of bond markets to the fiscal positions in terms of inflation expectation is unclear. The main issue would be the extent to which fiscal position and process of deleveraging in advanced economies would slowdown in their economies and also the global economy growth. The concerns of developing countries may thus relate to the impact of the fiscal position of advanced economies on their exports.

In some of the advanced economies, there may be a need to deleverage the financial sector, the private sector and the public sector simultaneously. In fact, the deleveraging process in the private sector even after shifting a significant burden of their deleveraging to the public sector may not be complete. This is also the time when financial sector may need more capital as per evolving global consensus to avoid future stress on financial stability. If the demographics of an advanced economy demand considerable expenditure on health and social security, the burden of managing public debt could be severe.

If the fiscal position is weak for a prolonged period in major economies, the head-room available for countercyclical policies will be less in these countries. In such a situation, it may be difficult for fiscal policy to supplement the countercyclical monetary policy that has been advocated as essential for global financial stability. In other words, the weak fiscal position will increase the burden of macroeconomic stability on monetary policy and regulation of the financial sector.

Paradoxically, fiscal authorities are most worried about the reaction of the financial markets and financial institutions to the growth in public debt, but these were the entities which needed to be bailed-out. Governments incurred huge debts to save the financial sector and now the rescuers have to be rescued.

It seems that countries need significant fiscal space to manage different levels of public debt in different countries. Increasing the globalisation of finance reduces fiscal space for countries since both tax and regulatory arbitrage need to be avoided. In other words, the huge public debt of countries incurred due to national policy actions for managing the crisis will necessarily involve strengthening national policies to manage the fiscal consequences. Managing fiscal consequences at the national level would be constrained by increased globalisation of finance. Perhaps the way forward could be either a greater globalisation of fiscal management or a recalibration of globalised finance.

Seventeen

Macroeconomic Frameworks and Financial Stability*

$\mathcal{I}$t is useful to clarify the concepts of macroeconomic framework and financial stability, since they are often used contextually. In the current context, discussion on financial stability is largely influenced by the global financial crisis and hence on avoidance of systemic risks to the financial system. However, it is appropriate to take a broader view of financial stability in a more normal circumstance and with a developmental perspective in the case of developing countries like India. The concept of financial stability was explained in the Indian context in June 2004 as follows:

> The concept of financial stability needs to be understood contextually also. For us in India, it means: (i) ensuring uninterrupted financial transactions; (ii) maintenance of a level of confidence in the financial system amongst all the participants and stakeholders; and (iii) absence of excess volatility that unduly and adversely affects real economic activity. Such financial stability has to be particularly ensured when the financial system is undergoing

* This chapter is an edited version of the presentation made at the Conference on Macroeconomic and Financial Stability in Asian Emerging Markets, organised by ADBI and Bank Negara Malaysia, Kuala Lumpur, 4 August 2010.

structural changes to promote efficiency. The structural changes relate to ownership, regulation and competition, both, domestic as well as external competition. Integration of financial markets is another dimension of the process: the integration of domestic financial markets is one aspect while global financial integration is another though a related aspect.[1]

The concept of macroeconomic framework generally refers to the set of comprehensive policy measures that are undertaken to pursue broad economic objectives. The objectives normally relate to economic growth, low or stable inflation rate and sustainable balance of payments. While the central focus is on welfare of people as reflected in what may be described as real sector, from the policy point of view, the macroeconomic framework generally refers to the conduct of monetary, fiscal and external sector policies. Policies relating to the financial sector, which were generally considered as part of the microeconomic policies have, after the global financial crisis, gained a distinct place in the set of macroeconomic policies.

In this background, keeping in view a practitioners perspective and Indian experience, the chapter comments on (i) the link between monetary policy framework and financial stability; (ii) the use of fiscal and regulatory policies for financial stability and (iii) external sector and capital account management for financial stability. This chapter is essentially forward-looking, keeping in view the tentative lessons learned from the global financial crisis.

LINK WITH THE MONETARY POLICY: INCREASING ROLE FOR DISCRETION

Inflation as the dominant objective of monetary policies has now been supplemented with concern for financial stability. In a way, the trade-off is no longer only between growth and inflation but also between the two, and concerns relating to financial stability. In this regard, there is a view that what may be considered as low and stable inflation so far might be too low for the effectiveness of countercyclical monetary policies. Experience in recent years has shown that on an average, inflation in developing countries has been higher than in advanced economies. There is a perception that in the future, central banks in advanced economies may tolerate a higher inflation than in pre-crisis period to enable management of huge public debt that has been incurred for bailout and stimulus operations during the crisis. Under the circumstances, it is necessary to explore whether a predominantly rule based system of monetary policy would continue to be preferred.

Greater scope for judgment and discretion for monetary authorities may be essential in EMEs for several reasons. First, the structural transformation in the economies of EMEs has considerable economic and broader socio-political complexities. In fact, identification of cyclical and structural components in the performance of the economy, and a fix on the potential output are more difficult in EMEs than in advanced economies due to rapid structural changes in the former. These dynamics call for greater role for judgments. Second, the information base and timeliness of data are matters that constrain adherence to a rule based system in EMEs. Third, EMEs are affected by the developments in advanced economies often without reference to their own economic fundamentals. In particular, their currency and debt markets are influenced disproportionately (and sometimes for a prolonged period) by developments in advanced economies. Hence precautionary or defensive measures against externally induced volatilities on domestic financial markets may be required from the EMEs. Fourth, the relative weights to domestic and global factors in monetary policy are subject to change, depending on the extent of de facto global integration that itself is rapidly changing in most EMEs. Fifth, it is possible that the global economic cycle may not always coincide with the domestic economic cycle. For example, as of now the pressures in advanced economies may be deflationary with large unutilised capacities, whereas in some EMEs like India, the pressure could be inflationary, rather than deflationary. In a globalised situation, the monetary policy will have to take a view on coordination of their macro-policies with other countries in the context of global trends, while simultaneously responding to the domestic situation. The divergence between the two is likely to be more acute in the near future with increasing uncertainties in the global economy and uneven recovery across the countries. Sixth, coordination of monetary action with fiscal authorities and regulators within a country becomes extremely important to maintain stability. It must be recognised that the fiscal headroom available to EMEs may be less than in advanced economies, if they are not in a position to raise sovereign debt in their own currency in the global markets. Further, in countries such as India which already have large public debt and persisting fiscal deficit, the scope for effective and significant countercyclical fiscal policies on a discretionary basis may be relatively limited. In such cases, the burden on monetary policy to maintain financial stability will be higher and the precautionary steps to be taken by monetary authorities will have to be actively considered in a timely manner. Finally, a word of caution to EMEs following the lead of advanced economies in prioritisation of financial stability may be necessary in this context. The monetary policy framework is being redesigned in advanced economies to the extent it had ignored the importance of financial stability in the past. Many EMEs, especially in Asia, have to emphasise the importance of developmental objectives in reviewing regulatory policy framework of the financial sector in the current context. In other words, the focus of financial sector reforms in EMEs, particularly in Asia, should still be on growth in view of their levels of development and also current assessment of potential for financial instability domestically.

USE OF FISCAL AND REGULATORY POLICIES

The most important component of macroeconomic policies in the context of financial stability is fiscal position. Fiscal position in the context of financial stability can be analysed in terms of the aggregate fiscal position and the management of public debt. The debt management of a sovereign has significant impact on financial institutions and financial markets.

Coordinated countercyclical policies require an agreement on the phase of the cycle, between monetary, fiscal and regulatory authorities. To the extent, judgments are involved about the phase of the cycle, there is need for an understanding and harmonisation between monetary, fiscal and regulatory authorities. The monetary authority has to make a judgment on the automatic stabilisers available for fiscal authorities and the headroom available for discretionary fiscal policy to enable conduct of countercyclical policies. The monetary authority should recognise not only macroeconomic realities such as public debt to GDP ratios but also the perceptions of financial markets on the evolving state of public debt.

The nature of sovereign debt is extremely important in terms of link between fiscal, monetary and regulatory policies, and the external sector. Some illustrations may be in order. To the extent the outstanding sovereign debt is significantly on floating rates of interest, the impact of monetary actions may be more than otherwise on the fiscal positions. If the sovereign debt outstanding is significantly on fixed interest rate terms, the impact of monetary actions may be more on the financial institutions that hold the government paper.

The currency in which the sovereign debt is dominated will also be important. If a major part of the sovereign debt is foreign currency denominated, the exchange rate becomes critical for financial stability (the example of Latin America may be relevant). Whether the holders of government debt are mainly residents or non-residents, is also important in regard to debt management because the resident holders are likely to have a domestic bias. In other words, in times of financial stress, there may be greater volatility in non-resident holdings of government paper. Examples of Japan and India on thr one hand, and Greece on the other, will be instructive for appreciating this.

The duration of the debt may also determine the headroom available to fiscal authorities to raise fresh debt because of the implications for increase in gross borrowing requirements relative to net borrowing requirements. In India, the banking system which plays a pivotal role has to hold about 25 per cent of its assets in the form of government securities as a prudential requirement. In addition, many banks are owned by the government. In other words, in an EME, an assessment has to be made about the linkages between the financial sector, in particular the banking sector and the fiscal position, with regard to public debt, in the context of interaction between fiscal and monetary policies.

The regulatory and monetary policies will interact more in future, mainly because of the acceptance of the significance of countercyclical policies in both monetary and regulatory policies, as also the macro-prudential aspects in the regulatory policies. In each country, an assessment may have to be made of the impact of monetary policy actions on the balance sheet of financial institutions, and in particular, of banks. The stress test to be conducted by the regulators should take into account not only market uncertainties, but also policy uncertainties. The changing transmission mechanisms of monetary policies in EMEs will have to be continuously assessed since the transmission of policies are essentially through financial markets, and to a larger extent, through financial institutions in EMEs, which are themselves in a state of rapid transformation.

In many EMEs, foreign banks play a dominant role in financial markets and to a lesser extent in traditional retail banking, though they may be relatively less dominant in Asia. Foreign banks have a significant scope for operating across markets, across tax regimes, and across regulatory regimes. Ensuring strict alignment of their operations with the intent of domestic regulators is often a challenge for regulators in EMEs. Way forward, due to global uncertainties, the issue may acquire new dimensions.

The role of regulatory policy will be central to financial stability in EMEs since sector specific issues in somewhat segmented real economy can be addressed by regulations. Further, institution specific issues, including those that are 'too large to fail' and market-specific (debt or equity) or instrument-specific issues can be managed by regulations. In EMEs, there may be activities that are credit constrained alongside some bank financing of asset bubbles, that requires regulatory attention. On the whole, monetary policy plays an active role in matters relating to business and credit cycles, and a supportive role or a complementary role in ensuring financial stability, broadly defined to include support to real sector, and maintenance of trust in the financial system.

External Sector Management

At a very general level it can be argued that an open capital account in a way constrains the freedom available for monetary policy, and this may in the ultimate analysis include freedom available for monetary policy to conduct countercyclical policies also. More important, the EMEs with persistent current account deficits will have to bear a significant pressure in times of stress on financial sector globally. If such EMEs have adequate forex reserves to manage the shocks, the impact on financial stability may be moderated. Thus, many EMEs may have to consider, as part of maintaining overall stability, the precautionary principle as an important factor in assessing the sustainability of the external sector.

Forex reserves do provide some self-insurance. The adequacy of reserves, however, has to be interpreted in a dynamic context and in terms of insurance against possible shocks, both on current and capital accounts. A national balance sheet approach, making an assessment of the liquidity as well as the return of aggregate external assets and liabilities, both on public and private sector account, will be useful so that monetary policy actions can assess the extent of precautionary steps that have to be taken.

The Way Forward

It should be recognised that globally public debt management is likely to be a challenging task for many economies, and in particular, advanced economies whose public debt to GDP ratios have risen to an all time high in peace time history. The implication of this dramatic development for public debt management of EMEs and consequently the implication for their monetary policies will have to be studied. Second, there has been considerable literature on the cost of holding forex reserves mainly because it was possible to somehow measure it, but there has not been much work on the benefits of reserves which are admittedly non-quantifiable. Recent events have shown the non-quantifiable benefits of reserves. Third, the point at which the forex reserve build-up ceases to be precautionary, and centres around exchange rate management, is extremely dynamic. Globally agreed arrangements such as safety nets by IMF or regional initiatives like Chang Mai may, if successful, provide some comfort to EMEs and reduce the level of precautionary needs for reserves. In other words, if the world in the near future is likely to be more uncertain than before, there are implications for reserve build-up and currency composition of reserves, from the point of view of EMEs. Fourth, in managing external sector, it is necessary to assess vulnerability to shocks, both on account of current account and on capital account. On current account, it will have to be essentially related to commodity prices which may affect export proceeds and import requirements. The sovereign wealth funds and commodity funds should in this regard be treated as a form of forex reserves or quasi-forex reserves. In respect of capital flows, the major issue is the composition of the stock of external liabilities and the volatility in the capital inflows as well as outflows. There is a hierarchy in the nature of such flows, the most vulnerable in terms of volatility being the portfolio flows. It is possible to conceive both price based measures and non-price based measures in influencing the composition of capital inflows and outflows.

CAPITAL ACCOUNT MANAGEMENT AND
PRUDENTIAL REGULATIONS

From the point of view of capital account management with a view to avoid volatilities that threaten financial stability, it may be useful to differentiate between the balance sheets and activities of households, corporates and financial intermediaries. If credibility of monetary stability, in particular, the trust in banking system and the exchange rate stability are assured, the household is unlikely to be a major source of volatility in inflows and outflows on capital account. Non-financial corporates operate significantly in current account transactions and, to some extent, in capital account transactions. In the case of such corporates, therefore, there is considerable scope for capital account transactions to take place in the guise of current account transactions. There is also some scope for cross-border operations by corporates, depending on the extent of cross border linkages of corporates, and openness of the capital account of the country. With regard to the financial sector, however, there is considerable scope for volatility in inflows and outflows. Experience indicates that the financial intermediaries may exploit opportunities for profit disregarding, to some extent, the currency mismatches and the maturity mismatches on their balance sheets. Hence, the focus of capital account management will have to be the financial sector, and in this critical sector, there is a large overlap between prudential stipulations on the financial sector and capital account management. Indian experience has shown that judicious use of prudential regulations as capital account management could be effective.

The Way Forward

It is acknowledged that there are growing uncertainties in regard to the global liquidity condition. Emerging markets economies, particularly in Asia, could face problems of large inflows with a potential for large outflows at some stage. In such a situation, public policy may be well advised to keep a number of options to moderate the impact of volatility in capital flows. A transparent willingness and a credible determination on the part of public policy to take recourse to capital account management may itself moderate market expectations of assured profit-making through currency trade, and hence may moderate the volatility in the flows. Options to impose Tobin Tax should be part of a policy package to contain volatility in flows.

NOTES

1. Y. V. Reddy, 'Financial Stability: Indian Experience', speech delivered at the Zurich University, Switzerland, 27 June 2004, BIS Review 40/2004, available at http://www.bis.org/review/r040713c.pdf, accessed 18 October 2010.

SECTION IV

*Global Financial Architecture:
The Debates*

Eighteen

International Monetary System: Issues and Options*

$\mathscr{T}$he focus of this chapter is on the quest for a reserve currency most suited to the needs of a global economy in the light of macroeconomic imbalances that have been associated with the current global financial crisis. The chapter is divided into four sections. The first section narrates the current status of the international monetary system and the context of the global financial crisis in which there is a debate on the subject. The second section highlights the alternatives to the existing system under consideration. The third section explains the proposals for improving the current system or current non-system on the assumption that the alternative systems are at present not feasible. The fourth concluding section explores the possible implications of recent developments in Euro on the international monetary system.

* This chapter is an edited version of the at the Indian Council for Research on International Economic Relations (ICRIER), New Delhi, 21 July 2010.

International Monetary System: Current Status

The international monetary system conceptually refers to the practices, rules and institutions that are prevalent for international payments. From a policy point of view, it refers to official arrangements to regulate key dimensions of balance of payments and international reserves including exchange rates, current payments and capital flows. In popular view, the international monetary system refers to the form in which foreign exchange reserves are held by national governments.

There has been a debate for several decades within academic and policy circles on the international monetary system. However, currently there has been a renewed interest in the subject in view of a search for improvements in the global economic and financial systems as a response to the global financial crisis. In particular, an active debate has been engineered by Governor Zhou's (Governor of the central bank of China) statement in 2009 on the difficulties being experienced by the global system due to the US Dollar being the main reserve asset for central banks. In a way, therefore, the debate has been triggered by the concerns of China about maintaining the role of the US Dollar as a store of value. The country having a large stake in the evolution of the international monetary system at the current stage is China because it is maintaining a large amount of foreign exchange reserves. Most of the reserves of China are denominated in US Dollar, which is the most dominant international reserve currency, if not the sole reserve currency for the global economy. Though the accumulation of reserves by China and the stake for China has triggered the debate, there are three fundamental reasons for the global community being interested in this subject now. First, continued prevalence of large current account imbalances that are partly responsible for the crisis and their unwinding, may affect the status of the current international monetary system. Second, there are volatile capital flows in view of the uncertainties in the global economy, which may affect the stability in the value of various currencies in the world. Third, there is a large build-up of reserves putting stress on the store of value function of the existing currency that dominates the international monetary system.

In addition to the context in which there is an interest in the international monetary system, fundamental reasons are advocated for a change in the current system. First, the current system is actually described as a non-system, since under the flexible exchange rate systems that dominate the world, there are no rules or framework that regulate the demand for or supply of reserve assets for the global economy.

Second, the system, as it exists, is primarily based on one currency, namely the US Dollar, which gives exorbitant privilege to one country, namely the US. The US or US Dollar becomes the centre, and the rest of the world, in a way, becomes the periphery.

Third, the interests of the global economy and that of the domestic economy that is issuing the reserve currency may not always coincide. In other words, the total supply of US Dollars will have to take into account the requirements of stability and growth in the US economy, and also the stability and growth in the global economy that is using the US Dollar as a reserve currency for themselves. For example, if the reserve currency issuing country does not have a deficit in its balance of payments, it may not supply the currency to the rest of the world. In such a case, there is a deflationary bias in the world. If, however, the country which is issuing a reserve currency has large deficits, there may be too much of the currency available to the rest of the world, and it may result in erosion of the value of the relevant reserve currency itself. The right deficit for the country concerned, consistent with its requirements for growth and stability may or may not be consistent with the full employment and price stability for the global economy as a whole. This phenomenon is called Triffin's dilemma. The dilemma refers to a situation when there are fundamental conflicts of interest between short-term domestic and long-term international economic objectives for an economy where national currency also serves as an international reserve currency. This dilemma was first identified by Robert Triffin in the 1960s, pointing out that the country issuing the global reserve currency must be willing to run large trade deficits in order to supply the world with enough of its currency to fulfil world demand for foreign exchange reserves.

Fourth, asymmetric adjustments are triggered during shocks. In general, the non-reserve deficit countries are forced to make adjustments in their macroeconomic policies in a significant manner to convincingly honour their commitments, whenever there is a shock, while the countries that issue reserve currencies can finance their deficits with some cushion. Those countries which generally have surplus current account, in any case, have headroom for adjustment.

Fifth, the benefits of globalisation of finance that are expected to accrue through market based capital account are undermined due to lack of level playing ground. In other words, the global capital flows towards the centre or the country that is issuing reserve currency whenever there are uncertainties. More broadly, market discipline does not operate on the country issuing reserve currency, the way it operates on other currencies. Hence, the benefits that accrue from market discipline in a globalised financial world are sometimes undermined.

Sixth, the centre, namely, the country issuing reserve currency, is not anchored or compelled to adopt reasonable policies either through market discipline in the absence of its credible contestability or through global rules and arrangements, despite surveillance by the IMF and G-20 frameworks. In other words, there is no compulsion from markets or from binding discipline or rules on the country issuing reserve currency to adopt macroeconomic policies that are generally consistent with global economic requirements.

Seventh, it has been argued that the current system is both unstable and inequitable. The instability arises from the deflationary bias in the current system and use of national currency as an international currency. The inequitable nature has been aggravated with the need for self protection through accumulation of reserves by developing countries, which was necessitated by highly pro-cyclical capital flows. It is inequitable because reserve build-up as self-insurance involves transfer of resources from developing to advanced economies carrying relatively low returns. Self protection was needed in the absence of appropriate arrangements for provision of liquidity as needed in the global system.

It will be useful to recognise the position of the US in this debate. In brief, it may be summarised as follows. The US is providing a service to the global economy through provision of global reserve currency and liquidity as appropriate to the global economy. In a way, the US is virtually providing global banking and payment facilities. In this direction, it is keeping an open capital account and promoting financial markets in an orderly fashion. The privilege that accrues to the US is only a charge for such services, and it cannot be treated as exorbitant. The responsibility of being an international reserve currency constrains its freedom in managing the domestic economy and the privilege is only a small charge relative to the responsibility. There is a view that is presently gaining popularity, which holds that the US is in fact paying a heavy price in terms of discharging its obligations as being the issuer of the international reserve currency. In this view, it would be in the interest of the US to exit from this onerous responsibility in a non-disruptive manner.

There are two important issues that will have to be considered in any exploration of changes in the current international monetary system. First, what are the options available at this stage in terms of alternatives? Second, how does the global economy transit from the present non-system to a new system or an improved system, recognising the burdens of adjustment on different countries involved?

The proposals under discussion are: (i) devise a new global currency; (ii) convert the existing mechanism of Special Drawing Rights (SDR) into a global currency; (iii) promote multipolar reserve currencies or several reserve currencies instead of depending entirely on one country's currency, namely, the US Dollar; (iv) replace the unipolar reserve currency, namely, the US Dollar, with another unipolar reserve currency where a country is likely to demand a less exorbitant privilege and (v) improve the current non-system to make it a rule based system.

New Global Currency

It can be argued that a truly globalised economy demands a global currency. Further, it is necessary to have an entirely new currency if all links between the international monetary system and the condition and performance of major economies in the world are to be avoided. In fact, all proposals other than issuance of a new currency involve a national currency or several national currencies. To illustrate, SDR and SDR denominated instruments need to be converted into a national currency for payments and interventions. A new global currency could replace all national currencies as was the case with Euro, or circulate a parallel with national currencies.

A single new currency replacing national currencies, described as fiat currency, would require a global monetary authority. A global monetary authority that issues a fiat currency would warrant a mandate, target or targets, and instruments. It would also require some agreements on the fiscal management in different countries and some mechanisms for coordination in policies relating to movement of goods, services, labour and capital. In a way, therefore, a fiat currency for the global economy as a whole, demands the creation of a global monetary authority, binding fiscal discipline imposed on all the countries, and credible macroeconomic coordination among countries. Invariably, several issues regarding the governance, independence and accountability for such a global monetary institution will have to be addressed. There is a consensus that the chances of getting an agreement at a global level for a fiat currency to replace national currencies would be extremely difficult for a long time.

One approach is to create a new reserve currency, say International Currency Certificates, which could be SDRs, that could be swapped with the IMF or a new agency to be created by central banks. There would be no backing for the global currency, except the commitment of central banks to exchange it for their own currencies. The system envisages close links between the new global reserve system and reserves of central banks with agreement on extent of creation of global liquidity and allocations among countries. In this arrangement, the global reserve currency and national currencies coexist.

It is possible to consider creation of a new currency that could be in parallel with national currencies. Such a new currency will dispense with exorbitant privilege to one or a few economies. There will be less uneven pressures for adjustment by different countries in the event of a shock. It is also possible to have an arrangement where the issuer of such a new currency can be a true global lender of last resort. To capture these benefits, formal global agreement is needed about the quantity of the new currency to be issued, to whom it will be issued, by whom it will be issued and under what conditions it will be issued. The pre-condition for creation of an authority to issue such an international currency in parallel are an agreement on the governance arrangements and a target in terms of prices of a basket of goods, services and assets for the global economy as a whole. Operationally, such a new global currency may have to be freely exchanged with national currencies, but countries should ideally agree to hold at least a certain share of their reserves in such an international currency. The issuer of such a currency would require authority to vary the quantity of the new currency to match the needs of a global economy from time-to-time, and to conduct necessary open market operations for the purpose. It is also necessary that the financial markets be willing to trade in the instruments that the new international currency offers in its open market operations. It should also have the mandate to be a lender of last resort. Being a lender of last resort also requires an ability to make an assessment about liquidity conditions and freedom to take solvency risk, if the judgment about the liquidity risk happens to go wrong. In other words, there may be some risks in being the lender of last resort and the arrangements should provide for the new authority to bear such risks.

On balance, there is a consensus that such an arrangement of international currency in parallel with national currencies would be a good solution, and the global community should work towards such a solution. However, there is a broad consensus that at the current juncture and for the foreseeable future, it is unlikely that the governments would be willing or capable of coming to an agreement on the institutional arrangements for such an authority to issue a new global currency.

CURRENT SDR BECOMES A GLOBAL CURRENCY

Special Drawing Rights was devised by the IMF as a unit of account based on weighted average of four currencies (US Dollar; Euro; UK Pound and Japanese Yen) that are most widely used in the global monetary system. The weights in the basket are updated annually. SDR is a reserve asset and a unit of account, and not an actual currency that can be used for purchase of goods and services. However, it is possible to conceptualise an SDR-based international monetary system. The advantage of an SDR-based-system is that it provides stability in terms of value because it will be based on a basket of currencies instead of a single currency. It can be aligned better to global needs when compared to one currency linked to the domestic economy of one country. It is in the realm of possibility to design and mobilise policy discipline on select countries concerned whose currency constitute the SDR basket. In any case, there will be no exorbitant privilege exercised by a single issuer of currency. However, there are several negatives in this regard.

The experience so far with use of SDR in global economy has been less than positive. In terms of governmental usage, SDR had limited success so far, and even, and the private sector has not accepted SDR in any noticeable manner. It is, however, possible to make a fresh attempt. Automaticity can be introduced in additional allocations of SDR on a temporary basis to meet contingencies. The currencies to be included in the basket can be expanded to make SDR more acceptable and more diversified. It is possible to design special arrangements for settlement in SDRs. It is also possible to encourage official sector to use the SDR denominated instruments to enable broader acceptance. The government's sovereign borrowing can be designated in SDR through an agreement between countries. The international financial institutions may be persuaded to issue financial instruments designated in SDR. It is possible to consider pegging some currencies to such an SDR, thus providing greater stability to such countries than if they were pegged to one currency. It is possible to make a smooth transition from the existing system to the new system by the mechanism of substitution account which was considered before. The substitution account is a mechanism by which countries can exchange with the IMF current reserve holdings denominated in a reserve currency such as US Dollar for SDRs. The existing institutional arrangement in the form of the IMF, enables pursuit of SDR based-system building on the existing expertise and experiences.

Cooperation of the existing issuer of reserve currency, namely the US, will be critical to acceptance of this proposal. Moreover, the governance arrangements for the institution which issues SDR, namely the IMF, must be made acceptable to major economies so that official use is popularised. Finally, the transition to the SDR-based system requires the unwinding of the current system. Technically a substitution account through which the IMF takes over the exchange risk of reserve currencies from countries holding reserves by substituting their currencies with SDR issued by it could be a route for this purpose. The substitution account, however, will essentially socialise the exchange rate risk. In other words, through a substitution account, the risks of holding the US Dollar reserves in substantial measures by some countries, in particular China, will be spread to the IMF and in turn to all the other member countries. In a way, therefore, it can be argued that the exchange rate risk that was voluntarily assumed by one or few countries in managing their forex reserves is now being spread to other countries who may not have contributed to the current problems in any way. Hence, the process of substitution account which may be necessary for unwinding global imbalances would require global consensus on burden sharing of the legacy problems on account of one dominant international reserve currency.

MULTIPOLAR RESERVE CURRENCIES

A system of multipolar reserve currencies implies that the global economy moves away from excessive dependence on a single reserve currency, namely, the US Dollar. It is argued that the multipolar reserve currency system will diversify the risks. Such a system will distribute the privilege that currently accrues essentially to one country. It also provides some sort of a competition among currencies to provide the services to the global economy as the reserve currency. It can be argued that a multipolar reserve currency system already exists. The official reserves are generally held not only in US Dollars but also in Euro and Yen currencies, though to a limited extent. There are some countries which hold a small part of their reserves in other currencies, such as Australian Dollar, Swiss Franc and the Swedish Kronor.

It is necessary to note that the relative importance of one reserve currency over the others in the global economy depends on several factors. These include deep and liquid financial markets, liquidity in forex markets, wide use by the private sector in trade and trade related financial transactions, credibility about stability of macro policies in the currency of the reserve issuing country, capacity of the economy of the country to absorb shocks, credibility in regard to governance in the country, etc. Further, from a public policy point of view, several issues will have to be resolved if one were to have a really effective multipolar system. All the reserve currency issuing countries will have to accept some policy discipline. Moreover, policy coordination will have to be ensured for minimising exchange rate volatility since volatility between major currencies could impose costs on credit and investment flows. Finally, it is possible that network externalities may drift the system towards mono currency even if there is a policy preference for multiple currencies, and there is no reason why such a mono currency would not be US Dollar. It is not unlikely that a comparison between US Dollar, Euro and Japanese Yen in medium to long-term, on these parameters, will continue to give advantage to the US Dollar to be a primary reserve currency.

In brief there are several conditions to be satisfied for success of the multipolar system. There is a need for a smooth transition for reserve holders in diversifying currency composition. The reserve currencies issuers should accept macro-policy parameters such as those to be agreed in the G-20. The reserve currency issuers have to coordinate their policies to minimise exchange-rate volatility among themselves. There should also be incentives to other economies to emerge as reserve currency issuers, especially among EMEs. It should be possible to consider emergence of currencies which become genuinely internationalised. The aggregate demand for reserves should also be kept reasonably low so that demands on supplies of reserves are not stretched.

REPLACE EXISTING UNIPOLAR CURRENCY WITH SOME OTHER CURRENCY

The most important precondition for a country to be a reserve currency issuer is that the currency concerned should be internationalised. It means basically that such a currency should be a unit of account, a unit of denomination, a unit of payment, and a unit of settlement in international trade and financial transactions. It should thus be used as a medium of exchange and an acceptable unit of account. In addition it should carry credibility as a store of value. One way of assessing these characteristics is to measure the share of a currency in invoicing global trade and finance, financial transactions, bond markets, and forex markets. Currently, the share of US Dollar in forex is around 86 per cent, while in currency reserves, it is about 64 per cent. In regard to its share in bond markets, in bank deposits and in bank loans, it is around 50 per cent. The share of the US in global GDP, however, is about 30 per cent.

Currently in terms of economic strength and all the above characteristics, Euro and Yen could arguably provide a challenge to the US Dollar to replace it. No doubt, the projections of growth in GDP place China's Remnembi ahead of these two economies for the future. However, the share of Remnembi in global trade and transactions is relatively less. China has swap agreements with central banks of Hong Kong, Korea and Argentina, in addition to being a major actor in the Chang Mai Initiative. China has internationalised its currency in terms of trade settlement with Vietnam, Mongolia, Cambodia, Hong Kong, etc.

In addition to the share of the currency in trade and financial sectors to carry credibility as a reserve currency, the financial markets would make an assessment about the fundamental debt sustainability of the relevant economy and in the capacity of the country to withstand shocks and manage risks. In regard to these two fundamental characteristics, the US is in a strong position. The overseas assets of the US as an economy or the value of the global assets owned by the residents of the US relative to others, is very high. The returns on these assets is significant for the US. In other words, the fundamental debt sustainability is impressive in regard to the US. As regards the capacity to carry large risks, it is necessary to assess the claims of the citizens on the economy. In other words, the per capita GDP or per capita income of a country is as relevant as its aggregate GDP, in assessing the capacity to withstand shocks. The US has significant strengths in this regard also.

Replacement of the current US Dollar position by another currency has to address several issues. First, whether such a replacement is desirable, since the problem appears to be the unipolar system rather than the particular issuer of the reserve currency. Second, whether such a replacement is feasible in terms of the relative claims of various currencies to be a dominant global reserve currency. Third, whether there could be regional arrangements that could supplement or supplant the existing unipolar reserve currency.

IMPROVING THE CURRENT NON-SYSTEM

Proposals to improve the current non-system are made in two directions, namely, reducing the demand for international liquidity and reserves, and diversifying as well as increasing the supply of such liquidity in the system. Adequacy of reserves was traditionally assessed in terms of the months of normal imports covered by reserves. With the growth of share of invisibles in the current account, more recently the adequacy was measured in terms of the requirements for payment obligations on account of all current account transactions that also include payments for imports. With the growth in cross border financial flows, the reserve adequacy was measured in terms of aggregate payment obligation over, say a year, without fresh borrowings. With large volatility in commodity prices and capital flows, the vulnerability of a country to shocks was added in assessing adequacy of reserves. Thus, the demand for reserves is essentially governed by the policy preference of individual countries to take precautions against stress on the smooth functioning of forex markets, and on the movements in exchange rates. In brief, demand for reserves due to self insurance or precautionary purposes, is normally on account of three factors, namely, trade shocks or volatility in current account, volatility in capital flows, and limiting exchange rate movements.

It is possible to reduce demand on account of precautionary purposes by several measures. There can be arrangements for surveillance and sharing of information which may provide comfort to various countries. It is possible to impose restrictions on inflows and outflows of capital, thus reducing the level of reserves needed to moderate volatility in exchange rate due to capital mobility. It is also possible to conceive or encourage third-party insurance against shocks. There can be appropriate borrowing arrangements so that the countries concerned need not build reserves or attempt self insurance. These borrowing arrangements on a shared basis may be made at regional level through regional pooling or at the global level. It may be possible to penalise excess demand for forex reserves by international agreement to impose un-remunerated reserve ratios beyond a threshold on reserves. This option would need a global view on adequacy of reserves of individual countries. Taxes on current account surpluses is another option which penalises persistent surpluses in current account while those with deficits could build buffers. It appears unlikely that agreements can be reached at multilateral level on several of these issues.

From the supply side, the availability of resources from the IMF can be enhanced. This can be done in terms of improving the aggregate resources available to the IMF, providing predictability for availability of resources, reliability, and above all, avoiding the stigma while approachig the IMF. There are several proposals under consideration in the IMF. These are broadly described as financial safety nets. They have three components, namely, availability of resources on an automatic basis with no conditionality; semi automatic availability in the sense that the liquidities available are automatic, but the conditionalities are imposed after the commencement of drawing of resources from the IMF; and access with conditionality imposed before the disbursements by the IMF. In other words, in the third option, liquidity will be available only when conditions are satisfied.

There are several ways in which a greater role for SDR as a reserve currency could be attempted. The SDR basket can be diversified further to reflect changing global economic realities along with realignment of weights. The SDR could be a monetary liability of the IMF and national currencies could be valued with reference to SDR. The IMF may have to develop markets denominated in SDRs, with instruments of varying maturities and also ensure cleaning and settlement mechanisms, in addition to promoting use of SDR in global trade and international financial transactions. In brief, if

SDR were to be close to a truly reserve currency, the IMF should be close to being a central bank. In case the issue is treated as one of merely protecting the value of reserve assets held by the central banks, the objective can be achieved by mutual agreement among countries with large holdings of reserves to mimic SDR weights in the currency composition of their reserve assets.

There are three issues in regard to the above arrangements giving primacy to the IMF. First, the governance structure of the IMF still does not command universal confidence. There is still stigma in approaching the IMF. There are, no doubt, encouraging signs of build-up of some trust in the IMF. In brief, the decision making processes relating to expanded use of SDR may have to be significantly different from the prevailing ones. Second, there is still a suspicion that the IMF has certain ideological predilections. However, there are signs of some change in this regard. Third, there may be difficulties in providing support in the quantities needed for some of the countries. For example, the IMF may not be in a position to command resources to supply the needed liquidity if there were to be a problem in a large economy, since the liquidity requirements even for relatively small economies under stress like Greece, are admittedly large.

EURO AREA DEVELOPMENTS

The reaction of financial markets to the unexpectedly large public-debt of Greece, in addition to concerns about the fiscal sustainability of several other Euro area countries has some implications for the future of the international monetary system. First, the Euro was expected to be a principal reserve currency issuer to challenge the pre-eminent position of the US Dollar. However, consequent upon the developments in Greece, Euro's capacity to withstand shocks is currently in some doubt. Second, while the persistent current account and fiscal deficits of the US have been a cause of concern for the external world, the Euro area as a whole has not contributed to global imbalances. Yet, events in Greece have called for a collaborative effort on the part of the ECB and IMF to manage stress on the banking system and financial markets in general. These events could call into question Euro's potential to be a store of valve. Third, the use of Euro currency as a medium of exchange does not seem to have diminished. Fourth, the importance of fiscal coordination and possibly financial sector regulation in any regional currency arrangements has been high-lighted by recent events. Fifth, most issues relating to international monetary system were considered in the context of provision of liquidity for developing countries. The recent events in the Euro area indicate that even with total flexibility in exchange rate regimes, the advanced economies may also need liquidity support under stressful conditions. Sixth, the IMF is collaborating with the ECB in the programme relating to Greece. It sets a precedent for IMF to collaborate with and supplement regional arrangements. Such a precedent is of particular significance for Asia where there are arrangements for regional cooperation, such as the Chang Mai Initiative and surveillance at the regional level. Seventh, there is better appreciation now of difficulties in measuring and enforcing fiscal coordination among countries in the absence of a central fiscal authority. These considerations would set some constraints on the benefits and risks of regional currency arrangements. Eighth, some analysts hold that there could be debt restructuring by Greece at some stage in view of the potentially extreme burden on the people to honour such magnitudes of debt. Arguments are advanced in favour of the banks that contributed to the sovereign debt bearing a part of the burden. These developments raise the broader issue of the need for a properly constituted standing global sovereign debt restructuring mechanism. The current situation encourages irresponsible lending to the sovereign, as evidenced by the events in Greece. Ninth, the nations constituting the Euro area, in particular Germany, have huge stakes in supporting the Euro as part of a broader political commitment to maintain peace within the continent. The resolve to strength the European Union may be reinforced by their pride in the European culture. Further, with the rise of Asia, both the

US and Euro area may see merit in reinforcing each other's strengths in the monetary system of the global economy.

Finally, the experience with the recent crisis in Greece has implications for the debate on the international monetary system. The chances of a global currency seem to recede after the experience of the Euro area in terms of serious difficulties in ensuring surrender of sovereignty especially in the fiscal arena by nations to gain advantages of a currency union. There are obvious difficulties in agreeing upon, measuring and enforcing fiscal coordination, as part of a successful currency union. Further, in view of the recent developments, Euro's capacity to withstand shocks is in some doubt. Thus, Euro's claim to dislodge US Dollar as the pre-eminent reserve currency has been postponed for the present. However, in view of the experience with the unipolar reserve currency, in the context of the crisis, there is merit for the global economy in promoting SDR-based or a multipolar monetary system within which the Euro area could emerge as a critical component. Euro is significantly more of an internationalised currency than Yen and Remnimbi. The global economy, therefore, has a significant stake in supporting the Euro area in its current crisis.

Nineteen

UN Commission on the Global Crisis: Working and Recommendations*

$\mathcal{T}$his chapter is divided into seven sections. The first section gives a background to the UN Commission on the global crisis. The second section narrates the approach adopted by the Commission and the basic principles that governed its deliberations; while the third section details the relevant macroeconomic issues. The fourth, fifth and sixth sections summarise recommendations of the Commission on regulation of the financial sector, reform of international financial institutions and financial innovations. The concluding section gives an assessment of policy actions taken and outlook for the future.

BACKGROUND TO THE COMMISSION

The global crisis became manifest on 16 September 2008 when Lehmann Brothers, a venerable financial institution in the US,

*This chapter is an edited version of Dr Waheeduddin Khan Memorial Lecture 2010, delivered at the Centre for Economic and Social Studies (CESS), Hyderabad, 13 August 2010.

collapsed. This event resulted in a panic in financial markets and has led to the worst worldwide economic calamity in eighty years. Soon after this development, the President of UN General Assembly decided to convene a panel of experts to discuss the implications of the crisis for developing countries in an interactive dialogue with the General Assembly. Subsequently, he decided to appoint an Independent Commission of Experts on Reform of the International Monetary and Financial System.

The mandate of the Commission was to analyse the causes of the crisis, to assess its impact on all countries, to suggest adequate responses to avoid its recurrence and to restore global economic stability. The Commission was headed by Professor Joseph Stiglitz, respected Nobel Laureate in Economics, and eighteen members with Professor Jan Kregal from the US as the Rapporteur. The membership was drawn from developed and developing countries. It had a mix of academics, policymakers and market participants. It had representatives from central banks, governors and the finance ministers of different countries, some serving and some retired. Diversity was ensured by drawing expertise from both large and small countries with appropriate geographical spread. The members participated in their individual and not in any official capacities, and made contributions on an honorary basis. The Commission was established by the President of the General Assembly in November 2008.

The purpose of constituting a Commission of Experts, was to ensure objectivity and forthrightness in the analysis of the causes without being constrained by diplomatic considerations. In suggesting solutions, the Commission had the liberty to broach new ideas without regard to official positions or influential interests, though such ideas may not be translated into policies immediately. The Commission was expected to take a long term view of the issues and set the agenda for the future. In a way, the Commission considered that the processes of the Commission and the policy initiatives in the G-20 (the group of 20 is an informal body of twenty of systemically important countries of the world accounting for about 80 per cent of the World's population, income, trade and wealth) would be complementary and mutually supportive, while providing inputs to the deliberations of the General Assembly of the United Nations. The Commission had its first formal meeting in January 2009, constituted itself into four working groups and provided its inputs to the General Assembly of the UN. A statement by the UN on the World Financial and Economic Crisis, and its Impact on Development adopted in June 2009 reflects, to a large extent, the inputs of the Commission, though it was inevitably a product of compromise and calculated ambiguity.

The report of the Commission remains the most comprehensive and objective account of the global crisis embodying a consensus of experts and expertise drawn from diverse backgrounds. Hence, a study of the report would be of interest to academics, policymakers, and indeed, a large segment of the population which is affected by the crisis.

APPROACH AND BASIC PRINCIPLES

The basic approach of the Commission to the crisis could be summarised as follows:

The crisis is both, a financial crisis and an economic crisis. It has both macroeconomic and microeconomic aspects. The visible failures in the financial sector were, to some extent, a result of underlying macroeconomic problems. These macroeconomic problems include both global imbalances and income inequalities within countries and between countries. The existing global institutions could not anticipate the crisis reflecting the inadequacy of the global institutional framework to respond to the challenges of globalisation. The crisis reflects inadequacies at the global level in both global market and non-market mechanisms that governed globalised finance. In this background, the approach to understanding the crisis as well as identifying the possible solutions should encompass consideration of economic doctrines and economic arrangements, both at the national and global levels.

The basic principles that governed the deliberations of the Commission were an outcome of the above approach. First, consideration had to be given for attaining a balance between market forces and regulation by the government, both at the national and global levels, to manage the crisis and to design the post-crisis arrangements. Second, greater transparency and accountability were required, particularly in undertaking discretionary actions in responding to the crisis to avoid collapse of the financial markets and depression. Third, in taking short-term actions to avoid such a collapse, their consistency with long run solutions must be ensured. For example, actions to bail-out large financial institutions should not result in creating larger financial institutions which could become too big to fail than before. Fourth, all the economic policies undertaken in the context of the crisis have impact on distribution of incomes and the policy actions including bail-out, restructuring and stimulus, should not exacerbate income and wealth inequalities. Similarly, the monetary policy actions should not impact adversely the incomes of large segments of the population who did not gamble on risky securities and invested their resources prudently. Fifth, measures introduced by individual countries to manage the crisis should not result in increasing global imbalances and asymmetries. In a crisis, the developed countries pursue countercyclical policies; but the developing countries may be compelled to pursue pro-cyclical policies in view of limited availability of resources at their disposal reflecting the asymmetrical situations. These considerations warrant global responses to the crisis. Sixth, there should be a careful assessment of the distribution and incidence of risk. For example, an aggressive stimulus policy may increase the risk of inflation, and the impact of inflation will be serious on large sections which have no hedge against inflation. Seventh, policies should recognise that some policy actions are reversible while others may not be easily reversible, and some mistakes may be easy to correct while others are not. The magnitudes of policy interventions are important in the sense that excessive interventions may be counter-productive. Similarly, timeliness is important since it may be easier to dampen inflationary expectations before the onset of hyper inflation. Eighth, the policy choices should fully recognise the importance of diversity of situations in different countries and in the possibilities of alternative approaches to manage similar problems. In other words, policy perspectives cannot rely entirely on economic doctrines, but should take into account the available empirical evidence as well as the institutional context of a country.

Finally, because the crisis is of a global nature, there is a need for a global response. At the same time, the unique problems of developing countries in the context of the crisis should be explicitly recognised in all initiatives for global coordination. The developing countries are disadvantaged for several reasons. The citizens of these countries have low levels of income and hence face acute hardships in coping with a crisis. They do not have social safety nets. Their capacity to borrow from the international financial markets may be constrained in uncertain times. They may be subjected to international obligations such as free trade agreements, bilateral investment treaties and WTO commitments which were designed for normal times, and not for the crisis. Such obligations may further restrain the policy space available to developing countries.

MACRO ECONOMIC ISSUE

There are several macro economic reasons for the crisis. First, there were a set of economic doctrines that governed the financial and economic policies in some countries, especially in advanced economies. This economic doctrine believes that economic agents are always rational and that governments are inherently less informed than economic agents. They hold that markets are efficient and stable with strong ability to absorb shocks while the governments are not motivated by sound economic principles. Second, several policies relating to taxation and expenditures were redesigned with a focus on efficiency, and in the process eliminated social safety nets, thus weakening automatic stabilisers in the society and economy. Further, the public policies allowed consumption to grow more rapidly than incomes in some countries, particularly the US. This had a cumulative effect on inequalities in incomes and wealth, and large indebtedness of households. Thirdly, the process of globalisation itself produced increased volatility in incomes. The process facilitated the movement of capital than of labour, thus contributing to global imbalances. In many ways, there has been a breakdown of social conventions that influenced corporate governance. Fourth, easy monetary policy and widespread use of financial innovations reinforced the ability of households to finance consumption by borrowing while real incomes were somewhat stagnant. Fifth, globalisation brought about volatility in commodity prices and capital flows that affected national policies. Developing economies built forex reserves as self-insurance against such volatilities. Finally, the global integration of economies resulted in the problems that originated in some advanced economies due to which ill-advised policies were transmitted to other economies, in particular the economies of developing countries.

In responding to the crisis from a macroeconomic perspective, it is very clear that fiscal policy in each country will have to play a critical role in enhancing aggregate demand and avoiding depression in economic activity and hardships. However, such actions will have to be taken in a globally coordinated manner so that all countries contribute to crisis management, share the burden, and benefit from the recovery. This process would minimise free rider issues. Second, it is necessary to ensure that there is strong social protection in the fiscal policy response. Social spending components in fiscal responses could not only provide protection, but can be designed to crowd in private investment. Third, monetary policy will have to play a role in providing liquidity, and these have to be coordinated across countries. Fourth, it is evident that conventional monetary policy measures to combat the crisis seem to have been exhausted in several major countries. Fifth, providing more liquidity to financial institutions in such a situation may not lead to expansion of credit, but, in fact, may result in a kind of liquidity trap. Sixth, recourse to conventional and unconventional monetary policies may, therefore, be appropriate, but the more difficult decisions will lie in the future about when and how to retract the liquidity that had been injected to avert a crisis, as normality is restored.

Several aspects of the conduct of monetary and credit policies have also contributed directly to the crisis. First, there was excessive reliance on a particular set of models in the conduct of monetary policy, making unrealistic assumptions concerning rational behaviour. These models ignored key aspects of the economy including the importance of information asymmetries, the diversity of economic agents and the behaviour of banking institutions. It is noteworthy that countries that have judiciously intervened in their foreign exchange and capital markets have fared better than those that did not. Further, the central banks were too focused on inflation, and sometimes ignoring the source of inflation, in addition to being insensitive to the consequences of asset bubbles. In this background, the correctives in future should include redefining of objectives, and recourse to multiple instruments, keeping in view the need for government intervention to influence the future evolution of the structure of the financial sector.

The Commission devoted considerable attention to the considerations that should govern bail-out of financial institutions and markets. It was noted that bail-outs could have been costlier than they might otherwise have been, and they may have been viewed to be very unfair. In a way, the crisis seems to have called for a response involving massive redistribution of wealth from ordinary tax-payers to those who have been bailed-out. Keeping in view these experiences, a set of principles have been evolved to guide the bail-out design.

A major challenge to public policy relates to alleviating the adverse impact on developing countries that may be described as innocent victims. In the context of the crisis, there may be a temptation for advanced economies to take recourse to protectionism which should be avoided. Recognising inadequate sources of funding available to developing countries to undertake aggressive stimulus and countercyclical policies, the Commission urged the countries to increase the resources available to them through global efforts. An innovative proposal has been made by the Commission to create a new credit facility. The new credit facility which could be established under the umbrella of existing institutions could be administered under more representative governance arrangements or through the creation of a new international economic institution. The new funding facilities could finance the needs of developing countries, partly by mobilising funds from countries that have large international non-borrowed reserves.

REFORMING REGULATION OF THE FINANCIAL SECTOR

One of the findings of the Commission was that the last thirty years have seen an undue deference given to financial interests by public policy. Having large and liquid financial markets were seen to be an end in themselves as opposed to a means to an end. Given this framework, policies were promoted to unfetter financial markets without adequate regard to the dangers of unregulated finance. Thus, strategies to push towards complete capital mobility, limiting public intervention in financial intermediation, and weakening of previously existing prudential norms were promoted. The result of these changes in regulation was to sharply compromise stability in many countries and in the global system as a whole. Arguments in favour of such deregulation were, in fact, being made at the same time when policies to fully integrate their financial systems with the global economy were being promoted.

The Commission recognised reasons to implement good regulations of financial markets, and two of them are paramount. First, regulations are necessary to protect consumers and investors who are considered unsophisticated and whose savings are in the custody of the financial system. Second, when financial firms fail, the fallout effects are very serious, as it can severely limit trust and confidence among economic agents. There will be attempts to evade regulations, but such attempts should not be the basis for doing away with appropriate and effective regulations. Equally important is the fact that regulations should be made to direct the function of the financial system and not financial institutions per se, that is, it should not matter if an entity is not called a bank, but is acting like a bank; it should be regulated in accordance with rule made for a bank. Similarly, there may be a need to regulate players like credit rating agencies, which are not financial intermediaries.

The report highlights the need to enhance the prevalent micro-prudential regulation. This refers to policies which are aimed at affecting the incentives and behaviour of individual firms and participants. Implementing a set of policies which enhance transparency by making information reporting mandatory and clear, and which limit excessive complexity in financial products (as will be defined by the regulator) is essential. Further, during the crisis, the incentives given to financial institutions were not aligned with the interests of the society or of their own firms. Incentive payments encouraged short-term strategies and prevented the actual aligning of personal reward with long-term stability and growth. When things were going up, financial executives prospered. When things went down, they were not punished to the degree they were rewarded. It is, therefore, necessary to redesign the financial compensation structure. Further, the commission mooted the idea of a consumer financial protection agency that can regulate the newly invented financial products. While financial innovations can be a positive, some instruments such as credit default swaps, despite their origins as risk spreading devices, have increased the amount of risk in the system and made the resolution of the crisis very difficult. Hence, there should be adequate regulatory safeguards in regard to their trading.

Macro-prudential regulation refers to policies that are focused on key components of 'systemic' risk. This refers to the risk inherent in the system when financial entities are borrowing and lending in large amounts. Thus, for example, the commission identified certain key issues, such as, setting the appropriate degree of debt to equity of large financial firms, the ways in which to limit the adverse impacts emanating from the failure of large interconnected institutions, and ways in which to limit the damage to stability from unregulated credit instruments.

As financial markets become global, it is imperative to have global coordination of regulation. The Commission highlighted the importance of avoiding race to the bottom and national focus, except where international coordination is essential. In particular, the Commission recommended strengthening host country regulation where there are cross-border operations. As far as the developing economies are concerned, the commission noted that there is a needs to serious rethink the value of capital account management as opposed to capital account liberalisation. The active management of capital flows is important for countries in their attempts to encourage desirable investment and financing arrangements, to expand the scope of policy autonomy, and to maintain stable and competitive exchange rates and other social goals.

Observations of the Commission on regulatory institutions are noteworthy. First, regulatory institutions have to be created with the recognition of the risks of capture by the interests and perspectives of those being regulated. Users of finance, such as consumers, small businesses, pensioners, etc. should be given a voice. Second, regulatory design needs to be able to resist attempts by the industry to influence regulators and to divert them from their core responsibilities, namely, consumer and investor protection and systematic stability. Third, the battle between the regulator and the regulated might seem to be unfair from the start, if the regulatory bodies are not in a position to attract and retain talented persons with appropriate compensation structures. The Commission advocates a financial sector tax to fund the regulatory bodies. Fourth, on the regulatory structure, the Commission conceded that there is no single model appropriate for all countries. However, a possible structure involving two apex bodies—one focussing on macro-issues in the form of a New Central Bank and the other on micro-issues in the form of a Financial Regulatory Authority is given as an illustration.

A well functioning financial market requires, in addition to financial sector regulation, accompanying sound arrangements, such as competition policy, bankruptcy procedures and corporate governance. The Commission advocated a financial policy that devotes attention to such concomitants for well-functioning financial markets, and in addition gives priority to ensuring credit for all, and in particular, the provision of credit for long-term development. Expanding lending to productive purposes should, therefore, be a part of financial policy thus broadly defined, and this aspect may be of special significance to developing countries.

INTERNATIONAL FINANCIAL INSTITUTIONS: REFORMS AND CREATION

The experience with the crisis demonstrates the inadequacy of the existing arrangements relating to international financial institutions. This calls for a review of their mandate, their governance structures, and the philosophies underlying their policies and operations. The IMF and World Bank are two of the most important institutions relevant to the financial crisis. The IMF in particular is in-charge of macroeconomic surveillance. However, the IMF did not provide early warnings about the impending crisis (though it flagged the issue of economic imbalances, it had misread the financial stability conditions) unlike the publications of the UN system, such as *World Economic Situation and Prospects*, and the *Trade and Development Report*. Surveillance of the IMF has not been even handed in the sense that the surveillance over systemically important countries has been very weak, and not demonstrably independent. The governance structure is skewed in favour of the US and European countries, with a disproportionate share in ownership and representation on the board. The developing countries as a group have seen reduction in their shares since their establishment. The heads of these institutions are not selected on the basis of merit. Further, the IMF in its policies has been captured by particular ideology which believed in efficiency of the markets, and unfettered globalisation of finance. In addition, the IMF does not have adequate resources to cater to the requirements of developing countries under stress. The Commission made recommendations for correction of these infirmities. In particular, there is a proposal to create a new credit facility to be administered under a special governance arrangement. Such a facility would benefit developing countries, and would also draw savings from emerging markets. These funds could be used beyond the limits of investment and may help in managing crisis of magnitude as the present one. The FSB which is an extension of the FSF is also commented upon. The Commission recommended that the FSB should be made more representative and more accountable.

In addition to the review of the existing institutions, two new institutions are proposed by the Commission. The existing system of international economic governance had relied on two basic principles, namely, specialisation and coordination. The specialised agencies include the World Bank, IMF and WTO. They were complemented by other agencies of the UN system such as the FAO, UNESCO, UNDP, etc. The overall coordination of UN activities concerned with economic, social and ecological affairs was to be entrusted to the Economic and Social Council—one of the UN system's main organ. The G-7 and G-20 are informal groupings which exclude a large number of countries, since the world consists of 192 countries. In order to fill the gap, the Commission makes recommendation for the creation of two institutions, namely, International Panel of Experts and Global Economic Coordination Council. The International Panel of Experts is meant to be an immediate step entrusted with the assessment and monitoring of both short-term and long-term systemic risks. The panel could serve as an internationally recognised source of expertise in support of better coherence and effectiveness in the global governance system. The panel would also be able to identify lacunae and deficiencies in the current global economic system, especially in the system of global economic governance. While its analysis would focus on economic issues, it would also take into account the social and ecological dimensions of economic trends and policies, keeping in view the long-term developmental implications.

A Global Economic Coordination Council is also recommended to be established in the longer term at a level equivalent to the UN General Assembly and the Security Council. The Council would have a mandate over the UN system in the economic, social and environmental fields, which would include all specialised institutions. It will also have the benefit of support of the International Panel of Experts.

INTERNATIONAL FINANCIAL INNOVATIONS

The Commission, after reviewing the current financial institutions, suggested several financial innovations. Of these, four are significant, namely, a global reserve system, a sovereign debt default and restructuring mechanism; innovative risk management structures, and innovative sources of financing global public goods.

Currently, the US Dollar performs function of the dominant international reserve currency. Simply stated, many countries hold a very large part of their foreign exchange reserves in US Dollar dominated assets. There is an inherent problem with a national currency operating as an international reserve currency. The extent of liquidity required for the global economy may not always be equal to the extent of liquidity that is generated by a national currency for use in the global economy. For example, if the demand for global reserves is very high, supply of reserves is possible only if there is a corresponding deficit in the US current account. Further, if the global demand for such reserves increases significantly, and the country, say the US, supplies such currency in abundance, there is a risk that the value of US Dollar will be under threat since supply of such reserves also means addition to external liabilities of the country. At the same time, being a reserve currency provides an exorbitant privilege to the reserve currency issuer since the country could mobilise debt in its own currency more easily than any other. The system is also inequitable since the poorer developing countries are transferring resources to the richer developed countries that issue the reserve currencies when they build forex reserves as an insurance against volatility in current account receipts and capital flows. The reserve currency issuing country may also be affected because their exchange rates are influenced by the actions of the reserve holding economies. Encouragement of a multipolar reserve currencies is possible, and it may provide benefits of diversification of risks in changes in value of reserve currencies, but as long as the link between some countries reserve currencies and the global currency system remains, many of the inherent problems of reconciling national interests of issuers of reserve currencies and needs of global economy persist. In this light, there has been a demand for consideration of instituting a new global reserve currency.

The Commission makes a recommendation for a new currency called International Currency Certificates which could be SDRs. The working of this arrangement requires acceptance by the countries of such a currency and freedom to the authority issuing the currency to vary quantities. The Commission also makes a detailed recommendation for transition from the existing non-system to a new system. In particular, the Commission indicates that the existing regional agreements such as the Chang Mai Initiative may also provide a way of evolving towards a global reserve system.

The sovereign debt crises have been a major source of difficulties faced by developing countries. The social costs of these crises have been large. Currently, there is no system of formal debt restructuring, and the only recourse is to approach the IMF or go through disorderly debt restructuring. There have been several cases of disorderly restructuring in the recent past, including Argentina. The Heavily Indebted Poor Countries' Debt Initiative and Multi Lateral Debt Relief Initiative are only partial and ad hoc. The Commission recommended the establishment of an International Debt

Restructuring Court, similar to the National Bankruptcy Courts. The recommendation for such a court could moderate irresponsible lending by financial markets to sovereign, which currently extends to odious debt. The proposals also contain assistance to developing countries in more prudent and sustainable management of that debt.

The third set of proposals relates to innovative risk management structures which are essentially market based. These include GDP and commodity linked bonds. The fourth set of proposals relates to innovative source of financing for provision of global and regional public goods, such as health programmes, combating climate change and sustaining global environment more generally. The sources of finance are taxes, insistence on payment for use of environment and public-private collaboration.

Outlook and Assessment

The global crisis has erupted in 2008 is a testimony to the failure of economic policies and institutions. But the response of public policies in avoiding a collapse of financial markets has been praiseworthy. However, almost two years after the manifestation of the crisis and uneven economic recovery that has been observed recently, the outlook for the global economy is unclear. The intellectual frameworks that would govern the future as well as the institutional structures that would be in place are at best still evolving. The report of the UN Commission provides a good reference for assessing the current status of efforts to create new sets of policies and institutions for a better global economic order.

There is a recognition in intellectual and policy circles that the causes of the crisis, and hence the cures, go beyond the financial sector. While role of state was critical in averting a disaster from the crisis, the underlying dominant philosophy now is that state intervention should be for emergencies and for exceptional reasons. The approach to public ownership of enterprises (including those in the financial sector) is somewhat similar, despite the example of successful China where public ownership continues to dominate. There is an agreement that there is a trade-off between immediate actions to avert the collapse and stimulate the economy, and long-run compulsions of correcting macroeconomic imbalances, deleveraging the balance sheets of households and the financial sector, and ensuring price stability. There is, however, a serious difference of opinion on optimal balance in these matters.

The importance of lesser inequalities as a stabilising force in economies has not been recognised. The stimulus in many countries has not been sensitive to the redistributive aspects of the stimulus. While the coordination of global policies was impressive in bail-out operations and stimulus packages, legitimate differences among different countries have come to the fore in matters relating to exit from coordinated stimulus packages.

Currently, the governments which were the rescuers of the financial sector that was crumbling are severely constrained in persisting with fiscal stimulus, in view of their dependence on the rescued financial sector to finance their public debt. Increasing popular support in advanced economies for a tax in financial sector is partly on account of this paradox.

The divisions between developed and developing countries are less clear now than before due to two reasons. The EMEs are leading the revival of the global economy and indicating robust growth prospects over the medium to long term. Further, developments in the Euro area, in particular Greece, and the involvement of assistance from the IMF in Greece, also exposed the potential for vulnerability in advanced economies.

Macro policies addressing short-term issues have been largely successful, but the quality of fiscal stimulus, in some cases, is in doubt. Similarly, while monetary policy has been effective in averting the crisis, pickup in credit is uncertain and fears of liquidity trap are looming large in some advanced economies. At the same time, inflationary pressures and threats of asset bubbles are evident in some EMEs.

Resources for the IMF and World Bank have been expanded, with some support from China and India, and they are playing a pro-active role in advising on the management of the crisis globally and assisting some needy countries. Though emerging economies contributed to the additionality of resources, the IMF supported programmes have been designed and are being implemented under the existing flawed governance arrangements and not on the lines of the New Credit Facility proposed by the Commission.

There is a better appreciation of the need to adopt multiple objectives, including financial stability, and monitor multiple indicators, including asset prices. Counter-cyclical policies are being supported, but it is doubtful whether such a support would be forthcoming if a tightening phase of monetary policy is intensified. Similarly, the intellectual commitment to adoption of macro-prudential regulation of the financial sector is yet to be tested in the upward phase of the trade cycle. There is an agreement on contours of prudential regulation, but the emphasis is on stability without adequate recognition of developmental dimensions involved in economies undergoing structural transformation.

There are serious differences on the extent of tightening of micro-prudential regulation among different stake-holders and among countries. But there is a broad agreement on the desirability of enhancing quantity and quality of capital base, restraining excessive risk taking, differentiating systemically important institutions, and regulating financial innovations as well as some non-banks. The proposals under consideration in the FSB include some of the UN commission recommendations. For example, there are much more reasonable capital standards being pushed forward and there are now countercyclical capital buffers that are required. This will certainly enhance the stability of the global economy, even if it reduces some arbitrage options and potential for large gambles for banks. In some countries, for example in the US, financial reforms have been undertaken which reflect some features of the Commission's proposals. This includes the strong presumption that derivatives be placed on exchanges rather than OTC and that there is strong consumer protection in the laws of the land. While in terms of acceptance in principle and formal approaches the proposals are consistent with recommendations of the UN Commission, there is a dilution through detail and stretched time table. It is not clear whether the public policy in some countries is still subject to some elements of capture by participants in the financial markets.

There has been no attention to the creation of new institutions to improve the GFA. However the G-20, that was formed in response to the Asian crisis, has been elevated to the position of a fourth pillar of economic governance, though it does not have a formal official status like the other three, namely, the IMF, World Bank and WTO. The operating arm of the G-20 continues to be the IMF. While the G-20 played a positive role in coordinating the global response to the crisis and in avoiding collapse or depression, recent experiences in regard to coordination of exit policies is ambiguous. It has the potential to evolve as an important body, but the non-G-20 nations numbering 172, do question its legitimacy, representative nature and accountability as a global body. The FSB is an expanded and empowered version of the FSF to include all members of the G-20 and is formally mandated to evolve global standards for financial sector regulation.

The role of the IMF in surveillance has been strengthened and marginal changes in governance are contemplated. However, there are signs that the IMF is reviewing its ideological positions while philosophy governing its operations and policies is tending to be less dogmatic, but not yet sufficiently open to a possible new paradigm. The IMF's role in surveillance has been strengthened and there is an attempt from within the IMF to make it less uneven handed. There is an unstated sense of urgency in reforming the International Monetary System. China has expressed its discomfort with the current status of US Dollar being the dominant reserve currency. The US itself has reasons to be concerned at the constraints imposed by its current status on the conduct of domestic policy. It is extremely difficult to design a global monetary authority that could issue a global currency. Replacing unipolar reserve currency with multi-polar reserve currencies does not break the undesirable link between national currency and global currency.

Resolution of the issue of reserve currency and mechanisms for enforcing fiscal coordination among countries are the two most critical elements for a less unstable process of globalisation of economies.

Twenty

G-20 Framework: Review and Prospects*

$\mathcal{T}$he first section of the chapter narrates the origin and evolution of the G-20. The second section reviews its contribution, while the third provides an assessment of and prospects for G-20. The fourth section mentions possible approaches to reforms of the International Financial Architecture. The concluding part elaborates on the new realities that the G-20 should take note of, and makes a brief reference to the importance of India in the process.

ORIGIN AND EVOLUTION OF G-20

The G-20 finance ministers and central bank governors was established in 1999 to bring together systemically important industrialised and developing economies to discuss key issues in the global economy. The inaugural meeting of the G-20 took place in Berlin on 15–16 December 1999, hosted by German and Canadian finance ministers. The G-20 is made up of the finance ministers and

---

* This chapter is an edited version of the paper presented at the Round Table on Global Economic Crisis and the Asia-Pacific Region: Sustaining Asian Dynamism in a Post-Crisis Worlds, organised by UNESCAP and Club de Madrid, Bangkok, 18 August 2010.

central bank governors of nineteen countries (since 2008 the G-20 is being held at the Summit level as well, in response to the global financial crisis). These are:

- Argentina, Australia, Brazil, Canada, China, France, Germany, India, Indonesia, Italy, Japan, Mexico, Russia, Saudi Arabia, South Africa, Republic of Korea, Turkey, UK, US of America.

The European Union, which is represented by the rotating Council presidency and the ECB, is the twentieth member of the G-20. To ensure that global economic fora and institutions work together, the Managing Director of the IMF and the President of the World Bank, plus the chairs of the International Monetary and Financial Committee and Development Committee of the IMF and the World Bank also participate in G-20 meetings on an ex-officio basis. In response to the criticism that it is not inclusive enough, each G-20 Summit now has up to five special invitees to improve outreach, namely Spain, and a representative each from Asia and Africa. The G-20 thus brings together important industrial and emerging-market countries from all regions of the world. Together, member countries represent around 90 per cent of the global gross national product, 80 per cent of world trade (including EU intra-trade), as well as two-thirds of the world's population. The G-20's economic weight and broad membership gives it a high degree of legitimacy and influence over the management of the global economy and financial system.

Unlike international institutions such as the OECD, the IMF or the World Bank, the G-20 (like the G7/G8) has no permanent staff of its own. The G-20 chair rotates between members, and is selected from a different regional grouping of countries each year. In 2010, the G-20 chair is the Republic of Korea, and in 2011 it will be France. The chair is part of a revolving three-member management Troika of past, present and future chairs. The incumbent chair establishes a temporary secretariat for the duration of its term, which coordinates the group's work and organises its meetings. The role of the Troika is to ensure continuity in the G-20's work and management across the host years.

It is normal practice for the G-20 finance ministers and central bank governors to meet once a year. The ministers' and governors' meeting is usually preceded by deputies' meetings and extensive technical work. This technical work takes the form of working groups, expert groups, workshops, reports and case studies on specific subjects that aim to provide ministers and governors with contemporary analysis and insights, in order to better inform their consideration of policy challenges and options.

The country currently chairing the G-20 posts details of the group's agenda, meetings and work programme on a dedicated website. Although participation in the meetings is reserved for members, the public is informed about what was discussed and agreed upon immediately after the meeting of ministers and governors has ended. After each such meeting, the G-20 publishes a communiqué which records the agreements reached and measures outlined. Material on the forward work programme is also made public.

Till the Asian crisis, the unstated global economic order had been that G-7/G-8 countries (Canada, France, the US, UK, Germany, Japan, Italy and Russia) constituted the centre and the rest of the world was essentially the periphery, which would have to adjust its economies to what happened in G-7/G-8. The Asian crisis made it clear that the impact was not necessarily one-way, and there may be occasions when there can be a transmission of risks from developing countries to G-7/G-8. However, there was a fundamental assumption that the ideologies, codes of practices based on the ideologies, and standards of governance and transparency of G-7/G-8 should be adopted by all countries, and that such an approach would reduce the risks to global economy. The FSF was thus created with membership of advanced economies and a few international financial centres, but it did not include large economies like India or China. In a way, perhaps as an afterthought, this lacuna was filled by the creation of G-20, which was expected to take a broader view of the inter-related aspects of global economy.

The G-20 meetings, which were somewhat ad hoc in the beginning, were formalized through the G-20 Policy Manual in December 2006. From 1999 till 2008, G-20 was essentially a discussion forum which ended in the issue of a communiqué. During this period, several events led to a situation when the resources of the IMF were not in demand, and some questioned the continued relevance of the IMF. The global economy seemed to be running in an impressive fashion without relevance to the active involvement of the G-20 or FSF or IMF. However, G-7/G-8 continued to have its premier role, although select representatives of important EMEs were invited to the meetings for essentially non-substantive events. There were, no doubt, some concerns about the persistent global economic imbalances, with the main focus on the deficits of the US and the surpluses of China.

The financial crisis of 2008 came as a rude shock to the global community, in particular to the advanced economies. First, the centre (G-7/G-8) became the origin of the crisis. Second, the periphery (developing countries) became innocent victims, but was less affected. Third, the financial crisis was spilling over into serious economic and, possibly, a social crisis. It was clear that the crisis in 2008 was essentially global in nature, and the policy responses had to be globally coordinated. These events led to the initiation of Summit Meetings of the G-20 in November 2008 in Washington DC, with the US and UK taking a lead in the process. Since then, there have been Summit Meetings at the level of heads of states or of governments. In the context of the management of the crisis and creating a post-crisis world that would be more secure and stable than before, G-20 evolved as the most important economic policy forum in the world. It has been formally declared by G-20 leaders as the premier international forum for global economic cooperation. It has also been described as the fourth pillar of global economic governance, the other three being the IMF, World Bank and WTOs.

REVIEW OF THE CONTRIBUTION OF G-20

The work of G-20 has been noteworthy after the global financial crisis. First, G-20 provided a forum for discussing the global financial crisis of 2008, and the necessary measures to be taken to avoid a collapse of the financial systems and the onset of deflationary tendencies and possible depression. There was a broad agreement on the policy measures to be taken on an immediate basis by different countries to stimulate the depression-threatened economies and avoid protectionist measures. Undoubtedly all the actions have been at the national level, but broad contours were agreed upon and monitored in G-20. There was a broad consensus in the G-20 Toronto Summit declaration of 26–27 June 2010 that these efforts have borne 'good results'. Unprecedented and globally coordinated fiscal and monetary stimulus has helped in restoring some private demand and lending, and thus avoiding depression in the global economy.

Second, at the recent meeting in June 2010, the exit from extraordinary stimulus measures was considered. It has not been possible to arrive at similar agreements on specific coordinated actions in the G-20 for exit. However, it was recognised that follow-up on existing stimulus plans may involve the continuation of stimulus in some countries, and the initiation of exit policies in some others. In any case, there was a broad agreement that fiscal sustainability was important to all countries. In brief, there has been some disappointment at a lack of agreement on globally coordinated actions, but there has been some comfort that fiscal sustainability as well as diversity in the economic conditions of different countries has been recognised.

Third, a framework for strong sustainable and balanced growth was agreed among G-20 countries. This essentially provides a broad agreement on what appears to be specific appropriate policy parameters for macro-economic management in each country, consistent with the needs of a globalised economy. It was also agreed that there should be a process of mutual assessment of relevant national-level economic policies in relation to the agreed framework. In Toronto, there was an agreement that the second stage of country-led and consultative mutual assessment would be conducted at the country and European level. It was also agreed that additional measures, as necessary, would be identified to achieve strong sustainable and balanced growth. It is significant that there is some agreement (i) on the best practices; (ii) on peer pressure through monitoring; and (iii) on the need for changes in the measures appropriate for each country to meet evolving situations.

Fourth, there has been a continuous focus on financial-sector reform. The reform agenda was admittedly based on four pillars, namely, strong regulatory framework; effective supervision; resolution and addressing systemic institutions; and transparent international assessment and peer review. The work of G-20 on these issues has been virtually outsourced to a newly established institution, namely, the FSB. It may be noted that a considerable convergence has been obtained in the country-representation between G-20 and the newly created FSB. Members of G-20, such as China, India and Indonesia, which were not members of the FSF, are now part of FSB. Some countries in G-20 have in the meantime initiated measures related to regulatory structures, macro and micro-prudential requirements, and incentive mechanisms. Much of the corrective actions under consideration have so far been directed at rolling back excessive deregulation, and the actions at the national level have mainly been in advanced economies where the financial sector has been severely affected. The US, UK and other European countries continue to dominate the thinking process on the regulation of the financial sector, and there are genuine apprehensions that the financial markets would exert a commanding influence on the outcomes. Currently there are three, somewhat contentious, issues in G-20, namely, the time span over which the new regulatory regime would come into effect, the treatment of systemically important financial institutions, and taxes on the financial sector.

Fifth, the reforms of international financial institutions have been on the agenda, both for meeting the immediate requirements of managing the crisis and for strengthening the International Financial Architecture. To that end, additional resources were made available to the IMF and multilateral development banks on the basis of indications given by the G-20. There has also been an agreement on the review of quota and enhancement of voice for developing countries. The G-20 maintains that it is committed to reforming the mandates and governance in the international financial institutions to reflect changes in the world economy and the new challenges of globalisation.

Even-handed, candid and independent IMF surveillance is emphasised by G-20, and the IMF is being encouraged to strengthen its bilateral and multilateral surveillance, including macro-financial linkages. The IMF is also being encouraged to work on important subjects, such as the International Monetary System and the scope for tax of the financial sector. In addition, the Finance Ministers and Central Bank Governors have agreed to prepare policy options on sound incentives to strengthen global financial safety nets.

Finally, broader developmental aspects such as financial inclusion, financing for small and medium industries, elimination of fossil fuel subsidies, and anti-corruption have also been on the agenda of G-20. Attention has been paid to the issue of tax havens and the scope for global taxes on the financial sector, but there is a lack of agreement on specific measures.

ASSESSMENT AND PROSPECTS FOR G-20

The G-20 has been welcomed by the global community for several reasons. There is a better representation of EMEs and a better reflection of changing economic realities at the global level. The group is fairly representative, covering about 80 per cent of population income, trade, investment, etc. Though it has not formally replaced G-7/G-8, it is increasing in its importance in providing a forum for agreement on cooperative actions in multilateral institutions, and coordinated policies at the national level consistent with the needs of an increasingly globalising economy. With the participation of chairs of International Money and Finance Committee and Development Committees in the meetings, there is effective representation of global bodies to assume a high level of coordination on matters relating to global economic governance.

There have also been several criticisms of the G-20 framework. It has been argued that G-20 cannot claim to represent all 192 countries that are members of the United Nations. It has no formal legitimacy in the sense that there is no law or treaty backing the G-20. In fact, they indicate that G-20 is an extra-constitutional authority operating like a cartel of powerful suppliers of what they consider global economic goods. Its operating arms, especially in the IMF, are admittedly suffering from flawed governance. Hence, its policies are likely to continue to suffer from credibility. There is a compulsion for communication at the end of every Summit, and hence the pressure is on agreement and transparency rather than problem-solving and structural transformation. The G-20 has been vague and circumspect in taking substantive initiatives on fundamental issues such as the international monetary system or coordinating exit policies, while it has been expanding its scope beyond the financial sector. Finally, it is argued that it is inappropriate to give the status of a fourth pillar to G-20 since the IMF, World Bank and WTO are products of international legal agreements with broad representation, formal governance structures, some accountability, and a permanent secretariat.

Against this background, the way forward for G-20 may take one or more of three possible directions. First, G-20 may emerge as the most important global forum on a continuous basis. However, it should be recognised that as long as the operating arms of the G-20 continue to be the institutions with deficit in governance and a bias in ideology, it will be difficult for G-20 to continue to be effective beyond the crisis period. However, the record of performance so far indicates that G-20 could emerge as a pillar of global economic governance. Second, as the impression of normality is restored, the process of G-20 may be diluted to revert to status-quo ante, and thus make G-20 virtually non-functional. This has happened before. Third, G-20 may continue in its present form during and beyond the crisis, but may be effectively used in the future to undermine the legitimate processes of WTO and the United Nations.

Agenda for Reform of International Financial Architecture

There are two possible approaches to the reform of International Financial Architecture, namely, a narrow or an operations-oriented approach, and a fundamental or strategic approach. A narrow approach would focus on the lacunae that might have been responsible for the crisis in 2008. The second could be a fundamental approach that addresses basic structural problems that tend to create instability and inequity in the global economy.

A narrow approach accords importance to the surveillance of systemic risks, both at the national and the global level in the context of existing institutional structures. It also focuses on the importance of coordination of macro-economic policies at the national or regional levels to avoid systemic risks to the global economy. Further emphasis would be on deficiencies in the standards of financial regulation at the national level and cross-border arrangements with regard to regulation. Finally, it would seek to make available appropriate liquidity for the global economy, particularly whenever external adjustments are needed by countries suffering from short-term liquidity strains. It may be observed that a large part of the initiatives in the G-20 agenda essentially reflect immediate priorities on operations-oriented lines, although good intentions are expressed in communiqués on some strategic aspects. It is not improbable that there is a deliberate choice in G-20 in favour of front-loading of the consideration of operational issues and back-loading of the consideration of strategic issues as a more practical sequencing of reforms.

A fundamental or a strategic view taken on International Financial Architecture may have to address five important issues. First, there is a need to agree upon an international monetary system that avoids exorbitant privilege to one or a few reserve currency issuing countries, and severe disadvantages to EMEs and developing countries with current account deficits. Second, there is a need to agree upon the mechanisms by which transition to a more viable international monetary system from the current non-system can be brought about. Such mechanisms have significant technical and political implications, in addition to the acceptability to global markets.

Third, the adequacy of all relevant existing global institutions should be considered in a comprehensive manner, in terms of mandate, governance and policies. These include not only the IMF and the World Bank, but also Credit Rating Agencies, the International Accounting and Standards Board, etc. More importantly, it may be necessary to consider the creation of new institutions to fill up the gaps, in particular to establish sovereign debt restructuring mechanisms. The existing practice of disorderly sovereign debt restructuring (except under the HIPC initiative) is costly and encourages, on occasion, irresponsible lending by the financial markets to the sovereigns.

Fourth, an international coordination of fiscal regimes would be critical for obtaining benefits from and minimising the costs of truly globalised economies. The recent events in Greece indicate the link between fiscal position, monetary independence and the functioning of the financial markets, including regulation.

Finally, in addition to national-level and global institutions relevant to global finance, regional-level arrangements such as the Chang Mai Initiative are now a reality. These arrangements are still evolving, and hence they continue to provide a central role to the IMF for macro-economic assessment. Over time, the relationship between regional arrangements and the IMF will necessarily be redesigned. The global system as it evolves should be rendering greater clarity and importance to the role of regional arrangements in the global economic order. In other words, the International Financial Architecture should encompass institutions and policies at national, regional and global levels. For example, financial safety nets may be enabled at all three levels, with greater emphasis on the national level for larger economies.

SOME PERSPECTIVES—NEW REALITIES

The G-20 has been playing an extremely important role in moderating the impact of the crisis through the global coordination of policies. Second, G-20 has been playing an active role in encouraging more responsible macro-economic policies through peer pressure. This includes the coordination of exit policies in the short run, fiscal sustainability in the medium to the long term, and prudent macro-policies in general. Third, G-20 has been emphasising reforms in the regulation of the financial sector with a focus on enhancing stability, combined with some recognition of developmental objectives in policies relating to the financial sector. Fourth, efforts are being made to strengthen the existing multilateral institutions, in particular the IMF, and multilateral development banks. Finally, G-20 remains an informal body which promotes discussion and an agreement on appropriate actions at the national level, and possibly coordination in multilateral organisations. A good record of performance so far has been, by and large, in the context of the current crisis, but its usefulness so far provides hope for building on the experience to bring about fundamental changes in the International Financial Architecture. More importantly, there is no credible alternative mechanism on the horizon to take up the task of considering fundamental changes in the International Financial Architecture.

In considering a strategic approach to changes in the global economic order, however, G-20 is yet to take cognisable initiatives. In this regard, some new realities are worth noting. First, EMEs, and in particular Asian economies, are critical to bringing about any change in the current state of economic balances or imbalances. Asia accounts for a large part of forex reserves. The EMEs, in particular Asia, have demonstrated a potential for strong economic growth and stability, and an increasing share in world output and economic activity. In brief, therefore, any agenda for fundamental changes in International Financial Architecture can be designed and implemented only with the active involvement of EMEs, especially from Asia. Intellectual inputs to resolve these complex problems will have to come increasingly from the dominant EMEs, especially Asia. The dominant paradigms of the economic order are yet to be related fully to the successful experience of Asia.

Second, the G-3 countries, namely, the US, Europe and Japan, who have been playing a dominant role in global money and finance, will continue to do so, but they have been exhibiting some weaknesses which cannot be easily overcome in the very near future. The US has persistent current account and fiscal deficits. The European Union is grappling with the problems of fiscal coordination and asymmetrical levels of productivity and resilience among the nations. Japan continues to disappoint expectations concerning the revival of growth. Significant changes in their macro-economic policy frameworks would be essential for a suitable and sustainable global economic recovery. A review of the appropriateness of some of the fundamental premises of the policies of G-3 so far should not be ruled out, both in the interest of each G-3 country and the global economy. Managing public debt and avoiding excess volatility in the movements exchange rate in the future are critical to a stable global economy. The EMEs, especially Asia, may consider taking initiatives on these issues and help set the agenda for reform.

Third, the role of regional arrangements in the reform of international financial architecture is evolving. The IMF's participation in the bailout of Greece sets an interesting precedent. Similarly, the participation of EU in the G-20 is yet another precedent. Several agreements of cooperation at the regional level are still evolving, and their participation in global forums is unclear.

Fourth, in seeking global economic coordination and global common policies and standards, the importance of diversity should be recognised. Diversity goes beyond the application of a standard approach to the country context and implies possibilities of alternate approaches or divergent assumptions for economic management. It is possible to imagine the damage that could have been inflicted on Asia if, during the recent decade, a global standard of monetary policy and regulation following the dominant Anglo-Saxon model had been imposed on all countries in the belief that global coordination warrants such common policy responses. In a sense, there is a trade-off between diversity and regulatory arbitrage. The current debate within the G-20 is focused almost exclusively on the latter without recognising the significance of the systemic importance of diversity. In addition, the current approach seems to ignore the importance of mechanisms at the national level, similar to voltage stabilisers and circuit breakers in energy networks.

Fifth, the balance between finance ministers and central bank governors has been rightly tilted in favour of ministers in view of the compulsions of crisis management. Exit strategies should perhaps include a reconsideration of the relative roles of heads of governments, ministers and central bank governors to be consistent with normal times.

Sixth, EMEs have been co-opted to the global governance arrangements at an informal level through G-20. The extent of their participation, their effectiveness and their contribution are yet to be demonstrated in a convincing manner. The EMEs would be doing themselves and the global economy a disservice if they remain content with symbolic equality with advanced economies. In particular China, India, Brazil, Russia, South Africa and Indonesia have experimented with several models of economic management in a reasonably successful manner, and they should be able to bring to the G-20 table their experiences, perspectives and vision on rebalancing between the state and the market, between national policies and the global order; and between growth and equity, which is underway at intellectual, policy and operational levels.

Finally, it is useful to recognise that India is a low-income country in the G-20. It has large segments of population below the poverty line. Its share in global trade, or global finance, is among the lowest in the G-20 countries. However, India has a unique position for other reasons. India has not contributed in any way to global imbalance. In the pursuit of its economic policies, particularly financial policies, it did not take extreme ideological positions. It has huge prospects for growth in the future. The overall governance structures in the management of the economy are essentially participative. These intangibles give India a position of respectability and credibility, and therefore influence. However, such influence is most effective only if it is exercised to either introduce new ideas or make a difference to outcomes. The fact that India is a co-chair of the Working Group on macro-economic framework bears testimony to the fact that it is already playing this role. Maintaining a position of importance for India in the G-20 will require that India remain a source of diversity in thought, participative in process, and interactive in its actions on all major economic issues. In fact, India should project itself as a legitimate voice of many of the countries not represented in the G-20, but which are developing and, in the process, influence the setting of agenda.

Twenty-One

The Managing Volatility in Capital Flows[*]

$\mathscr{V}$olatility in private capital flows has been recongised as a reality for most EMEs. Managing volatility has become an important challenge for policymakers, particularly in emerging Asia. It is increasingly recognised that excess volatility in capital flows has harmful effects on the real sector output and macroeconomic stability. Policymakers are, therefore, grappling with a variety of options to minimise the adverse impact of such volatility while taking advantage of the benefits of a liberalised capital account. The use of capital controls is only one instrument for policymakers. It is, therefore, necessary to identify a policy framework that would enable optimal management of their capital account in times of volatility. This chapter is divided into three parts. The first part explains multidimensional aspects of volatility in capital flows. The second narrates policy options and policy dilemmas in managing the capital account. The third and concluding part consists of some

* This chapter is a consolidated and edited version of presentations made at the MAS/IMF conference on The IMF and International Financial Systems: The Post-Crisis Agenda, Singapore, 24 September 2010, and in the Development Debate on How to Manage Capital Flows?, organised by the World Bank, Washington DC, 7 October 2010.

comments on policy questions involved in managing capital flows in EMEs.

VOLATILITY IN CAPITAL FLOWS

Volatility and Size of Flows

The size and volatility of capital flows are related, but they are different in terms of challenges they pose and policies they require. In regard to the size of net capital flows, the major issue for policy purpose relates to a sustainable level of current account over the medium term. The reality of the global economy and financial markets is that there are risks for a country to have a persistent current account deficit beyond a threshold, though it is not easy to determine the threshold. Furthermore, it is recognised that from the point of view of avoiding serious global economic imbalances, neither persistent large current account deficits nor current account surpluses are desirable. In other words, the size of capital flows of a country that is consistent with the goals of growth and stability of the concerned country, and also consistent with the stability of the global economy, imposes a limit on the desirable size of capital inflows into the country over the medium term. Policymakers of each country recognise the limit in order to attain a sustainable level of capital inflows corresponding to a sustainable level of current account deficit over the medium term.

Policymakers need instruments that manage volatility in capital flows as distinct from the desirable size of such capital flows. Such instruments would not be needed if policymakers believe that the markets will always adjust in a smooth and relatively costless manner. Excess volatility connotes short term movements that signify higher costs relative to benefits and hence is of policy concern. The choice is between benign indifference to excess volatility or acquiring policy instruments to manage capital account. Thus, excess volatility is a concern for public policy, and that the policy response to volatility will have to recognise the difference between managing volatility and managing the size of capital flows.

Volatility in Flows and Flexibility in Exchange Rate

The exchange rate is an important instrument for managing capital flows but stability in exchange rate is also one of the objectives. Dr Bimal Jalan, as Governor, RBI, articulated in 1997 the importance of a policy that restricts volatility in exchange rate, but allows flexibility while there was no target or a band for exchange rate of rupee. Since then an intermediate regime allowing for some flexibility but combating excess volatility had served India well and proved to be an important instrument for managing capital flows.

It needs to be recognised that the distinction between flexibility and excess volatility in exchange rate movements is dynamic. In other words, as financial markets develop, larger movements in exchange rate can be tolerated with less serious impact on the real economy. Thus, over a period of time, as financial markets and flexibilities in the real economy develop, what appeared to be excess volatility may be acceptable as flexibility that can be tolerated. It is increasingly recognised that the central bank can combine intervention with some appreciation of the currency to manage volatility while allowing flexibility in the exchange rate. The distinction between volatility and flexibility is in some ways, judgmental since it is difficult to subject it to rules.

Volatility: Composition of Flows and Stock

Before the Asian crisis, there was a belief that all global financial markets are integrated and it is not possible to distinguish between different types of capital flows since they were totally fungible. However, Dr C. Rangarajan, then Governor, RBI, articulated in 1993 that there is a hierarchy in capital flows. In the Indian context, he advocated a policy that would open up equity markets for institutional investors, while keeping external debt under control and discouraging short-term credit unrelated to financing of trade transactions. This approach has served India well. After the Asian crisis, there was global recognition of the hierarchy, in particular, the importance of containing short-term debt obligations and the desirability of attracting direct investment flows since it is less volatile. The distinction between debt flows and equity flows is important since in regard to the latter, there are greater elements of risk sharing between foreign capital and domestic condition. A popular formula for assessing adequacy of forex reserves is based on short term obligations and implicitly therefore there is a role for policy in recognising a hierarchy in capital flows and in the level of reserves.

The potential for volatility is related not only to the composition of flows but also to the stock of external assets and liabilities of a country. In other words, if the stock of external financial liabilities of a country has predominant portfolio flows, there is a greater potential for volatility even if the current flows are predominantly less volatile. In determining the adequacy of reserves, the composition of stock of external liabilities in terms of potential for volatility is also relevant. A forward looking policy on volatility has to recognise the potential for volatility in the stock of liabilities. In brief, for the purpose of policy it is important to understand volatility both as flow and as stock, in addition to recognising the inflow and outflow dimensions of capital flows. Further, the tendency for capital outflows is often but not necessarily significantly more rapid and massive relative to inflows.

Volatility and Current Account

The high level committee on balance of payments in India chaired by Dr C. Rangarajan recognised in 1993 that it is possible that capital account transactions take place in the guise of current account. The committee recommended safeguards against this contingency through procedural stipulations in current account transactions. Though transactions are fully convertible on current account, there is a requirement to restrict the advancement or deferment of payment obligations in current account to a maximum period of one year. This is operated through insistence on repatriation and surrender of export earnings. It is possible to have huge leads and lags in effecting payments for imports and exports on the basis of expectations of movements in foreign exchange. Expectations that exchange rate movement will move in one direction has an exaggerated impact on the supply and demand of foreign exchange in forex market on current and capital accounts combined.

Volatility and Balance Sheets

It is possible to differentiate the balance sheets of households, corporates and financial intermediaries in terms of their incentives to take positions in foreign currency. Households generally have domestic currency bias, unless the trust and confidence in domestic currency or banking is lacking. The non-financial sector corporates are inclined to relate their foreign currency transactions to their non-financial sector activities. The financial intermediaries have maximum skills and opportunities to take positions both in terms of maturity, currency and instruments in the forex market. Volatility is often injected into the forex market by the participants in the financial sector. It can be argued that while the financial sector provides depth and liquidity to the forex market, they are also inclined towards herd behaviour and speculative positions which may tend to inject volatility and enable an exchange rate unrelated to fundamentals for a prolonged period. The instruments for managing capital flows may have to focus on the activities of financial intermediaries.

Excess Volatility and Market Failures

It is possible to argue that all movements in exchange rates are means of price discovery and that the real economy should be able to adjust itself to movements in the financial market. It assumes that the market mechanism is efficient in price discovery at all times and rules out the possibility of such a rate being inconsistent with the fundamentals for a prolonged period (it also assumes that adjustments in the real economy can also take place in a relatively smooth or costless manner). However, global financial markets in point of fact are less than perfect. The international monetary system does not provide level playing field in currency markets. There are some countries which are in a position to raise resources in their own currency in the global financial markets. In the event of shocks, the adjustment process is asymmetrical since those with current account deficits, and not able to raise money in their own currency, have to bear the total burden of adjustment. Financial markets are aware of this unlevel playing field. The unlevel playing field gives rise to market failures. Further, global financial markets are dominated by very few credit rating agencies and very few leading news services. Hence, excess volatility may also reflect functioning of imperfect markets in global finance.

POLICY OPTIONS AND DILEMMAS

Options

Policymakers have taken recourse to several measures to address the problems arising out of volatility in capital flows but they have been conscious that each of them has some costs also. First, some adjustments could be permitted in the exchange rate which essentially implies that the impact of volatility in capital flows is reflected in the exchange rate with possible consequences for the real economy.

Second, there may be intervention in foreign exchange markets in order to contain the impact of volatile flows. Such an intervention, not accompanied by sterilisation, has an impact on liquidity of the domestic currency, whereas if it is accompanied by sterilisation, there are fiscal costs apart from the possible impact on interest rates, which would attract more capital flows.

Third, financial market development is often advocated as one of the measures for reducing volatility in capital flows. Policymakers recognise that the development of the financial sector is a longer term solution to enhance the capacity of the system and to absorb volatility, but volatility is often an immediate problem while development of the financial sector is a medium term solution. Further, the objectives of deepening and strengthening financial markets like, growth, financial inclusion and financial stability, and absorption of capital flows, are only be a means to such broader objectives.

Fourth, prudential measures can be undertaken in respect of financial sector to limit the exposures of regulated entitled and their clients. Such measures need not be in consistent with the development of the financial sector.

Fifth, price-based measures include un-remunerated reserves and tax on short term gains. It is argued that these measures may not have an effect on the size but only on composition of flows. However, the composition of flows has some relevance for potential for volatility. Administrative measures may be taken as part of capital controls on capital inflows and outflows, and controls may stipulate the conditions under which each such transaction can take place. Administrative measures are also useful but may result in distortions in incentives if the enforcement is arbitrary.

Sixth, in case volatility is observed in terms of persistent capital inflows, liberalisation of outflows is often advocated. However, the liberalisation of outflows may not result in an outflow of capital at a time when the global perception is one of greater confidence in the economy concerned. In fact, liberalisation of outflows may attract more liberal inflows in the short run.

Seventh, monetary policy measures in terms of aligning interest rates better with global interest rates, can reduce the pressure of inflows and outflows. However, such and actions have consequences for the domestic economic activity.

Eighth, fiscal policy has a role in managing demand, but while tackling the issue of volatility it may play a very limited role. A price based fiscal measure is taxation of short-term capital gains. However, countries which have a fixed exchange rate regime will have to use fiscal option intensively along with macro-prudential regulation. A common instrument to manage volatility is taxation of short-term capital gains.

Ninth, monitoring of capital account transactions particularly by large intermediaries and corporates should help in undertaking corrective actions through several instruments available to the policymakers. Monitoring of financial markets and financial intermediaries by itself may reduce incentives to take positions if there are credible threats of policy or administrative corrective actions.

Finally, it is often argued that a country should increase the absorptive capacity of the domestic economy so that capital inflows are productively utilised. It is possible that policymakers devise a policy framework which will generate current account deficit that will absorb capital flows, provided they are on a sustainable basis. However, it will be impossible to vary the absorptive capacity in the short run through policy interventions, and in any case, the absorptive capacity of an economy cannot be calibrated to match the volatility in capital flows. In brief, policy of influencing absorptive capacity is perhaps relevant to address the issue of desirable size of capital flows over the medium term and not volatility in capital flows.

Dilemmas

It is often argued that policymakers should try to counter the ill-effects of temporary flows but should not try to influence the more permanent flows. From an operational point of view, it is difficult to categorise capital flows as temporary or as permanent and a more appropriate way of looking at the nature of capital flows is the potential for volatility. For example, portfolio flows in relative terms may be more volatile than Foreign Direct Investment (FDI), but it is not as if FDI is permanent; it is at best less temporary. Further, there will always be some more temporary and some less temporary components in all flows. However, the basic issue is whether the exchange rate appears to be out of alignment with economic fundamentals, and whether such movements are taking place due to herd behaviour. It is true that policymakers are not equipped to determine a right exchange rate, but policymakers should be able to sense huge movements in exchange rate mainly caused by volatility in capital flows.

There are two types of judgments involved in policy interventions to combat volatility in capital flows, namely whether the flows, either inflows or outflows, are relatively temporary or not; and whether correction by market forces is less costly than policy intervention. The judgments are necessarily contextual, but analysis helps in making well informed judgments. Very often, a presumption has to be made by policymakers as to whether the flows are more temporary or more permanent. In deciding whether the flows are essentially temporary or permanent an assessment of the extent of push factors relative to pull factors in the capital flows would be useful. The push factors are generally caused by the short-term changes in the conditions of the global financial markets, while the pull factors usually relate to the economic fundamentals of the country.

It is not appropriate to view each instrument of managing capital flows in isolation and evaluate its effectiveness. Each of the instruments has its own limitations, but it is possible that each instrument could be effective within some limits. Further, the use of each instrument will have an impact which may not be restricted to influencing the capital flows. Moreover, with an appropriate combination, the instruments may be far more effective than using them in isolation. It is important to consider an appropriate package of measures in a dynamic manner after taking into account the costs and benefits in a given context. Thus, for instance, it is possible to have a combination of more adjustments in exchange rates, combined with sterilised interventions, to supplement prudential measures as well as administrative controls. The package of measures and instruments will have to be consistent with the monetary policy measures that might have already been implemented to curb potential volatility.

There are two approaches to pre-commitment in regard to management of capital account. One approach would be to make a commitment for free capital flows and keep the option open of using the instruments to manage capital account when the circumstances warrant. The second option is to make a formal commitment to manage the capital account whenever considered necessary or as long as it is useful so that the markets themselves expect policy intervention against volatility. There is merit in financial markets being aware of the determination of policymakers to use policy tools to curb excessive volatility since such an awareness on the part of financial markets itself may moderate the potential for volatility.

MANAGING CAPITAL FLOWS: COMMENTS ON POLICY QUESTIONS

A broad generalisation is that private capital flows to developing countries are beneficial since they constitute a welcome supplement to domestic savings. It is interesting to note that most of the countries that recorded impressive growth in Asia have, for most part, domestic savings in excess of their investments or as in the case of India a very marginal supplement to domestic savings. Perhaps it is the nature of opening to capital flows and not the extent of capital inflows that promotes growth with stability.

Many developing countries which depended on foreign savings to supplement domestic savings in a significant manner (those with large and persistent current account deficits) had experienced considerable instability—especially during generalised shocks in global liquidity. Hence, there may be a safe quantitative limit on the extent of supplements of domestic savings by foreign savings.

De jure open capital account does not necessarily result in large amount of capital inflows. In fact, a large part of net cross border capital inflows to developing countries happen to move to countries with less open capital accounts than to many others with relatively more open capital account.

Empirical evidence indicates that domestic economic conditions, mainly inherent attractiveness or vulnerabilities, dominate the size and nature of flows. Volatility in capital flows, both inflows and outflows, are predominantly though not wholly due to global conditions and far less frequently due to domestic episodes. Synchronisation of booms in financial markets in several developing countries over a prolonged period is indicative of this.

Addition to foreign exchange reserves as a precautionary measure should be relatable to the potential for volatility in the stock of external liabilities and capital flows. For example, FDI in green field projects would warrant far less precautionary reserves relative to portfolio flows. The problem in assessing cost and benefits of accumulation of foreign exchange reserves is that costs are in a way measurable like the cost of insurance, and benefits are difficult to measure. Experience shows that significant benefits from adequate level of forex reserves do accrue from (i) the weight to reserves that credit rating agencies give for sovereign ratings and (ii) the availability of liquidity to mange shocks in the current account (due to commodity price movements) and the capital account (volatile capital flows). The resilience of economies to the recent financial crisis gives empirical support to benefits of holding adequate reserves.

Macro-prudential regulation has a critical role to play in managing volatility since open position on currency is mainly taken by financial intermediaries. Further, countries that had adopted countercyclical policies in financial regulation withstood the crisis better than others, unless there were other macroeconomic vulnerabilities.

The problems of volatility in flows and effectiveness of policy responses at the national level during a globally synchronised volatility in capital flows are different from country-specific volatility in capital flows. With the benefit of empirical evidence, it is possible to explore the nature of policy interventions that optimise benefits of open capital account in a credible manner. The main carriers of volatility in capital flows are globally active financial intermediaries—ranging from well regulated international banking giants to hedge funds. Volatility in cross border capital flows to EMEs can be appreciated better if the global players and global factors that engineer volatility (through advice and financial flows) and take excessive risks are monitored and studied. Such studies would help strengthen regulatory regimes over such systemically important (for cross-border capital flows) financial intermediaries.

There is a multilateral dimension to the issue of volatility in capital flows. As mentioned above, empirical evidence in regard to developing countries should be studied. There should be a focus on research and monitoring of actions to be taken by systemically important countries to ensure that liberalised capital flows benefit the global economy. Measures for encouraging financial activity within the territory of an advanced country or a tax haven through tax concessions or soft regulation may influence the volatility in capital flows. Distortions in the international monetary system, that impinge on the efficiency of global financial markets, should be analysed as part of enhancing benefits from open capital accounts to the global economy. There is merit in studying the regulatory practices in both major advanced economies and EMEs that may encourage volatility and those practices that moderate or discourage volatility.

Twenty-Two

The New Global Financial Architecture: Approaches and Issues*

*T*his chapter is divided into four sections. The first section describes the pillars of the Global Financial Architecture (GFA), while the second section explains the context in which the new GFA is being considered and past proposals as well as initiatives. The third section elaborates the current approaches under consideration and undertaken new initiatives. The concluding section lists a few issues relevant to the new GFA.

PILLARS OF THE GFA

The IMF and World Bank group constitute the most important pillars of the GFA. The two institutions are inter-governmental organisations generally referred to as Bretton Woods institutions.

---

* This chapter is an edited version of the 4th I. G. Patel Lecture, organised by The London School of Economics and Political Science in association with the Administrative Staff College of India, delivered at the Jubilee Hall, Public Gardens, Hyderabad, 25 October 2010.

They have as members the governments of almost all the countries. They are cooperative institutions, but the members have unequal voting strength within the two organisations. Representation on the Board of Directors that manages day-to-day affairs is skewed in favour of advanced economies, in particular European economies. Major decisions require special majorities, and this bestows virtual veto on important matters to the US, the single largest shareholder.

The IMF's main functions are, monitoring global economy, surveillance over exchange rate and related policies of individual countries, and providing liquidity support to countries to overcome temporary problems of balance of payments. The IMF also provides technical assistance to some member countries to improve their macroeconomic management. The members of the IMF have to observe some obligations such as avoiding dual exchange rate, subjecting themselves to surveillance, and enabling full convertibility of their currency on current account. The IMF's core competence and responsibility relate to global financial system, in particular balance of payments, exchange rate and related macroeconomic policies. The IMF derive its resources mainly from the contributions of member countries, which are supplemented, as necessary, by borrowings from member countries.

The World Bank consists of two entities, namely the International Bank for Reconstruction and Development (IBRD) and International Development Association (IDA). The World Bank is also an intergovernmental organisation with governance arrangements similar to the IMF. The World Bank provides resources and advice to developing countries for economic development. The World Bank group includes private sector affiliate, like the International Finance Corporation and others. The IBRD operates with capital provided by the members and by borrowings from financial markets. The IDA draws its resources from member governments, the IBRD, and repayments and retained earnings.

The WTO, as a third pillar, deals with the subject of international trade and is designed to bring down barriers to trade. The WTO covers, apart from trade in goods, subjects like trade in services and minimum standards for intellectual property protection. The General Agreement in Trade and Services (GATS) of the WTO is designed to establish a multilateral framework of rules for trade in services with a view to ensure expansions of such trade under conditions of transparency and progressive liberalisation. One of the services covered by GATS is financial services. Financial services cover a wide range of insurance, reinsurance and other insurance-related services as well as a host of banking and other financial services. The WTO is unique as far as its decision-making methodology is concerned, since members have equal voting weights. The WTO continues the practice of decision-making by consensus, which is defined as absence of formal objection. Since voting is seldom resorted to in practice, in a sense, every WTO member enjoys veto power.

Recently, the G-20 has been described as a fourth pillar of the GFA. The body is an informal group of select twenty countries, and its deliberations are operationalised either through actions at national level or though the three pillars of GFA, especially the IMF.

The BIS is an international organisation with some (not all) central banks as members. The BIS fosters international monetary and financial cooperation and serves as a bank for central banks. It acts as a forum to promote discussion and policy among central banks and the international financial community. Its customers are only central banks and international organisations. The BIS plays a critical role in enabling the evolution of standards of capital adequacy for the banking system, and was instrumental in developing Basel standards. The operating arm for this work is the BCBS, which is hosted by the BIS.

There are a host of other international organisations that are also part of the GFA but may not be described as pillars. These are the FSF (replaced by the FSB after the global crisis); the Financial Action Task Force (FATF); the International Organization of Securities Commission (IOSCO); the International Association of Insurance Supervisors (IAIS); the Joint Forum of national regulators in banking, securities and insurance; and the International Accounting Standards Board (IASB). Credit rating agencies which are for profit organisations, are also considered by some to be one of the pillars of the GFA.

CONTEXT FOR THE NEW GFA

The global financial crisis has several dimensions but there is a consensus that the GFA was one of the relevant factors in causing the crisis. First, macroeconomic imbalances developed, which were a source of financial instability. Second, the surveillance of systemic risk for the global economy was obviously less than adequate. Third, financial markets have been globalised and financial institutions have been operating cross-border finance without adequate global coordination of regulations. In other words, the cross-border arrangements for financial regulation were non-existent or inappropriate. Fourth, the institutional arrangements for the provision of liquidity support to countries that suddenly faced serious difficulties, and to smoothen the necessary adjustments against shocks were not available. Fifth, infrastructural arrangements such as credit ratings and international accounting standards proved to be pro-cyclical and hence sources of instability. Broadly speaking, the inadequacies relate to macroeconomic policies, financial sector regulations and institutional set up to deal with globalised financial markets. With regard to macroeconomic policy in particular, it was felt that the international monetary system and the exchange rate arrangements were responsible for the generation of macroeconomic imbalance and their perpetuation without necessary correctives. In view of the global crisis, several proposals have been made for improving the GFA to avoid instabilities in the future and minimise the costs of adjustments in response to the crisis.

The gross inadequacies of the GFA were brought into focus as a result of the crisis. With regard to the IMF, there is a recognition that surveillance by the IMF was not sufficiently objective, in the sense that too much faith was placed in a particular ideological position that trusted unfettered markets. It was also felt that the surveillance failed to take account of systemic risks that were building up, in particular the risk to financial stability. Moreover, the IMF has not been even handed in its surveillance in so far as it has not brought out clearly some of the weaknesses in major advanced economies. When the crisis occurred, it was noticed that lendable resources available with the IMF were inadequate to meet the requirements of a number of developing economies. Many of these developing economies had been impacted by the financial crisis mainly because of global circumstances, and not because of their own weaknesses. Finally, the IMF was not in a position to command adequate legitimacy and trust in view of its reputation built on past experiences. The ownership rights, the design of governance and the composition of the Board were responsible for the infirmities in governance of the IMF, and in any case, did not reflect the changed global economic realities.

In respect of the World Bank, according to many, its contribution in realising the objectives of development, have not been cognisable, though its contribution to thinking on developmental issues is arguably significant. In terms of flow of resources for development, it was playing an increasingly smaller role in relation to private capital flows. When the crisis occurred, the resources available with the World Bank were less than adequate to meet the demands of developing countries. Above all, the governance structure of the World Bank suffered from weaknesses similar to the IMF. In regard to the WTO, many members have undertaken commitments for liberalising the financial services sector. The push for such liberalisation through the WTO could have been one of the contributory factors to the global crisis.

Within the BIS, which has restricted membership, there is a domination of North America, Europe and the UK, and their ideological preferences. The regulatory standards evolved under the aegis of the BIS described as Basel II could not prevent the financial crisis, in particular, the banks' balance sheets. The FSF constituted for the Asian crisis in 1998, which was the watchdog of the Global Financial Stability had not anticipated the crisis and had not taken any steps to mitigate the impact. Similarly, the G-20 which was also brought into existence in 1999 after the Asian crisis has failed to appropriately anticipate the forces that led to the crisis. These realisations have led to a serious reconsideration of the GFA.

PAST PROPOSALS

It is necessary to recognise that the inadequacies in the GFA are not entirely new. There was a realisation that inadequacies existed. The first and foremost effort to set up a GFA was undertaken after the Second World War. This initiative led to the creation of Bretton Woods Institutions. When US Dollar's link with gold was broken in 1971, there were discussions on the International Monetary System. However, no significant change took place. The major review of the GFA took place consequent upon the Asian crisis. There were several proposals, particularly within academic circles. It was noted that during the 1990s, the G-7 group of industrialised countries, i.e. the US, Japan, Germany, France, UK, Italy and Canada acting in close coordination with the IMF and World Bank, had performed the functions of the global lender of last resort. It was, however, observed that the resources available for the lender of last resort were grossly inadequate. It was felt that a larger fund for the IMF as a lender of last resort may encourage banks in industrialised countries to take more risks and, at the same time, encourage developing countries also to take on huge external liabilities. No significant progress was made in increasing resources for the IMF. An international financial manager was proposed. The crisis manager may not necessarily need large resources, but should be in a position to provide comfort to the international community. The issue was whether functions of the crisis manager and lender of last resort can be separated.

Another proposal was to set up an International Bankruptcy Court in order to adjudicate debt issues between sovereign debtors and their creditors. This was expected to be similar to Chapters 9 and 11 of the US Bankruptcy Law. There is, however, a difference in the sense that in regard to a domestic bankruptcy, fixed assets can be seized and action can be taken against the Board of Directors of the company. No such options are available in regard to a country. However, there was a major difference, namely, countries have a sense of continuity and, therefore, there were strong incentives to honour their debt obligations so that they continue to be credit worthy. The International Bankruptcy Court, however, may help in coordinating expectations about a good international sovereign borrower and a good international sovereign lender. An international authority to insure institutional investors against debt defaults was proposed. The authority would insure loans in advance when they are floated, and the G-7 would deny bailouts of loans that were not insured. There was a view that there should be no lender of last resort at all in global finance so that both lenders and borrowers are prudent.

Some proposals are related to a global financial regulatory authority to be run by investment professionals to oversee both banks and non-bank financial intermediaries. It was felt that this would help harmonise standards of global regulation. Increasing transparency and improving financial regulation in developing countries was a more acceptable proposal. An international deposit insurance corporation to insure sovereign debt issues with floating rates was another suggestion.

A world monetary authority akin to the ECB but on a global scale, was also proposed. The world monetary authority would have the ability to issue currency to address global liquidity flows. In addition, proposals to impose controls on capital flows were also propagated. This will control capital inflows or capital outflows, or both. Build-up of higher level of foreign reserves was considered as yet another option. Opening up more to foreign banks was suggested to reduce the costs of any bailout after the crisis. Yet another suggestion was that there should be a correction to the bias in favour of debt-financing. There is a bias towards debt-finance since there is no risk sharing, and international debt contracts are often enforced through creditor country codes and G-7 institutions.

PAST INITIATIVES

It is interesting that almost none of the above proposals or improvements in the GFA were considered seriously among policy circles. The problem at that time was considered to be essentially one of the debt of developing countries, and one of inadequate development of financial markets and weak regulation of the financial sector. The problem was also thought to be one relating to currency markets and relating to the banking sector of developing countries. In brief, the problem was essentially local and marginally of global significance. Accordingly, three changes were brought about in the GFA. The FSF, a forum of select advanced economies and important financial centres, was brought into existence to monitor financial stability. This was working mainly under the aegis of the BIS. The G-20 was constituted consisting of both developed and developing countries. The objective was to bring together systemically important industrialised and developing economies to discuss key issues relevant for global economic stability. This had both, finances ministers and governors of various countries. The BIS, IMF and World Bank took initiatives to have a set of internationally acceptable standards and codes in regard to the financial sector. The Financial Sector Assessment Programs (FSAPs) were initiated in respect of most countries. A very modest beginning was made to change the composition of voting strength in the IMF and World Bank to reflect changing global realities in economies and trade.

CURRENT APPROACHES

As a result of the current global financial crisis, some of the proposals which were originally mooted soon after the Asian crisis are, in a way, being revisited more seriously than before. There is better appreciation of the problem as being global in nature, though in reality the problem was in advanced economies but was transmitted through contagion to many developing economies. It is interesting that the role of two new institutions in the GFA (G-20 and FSF, constituted in 1999) which were created consequent upon the Asian crisis, and which failed to address the issue of financial stability has now been expanded and strengthened.

It is also necessary to note that during the period between Asian crisis and the current crisis the role of the IMF in handling the Asian crisis had come in for severe criticism. The stigma attached to obtaining resources from the IMF was intensified on account of its role in Asia. Subsequent to the Asian crisis, there have been crises in developing economies, in particular, in Latin America, which required support from the IMF. However, as the global economy picked up considerable growth momentum, the demand for support from the IMF waned. Operational income of the IMF was unable to maintain its expenses. There was a feeling in some circles that the IMF has become somewhat irrelevant while many felt that it was necessary to have a global institution conducting economic surveillance over countries and over the global economy.

Asian economies in the light of experiences from the crisis of 1997 improved their performance in a dramatic manner, and they built significant reserves as a deliberate policy of self-insurance. The World Bank was, in the meantime, not in a position to significantly increase its net transfer of resources. The BIS expanded its membership to include some central banks of developing countries. In brief, the GFA almost went out of active agenda in the consideration of the global economy in the events leading to the current crisis. The crisis brought the GFA back into sharp focus.

There are two possible approaches to the design of the new GFA under discussion, namely, to create new institutions to replace or supplement the existing global institutions. These include institutional framework for a new global reserve system including establishment of a global central bank, a global economic coordination council, an international debt restructuring court, and above all a new Bretton Woods conference to consider a new GFA. Those who advocate in favour of new institutions argue that the existing architecture cannot be improved through marginal changes, in view of the inherent structural weaknesses in the institutions, their lack of credibility, their poor track-record and above all their resistance to divert, in the substance and style, from the entrenched interests in existing institutions. They also argue that such a process of designing a new GFA should not be difficult since the world is far more conducive to global cooperation now than before. On the earlier occasion, discussions took place soon after the Second World War and it was possible to come to an agreement through intellectual exercise backed by political considerations. The current crisis is of such magnitudes that a fundamental change in the institutional structures is called for, and hence a new GFA is required.

An alternative approach is to proceed on the assumption that creating new institutions would be an extremely complex process and hence it would take time. It would also divert attention from the immediate tasks. More important, the existing institutions are repositories of talent, skill and experience which could be built upon. Hence, it is also argued that since there is a clear recognition of the problems arising out of the crisis, it is possible to effect improvements to the existing institutional structures and their way of functioning, with a proper mandate and direction. On balance, the consensus appears to be in favour of reforming the existing institutions. In other words, the current approach is that a new GFA should be through reforming existing institutions rather than building new institutional structures.

The fundamental weaknesses of the International Monetary System which is closely related to but not exactly a part of the GFA, have been placed on the table as an issue. It has been recognised by most analysts that it is an issue which has to be addressed, but it is not easy to find technical solutions that would be politically feasible, and in any case, the transition would be complex. However, in view of the urgency as well as the necessity to explore improvements in the International Monetary System, ways are being explored by which

SDR or SDR like mechanisms can be strengthened and utilis
the IMF playing a critical role. Such a critical role could be t
sub-structures of the IMF. This is an issue on which consia
debate should be expected in the near future.

NEW INITIATIVES

Several initiatives have been taken by the IMF for internal reform
under the overall direction of the G-20. First, the IMF has initiated
a process of reappraisal of its policies as evidenced from several
research documents. It is not very clear whether the open mind and
objective approach, as found in the research documents, is being
reflected in the IMF operations.

Second, in regard to surveillance, the coverage of the financial
sector has been increased and its assessment is being integrated into
surveillance mechanisms. There is greater effort to address systemic
issues in the surveillance while ensuring even handedness. In fact,
in September 2010, the IMF made it mandatory for twenty-five
jurisdictions with systemically important financial sectors to undergo
financial stability assessments under the FSAP every five years.
Selection of countries for mandatory assessments has been based on
the size and interconnectedness of their financial sectors, and will be
reviewed periodically to make sure it reflects developments in the
global financial system.

Third, lendable resources have been enhanced through several
channels in particular through additional borrowings under the
IMF's New Arrangements to Borrow.

Fourth, global safety nets are being put in place. For countries
which have strong policies and fundaments, there is an option of an
assured resource by opting for flexible credit line. For countries which
have policy strengths in most areas, they may opt for precautionary
credit line which will make resources available but with ex-post
(after disbursement) conditionality. The IMF is also examining the
possibility of global stabilisation mechanisms as part of the global

safety nets. It is not clear whether the possibility of collateral lending to supplement conditionality is being explored. Above all, effort is being made to erase stigma associated with approaching the IMF.

Fifth, with its program of lending to Greece in association with the ECB, the attitude of the IMF to link with regional bodies is under reappraisal.

Finally , in regard to governance, agreement has since been reached in G20 on October 23rd, 2010 for a shift in quota shares in favour of dynamic EMEs and under-represented countries of over six per cent while protecting the voting share of the poorest. India's quota share will improve from 2.44 per cent to 2.75 per cent. Europe will give up two if its seats on the Board. In the World Bank also, the voting power of developing countries is being increased and an additional Board seat for sub-Saharan Africa was agreed.

In 1978, the Articles of Agreement of the Fund were amended to allow the setting up of a Ministerial Council of the IMF. Unlike the IMFC which is an advisory body, the Council would be a decision-making body with voting based on the current vote shares in the IMF. The composition of the Council is similar to the Executive Board. The Council will also have powers delegated to it by the Board of Governors. The activation of the Council requires a majority of 85 per cent of the voting power of the Board of Governors. The activation of the Ministerial Council has been recommended by the Independent Evaluation Office of the IMF and an Expert Group chaired by Trevor Manuel, the former Finance Minister of South Africa. However, there is no indication of action on this part.

In regard to the World Bank, lendable resources have been enhanced. The voting shares of developing and transition countries are being increased by 3.13 percentage points (from 44.06 per cent to 47.19per cent). Authorised capital of the bank is also being raised. For multilateral development banks as a whole, the capital base is being increased by 85 per cent. During the crisis, the World Bank had extended assistance to several developing countries and there has been front loading of IDA disbursements. There is however, resentment among several less developed countries that several

countries like China and India continue to draw resources ¡
IBRD and IDA on a significant scale.

As regards the WTO, there has been no significant ᵗ
on the implications of the financial crisis. In its functioninᶢ
commitment of the members, the FSF has been expanded to incₗ
several developing countries virtually mirroring the compositior.
the G-20. The FSB has been functioning as the operating arm
the G-20 in regard to the financial sector. This includes monitorinₜ
of standards and codes, and setting up regulatory standards. The
recently released BCBS guidelines on Basel III focuses on five aspects
of financial sector regulation, namely, macro-prudential regulation
specially for capital adequacy; macro-prudential regulation in terms
of countercyclical measures; addressing liquidity issues; improving
trade practices in regard to financial markets; and special provision
for systemically important institutions.

The G-20 has been holding meetings regularly and considering
coordination of various issues. These include issues relating to the
GFA. However, the decisions of the G-20 are made operational
through the existing global institutions and actions by respective
national governments in their relationship with existing institutions
that comprise the GFA.

SOME RELEVANT ISSUES

There are several issues that would determine the outcomes of the
new GFA. First, the changes that have been brought about so far
are addressing the infirmities observed in the existing institutions
and their functioning. There is no evidence of a fundamental
review of the ideological base of the global economy and global
finance. Second, the actions taken so far relate to operational
aspects within the existing institutions with some indication of
a possible shift in governance. As per all indications, the shift is
likely to be very marginal. In other words, the new GFA is new
only in operational terms but not in strategic terms. Third, the

approach so far is proceeding with only two layers, namely, national and global. However, the three layer approach involving regional arrangements such as in the Euro area and in Asia, may be more appropriate. In particular, safety nets should be considered at national, regional and global levels, taking into account the circumstances of different countries and regions. Fourth, the link between the financial and real sectors has not been explored adequately. There is still an assumption that real activity will have to necessarily adjust to financial markets. Fifth, the trade-offs between growth, stability and regulation, have not been sufficiently explored in the design of improvements to the GFA. In particular, the design seems to aim to address stability issues of advanced economies rather than structural and developmental issues of developing economies. The missing element in regulation is the inter-connected and cross-border financial processes especially in the activities of international banks. Highly leveraged private institutions operating in cross-border markets remain somewhat unregulated. Sixth, while the G-20 has flagged the issue of tax havens and tax secrecy, the importance of global fiscal coordination has not been adequately addressed. There is a review of progress in Tax Information Exchange Agreements but they only refer to quantitative aspects. Quality of agreements signed, relevant partners, domestic regulation of tax-haven jurisdiction, etc. are not addressed. The GFA is incomplete without binding institutional structures for coordinating tax regimes since tax regimes and regulatory regimes of financial sector impinge on each other closely. Seventh, no serious effort has been made to revisit the financial services commitments undertaken with the WTO. It can be argued that the commitments already undertaken with the WTO need to be reviewed to ensure the integrity and stability of the financial system and that since the problem is not relatable to a single member or a group of members only, it is desirable to adopt a ministerial declaration enabling the members to revise their schedule. In fact, the preamble to the GATS recognises the right of members to regulate and to introduce new regulations on

the supply of services to meet national policy objectives. M
may have to roll back some of their commitments in the fii
services sectors under GATS on the way forward to pi
recurrence of global financial and economic crisis.

The question that remains unanswered so far is how new \
the new GFA be? Much will depend on the functioning of a reviv
IMF and a rediscovered G-20 which happen to be the cognisabl
new elements of the new GFA.

There are three distinct challenges for both the IMF and
G-20. First, how to manage the asymmetry in the extent of global
integration of labour, capital and financial regulation? Second, how
to design global governance that is equitable to people at large with
unequal nations, unequal in terms of economic strength? Third,
how to reconcile the public policy autonomy needed for national
governments essential for their accountability, and the arrangements
for governance at the global level? In addressing these issues, it is
essential to recognise that developments in technology have a
tendency to favour globalisation in general.

India has an important role to play in the evolution of the
new GFA. India is unique among major economies is not causing
the macro imbalances and not contributing to the financial crisis.
India adopted pragmatic policies successfully and hence India can
be objective and impartial in the deliberation of the GFA. This has
been recognised by the global community and the Prime Minister
of India has emerged as a global economic statesman. There is every
reason to be cautiously optimistic about a desirable and acceptable
new GFA.

SECTION V

India:
Performance and Prospects

India's Financial Sector in Current Times: Priorities for Reform*

$\mathcal{T}$his chapter initially explains the need for reforms in the financial sector of India, taking into account India's experience and lessons from the global crisis. In particular, the global crisis has underlined the need to focus on some factors that are critical for the efficiency and stability of the financial system. The chapter comments on India's strengths and vulnerabilities vis-à-vis these critical factors, namely, macro-economic management, monetary policy, regulatory coordination, appropriateness of incentive systems, excessive financialisation, and the banking system. From the narration, it is possible to infer major areas that need the immediate attention of policymakers and regulators in the Indian context at the current juncture.

---

* This chapter is an edited version of the S. Guhan Memorial Lecture, organised by the Citizen Consumer and Civic Action Group (CAG), Chennai, 22 October 2009.

NEED FOR REFORMS

The current global financial crisis has unsettled views concerning the right model of the financial sector, and has imparted great uncertainty to what it should ideally be. Most countries, especially those leading the way for the others, like the US, UK, and other European countries, have embarked on a mission to reform their financial sectors, while a group of twenty leading countries of the world is attempting the coordination of policies at the global level. In this scenario of heightened uncertainty and search for optimal models of the financial sector at the global and at national levels, it is relevant to look at the positioning and directions of India's financial sector.

India has largely escaped the travails of the global financial crisis. Some say that this was possible only because the policy was conservative and did not act to improve the efficiency of the system. This view is incorrect because India was active in policy interventions in both monetary and financial sectors. The RBI adopted an active countercyclical policy unlike other central banks, which failed to intervene. Hence, these policies need to be pursued as appropriate to evolving circumstances.

India's relative success does not obviate the need for reforms in the financial sector. However, there is a problem now with acting rapidly or comprehensively on reform since there is no agreement on a right model for the financial sector. It is therefore desirable to look carefully and pragmatically at specific and urgent issues that need attention.

Maintaining the status quo in the Indian financial sector would be a mistake since India's financial system suffers from several inadequacies, ranging from an inappropriate credit culture to financial exclusion and poor service. Although serious infirmities that could cause a crisis may be absent, the financial sector is yet to fully serve the needs of the real sector. The needs of the real sector can be met only when there are synchronised reforms in both real and financial sectors.

The importance of synchronised reforms in real and financial sectors may be illustrated through finance for housing. Housing is

a priority for India, given its demographics, trends in the gro
the GDP, and rapid urbanisation. Hence, housing finance ou
be encouraged. But for housing finance to be viable and effic.
there should be reasonably good housing markets, prefera
liquid markets. Unfortunately, housing markets are generally ve.
complex and illiquid in India due to the existence of a combinatioı
of formal and informal construction activity as well as its financing
models. There are also high transaction costs in terms of registration
fees, difficult tenancy laws, non-standardised layouts, inadequate
processes of price discovery, unrealistic loan to rental value ratios,
etc. Hence, developments and reform in housing products and
housing finance products should be reviewed together while seeking
rapid growth in housing finance and innovating related financial
products.

It should be recognised that the lessons that are still being
learnt from the global crisis are of a fundamental nature and not
merely incremental. They call into question the intellectual basis
of some of the reforms under consideration in India prior to the
crisis. Take for instance the attitude to the Tobin Tax. In 1978,
James Tobin suggested the levying of a small tax—say 0.5 per cent
of the turnover—on foreign exchange transactions in order to
discourage speculative transactions in foreign exchange. This was
considered retrograde and impractical till recently, both in India
and globally. Now eminent persons in finance, such as former US
Fed Chief Paul Volcker and current chief of UK FSA, Lord Turner,
are suggesting the consideration of such a tax even for domestic
financial transactions.

What does this mean for India? This idea could be examined
to suitably modify the STT system and extend them to transactions
in participatory notes, although they are traded abroad, by insisting
on such transactions being recorded in India. Similarly, issues of tax
arbitrage and tax havens are being revisited globally, and the related
levels are being reviewed. The disclosure of information being
insisted upon by the US from some accounts in Swiss banks is an
example of such a review.

Although there is no universal agreement on the appropriate reforms in the financial sector in the light of the global crisis, the crisis has revealed some fundamental factors that are undoubtedly critical to the efficiency and stability of the financial sector. These critical factors or questions, raised in global debates, should be factored into the reassessment of India's financial system. The global debates relate mainly to macro-economic management, monetary policies, regulatory coordination, incentive systems, excessive financialisation, and the banking system.

MACRO-ECONOMIC MANAGEMENT

Macro-economic management in India is by and large reasonably balanced. There are no excessive current account imbalances; no excessive dependence on exports or external demand; no excessive reliance on investment or consumption expenditure; and no excessive leverage in most households, corporates or financial intermediaries.

There is, however, vulnerability of the macro economy due to the potential for shocks on four fronts: fuel, food, fiscal and external finance. The vulnerability of the economy on account of fuel is due to the significant dependence on imported fuel. The impact of drought or floods on the availability of food items, their prices, and the import bill is well-known. On the fiscal front, the quality of fiscal management and the consequent subordination of both monetary policy and the financial sector to fiscal compulsions continue to be concerns. In external finance, the volatility in such flows due to heavy dependence on portfolio flows and the quality of such capital flows continue to be an area of concern. In particular, the quality of FDI deserves a closer look, in terms of the extent to which they are financing green-field projects. A green-field investment is the investment in a new venture or in an area where no previous facilities exist, while FDI in a non-green field project adds only to the financial inflows.

MONETARY POLICY

The conduct of monetary policy is by and large sound and comma credibility. The objectives of growth, price stability and financ stability have been well-articulated, and have for the most part bee achieved. India's regime of multiplicity in indicators, objectives and instruments has gained respectability globally. The successful management of the impossible trilemma has also been recognised.

Three challenges will continue to confront the monetary policy: (i) fiscal dominance; (ii) public policy, especially in relation to administered interest rates that inhibit the transmission of monetary pressures and management of the capital account; and (ii) reliance on wholesale price index as headline in contrast to the practice in the rest of the world.

REGULATORY COORDINATION

Although the current mechanisms for regulatory coordination in the financial sector are broadly adequate, they leave some scope for improvement. A high-level committee (assisted by inter-regulatory technical committees) on financial markets presided over by the Governor, RBI, with other regulators and the Ministry of Finance as members, is in place. The interesting feature, however, is that the secretariat to this committee is provided by the Ministry of Finance (which has close ties to participants in financial markets, including the large public sector), while the RBI is expected to assume responsibilities for financial stability. The Governor chairs the meetings.

INCENTIVE SYSTEMS

A systematic study may be needed to determine whether there are incentive systems in India that are inappropriate for the stability of the financial system and the interests of depositors and retail investors.

The case of the mutual fund industry would be illustrative of the possibilities of conflicts of interests. Mutual funds are institutions meant to serve the interests of several small investors who may not have the time, experience, expertise, or means to manage their investment portfolio directly. So, the savings of individual investors are pooled into a fund with a genuine mutuality. Contrary to this objective of serving small investors, in India corporates, non-bank financial companies (NBFCs) and banks are permitted to invest in mutual funds, and they even enjoy tax benefits. In fact, it seems that an overwhelming part of the contributors to mutual funds in India are corporates and banks, and not individual investors. As mutual funds, which are meant to service individuals, are permitted to raise funds from institutions, their managements tend to cater to the interests of these large institutions possibly at the expense of the interests of individual retail investors. In fact, if mutual funds are sponsored by such large institutions, there may be incentive to dilute the focus on individual retail investors` interests, to the point of their subordination to the interests of sponsoring institutions.

This raises the broader question of conflicts of interest in the financial sector, which requires detailed studies and assessments. Events in India during the crisis have shown that extraordinary liquidity facilities had to be provided by the RBI for mutual funds and NBFCs, which may be indicative of their vulnerability. It is also noteworthy that some mutual funds and NBFCs have close affiliations with large corporates. No doubt there could be what may be technically termed firewalls, but a detailed study of their inter-linkages, actual operations in concert or clusters with each other, and in the equity and corporate bond markets would help to provide reassurance that serious conflicts of interest with systemic consequences are not pervasive.

Excessive Financialisation

Excessive financialisation may be occurring due to the proclivity of financial markets and institutions for a multiplicity of transactions,

since many of them obtain incomes through margins on tra
Generally speaking, when multiplicity in financial transactions t<
place with no visible signs of redistributing risk or greater efficier.
in reallocating resources, it amounts to excessive financialisation. *
the absence of large-scale derivatives, structured products, etc., there
may be no prima facie reason to suspect excessive financialisation,
but eternal vigilance is the price to be paid to ensure stability.

One area which may need study relates to the financing of
infrastructure. Consider one scenario in this regard. The Indian
Infrastructure Finance Company Limited (IIFCL) is a 100 per cent
Government of India-owned agency to fund infrastructure. It raises
bonds to raise resources for lending to infrastructure. Commercial
banks, especially public-sector banks, possibly contribute to a
large part, say 70 per cent of these bonds. Suppose that the IIFCL
in turn offers to refinance the banks to the tune of, say, 70 per cent
of their lending to infrastructure. Of course implicitly the lending
risk is borne by the banks. Banks thus lend to infrastructure by
first giving resources to IIFCL and then again getting the refinance
for IIFCL, while retaining the attendant risks for themselves. In
this arrangement, the primary risk remains with the bank and the
overall risk with the government, which may or may not formally
extend guarantees to the bonds issued, but owns both the IIFCL
and public-sector banks. In refinance, lending decisions are made
by banks. There is no evidence of any additional availability of
funds for infrastructure, but there could be transaction costs for the
issue of bonds and trading in bonds, adding to the multiplicity of
financial transactions. To this scenario may be added the additional
dimension of guarantees extended by banks, especially public-sector
banks, to the external commercial borrowings by the same private
entity that it is financing. These may be hypothetical scenarios, but
studies relevant to excessive financialisation would provide comfort
to the systemic stability in view of the size of the transactions.

Fortunately, there is no direct evidence of any large-scale
lending in India that could be characterised as irresponsible or sub-
prime lending. But a study should be made of commercial banks'

lending and support to micro-finance institutions that are profit-seeking (MFI-PS). Here, too, one can describe a possible scenario. A commercial bank may legitimately prefer to lend to an MFI-PS at a rate far higher than is permitted for lending to low-income customers. Bank lending to MFI-PS has the benefit of being treated as priority-sector lending. The MFI-PS in turn charges market-based rates of interest, without attracting the jurisdiction of laws relating to money-lending or usury. Micro-finance is a respectable area, and the impressive profitability of MFI-PS in India has attracted investments from private equity funds globally, with a huge premium. There may therefore be merit in a detailed analysis in a sort of supervisory review, in order to check any incipient tendency towards irresponsible or usurious lending through MFI-PS.

There are fortunately no visible signs of a lack of integrity in the financial system. However, a deeper study of the integrity of two of the markets may be warranted. First, the corporate debt market continues to be dominated by private placement and select players, and the process of price discovery is yet to gain full credibility. Second, in the money markets, short-term instruments exchanged between corporates, insurance companies and mutual funds may be large in magnitude, posing issues relating to conflicts of interest and systemic stability in the absence of an appropriate regulatory framework.

BANKING SYSTEM

India, like many developing economies, has a bank-dominated financial system. There is broad agreement about its strength and the resilience of banks in India, while there are debates on the level of efficiency in the context of externally imposed policy constraints and governance standards. There is, however, a need to assess whether there is a serious hollowness in banking services in our country. This does not refer to the issue of financial inclusion or efficiency of customer service, although both are important and need attention.

It refers to the missing elements in the core functions of a b
namely taking deposits and providing credit, especially for work
capital and for other productive sectors.

Over a quarter of the asset base of banks in India is earmarkec
for securities issued by the government. Banks are encouraged by
public policy to participate in bond markets, establish private equity
or venture capital subsidiaries, and step up lending to infrastructure,
as well as housing. They are also being persuaded to invest in equity
markets more aggressively. Banks also invest in mutual funds. As a
result, there is a reduction in advances towards working capital and
other funding, especially to agriculture, small business, and small and
medium industry. But these are the sectors that need bank funding
the most, and their access to new forms of funding through capital
markets is limited. Banks are expected to have special retail skills to
make such advances. The main justification for issuing a banking
licence is precisely to primarily conduct traditional retail banking
activities that are vital to economic growth at India's current stage
of development.

A study on this emerging hollowness in bank lending is essential.
There is a need to consider policies that will promote a banking
system which serves India's needs at this stage of development. Such
policies would mean emphasis on lending by banks to real-sector
activities, especially to directly productive sectors like agriculture,
small trade and industry, rather than, say, subscription to further
financialisation of the funds that depositors place in the bank. A
movement in this direction of immediate study may also avoid the
pitfalls that were observed in the extensively practised 'originate to
distribute' model of lending by banks.

Twenty-Four

Macro Framework, External Sector and Financial Sector*

$\mathcal{T}$his chapter is divided into five sections. The first section is devoted to a description of macro policies that are proving to be a source of comfort for India during the global financial crisis. The second section is devoted to the management of the external sector, which contributes to growth with stability and is also exhibiting its resilience to the stresses of the global crisis. The third section is devoted to the regulations of the financial sector in India that enabled India to moderate the boom-bust cycle that the world is witnessing. The concluding section is a brief account of the way forward.

MACRO FRAMEWORK

India's macro policies give high priority to the avoidance of serious macro-economic imbalances for several economic, social and geo-political reasons. India does not figure in debates on the global

* This chapter is a condensed and edited version of the Anand and Jeet Khemka Distinguished Lecture, University of Pennsylvania, New York, 12 November 2009.

economic imbalances arising out of excess savings or excess c
sumption by select countries. An avoidance of persistent imbalanc
between saving and investment, consumption and investment de
mand, domestic or external demand, and in the current or capital
account of the external sector are the results of the public policy.

Avoiding serious imbalances is very important for India in view
of the country's vulnerability to four important sources of shocks.
The first and most important source of shock is fuel. The prices of
petroleum and petroleum products are highly volatile, and since
the country is to a significant extent dependent on imported fuel,
this volatility has a huge impact on the whole management of the
economy, in particular the balance of payments. The second source
of shock is food supplies. While India is broadly self-sufficient
in food, it is susceptible to drought and, on occasion, floods. So
whenever there is a deficiency in the domestic availability of food
items—even if the deficiency is small in relation to India's supply-
demand position—its impact on prices in the global market is large.
These two shocks—on account of fuel and food—are essentially
current account shocks. The third source of shock is related to the
finance of government, namely, the large amount of public debt as a
proportion of the Gross Domestic Product and persistence of fiscal
deficit. The fiscal stress is structural, in the sense that it did not come
about to tackle a temporary problem. Since India's debt-to-GDP
ratio is over 70 per cent of GDP, the manoeuvrability for public
policy in times of any stress is restricted.

The fourth also relates to finance, but is an external finance
problem that essentially relates to capital flows. It is not only the
quantity but also the quality of capital flows that one needs to look at,
and after the Asian crisis, one looks at the stability of capital inflows
and outflows. India has a high dependence on portfolio flows relative
to less unstable flows such as those on account of FDI. Further, the
data on FDI in India should be taken with some understanding
of the difference between investments in green-field (such as new
factories) and non green-field ventures (buying of existing business
by foreign capital). Ventures that are not green-field relate to the

transfer of existing domestic shareholdings to foreign capital, and if there is already a capital account surplus, such flows merely add to the surplus in the balance of payments. By distinguishing between green-field and others in FDI, the differences in terms of their impact on the real economy become clearer.

Just as the macro-economic framework avoids imbalances, monetary policy in India is characterised by pragmatism and being proactive. The objectives of monetary policy are not explicit; the mandate is vague in the RBI Act. In fact, it may be amusing to note that in 1935 when the RBI Act was approved, the Preamble said that in view of the very difficult and uncertain global conditions, the law on RBI was being enacted as a temporary arrangement. That temporary arrangement continues till today. And it is interesting that what was said then in the preamble is being reinforced now by the global financial crisis in the seventy-fifth year of the forming of the RBI!

The RBI interpreted the broadly stated mandate to be price stability and availability of credit for productive purposes, the relative emphasis being dependent on evolving circumstances. In brief, the twin objectives are output growth and employment, and maintenance of price stability. In recent years, the RBI has announced a self-imposed objective of keeping inflation below 5 per cent per annum over the medium term and to reduce it to 3 per cent over the longer term, so that India's inflation is broadly in alignment with global inflation. This is to enable India's smooth integration with global inflation. The assumption is that the persistent large inflationary difference between India and the global economy could be quite disruptive to the Indian economy when India was fully integrated with the global economy. Price stability was articulated by the RBI in this manner; although there was no formal inflation target in the normal sense, this articulation helps set inflation expectations. The RBI also announced a few years ago that financial stability was an objective as well. No doubt it is in a way implicit in the objective of output and price stability, since one cannot think of output and price stability without financial stability. Financial stability generally

transmits itself to output and price stability. Yet financial stab.
was formally articulated by the RBI as a self-declared objecti\
although there was no formal mandate from the government fo
financial stability.

In its articulation of monetary policies, the RBI made it clear
that the weight for financial and price stability has to be higher in
India. When one takes the relative weights between growth and
stability, it is true that growth is important for a developing country;
however, in a country with a large population and a large number
of poor people who do not have hedges against inflation or social
security, inflation is a very serious human problem. The problem is
that growth trickles to the poor with some time lag, but instability
impacts the poor immediately. In fact, the reform process is sustained
only if there is assured growth without instability. The popular
support for reform itself will be undermined if there is even one
serious event of instability. Therefore, the RBI emphasised that at
this stage of structural reform of the economy, in order to maintain
public support, it is necessary to give a higher weight to price and
financial stability when evaluating the risks. So policy inevitably
becomes countercyclical, because if one emphasises stability, one
moderates the booms and busts. In fact, in 2002–3, there was some
criticism that India has lazy banking; and after some actions were
taken by the RBI, there was a feeling that the issue had become one
of crazy banking. But neither lazy nor crazy banking actually resulted
in serious instability. That is a tribute to the successful management
of policy, whereby you do not eliminate cycles but you contain
volatility within acceptable limits.

While conducting countercyclical policy, the dominance of
the domestic economy in India relative to the global economy
was kept in view. The enthusiastic globalisers preferred Indian
monetary policy to follow the relatively easy monetary policy
stance of global economies, especially the US. In fact, the monetary
policy recognised the linkage of Indian economy with the global
economy, but gave greater weight to domestic considerations. For
the first time, at least since independence in India, the words 'early

signs of over-heating' were used in the monetary policy. When an economy grows at 9 per cent and there are not enough roads or adequate ports or dependable power, it is evident even to a layman that there are supply rigidities and that these may be early signs of over-heating. After using the word once, the RBI was persuaded not to use it again, but in practice it pursued a policy that responded to over-heating.

The burden of countercyclical measures on monetary and financial-sector policies becomes more if the fiscal headroom is less. If the fiscal deficit is already high and there is a strong component of structural fiscal deficit, then the manoeuvrability of the fiscal policy to manage cyclical features is less. However, fiscal authorities should be willing to tolerate countercyclical policies in monetary management, if they are to be effective. The experience during the recent years of boom in India is complex in this regard. For the first time since independence, India was seeing a rate of growth that was respectable. So there was a huge political commitment to ensure that such a growth rate was not derailed at any cost. The leadership said, 'For heaven's sake, don't do anything, we can't take the risk! Never since independence did India have this high a rate of growth!' There was almost a fear that the RBI was risking the growth with its countercyclical policy. Naturally, from a political angle, the time horizon is short, and financial markets also have somewhat similar, if not shorter, horizons. And if they reinforce each other, the tasks of monetary authority and a regulator in the financial sector are not easy.

The pursuit of multiple objectives of monetary policy rather than the single objective of price stability was reinforced with the adoption of the multiple indicators approach to monitor the economy and govern the policy responses. In the multiple indicators approach, several variables, including money supply, prices, exchange rate and growth of credit are monitored and analysed carefully. One of the important things tracked in this approach was credit growth. When credit was expanding too fast by several indicators during the boom that preceded the crisis, there was a need to worry. If one looked at the loan-to-value ratio, one could easily find signs that people we. betting on asset prices increasing in the future.

The issue before the policymaker in the boom period was whether they should expect the booming markets to correct by themselves or whether they should do something about it. Financial markets could be ultimately self-correcting, but such a process of self-correction after an occurrence of extremes could impact the real sector adversely. For example, an exporter could go bankrupt due to a large, unanticipated appreciation of the currency. After she goes bankrupt, she can't become 'un-bankrupt' in a cost-free manner since one cannot re-start a factory again without cost, or soon, or even retain the market. Adjustments in the marketplace, which are possible with minimal friction in the financial markets, may not happen smoothly in the corresponding real sector. In the real sector there are adjustment costs; if the bones are broken, they are never fixed perfectly in the real sector. And therefore the RBI decided that policy had to take into account the whole issue of very rapid growth of credit and also of bubbles in asset prices rather than expect these to correct smoothly if they were excessive. The issue was one of judgement on how painless the correction in financial markets of non-quantifiable excesses would be, and their cost if public policy did not interfere, against how much such intervention of public policy would undermine market efficiency and hurt growth, if it turned out that there were no excesses or market failures.

The policy used multiple instruments of intervention by looking at multiple indicators to achieve multiple objectives. The prevailing belief globally was that there should be a single objective and a single instrument to achieve that objective in order to optimise policy. It was judged that in India, the reality was complex, particularly with regard to the institutional context. So it was not a question of using either one or more direct or indirect instruments; the policy had to use both sets.

India had anticipated a possible surge in capital flows even in 2004, and it was decided to be prepared were these large capital flows to occur. For that, a range of instruments was devised. One of them was the refinement in Liquidity Adjustment Facility. Basically, what the Liquidity Adjustment Facility does is that virtually every day, the RBI is prepared to put money into the banking system, and if need be, is prepared to take money out of the banking system. There is a corridor of interest rates within which these operations are conducted. If there is great uncertainty in the markets, the spread between interest rates to take and give the money increases. Sometimes the RBI also increases the spread to show that there is uncertainty. In a way, under these mechanisms, the RBI does not guarantee predetermined absolute interest rates at any cost, but tries to contain excesses in the movement of interest rates in either direction.

An innovative instrument called the Market Stabilisation Scheme was introduced to specifically manage capital inflows. When there is an excess of capital flow, as reflected in a possible steep appreciation of the rupee, the RBI intervenes to buy dollars with rupees, and then has to sterilise the rupees thus injected by borrowing the excess rupees used for the purpose. There is a cost of servicing such borrowing through sterilisation when the RBI intervenes, but this cost is incurred to avoid the adverse consequences of excess rupees floating in the system. In this process of sterilisation, money is taken out of the system; one can't use such money, but has to still pay interest on it. A sterilisation cost has to be incurred if excesses in capital inflows are not checked, and an unacceptable appreciation of the rupee has to be avoided by intervening in forex markets to buy foreign currency. These operations could be conducted by the RBI in the normal course if capital flows were not hugely excessive and persistent. But ultimately the cost is borne by the government because any cost or losses on account of these operations have to come out of the profits of the RBI, which belong to the government. It was expected even in 2003–4 that magnitudes of capital flows in future could be large, and costs of sterilisation could be huge over a longer period. Under this Market Stabilisation Scheme proposal, the government issues bonds and takes over the excess liquidity; the amounts raised are just kept in the government and cannot be used.

Liquidity is released if conditions change, say if there is a reversal of capital flows. In such a case, the process is reversed. When a reversal of capital flows happens, the RBI sells US dollars; and by unwinding the unused rupee balances under this arrangement, rupees are provided to help the markets buy US dollars. So serious volatility in both the foreign exchange and rupee markets is avoided by this arrangement, but these operations may involve costs. The RBI's proposal was that the government should indicate the overall limits to such operations and bear the costs of such special operations. Once the limit is agreed upon, the RBI would calibrate the size of intervention and sterilisation policies.

There was initial opposition to this proposal in the government. The arguments against the RBI's proposal was that the exchange rate has to be managed by the central bank, and it must have the independence to decide what it wants to do and bear the costs from its balance sheets. The RBI's response was that such independence is not desirable when the fiscal implications are serious. It argued that the people of India have to pay the potentially large costs of intervention and sterilisation, and it is only the government who should take a view on how much the people of India should pay for the combined effect of allowing excess capital inflows and the desired exchange rate. These are the two related issues, and they are too important to be left to an independent central bank. Further, the government was deciding the extent of capital inflows, and since that may affect the costs of sterilisation, only the government should take a holistic view. After some discussions, there was agreement on the proposal. Thus, under the Market Stabilisation Scheme, a ceiling is fixed on the amount to be sterilised through this scheme from time to time, and the ceiling keeps going up and down based on mutual agreement between the government and the RBI depending on the circumstances. Similarly, the management of capital account is a joint responsibility.

To manage liquidity conditions due to excess capital inflows, it was also necessary to impose a burden on the banking system through CRR. The banks had to place the money with the RBI as CRR, for which they were being remunerated till recently. The medium-term objective of the RBI was to reduce the CRR. However, the RBI took the view that if one really wants management of liquidity to be effective, banks should not be remunerated for their deposit under the CRR. The RBI urged the government to pass a law in Parliament removing the requirement of a prescribed minimum for the maintenance of a CRR, and also to the effect that if the CRR were imposed, no remuneration would be paid to the banks by the RBI. Each of the instruments, namely, Liquidity Adjustment Facility, the Market Stabilisation Scheme and the CRR, also has a time dimension (with LDF operating at the short term and CRR at the longer end of liquidity) and distribution of burden between various stakeholders, namely the RBI, the government and the banking system (on account of Liquidity Adjustment Facility, Market Stabilisation Scheme and CRR, respectively).

Fiscal management during the boom years prior to the crisis was also conducive to countercyclical policies. No doubt the public debt to GDP ratio has been high—as has the fiscal deficit—but during the boom period, fiscal deficit was on a downward path, notwithstanding some off-budget items such as the issue of oil bonds by the government. In addition, the Fiscal Responsibility and Budget Management Act (FRBM) had special provisions for managing extraordinary situations. Prior to its enactment, automatic monetisation was the norm, and under this arrangement, whenever the government wanted financial accommodation, the RBI had to extend it on concessional terms of interest, and the central bank would also participate in primary markets for government banks through private placement to itself. This system was discontinued under the FRBM, but a provision was incorporated within the FRBM stating that in extraordinary situations, the RBI may directly contribute to the government's borrowing programme.

In India, the debt of the state governments is also managed by the RBI. The limits on borrowing by states are in fact set by the central government, and state governments cannot directly borrow in foreign currency. The RBI has managed to enable a fairly reasonable stability in state finances, and debt default even by distressed states is very rare and, at best, temporary.

In general, the public policy has several instruments at its command, and one of the basic principles of this reform, as managed in the Indian financial sector, has been the ability of public policy to intervene with some sense of accountability when it becomes necessary. A public policy instrument is a constraint on the market, and the freedom of the market is a constraint on the policy. So a dynamic balance between the freedom of and constraints on markets is what is needed. What is done in normal times may have to be altered in extraordinary times, and the innovation in Indian public policy is to provide legal mechanisms to meet such extraordinary situations.

EXTERNAL SECTOR

Under the Foreign Exchange Management Act (FEMA) that was enacted as part of the reforms, current account transactions are free from restrictions—except in extraordinary circumstances—but the capital account is managed. In other words, rupee and foreign currency are fully and freely convertible for all legitimate transactions, provided they do not involve future financial obligations in the nature of capital transfers. Capital transfers such as loans and investments are governed by well laid-out rules, and flexibly managed from time to time. The most important policy consideration in the management of the current account is a sustainable current account deficit over the medium term. In other words, the current account deficit should be such that the capital flows will normally meet the deficit over the medium term. The concept of adjusted current account deficit was also introduced for analytical purposes. The adjusted current account deficit is computed by deducting the remittances by non-resident Indians from the receipts on account of invisibles in the current account. Remittances from non-residents are similar to regular gifts within a family, and do not reflect the strength of the resident household or the domestic economy. The gifts help better manage the households in India or the external finances of the country, but do not reflect the inherent economic strength of the household or the country's economy. The adjusted current account deficit helps one to appreciate the relationship of the domestic economy with the exchange rate and its impact on the economy. India had a trade deficit in recent years on an average of around 7 per cent of the GDP, and a current account deficit of around 1 per cent. But the adjusted current account deficit has been around 4 per cent. The difference between the large trade deficit and the modest current account deficit may be attributed largely to remittances from non-resident Indians and the export of services.

The Indian currency is fully convertible with regard to current account transactions, while some capital account transactions are subject to regulations. However, there has been a process of the gradual liberalisation of the capital account, both in terms of capital inflows and capital outflows. A distinction is made between households, corporates and financial intermediaries with regard to the nature and extent of liberalisation of the capital account. As far as households are concerned, it was felt that a flexible exchange rate was desirable not only among the markets, but also in the minds of people, and that confidence in a currency is achieved when there is a two-way movement in exchange rate for a reasonably long period. As long as there was only a one-way movement, say a depreciation of the rupee for a long time, people simply held on to US dollars in preference to rupees. Once two-way movement was achieved, outflows on account of household could be liberalised. In the case of corporates, there is normally an underlying real economic activity. Significant liberalisation for corporates was therefore possible with regard to both inflows and outflows of capital. As a result, Indian corporates have acquired overseas entities or expanded their operations externally. As regards financial intermediaries, there is considerable caution in the management of capital account since they are (i) leveraged, (ii) the relationship with real activity is not very clear, and (iii) a currency mismatch is introduced in their balance sheets with attendant risks.

Further, with regard to financial intermediaries, a differentiation between prudential regulation and capital controls is difficult. So it was the financial sector that was subjected to significant constraints in capital account relative to others.

The exchange rate in India is not managed with a target rate in view; the RBI intervenes in the forex markets as and when needed to avoid excess volatility. In deciding on its intervention in the forex markets, the RBI does not keep in view a fixed exchange rate or band, but keeps in view the desirability of a broad alignment of the exchange rate with the fundamentals. It is indeed difficult to define excess volatility or alignment with fundamentals. Judgements are involved, but as was articulated repeatedly, there is often no need to define what is right in order to recognise what is patently wrong. Similarly, something does not become less relevant for policy action simply because it cannot be defined or measured.

FINANCIAL SECTOR

The deregulation of the financial sector should be related to the functioning of markets in the real sector since a deregulated or marketised financial sector is supposed to allocate resources efficiently in the real sector. If the real-sector markets are distorted— if there are restrictions on trade, if there are controls, etc.—then the financial sector will also misallocate the resources. In other words, there should be harmonisation between the extent of reform in the real sector and that in the financial sector. The idea that the financial sector will by itself stimulate competition and efficiency in the real sector is questionable. In India, there are restrictions on agriculture, on commodity movement—especially important commodities— as well as rigidities in infrastructure. These restrictions on the functioning of domestic markets in the real sector place limits on the benefits of deregulation of finance relative to costs.

The financial sector is used extensively by the government to administer policies and programmes for development, and to that extent there are limits to deregulation. To illustrate, 25 per cent of a bank's deposit should be invested in government securities and 40 per cent of the rest be lent to the priority sector, with the result that there is little room left for real, traditional market-based banking. Further, a large part of the administered lending is subject to interest rate prescriptions. The interest rates on savings schemes in Post Offices and Provident Funds are also regulated. There are other types of moral suasions to lend at their behest and are at terms indicated by the government, especially through public-sector banks. Thus, two things to which importance was given in the financial sector were precautionary and developmental dimensions. Precautionary measures were taken due to the large stakes the poor had in stability. Second, development is not merely an accumulation of capital, but is also the enhancement and enlargement of opportunities to large sections of the population through the financial sector.

In 2003–4, a decision was taken to address issues relating to weak banks that had been allowed to operate even when their capital adequacy was low. The first to gain the attention of regulation was a small but high-profile commercial bank endowed with all modern financial instruments and technology. It was systemically important, but had weaknesses in the balance sheet that, with the connivance of the auditors, were initially not disclosed. After exploring with the major stakeholders the possibility of obtaining additional capital from acceptable sources, the bank's operations were frozen, and it was compulsorily merged with another bank at the instance of the RBI. The operations for freezing, which commenced on a Friday evening, were done over the weekend, and the merger was announced before noon on Monday. At that time, the accusation was that the RBI was non-transparent because the operations had been conducted over the weekend. The RBI was questioned in courts right up to the Supreme Court, but ultimately RBI won the case. It was a merger where the shareholders of the weak bank lost out. After the crisis, such things are done routinely in the financial sector over the weekend all over the world, and often with fiscal support. There were a number of other weak banks as well, and these were either merged or closed, and the first move on a high-profile bank made subsequent regulatory actions very effective.

In India, there are Regional Rural Banks (RBIs) to serve rural areas. They had to be recapitalised and revitalised, and some of them had to be merged. The rural corporative sector was another weak sector, and cleaning up had to be done here too. Removing weaknesses in the banking system and eliminating weak banks were the first steps in the RBI's effort to strengthen the banking system. This was executed over five years, and there was virtually no commercial bank with capital adequacy of less than 9 per cent.

A countercyclical policy was adopted in the regulation of the financial sector, especially the banking sector, for several reasons. First, risk does not arise after a loan becomes a non-performing asset; it arises basically when the loan is extended. A close monitoring of credit growth was therefore considered essential to assessing how risks were being generated, and how they were likely to be managed. Second, risk is not necessarily one-dimensional; there are many dimensions to risks, both micro and macro. Third, risk is very difficult to assess in a country where significant structural transformation was taking place. Fourth, risk could vary between different sectors, depending on the extent of efficiency of each sectoral market. Whether the relevant markets are liquid or not is also important. For example, in India the housing markets are not very liquid and transaction costs such as taxes and duties are well over 10 per cent, while tenancy laws are rigid. Depending on the changing assessment of these multiple factors, it was necessary to have both general and sector-specific prescriptions of the capital charge. It is true that judgements are involved in such discriminatory prescriptions, but complexity by itself does not absolve the regulator of the responsibility assigned.

Basically, excessive risks in the banking system have serious consequences, and that is where the emphasis on precautionary motive becomes relevant. Several instruments were used as countercyclical precautionary measures. In 2002, an IFR was created. Limits were prescribed on banks' investment in risky assets associated with specific activities, such as consumer lending, stock markets and real estate. Universal banking was acceptable, but was permitted in a constrained sense since retail banking, and not wholesale deposits or non-deposit resources, had to be the core activity of banking—the main purpose for which a bank license has been issued. A supervisory view of select banks was conducted and bank-specific restraints on exposure to risky assets imposed. Some banks, especially the new private-sector banks, argued that countercyclical policy was not warranted and that, in any case, the RBI did not have a formula-based approach for countercyclical policy. The RBI was of the opinion that it could not afford to wait for formulas and had to do something when, in its view, a problem was likely to arise.

Along with countercyclical regulatory policy, there is another area that is now discussed globally, namely off-balance sheet items among banks. The RBI has also been monitoring off-balance sheet items of individual banks and identifying where the excessive growth was. For this, a credit conversion factor is critical. A credit conversion factor, simply stated, is arriving at a ratio between the credit equivalence of off-balance sheet items for regulatory purposes. In computing a credit conversion factor for off-balance sheet items, caution was exercised. Further, many banks want some borrowed money to be treated as capital. The RBI adopted international norms, but with a little more caution. The argument against many of these actions was that the RBI's regulation was burdensome on the banks. It was explained that actions would obviously not be burdensome if the share values of banks were increasing manifold. When share values and bonuses are up across the board in the industry as a whole, one cannot say that there is an excess regulatory burden.

The scope of regulation is another issue that has come up in recent debates. It is now argued in global discussions that investment banks were not deposit-taking institutions, and therefore ended up unregulated. Now, in global debates, it is held that all systemically important financial companies ought to be monitored and regulated, and their leverage prescribed to assure financial stability. In 2004, there was a proposal before the government to amend the existing law to remove the RBI's powers to regulate non-public, deposit-taking, non-bank finance companies on the grounds that such regulations are intrusive and not common in most countries. It was explained that the RBI had no intention of regulating all such companies but should have the powers to monitor all NBFCs; and—if and when required—it should have the power to regulate systemically important ones among them. Fortunately the government agreed to drop the legislative proposal, and hence the RBI continued to remain in a position to monitor and take some corrective actions to avoid the perils of shadow banking in India. The RBI regulated and supervised well-defined—defined on the basis of the size of balance sheets—systematically important NBFC.

In India, the banking system is dominated by public-sector banks, although there is a mix of private shareholders and some private-sector banks. Prudential regulation is totally common to both. The private sector, to put it politely, is a little more innovative in minimising the burden of regulation. In terms of regulatory standards, there was little or no interference from the government as far as public-sector banks were concerned. On governance in banks, matters relating to the governance of the private sector are with the RBI, but governance issues of the public sector are with the government. Under the relevant statutes, whenever there was a concern with governance in public-sector banks, the RBI took the matter up with the government. With regard to governance in private-sector banks, the RBI has jurisdiction. The RBI evolved and announced guidelines on ownership and governance of private-sector banks in 2004. The justification for these guidelines was that deregulation of banks should be accompanied by enhanced comfort vis-à-vis their governance standards. The RBI tried to enforce these, albeit within some constraints, and within the limits set by law on the RBI's powers. Another issue coming up for discussion after the global crisis is the remuneration of Chief Executive Officers (CEOs). As far as banks are concerned, the CEOs' remunerations have to be approved by the RBI under the law. The RBI had approved neither a signing-in bonus nor a signing-out bonus, but only the salary and shares options.

Consolidation of banks is another issue to come up in India. The RBI's view has been that consolidation to achieve enhanced efficiency, economies of scope and greater resilience should be a priority and mergers should be instruments and not ends, while being mainly market-led. The government was enthusiastic about consolidation in the public sector to merge and create large-sized banks. With regard to mergers, the RBI wanted to be assured of the benefits of the idea that 'bigger is better', and it was in favour of consolidation only it could improve the health, and not necessarily favour mergers and acquisitions. As a result, a number of mergers and acquisitions in the private sector took place as a process of eliminating weak private-sector banks.

The RBI examined the issue of financial inclusion and pioneered it. It was not only the dispensation of credit that was considered important; financial inclusion was also emphasised. Financial inclusion means effective access to a whole range of financial services, especially the payment system. The banks are licensed to accept non-collateralised retail deposits and are highly leveraged. They are essential to the life of the community. Economic systems require a payment system and, more importantly, some place where people, especially poor people, can keep their money safely. For most people in India, especially the women of the villages, what is needed more than loans is a place to keep money safe, particularly from their husbands. The deposit-taking and payment system is a basic necessity of life for a common person, and it was felt that regulators have a duty to spread the penetration of banking services as part of the process of development.

With regard to financial innovations, proposals have now been made in several countries to constitute authorities for the safety of financial products; however, in the RBI the responsibility for regulating the financial innovations in which banks participate was assumed as part of bank regulation and the regulation of money, government securities and forex markets. The RBI took a relatively cautious approach and has been keen to identify the link between the derivative and the underlying original transaction. In fact, with regard to derivatives, onus was placed on banks to assess the capacity of clients to undertake it. As a general practice, safeguards were deliberated between the RBI and market participants in technical committees before permitting them.

For consumer protection, the RBI introduced and strengthened a scheme of Ombudsmen. It also devised a standards board following the UK model, in which the banks themselves indicate the consumer's rights and standards they practice. The Board is conceived as a voluntary body promoted by the RBI in collaboration with the Indian Banks' Association to evaluate banks` services with reference to the standards set by the banks themselves. While the RBI promoted it, the roadmap is for the RBI to divest the role, as happened with earlier refinance and trading institutions.

Finally, with regard to the regulatory structure, there is a debate in the US—and to some extent in the UK too—on the appropriateness of the prevalent regulatory structures. The stand taken by many in this debate is that coordination is important, whether it be a system of multiple or single regulators. One can have a single regulator but different departments pulling in different directions, or one can have multiple regulators cooperating. In India, the dominant view has been that coordination is important, and it is done though administrative arrangements. There is a high-level committee on financial markets, presided over by the Governor, with all the heads of financial regulators and the finance ministry as members. This has been working fairly well, and there has been a long-standing proposal to make the Committee legally binding. However, it has served the nation well even without being legally binding.

THE WAY FORWARD

On the way forward, there are several priorities for urgent action and a few vulnerabilities to be addressed for India. One, financial inclusion, since not many people are included in the financial system. Second, customer service and protection is still poor. Third, credit penetration is low since a very large number of people and activities that are eligible do not get credit, and certainly not on terms appropriate to the risks. Fourth, the credit 'culture' in India is generally poor. Contracts relating to credit extended by banks and non-banks are often not transparent, not equitable, and not easily enforceable. A series of subsidies and the periodical write-off of credit and repeated corporate restructuring on a discretionary basis tend to undermine the evolution of a sound system of institutional credit.

No serious vulnerabilities are identifiable in Indian financial systems, but there are some basic issues that have to be considered urgently. The first is the appropriateness of incentives in the financial sector. The whole concept of a mutual fund is that there are individuals who come together and ask somebody else to manage it—to assess risks and returns—since they are small investors. In India, mutual funds are dominated in reality by the corporates and the banks. So the incentive for the funds is to attend to the interests of the corporates and the banks, who account for a major share of their resources, rather than that of individual investors. Second, conflicts of interest are troubling in the financial sector, particularly between mutual funds, NBFCs and corporates who promote them, apart from some banks as well. Third, there may be excessive financialisation in India. To give an example, there may be a refinancing body that will issue bonds. This refinancing body takes money from banks through the bonds with a guarantee by the government. Then the refinancing body refinances the banks up to 70 per cent. The risk underlying the credit continues to be with the bank or the government, as it had been before the whole process. These are just multiplications of financial transactions, and there is an understandable interest in the financial sector for multiple transactions because that is where the margins lie for the players. Fourth, there are the beginnings of irresponsible lending, like sub-prime in the for-profit micro-finance institutions.

CONCLUSION

There is a new global consensus on issues relevant to the regulation of the financial sector and related macro-aspects. While the consensus does not pertain to all solutions, there is consensus on issues that are important. Looking at the trends, it is clear that there should be both re-regulation of finance and some recalibration of the globalisation of finance. For India, while going forward, caution in public policy is extremely important in the financial and external sectors because there are considerable uncertainties regarding the right model of regulation in the financial world. At the same time, there are several other areas where urgent policy initiatives are needed, and these relate to the real sector, infrastructure and the fiscal sector.

Twenty-Five

Financial-Sector Regulation in India: Review and Proposals for Reform[*]

$\mathcal{I}$n the first section, this chapter draws attention to the major issues being considered in global debates on revamping the regulation of the financial sector, and reviews the status in India with respect to each issue. The second section is a brief narration of a critique of the Indian experience, and its justification. The third section analyses three important proposals for reform, namely the establishment of a Commission on Legislative Reforms, a Financial Stability and Development Council, and the issuing of new bank licences.

GLOBAL DEBATE AND STATUS IN INDIA

There is an ongoing debate on the ideal approach to the regulation of the financial sector based on the experience with the global financial

* This chapter is an edited version of the Khusro Memorial Lecture organised by the British northern universities (Universities of Lancaster, Leeds, Liverpool and Manchester), and the India Forum, delivered at Bella Vista, Hyderabad, 23 March 2010.

crisis. This debate has already unveiled some general desirable approaches, although there is no unanimity or finality to them. Nevertheless, a review of the status in India with regard to these desirable approaches would help us to appreciate the challenges for reforms in the financial sector, and also assess the current proposals for reform.

Countercyclical policies are now emphasised in global debates as being essential for financial stability. In India, monetary policy was largely countercyclical during the years preceding the crisis, especially after diagnosing early signs of overheating in the Indian economy. This facilitated a similar approach to the regulation of the financial sector. As credit was growing very rapidly after the slack in 2003 and as asset prices were escalating steeply, a series of precautionary steps were introduced from time to time to protect the banking system from undue stress. An IFR for banks was introduced in good times in 2002. Restrictions on the exposure of banks to equity markets have been rationalised and reinforced since 2004. Risk weights were increased for sensitive sectors like real estate and consumer credit from 2005. Provisioning norms for standard assets other than agriculture, small and medium enterprises, and a few other sectors were tightened during 2005 and 2006. Bank exposures to risky assets like venture capital were severely limited, while exposures to Non-Banking Finance Companies were brought under scrutiny and thus contained. Considerable recourse was taken to moral suasion and supervisory review of individual banks and NBFCs so that norms could be further tightened or liberalised for specific banks, as warranted.

Countercyclical measures with regard to the regulation of the financial sector during the boom period served to minimise the impact of the global downturn. It also provided the required headroom and appropriate instruments which could be utilised to meet the downturn in the cycle due to the global crisis. It was possible to unwind or dilute many of these regulatory stipulations with the onset of the global financial crisis and its consequences for India. The unwinding of the tightening measures in regulation yielded positive and prompt results in the management of the crisis.

A Macro-Prudential approach is now being recommended in global debates since the safety and solvency of individual institutions do not guarantee systemic stability. As a necessary adjunct to countercyclical policies, the RBI has been undertaking macro-prudential assessment of the financial sector and placing it before the BFS for overall guidance. Banks' access to inter-bank money markets was restricted in relation to their respective net worth. There are limits to the shareholding of a bank in another bank (set at 5 per cent). The exposure of banks to NBFCs is subject to monitoring and guidelines, while all systemically important NBFCs are subject to more stringent prudential measures than others. Large conglomerates are supervised through cooperation between all regulators, under arrangements put in place in 2005.

With regard to micro-prudential aspects, the focus of the global debate is currently on the enhancement of the quantity and quality of bank capital, the extent and quality of off-balance sheet items, the incentives to management with regard to risk-taking, the dangers of principle-based regulation, and the consequences of very large financial institutions (that is, too big to fail). In India, capital in all banks is in excess of the relevant Basel norms of capital adequacy. This was accomplished over a five-year period ending in 2005, through compulsory or voluntary mergers, infusion of capital, and in a few cases by liquidation. The payout during this period of restructuring from deposit insurance for depositors in banks that had to be wound up or restructured was unprecedented in Indian history. Special packages were prepared for what may be termed local banks in the cooperative sector. Banks were permitted to adopt innovative measures to raise capital, especially tier 2, consistent with global trends, but with an approach that did not give undue weight to the saving of regulatory capital. On large-sized banks, the RBI's effort was consolidation through a process of mergers and acquisitions as a measure to eliminate weak banks; however, it was not keen on consolidation merely as a means of a presumed increase in efficiency through assumed economies of scale and scope.

The growth in off-balance sheet items has emerged as a matter of concern. Such a growth was observed in India too, mainly in the private sector and in branches of foreign banks. Whenever this phenomenon was noticed in select banks, supervisory concern was conveyed to them. More generally, a higher than normal credit equivalence for prudential purposes was considered to discourage them in this regard. The incentive systems, especially remuneration systems that encourage risk-taking, have become a matter of concern. In India, the pay of chief executives of private-sector banks is subject to the RBI's approval. This responsibility was taken seriously and entry or exit bonuses were not approved, while the approval of bonuses was subject to specified guidelines.

Excessive reliance on principle-based regulation was also considered one of the reasons for the slack in regulation. The RBI insisted that principle-based regulation should be adopted gradually and selectively, in particular after reasonable assurance of sound practices of governance in the banking system as a whole.

Recommendations on best governance practices were prescribed with an insistence that progress in deregulation would be coterminous with improvements in standards of governance. Formal guidelines were issued on desirable ownership and governance, in particular on the fit and proper criteria for members on the boards. These were applicable to private-sector banks, since such governance aspects with regard to public-sector banks are prescribed by the respective statutes.

The usefulness as well as risks of financial innovations, especially of credit derivatives and over-the-counter trading, are under discussion in global debates. The RBI has been cautious in all these matters, partly reflecting its bank-dominated system and its preference for concentrating on the flow of resources to government securities and for lending into the priority sector. Since the performance of Indian banks, both in the private and public sectors, has been consistently high and improving—as reflected in returns to capital in equity markets—there was no compulsion to encourage banks to participate actively in financial innovations. Further, their positive contribution to overall efficiency and stability of output was acceptable in the Indian context.

The regulation of financial innovations is an area engaging the attention of reforms at the global level in view of the experience with derivatives. The focus of the debate is now on the establishment of an authority to certify the safety of financial products and to insist, as far as possible, on exchange trading and centralised settlement in complex products like derivatives. In India, instruments offered by commercial banks should either be explicitly enabled by legislation and rules, or should be specifically approved or not have been disapproved by the RBI. Traded instruments are governed by the regulations of the securities regulator. However, due to the continued dominance of commercial banks in financial markets, mainly by virtue of confidence and credibility, banks dominate most of the financial instruments. In any case, a financial innovation does not get actively traded unless the RBI, as banking regulator, approves or permits banks to hold or trade in them. Similarly, over-the-counter trade in some instruments is possible only when the RBI does not disfavour banks taking recourse to them. The RBI's approach in this regard has been to accord approval to those activities, practices and instruments vis-à-vis which it is in a position to reasonably assess the risks and benefits.

It is not unusual for banks and market participants to initiate innovations and continue unless or till the RBI places conditions or safeguards, or prohibits them. The RBI views those innovations where trading in exchanges is not active with serious caution. The overall safety of the products traded in stock exchanges is within the jurisdiction of the securities regulator, but the regulatory framework governing money, government securities and forex markets vests with the RBI. While public policy and the securities regulator were keen to develop the derivatives market, the RBI through its unique position was able to moderate the pace of such innovations to suit Indian conditions. It is useful to note that the RBI retains the option to intervene in all these markets. This enables it to address the issues of maintaining stability and ensuring a harmonised development of markets.

The objectives of regulation are now sought to be extended to include the stability of the financial system in view of the experience with the crisis and the existing emphasis on the solvency of individual institutions, providing a level playing field to the regulated entities. Consumer protection is also being extended to cover consumers of financial products. Formal mandates for regulators usually focus on depositors' or investors' interests, and the RBI was no exception. However, the RBI had interpreted the objectives of regulation to include stability of the system and quality of service to consumers, in addition to sub-serving development through prioritisation of credit flow and through incentives for financial inclusion.

There is a general agreement now that the scope of regulation in most countries had been restricted to banks in the past, and that it should now be extended to non-banks as well as to the shadow banking system. The scope of regulation in India currently includes NBFCs in addition to Insurance, Pension Funds and Mutual Funds. The RBI monitors and regulates deposit-taking NBFCs and capital requirements are related to the nature of business as well. Systemically important NBFCs, defined by size, are more intensely regulated. In spite of the RBI's regulations, however, during the crisis there was significant pressure on the liquidity of NBFCs and Mutual Funds, warranting special windows of refinance by the RBI. The RBI also identified conglomerates for purposes of supervisory coordination, led by a 'lead regulator'.

Currently, there are proposals at the global level to treat retail banking as a public utility and to at least prohibit banks from undertaking excessively risky businesses. The existing legal provisions enable commercial banks in India to carry out universal banking, with the RBI having considerable regulatory discretion in permitting investments in other financial intermediaries, or in undertaking activities other than the core retail deposit-taking lending and investing in government securities. These discretionary powers have been used by the RBI to prohibit, restrict or permit risky non-core-bank activities by banks. Over a period, banks have diversified significantly into financial activities other than banking, but within the conditions and limits prescribed by the RBI. Hence, the current preference in global debates for restricting banks to 'boring banking' (that is, traditional retail deposit-taking and extending credit) has been observed by the RBI in exercising the discretion given to the banking regulator on this issue.

Although the global crisis hit several countries, it did not seriously affect many others in the context of a wide variety of structures of regulation. There is now a focus on reforming the regulatory structures, particularly in the severely affected countries. The proposals range from restoring the regulation of banking to central banks, to formal new institutional arrangements for ensuring financial stability. With regard to the latter, the relative roles of central banks and governments are under discussion. A separate agency for ensuring the safety of financial products is also under consideration.

In India, the function of the regulation of banking has been assigned to the RBI by a separate legislation. The RBI has interpreted its mandate to mean that the responsibility for stability rests with it. Its role has been facilitated by existing arrangements for coordination through the High Level Coordination Committee on Financial Markets, over which the RBI Governor presides, with the Finance Secretary for Government and heads of insurance, securities and pension regulators as members. The secretariat for the committee vests with the government and by convention, the Finance Minister informally approves the minutes of the meeting before it is formally approved by the governor as Chairman of the Committee.

A Critique of the Indian Experience

It may be useful to consider some major criticisms of the regulation of the financial sector in India. First, it is said that in the trade-off between growth and stability, India sacrificed growth due to its very stringent or intrusive regulation of the financial sector. It is difficult to assess the foregone benefits of a more liberalised financial environment, but the record of overall growth is certainly not inconsistent with the prevalent underlying savings, investment and productivity trends during this period. Sometimes it is held that the RBI's policies were conservative because it preferred to preserve the status quo. It is obvious that the RBI was active, inasmuch as it took several countercyclical measures.

Second, it is held that the goals of financial inclusion and deepening have not been achieved. It is true that there is significant scope in this regard, and more has to be done in this direction. However, the RBI can be justifiably proud of being a pioneer in this field, and for leading in innovative approaches with close collaboration with state governments. Views may differ on the extent to which these pioneering and enthusiastic efforts helped the cause of financial inclusion, and the extent to which regulatory approaches hindered the process of market-led financial inclusion. An interesting issue to be deliberated is whether more freedom to banks and financial markets than has been provided so far would achieve such objectives better or sooner.

It is also argued that the development of financial markets, especially in terms of deepening such markets and encouraging bond, currency and derivatives, has been hampered by the conservative regulation of the financial sector. The jury is perhaps still out on whether derivatives on a large scale in financial markets add to economic development. Similarly, it is not yet clear if the RBI's lack of support to making India a regional financial centre of the world was inappropriate. As of now, the RBI's judgement seems vindicated.

Third, it is mentioned that stability was a by-product of the dominance of the public sector in banking, and not a product of the regulation of the financial sector. It is true that the nature of governance and incentive frameworks in public-sector banks do not encourage excessive risk-taking. However, it can be pointed out that large private-sector banks and branches of foreign banks do operate in India, and that their operations in India were affected by the global crisis only very marginally. At the same time, the balance sheets of some branches of Indian private-sector banks outside the country were adversely affected, partly reflecting the regulatory environment in those jurisdictions relative to India. Thus, empirical evidence shows that the regulatory environment in India, which is common to both the public and the private sectors, has been conducive to both efficiency and stability.

Fourth, regulatory restrictions on banks, which dissuaded them from taking excessively risky exposures, are also criticized as having hampered economic growth. In this context, one may point to recent debates questioning the benefits of universal banking that imply larger risk-taking with depositors' funds or relying on volatile wholesale sources of funds.

Fifth, there is a view that the overall regulatory structures and framework are archaic and that the reform of the financial sector has been slow to meet the growing future needs of the country. This is a far broader question, and goes beyond the conduct of the regulation of the financial sector in the available legislative frameworks. However, many of the assumptions behind the accelerated reforms of the financial sector advocated in India, particularly by globally active financial institutions or official committees dominated by representatives of such institutions in the pre-crisis era, are being questioned and revisited globally. It is difficult to assert that what is described as 'gradual cautious deregulation' as practised in India was inappropriate when in other countries the current reform is towards the rollback of some deregulations. Clearly the 'right level' of regulation in the setting of a particular country is yet to be determined.

REFORMS IN INDIA: CURRENT PROPOSALS

Economic reforms as we know them now have been under progress since 1991, and the financial sector constitutes one element of such reforms. The performance of the financial sector, in terms of its contribution to growth and stability, is rated among the most impressive of all the sectors in India. The current proposals announced in the budget of 2010–11 are in many ways part of the continuing process. Yet, the elements of continuity in ideas and actions relating to reform have to be balanced with the lessons learnt from the experience of the global financial crisis and India's needs. It is necessary to view the current proposals as a mix of continuity and change in the given context.

There are three major sources of inspiration for the proposed reforms in the financial sector. First, there is an expectation that India will follow the G-20 consensus on reforms, even though many recognise that such consensus may not fully capture the prevailing country contexts. Actions of individual countries are also monitored in the G-20. Second, there is an overhang of reforms recommended by past committees appointed by the government on the subject. While it may be difficult for the government to totally dissociate itself from their recommendations, the emerging new global realities require a more nuanced response to their somewhat dated suggestions. The IMF is itself, however reluctantly, modifying its stance on several basic paradigms governing the financial sector, which had formed the basis of many of the recommendations made in the past.

Third, there are several domestically generated proposals for reform on the ground that the future needs concerning the growth of the Indian economy warrant reforms in the financial sector, although it has served India well so far. It is also said that the proposed reform should advance the cause of financial inclusion and, more broadly, that of inclusive growth. This approach recognises a far more complex mix of a more efficient functioning of markets through deregulation, and a more explicit recognition that finance and its regulation need to be treated as instruments of intervention of the state to facilitate development.

The current proposals reflect the government's intention as announced in the budget of 2010–11. These relate to (i) the establishment of a commission for legislative reforms in the financial sector; (ii) the establishment of a financial stability and development council; and (iii) the issue of licences for the establishment of new banks. It is essential to deliberate on each of these and explore ways of making a success of these ideas to which the government is already committed.

In implementing the decision to establish a commission on legislative reforms, it may be desirable to pay attention to some relevant factors that are mentioned below. First, there are already several legislative proposals made by the RBI and other bodies that have been before the government and the Parliament for several years. A review of the logic underlying them and the reasons for the delay in enacting them would enhance an understanding of the political economy of economic legislation in India. Second, the Financial Sector Assessment recently undertaken by the government and the RBI captures the desirable framework for legislative changes. These reflect the views of several eminent domestic and global experts, market participants and public policy, multilateral bodies and academics. A study of this will help to provide a sound basis for evaluating the principles underlying the approaches to reforms.

Third, an examination of the observed lacuna in existing legislations and the consideration of appropriate amendments can bring about immediate improvements in the legal framework. Fourth, global debates on optimal frameworks for the financial sector are as of now contentious. However, there is a preference for coordination among countries, especially of the G-20, in the framework for the regulation of the financial sector to the extent that it has cross-border significance. It is likely that some of the proposals, for instance the Tobin Tax or other forms of cross-border regulation, may warrant legislation at the national level in the future. The progress of the Commission's work will have to await these developments, particularly since there are no convincing or serious problems in the domestic situation that compel immediate action. In many ways, the work of the Commission has to be futuristic, and not a once-for-all time-bound exercise.

Finally, the scope of such a Commission needs to be carefully determined. The legal hurdles facing an efficient financial system often lie outside the regulation of the financial sector, as for instance the enforcement of property rights, tenancy legislation, dispute resolution, insolvency, etc. These are perhaps areas that are in need of urgent attention and priority in the Indian context. Hence, defining the scope, priority and time schedule are important tasks. The composition of the Commission and its terms of reference would naturally be consistent with such a defined comprehensive framework.

There appears to be a broad agreement in global debates that arrangements, where they do not exist, should be put in place to (i) ensure a better focus on financial stability by the monetary authority, the regulators, and also by the government; (ii) enable a greater degree of coordination among them; (iii) strive for greater accountability; and (iv) avoid any dilution of the operational autonomy or authority of the regulators. The proposal for a Financial Stability and Development Council is presumably addressed to putting such an arrangement in place in India.

First, the proposed arrangements in India would naturally devise innovations to ensure that the above objectives are better met than the existing mechanisms, which fortunately have not been found significantly wanting so far. Second, it may be useful to consider the logic behind the Deepak Parekh Committee's views that sought a statutory basis for the current arrangements, namely, a High Level Coordination Committee. Third, despite the initial enthusiasm in some countries to have the government take central place in the proposed new arrangements, the recent trend seems to be to put central banks in the central place. Fourth, as the recent crisis has shown, central banks play a critical role in crisis management. Hence it can be argued that they have a greater stake in maintaining stability relative to any other agency.

Fifth, in India, the RBI has a unique position in the sense that in addition to being the monetary authority, it has been assigned functions to regulate banking—admittedly the most vital of institutions—and some of the financial markets. In fact, it is already performing the functions of several regulators by itself, and is endowed with both the expertise and an enviable track record. Hence, the proposed arrangements should try to build on these proven strengths. Sixth, unlike the RBI, the boards of regulators of the financial sector are dominated by serving officials of the government, and so the proposed arrangements should avoid giving the unintended impression that the RBI's role is being eroded by equating it with others, since the RBI's governance permits only the sole nominee of the government to participate. The perceptions are important since, according to all global analysts, the RBI is one of the least independent central banks in the world as per the provisions of law. In any case, in India, as in other parliamentary democracies, the central bank is not a body provided in the constitution and it is accountable to the parliament through the Finance Ministry. Seventh, there were occasions in the past when there was some political instability that threatened the stability in financial markets. A relevant example is the flow of events in mid-May 2003, when soon after the elections there was a sort of vacuum—in fact, albeit not in law—in the political executive in New Delhi. The RBI took charge of the situation, took coordinated actions and credibly restored stability. It is essential to ensure that the proposed arrangements do not undermine the ability and authority of India's central bank to meet challenges to financial stability in times of purely temporary political uncertainties.

Finally, it is necessary to overcome the serious problems of design of a council that combines financial stability and regulation with development. While a focus on development in the conduct of monetary and regulation of banks is essential, public funding of development has to be essentially a fiscal responsibility. Hence, it is necessary to ensure that the proposed arrangements do not give the impression that India is moving back to the pre-reform era of using the financial sector as a means of funding the programmes of the government, or cross-subsidising at the behest of the government.

The announcement in the budget of 2010–11 that the RBI, which has the statutory responsibility for granting banking licences, would consider issuing new licences is welcome at this juncture. However, it is critical to ensure that such licences will necessarily serve the developmental objectives announced in the budget, although they could also potentially add to the efficiency and stability of the banking system by inducing more competition. The proposal is timely because the major private-sector banks operating in India are now incorporated in India, but are predominantly owned by foreigners. In view of the ample supply of domestic savings to meet well over 90 per cent of the demand for funds, the impressive technological capabilities and the high level of human skills, Indian-owned and Indian-incorporated banks have the potential to improve Indian banking to the best standards globally, and also become a force to reckon with in the global economy, provided the objectives behind giving new licences are realistic and the processes of granting licences are sound.

To ensure that the new banking licences serve the purpose of improving Indian banking, making it globally competitive and strong with a global reach, several studies and actions will be needed. First, the underlying reasons for the nationalisation of banks in 1969 have not entirely lost their relevance. They should be studied. Second, a detailed study of the fate of each bank licensed in the early 1990s in both the first batch and the second round will be useful. The unutilised bank licence also provides lessons that will be instructive. Third, experience has shown that the promises made by the licensee at the time of issue of the licence and their subsequent compliance are often at variance, and the RBI has little authority to take corrective action, especially in a deregulated environment. Cancellation of the licence of a bank that commences business is often an impractical proposition under the current legal framework. A study of compliance with the conditions imposed on bank licences issued, including promises of priority to, say, agriculture, would be helpful in devising correctives and pointing to a way forward.

Fourth, there have also been instances where full and reliable information on the fit and proper ownership of promoters was not brought to the notice of the RBI before the issue of licence. Perhaps placing every application and its accompanying information at every stage in the public domain would safeguard against such misleading representations. Fifth, the guidelines on ownership and governance issued in 2004 have helped to improve the consolidation and strengthening of private-sector banking. Hence, the issue of new licences could ideally be considered broadly, as per the guidelines already in position. Sixth, legal aspects, both in letter and spirit, cannot be ignored. As per the current legislation governing banks, voting rights are restricted to 10 per cent, whatever be the extent of actual ownership. When the RBI stipulates a higher percentage for a promoter's ownership, artificial slicing of ownership often becomes an operational necessity, and the RBI becomes a willing party to such slicing, thereby in a way undermining the intent of law. Amendments to the existing Act also envisage strengthening the regulatory authority of the RBI, consistent with global best practices. In view of the recent global experience with the banking industry and Indian's own experience, the proposed amendments to the law could ideally be carried out first and the new bank licences issued thereafter, so as to reduce uncertainties for all concerned.

Seventh, there is a global consensus that banks that are 'too big to fail' are sources of serious risk to financial stability. It is also recognised that it is not simply the size but a bank's systemic importance that makes them 'too big to fail'. Thus, if links are permitted between large corporate houses and banks, they become too important systemically to be allowed to fail. Globally, there is also a discomfort even with current proposals to allow such big banks with safeguards for two reasons: first, the formal recognition that they are 'too big to fail' encourages them to take excessive risks; and second, in any case regulatory capture is far more likely by such large entities. There is a preference to avoid such banks from emerging, and the feasibility of breaking up banks that are 'too big to fail' is being considered. In fact, there is a movement that insists that banks that are 'too big to fail' are 'too big to exist'. These considerations are reinforcing the global mood to deny a bank licence to real-sector entities like, say, General Electric in the US. Recent developments call for reinforcement rather than dilution of guidelines on appropriate ownership and governance. Eighth, the global trend has been one of serious discomfort with the combination of non-bank functions with traditional banking. In the US, there is a serious proposal to reverse the trend and move back towards narrow banking. The legacy of a non-bank cannot be ignored when it sponsors or becomes a bank. These lessons at the global level, learnt after a heavy price, would also provide guidance for us in India.

Finally, it is not clear whether a licence would be granted for injecting private capital and management into select RRBs. This could be in the form of public-private participation, by replacing the existing sponsorship of public-sector banks with the dynamism of the private sector to serve rural areas in a limited jurisdiction. This approach can be the beginning of a decentralised but focused developmental banking to rural India through public-private partnership.

CONCLUSION

Financial-sector reform has taken on new meaning all over the world. Until the crisis, reform of the financial sector meant deregulation. That was yesterday's reality, but today's truth is that reform of the financial sector globally refers to elements of re-regulation and improving quality as well as the effectiveness of regulation.

India may feel relieved to have avoided the worst effects of the crisis in the financial sector. That is not enough. In order to move forward, it must appreciate both global realities and the Indian context. In moving forward with appropriate reforms in the financial sector, the following factors must be borne in mind: (i) the financial sector and its reform is not an end in itself; (ii) the risks are amplified if the reforms in fiscal and real sectors are not in consonance with the pace of reform in financial-sector regulation; and (iii) the highest priority should be accorded to efficient intermediation of domestic savings and domestic investment with a wide participation of the people of India.

India, Asia and the Global Economy: Resilience and Recovery*

*A*sia, and in particular China and India have shown remarkable resilience during the crisis and contributed impressively to the global economic recovery. The first section of the chapter identifies the reasons for such resilience followed by an assessment of prospects and challenges, in the second section. The third and fourth sections analyse the future of two distinguishing characteristics of the Asian model, namely export-led growth and bank-dominated financial sector. The concluding section brings together lessons from the Asian experience and its increasing claims for leadership in the global economy. In the narration, Indian experience is contrasted with experience of other EMEs of Asia.

* This chapter is an edited version of comments made at a High Level International Conference on Asia, organised by the Republic of Korea and the IMF, Daejeon, 12 July 2010.

REASONS FOR RESILIENCE OF INDIA AND ASIA

India's resilience during the crisis may partly be attributed to recognition of its vulnerabilities and the precautionary steps taken in macroeconomic management as well as regulating the financial sector during the pre-crisis period. In view of the high fiscal deficit and large stock of public debt, a calibrated approach was adopted in dismantling the regime of financial repression that enabled smooth management of public debt. In opening the debt markets to non-residents a gradual approach was adopted. Similarly, in the external sector the policy preference was to contain current account deficit at moderate levels despite the attraction of a far higher current account deficit that could be funded through strong capital inflows. Thus, liquidity buffers were built both in domestic and foreign currencies during boom time, keeping in view the difficult balances needed between objectives of growth, price stability and financial stability.

A precautionary approach was built into the regulatory polices by adopting a countercyclical approach and by enlarging scope of regulation beyond the confines of banks. At the same time, growth in credit was encouraged in some sectors while it was discouraged in some others sectors like real estate and equities. This precautionary approach was buttressed by fiscal consolidation, that was underway, and high domestic savings, in addition to the supportive monetary policy measures.

In contrast, the other emerging economies of Asia, including China, had the benefit of a strong fiscal position, and in general current account surpluses. Financial sector however displays greater diversity, though, as in India, traditional banking dominates in most large economies. Consequent upon the Asian crisis, banking system was strengthened and greater reliance was placed on retail of traditional banking business in East Asia and Korea. There are strong similarities between India and the rest of emerging Asia in regard to dominance of traditional banking. However, in China and India public sector dominates the banking activity. There are also similarities between India, China and the rest of emerging Asian in regard to high level of domestic savings, in particular the level of household savings.

There are differences of opinion as to whether it was the macroeconomic management or the state of financial sector that contributed to the resilience of the Asian region. However, there is a recognition that prompt and effective action was taken by policymakers in Asia to moderate the impact of crisis and lead the way for rapid recovery. Social factors, geopolitical considerations and the recent experience with the crisis in East Asia may have contributed, in different measures, in determining the actions taken by different countries at the national level. In brief, the policy measures in emerging Asia were precautionary before the crisis and effective during the crisis.

PROSPECTS AND CHALLENGES

The prospects for India appear bright for several reasons. The impact of the global crisis on the Indian economy has been less than what it was in most of the EMEs. The impact could be less than what the movements in GDP indicate, mainly for two reasons. First, the global crisis coincided with deceleration in growth of agriculture due to seasonal factors. Second, there were policy perceptions of overheating prior to the crisis, and hence policy actions were taken to cool the economy. Hence the domestic cycle was also undergoing some correction by the time the crisis erupted. In addition, in India there is impressive balance, in macro terms, between savings and investments, investment demand and consumption demand, and domestic and external demand. The current account deficit appears sustainable despite the recent increases in the deficit. The financial sector's capacity to cater to the needs of development while maintaining stability is not in doubt, though there is scope for improvement. Corporate sector in India is often credited with impressive capacities to innovate, and such skills are particularly precious during periods of stress. Finally, the stimulus, both fiscal and monetary, was prompt, ample and effective.

There are, however, significant challenges ahead for India. In regard to the fiscal position, the structural component of the fiscal deficit remains high. While the extent of fiscal stimulus was not as high as it was in the case of some other Asian economies, much of the stimulus at the time of the crisis appears to be more structural than cyclical. The structural factors include the hike in the civil services pay and the rural employment guarantee scheme. Hence the scope for withdrawal of the fiscal stimulus may be somewhat constrained. To that extent, the burden on monetary policy will continue and may even intensify. Secondly, India has been experiencing high inflation at a time when many countries were faced with deflationary pressure. In some ways, India along with the rest of emerging Asia, is beginning to face early onset of inflationary pressures. Thirdly, the external position is vulnerable to possible commodity shocks especially in the area of fuel prices. The current account deficit is reaching an uncomfortable level of 3 per cent of GDP even after the comfort of remittance of non-resident Indians to the tune over 3 per cent of GDP. Overall, the major challenges on the way forward during the medium term relate to the management of the domestic economy and balance of payments. The management of the domestic economy requires attention to physical infrastructure such as power and roads, social infrastructure such as education and health, and institutional development, including in particular, governments.

The prospects for the rest of emerging Asia, as a whole, appear particularly bright due to a strong fiscal position and a reasonably robust financial sector. The stimulus has been prompt and effective, and the withdrawal from the stimulus commenced relatively early as compared to the rest of the world. The main challenges to the region relate to managing the external sector both on current and capital account, and inflationary processes including upward movement in asset prices. Most of them are dependent on the external sector for maintaining momentum for growth. Moderation in aggregate demand due to the crisis and uncertain prospects of growth in US and Europe, and recent developments in the area using Euro as currency, add uncertainties to the outlook for external demand. Any effort by China to shift from external demand-driven economy to domestic demand-driven economy, will not only result in a reduction in exports, but will also result in import reduction, particularly from rest of Asia. In other words, the import intensity of China's export sector may be far more than the import intensity of China's domestic demand. In such a scenario, the Asian economies dependent on China for the large part of their export demand may be adversely affected due to moderation in growth of demand for their products, both in advanced economies, and to some extent in China. Options for Asia to meet shortfall in export demand include expanding domestic demand and intra-regional trade. In doing so, a choice has to be made between emphasis on investment demand that adds to potential output necessary for developing economies and consumption demand that could impact domestic savings.

There is some diversity in challenges between India and the rest of emerging Asia in the management of current account. The strategy for India may have to be to attempt an increase in exports in view of its large trade deficit. The trade deficit, which is approaching 10 per cent of GDP is particularly challenging for India. It is possible that sustained growth in India will facilitate significant imports from other Asian economies.

In regard to the capital flows, it is likely that there will be a common challenge for India and the rest of emerging Asia, because of the region's attractiveness relative to other parts of the world in terms of both growth and stability. In particular, the relatively easy monetary policy and fiscal policy adopted by advanced economies may continue while tighter monetary policies may be warranted in Asia, thus providing a window of opportunity for strong capital inflows. While the challenge is common for India and the rest of Asia, policy challenges are daunting for India for two reasons. First, the current account deficit is already almost 3 per cent of GDP, and is likely to persist if the anticipated impressive growth materialises. Hence India, unlike most other Asian economies, is dependent on some capital flows, but will have to avoid excess capital flows. A fine balancing of the level is complex in managing capital flows when they are driven by push factors from the rest of the world with no changes in domestic fundamentals. Secondly, India is dependent on volatile portfolio flows and share of short-term component of external liabilities has escalated in recent past.

Inflationary pressures are common to India and the rest of emerging Asia, though they seem to be stronger in India. The boom in asset prices appears to be higher in the rest of emerging Asia. Inflationary pressures have set in emerging Asia as a whole, and the pressure on asset prices, in particular equity and real estate pose a challenge to policymakers since the growth in bank credit to directly productive sectors is yet to gather momentum.

Indian economy is likely to be less affected due to Euro developments, relative to the rest of Asia since its trade is more diversified and its dependence on export of goods is relatively less compared to the rest of Asia. In regard to services and remittances from non-resident Indians, the impact is also likely to be moderate. The financial markets are likely to be jittery, and to that extent, the uncertainties will impact India also. In particular, the volatility in regard to portfolio flows may be large. The rest of Asia is likely to be impacted through their dependence on exports though its exposure to Europe is not as high as it is to the US. The rest of Asia is also subjected to pressures of volatility in capital flows but, the preponderance of FDI in their inflows is likely to moderate the extent of volatility. In addition, the initiatives taken for integration at the regional level through the Chang Mai Initiative are likely to provide a sense of confidence and some safety net to the rest of Asia, relative to India.

WILL THE ASIAN EXPORT GROWTH MODEL WORK?

Most economies of Asia, including India, have demonstrated the benefits that could accrue to a developing country by adopting the export growth model. However, in view of the global crisis, there is a debate now as to the extent to which it would continue to be attractive. First, everyone cannot export, and someone has to import. If Asia is emerging as a dominant economy in the world, it is inevitable that the prospects of export to the group of less dominant economies will be modest. Secondly, in recent years, there was considerable substitution of domestic production by imports in the global economy, but such a substitution is not inexhaustible. No doubt, developments in technology expand scope for such substitution, but new entrants to the export growth model may face more difficult terrain to capture export markets. In brief, the growth in tradable goods in world trade may not continue at the level at which it has been in the past. Thirdly, the growth in world trade may be moderate since the GDP growth of the world is moderating in the short-to-medium term. Fourthly, in view of the large public debt in the US and UK, some austerity measures are inevitable and they may also moderate the demand for exports from Asia. Some protectionist tendencies by advanced economies should not be ruled out. Finally, the skills that are needed to be globally competitive may become even more demanding than in the past, since there are many other countries including South Asia and Africa, which will be competing with emerging Asia by adopting export growth model strategies for a pool of exports.

As against these constraining factors, there are compensating factors which may indicate reasonable prospects for the export growth model. The scope for services exports is increasing. Second, technological developments are making transport and communication easier, more economical, and hence amenable to world trade. Third, as countries such as Korea and China, are moving towards higher labour costs, other economies may see opportunities to expand their exports. This had happened when China replaced Japan and Korea as the major exporter from Asia. Finally, it is possible for countries to have more exports and more imports, and thus have value-added to the advantage of both economies, provided there is no recourse to increased protectionism.

WILL THE ASIAN FINANCIAL MODEL WORK?

The basic characteristic of the Asian financial sector model, which indeed is common between India and rest of emerging Asia, is the domination of commercial banks. Hong Kong and Singapore are, no doubt, exceptions. One view is that domination of traditional commercial banks is not the most efficient form of intermediation in the financial sector. Generally, a banking system demands significantly larger capital than financial markets, to finance the real economy. A bank-dominated system has been described as essentially an over-regulated system and, that in any case, excessive regulatory capital hurts financial intermediation and makes it expensive for the real economy. It is also argued that banks by themselves do not add to the maintenance of stability, as the recent global crisis has shown. It is argued that a diversified financial system with multiplicity of institutions and instruments is more effective and adds to stability.

As against these arguments, the empirical evidence of emerging Asia so far indicates that the bank-dominated system has enabled the region to maintain a high rate of growth and, at the same time, maintain stability, particularly after the necessary correctives in terms of improving the banking system consequent upon the Asian crisis of 1997. Cross country comparisons of developments in the financial sector among EMEs do not indicate conclusively that those with diversified financial sector performed better in growth, level of savings, investment and productivity. There has been no evidence that bond markets are essential for economic growth, since Europe, Japan and much of Asia, which have developed their infrastructure though bond markets did not really thrive. Even in UK, the financing of infrastructure was mostly in the public sector, and bond markets played only a marginal role. Even where the financial markets existed in other EMEs and even in Asia, the intermediation in financial markets was essentially through the direct operations of banks themselves or through the indirect use of bank deposits. For instance, during the recent crisis, it has been observed that the ultimate burden of excessive leverage in the financial sector as a whole fell on the banking system. If the proprietary trading by banks is not permitted, it is not clear whether such diversified financial markets will have enough depth, particularly in EMEs—barring financial centres like Hong Kong and Singapore.

It is possible to argue that many of the prescriptions for regulatory reform in advanced economies are tilting the balance towards traditional banking in the financial sector. Asian economies may be conscious of the benefits of continuing with the traditional bank-dominated system and, in particular, retail bank domination. It is very difficult at this stage to assess whether the Asian financial model will work for the rest of the world, but the tilt within the financial sector reform around the world is towards the features representing the Asian financial model.

ARE THERE LESSONS FROM THE ASIAN EXPERIENCE FOR THE GLOBAL ECONOMY

It will be useful to compare the experience of EMEs and developing countries of Latin America, Eastern Europe and Africa, with the experience of Asian economies. This may bring out clearly the factors that appear most relevant for the strength and resilience of Asian economies while recording significant GDP growth. First, it is very clear that from a macro point of view, Asian economies relative to many other EMEs have a strong domestic savings component in the GDP and, in particular, household savings are high as a proportion of the GDP. Second, relative to other EMEs the strength of fiscal position is clear except in the case of India. Fiscal strength gives headroom for action at the time of the crisis and fiscal authorities are the ultimate bearers of all risks. Third, in most Asian countries including Japan and India, government securities are held by residents. This may be contrasted with experience of Greece and other transition economies, where non-residents were the main bondholders.

Fourth, many Asian economies including India built significant levels of foreign exchange reserves which provided comfort to the countries and markets. Their actual utilisation may not fully reflect their value during stress or crisis. Fifth, most of them maintained current account surplus or marginal current account deficit. Current account deficit is a sign of dependence on the external world for sustainability and growth. Obviously, excessive dependence on foreign savings for a prolonged period brings instability. Sixth, the domination of domestic banking system, in particular retail banking in the financial sector in most economies, except in Singapore and Hong Kong, helped rendering stability. Asian economies which suffered during the Asian crisis seem to have strengthened their banking system by reducing dependence on wholesale deposits and both serious currency and maturity mismatches. Finally, the share of foreign banks in banking activity is relatively low in emerging Asia compared to other EMEs. It is essential to undertake in-depth study of the relative importance of each of these distinguishing features in imparting efficiencies and resilience to emerging Asia so far.

In Asia, by and large, there is a better balance between the growth of real sector, as a source of employment, and stability with the financial sector, playing an enabling and supporting role. The political leadership was not exhibiting any perception that it was afraid of the power of financial markets. Regional cooperation in Asia has demonstrated the advantages of such cooperation and by itself could provide stability without necessarily undermining the forces towards benefits of global integration. Asian economies in general have demonstrated the importance of diversity in policies. Many countries have been following different policies and do have different fiscal positions and the degree of openness to global finance. In addition, Asian economies followed a prescription of a development model which was not the standard model advocated at a global level, and in particular, by the IMF. It is the diversity in the global macroeconomic management and financial sector policies that has helped Asia with its growth and stability. This is an important lesson for the global economy that diversity by itself has some advantages. If a globally unified policy and regulatory framework for financial sector was agreed upon and imposed on all countries during the past, it is quite possible that Asia would not have been able to sustain its growth and provide stabilising elements that it has been able to do in the context of the current global crisis.

ASIA AND THE IMF

What has been the role of the IMF in Asia? India faced a crisis in 1991. It received assistance from the IMF. There was agreement about the need for significant economic reforms, but India followed its own trajectory of reform. The role of the IMF in India has been, by and large, successful, and their relationship has been positive. No doubt, popular opinion in India is still similar to most other countries in terms of the stigma attached while seeking any assistance from the IMF. In the case of East Asia, the IMF conditionality is considered severe and, in fact, the Asian crisis is described as the IMF crisis in East Asia. In these countries, there are bitter memories of any association with Asia. There is also a perception that the conditionality imposed on Asian economies was far more severe than in Latin America. However, after the onset of the crisis emerging Asia is confident of its resilience, strength and bright future.

The IMF itself became virtually irrelevant on the eve of the crisis. The IMF appears chastened by its experiences, and there are signs that it is now open to new ideas. There is a deliberate effort on the part of IMF to reach out to EMEs and in particular to the development experience of Asia. The IMF has fully realised the stigma that is attached while approaching the IMF for assistance—even in advanced economies, and perhaps even more than the developing countries. The IMF's relationship with regional arrangements has changed since the time it was opposed to the creation of the Asian Monetary Fund. Recent arrangements in regard to tackling the debt crisis of Greece in Europe in collaboration with the ECB, illustrates the inevitability of the IMF working closely with other regional arrangements. While governance arrangements are yet to change for the better, the IMF as an institution is attempting to be significantly more heterodox. It has started being open to diverse ideological positions relating to growth and stability. Finally, in the G-20 that has acquired significance more recently, Asia has noticeable representation, and as an important operating arm of the G-20, the IMF is trying to demonstrate its even handed approach towards Asian countries.

Will Asia assume leadership in the global economy? The countries of Asia, as a whole, have significant diversity in political systems and economic management. The region contains some OECD countries, such as Japan and Korea; important financial centres such as Singapore and Hong Kong; fast growing economies like Vietnam and Indonesia; and very large economies like China and India. The ASEAN is an economic forum to reckon as a region, India accounts for significant economic activity, but it also has a large and diverse population. The demands on climate, globally competitive skills, and above all, governance, are likely to be intensive for almost all parts of Asia. Since the crisis, the issue of inequality, especially increasing inequality, is disturbing. Even as the region grows, the per capita incomes for many countries will remain lower than the US and Europe. In a globalised world, income and inequality have to be measured in global terms and not just within the nation, and on both counts, Asian economies have big challenges.

Close regional cooperation in Asia, particularly in trade and investment can boost their economies individually and collectively. Such cooperation and economic integration will strengthen their position in the global economy. There are strong complementarities between large economies. For instance, India has fiscal and current account deficits while the rest of emerging Asia has surpluses on both accounts. India's infrastructure deficit can absorb private investment flows and expertise from the rest of emerging Asia. The central banks can diversify their currency composition of their reserves by investing in each other's government securities. While India has strength in services, the rest of emerging Asia has a strong manufacturing sector. Hong Kong, Singapore, Shanghai and Mumbai have strong financial infrastructure. Asia is rich in resource endowment. In brief, Asia is and will continue to be in the forefront of global economic activity which is a matter of satisfaction. Regional cooperation and economic integration will be of great value to the economies and may makeup, to a limited extent, loss of growth momentum from the US, U.K and Europe. Regional cooperation will help Asia's public policies in tackling severe challenges in managing the large population infused with unprecedented hopes and aspirations of a far better future. Such close regional cooperation will pave the way for Asia to be a part of the global leadership in the global economy.

Twenty-Seven

The Global Crisis and Exit Strategies: An Indian Perspective*

$\mathcal{T}$he exit strategies of any country, from stimulus and other extra ordinary measures taken to combat a global crisis, have to be viewed in the context of the entry measures taken to manage the crisis from which exit is sought. In reality, the exit strategies could also include some pre-crisis policies that were responsible for the crisis. Ideally, exit policies should be considered as an extension of a review of policies adopted in the pre-crisis period and the measures taken during the crisis period. The first section of the chapter highlights the perceptions on the Indian economy prior to the crisis as one of the riskiest to being one of the most resilient when the crisis materialised. The second section gives a brief account of the three phases of Indian economic policy, namely pre-crisis, crisis and post-crisis, which correspond to the initiation of exit measures. The third section explains monetary measures and exit strategies; while the fourth, fifth and sixth sections give an outline of regulatory, fiscal and

* This chapter is an edited version of a presentation made at the International Conference on Economics, sponsored by the Turkish Economic Association, Girne, 2 September 2010.

external sector policies in relation to exit strategies. This is followed by locating some issues that appear to be common to exit strategies in many countries, keeping in view Indian experiences so far. The concluding section lists some challenges specific to managing exit from the extraordinary measures taken to mitigate the impact of the global crisis.

FROM RISKY TO RESILIENT: PERCEPTIONS ON THE INDIAN ECONOMY

Not long ago, India was ranked among the riskiest economies, as the following extracts from *The Economist*, 17 November 2007, would show: "The riskiest economies, all with current-account deficits and relatively high consumer-price inflation, are India, Turkey and Hungary"; "Economies where inflation and credit growth are already high and budget deficits large, such as India, have less room to ease monetary or fiscal policy if the economy weakens"; "Instead, India's poor risk-rating should ring alarm bells"; and "China's economy looks less risky thanks to a small official budget deficit (many reckon that it really has a surplus) and its vast current-account surplus and reserves. The other two members of the so-called BRIC group, Brazil and Russia, also have a better risk-rating than India".[1]

In 2010, India is credited with having weathered the crisis better than many, and continues to register a commendable growth in GDP. The answer to this paradox is partly explained by extracts from a speech that referred to the observation in *The Economist* and the precautionary steps taken to minimise chances of perceived risks materialising.

> The reform process in India, lays emphasis on appropriate sequencing of reforms. Firstly, the Reserve Bank, in particular, has been treating reforms in financial and external sectors as a means to broader objectives of accelerated growth with stability rather than as ends in themselves. Secondly, reform in external sector makes a clear distinction between the costs and the benefits of

trade liberalisation, and between the risks and rewards of capital account liberalisation. Thirdly, a hierarchy in capital flows is recognised and management of capital account is advocated on that basis. Fourthly, the pace and content of reform in financial and external sectors are calibrated after taking into account reforms in real, fiscal and public sector as a whole.

These approaches to reform have had a salutary impact on the preparedness of financial institutions, financial markets, public policy and above all, public opinion to participate gainfully in the reform process.

Way forward, there is a considerable merit in persisting with these approaches that have ensured macro-stability, while fine tuning them to the changing times and global challenges. Reserve Bank will, in regard to both growth and stability, continue to pursue its policy of being enlightened by theory, educated by global experiences, and conditioned by domestic realities without being bound by any particular ideology.

Way forward, with a view to mitigate the potential risks, there is clearly a case for continuing with such a well nuanced and coordinated policy of management of public debt, as long as fiscal vulnerability persists, while at the same time, responding to changing circumstances.[2]

The approach to economic management described above provides a back-drop to the strategies for exit from management of global financial crisis also.

PRE-CRISIS, CRISIS AND POST-CRISIS

During recent times, three distinct phases of Indian economic policy are discernible, namely, the pre-crisis period (2003–8), the crisis period (2008–9) and post crisis period (October 2009 onwards) which corresponds to the operation of exit strategies. Before encountering the contagion from the global economic crisis in 2008–9, the Indian economy exhibited five successive years of high growth (averaging at about 8.9 per cent) with moderate inflation (averaging at about 5.3 per cent) and macroeconomic stability during 2003–8 (the fiscal year in India is from 1 April to 31 March). In the period preceding the crisis, the policy challenge to deal with large capital inflows, high inflation and risks posed by high credit growth was met by monetary tightening, countercyclical risk weights and provisioning norms while persisting with reforms. These policies were supplemented by some moderation in mounting fiscal deficits as well as current account deficits, active management of capital account and build-up of forex reserves.

As the domestic macroeconomic conditions changed significantly since August–September 2008 under the impact of the global financial crisis, the policy attention shifted to crisis management. In order to contain the adverse effects of the contagion from the global economic crisis the government necessitated monetary and fiscal stimuli with a view to moderate the pace of slowdown in growth, preserve domestic banks and financial institutions, and maintain orderly and well functioning markets.

This period of crisis management was followed by policy focus on managing the recovery. In the second half of 2009–10, despite a deficient monsoon and an adverse global environment, the domestic economy exhibited robust recovery, and at the same time inflationary pressures started to become more evident. Keeping in view the changes in the domestic as well as global economic factors, the policymakers in India, from October 2009, commenced an exit strategy by withdrawing support measures. This exit process is still underway.

MONETARY POLICY MEASURES AND THE EXIT STRATEGIES

In 2004, the RBI took measures to modulate the monetary overhang that was building on account of sustained expansion in money growth. The withdrawal of monetary accommodation commenced in 2004 with gradual increase in both repo and reverse repo rates. Despite the easy monetary policy prevalent in many global economies, the RBI continued with monetary tightening to modulate any build up of inflationary expectations as well as asset bubbles, and this process continued till the global crisis in September 2008. While the repo rate under the Liquidity Adjustment Facility (a facility under which the RBI injects or absorbs liquidity on a daily basis through repo and reverse repo operations to influence the overnight interest rates in money markets) increased from 6.0 per cent at end-March 2004 to 9.0 per cent at end-July 2008, the reverse repo rate increased from 4.50 per cent to 6.0 per cent during the same period. The CRR (the ratio of minimum statutory cash reserves to be kept with the RBI) was also raised successively from 4.50 per cent at end-March 2004 to 9.0 per cent at end-August 2008. This increase was enforced due to extraordinary liquidity conditions despite the medium-term commitment to bringing the CRR to less than 3 per cent, as part of removing policy constraints on the banking sector.

In addition, significant intervention in forex markets as part of the open market operations was undertaken to mop up excessive and volatile capital flows, resulting in build-up of forex reserves. Simultaneously, sterilisation operations were undertaken. Since the RBI is not permitted to issue bonds on its own account, the government consented to authorise the RBI (within limits prescribed from time to time) to issue bonds on behalf of the government under an agreement entered into in 2004. These bonds are no different from treasury bonds except that proceeds cannot be used by the government as long as they continue to be held under the scheme, called the Market Stabilisation Scheme. In brief, the excess liquidity, both in forex and rupee, stood stored up for use in future, as and when needed.

As the global liquidity crisis deepened in September 2008, the RBI pursued an accommodative monetary policy. These included augmenting domestic and foreign exchange liquidity and sharp reduction in the policy rates. The RBI used multiple instruments such as the Liquidity Adjustment Facility, open market operations, CRR and securities under the Market Stabilisation Scheme to augment the liquidity in the system. In a span of seven months between October 2008 and April 2009, the policy activism during the crisis phase was reflected in: (i) the repo rate reduced by 425 basis points, from 9 per cent to 4.75 per cent, in pre-crisis phase; (ii) the reverse repo rate reduced by 275 basis points, from 6 per cent to 3.25 per cent, in pre-crisis phase; (iii) the CRR reduced by a cumulative 400 basis points, from 9.0 per cent to 5.0 per cent, in pre-crisis phase and (iv) the potential provision of primary liquidity being of the order of 10.5 per cent of GDP.

For enhancing the availability of domestic liquidity, besides the usual reduction in CRR, greater access under the Liquidity Adjustment Facility through repos, and unwinding of the Market Stabilisation Scheme securities, several other conventional as well as unconventional instruments were also used. The choice of instruments was based on the nature and expected magnitude of the demand for liquidity, from time to time, such as a second Liquidity Adjustment Facility window providing access to liquidity in the afternoon as against the normal Liquidity Adjustment Facility access in the morning, a special 14 days repo facility using the eligible securities up to 1.5 per cent for meeting the liquidity needs of non-banking financial companies (NBFCs), housing finance companies and mutual funds, increase in export credit refinance limit for commercial banks, and special refinance facilities for specialised public sector financial institutions. At the request of the government, money was released, as a temporary advance, to the banks equivalent to the amounts due to the banks from the government. The additional liquidity that was made available by the end of the year amounted to 7.9 per cent of GDP.

There are several features of these special liquidity measures that accompanied the softening of interest rate. First, refinance was provided to the banks on collateral basis, to enable the banks to fund the immediate liquidity needs of development finance institutions, mutual funds and NBFCs. The banks were obliged to assess risks in providing liquidity to these institutions. Second, refinance facility was time bound, and thus exit was in a way built-in. Third, the advance to banks towards dues from the government was in the nature of temporary ways and means advance to the central government, being a sort of targeted creation of temporary liquidity for the government by the RBI. Fourth, the amounts utilised under refinance were modest since the announcement of large facility had the effect of comfort of liquidity in the markets and for the institutions. Fifth, refinance ensured that liquidity was provided by the central bank in quantities that were sought by markets and institutions, and such liquidity has inbuilt scope for automatic exit. In brief, the multiplicity of instruments in place and those already utilised in the direction of tightening, could be resorted to and used in the opposite direction of easing, with little loss of time, energy or credibility. Indeed, all these crisis-management measures were undertaken with instruments that were already in place and efforts were made to ensure that these instruments were either time-bound or easily reversible, as and when considered necessary.

The RBI began the first phase of exit in October 2009. The first exit strategy was the withdrawal of the unconventional measures taken during the crisis period. This was followed by the increase in CRR and policy rates. In October 2009, the RBI announced the first phase of exit from the expansionary monetary policy by terminating some sector-specific facilities (such as the special refinance facility and the term repo facility) and restoring the statutory liquidity ratio (SLR) of scheduled commercial banks to its pre-crisis level. The CRR of scheduled banks has been raised by 25 basis points from 5.75 per cent to 6.0 per cent of their net demand and time liabilities effective from April 2010. Subsequently, as a part of the calibrated exit strategy the Liquidity Adjustment Facility repo and reverse repo rates were increased successively to 5.75 per cent and 4.5 per cent, respectively, effective from July 2010.

REGULATORY POLICIES AND EXIT

Since April 2005, the RBI has been concerned over the rapid growth in credit, and the overdrawn state of the banking system to sustain credit disbursement, given the mismatches between the source and the use of funds, and the associated increase in credit-deposit ratios for certain banks. Recognising the unprecedented credit growth to the real estate sector during 2004–7, the provisioning requirements and risk weights were increased as countercyclical regulatory measures to prevent a build up of asset bubble. Illustratively, the risk weight on the commercial real estate exposure was increased from 100 per cent to 125 per cent in July 2005. Given the continued rapid expansion in credit to the commercial real estate sector, the risk weight on exposure to this sector was increased to 150 per cent in May 2006. The provisioning on standard commercial real estate advances was increased from 0.25 per cent to 2.00 per cent in stages. In order to ensure that asset quality was maintained in the light of high credit growth, risk weights and provisioning requirements on standard advances for banks' exposures to the sectors showing above average growth had been progressively raised during the last 3–4 years, as a countercyclical measure. The general provisioning requirement of residential housing loans beyond Rs 20.0 lakhs was raised from 0.40 per cent in May 2006 to 1.0 per cent in January 2007.

However, with the global financial crisis starting to affect the Indian economy from September 2008 onwards, the RBI reversed some of the earlier countercyclical measures. In view of the growing concern of possible increase in stress in the Indian banking system, certain modifications were made to the guidelines on restructuring of advances in August 2008 as a one-time measure and for a limited period. In November 2008, as a further countercyclical measure to counter the downturn, the provisioning on standard commercial real estate advances was brought down to 0.40 per cent.

With the restoration of normal conditions, the focus of regulatory policy in India has once again shifted to improving the provisioning cover and enhancing the soundness of individual banks. It was decided in October 2009 that banks should ensure that their provision coverage ratio (consisting of specific provisions against NPAs and floating provisions) is not less than 70 per cent by end-September 2010. This stipulation is a part of a countercyclical provisioning policy on which work is underway. The final policy is expected to deal with build-up of provisioning buffers and their utilisation.

FISCAL POLICY AND THE EXIT

As part of the reform process, fiscal consolidation was taken up taking advantage of the buoyancy in the economy. The gross fiscal deficit of the central government as a percentage of GDP, which was 5.9 per cent in 2002–3 was brought down to 2.7 per cent by 2007–8. Revenue Deficit which was 4.4 in 2002–3 was brought down to 1.1 per cent by 2007–8. There was a dramatic improvement in the finances of state governments also. The combined fiscal deficit of the Centre and the states was brought down from 9.6 per cent to 4.3 per cent during the corresponding period. The public-debt to GDP ratio, which has been one of the highest in the world at about 80.3 per cent of GDP in 2002–3, showed some improvement during this period and was brought down to 72.0 per cent in 2007–8. No doubt, level of public debt and fiscal deficits continued to be a cause for concern, but their reduction in the years preceding the crisis provided some headroom to inject cyclical fiscal policies. Further, almost the whole of public debt of India is held by residents, especially banks, and is mostly denominated in domestic currency and issued at fixed coupon rate. These characteristics helped the RBI to manage stress on the market.

To counter the negative fallout of the global slowdown on the Indian economy, the government responded by providing focused fiscal stimulus packages during 2008–9 in the form of tax cuts, increased expenditure on government consumption and enhanced investment in infrastructure. Conforming with the prevailing tax policy, during 2008–9, the corporate tax rates were kept unchanged, while the threshold limit of exemption for Personal Income Tax

(PIT) was raised and the four slabs of tax were revised upwards. With regard to indirect taxes, the budget of the government announced reduction in general Central Value Added Tax (CENVAT) on all goods from 16 per cent to 14 per cent with a view to providing stimulus to the manufacturing sector.

The expansionary fiscal stance continued to support aggregate demand during 2009–10. The general CENVAT rate was further reduced by 4.0 percentage points and 2.0 percentage points in December 2008 and February 2009, respectively, to 8 per cent. Additional expenditure amounting to 3.0 per cent of GDP was authorised during October 2008 and February 2009. Of the expenditure measures, revenue expenditure constituted around 84 per cent and the capital component accounted for the rest. On the whole, the fiscal stimulus measures appear to have given more emphasis to supporting consumption demand rather than investment demand.

The fiscal stimulus led to an increase in gross fiscal deficit of Centre from 2.7 per cent in 2007–8 to 6.7 per cent of GDP in 2008–9. The revenue deficit increased from 1.1 per cent to 2.7 per cent of GDP during the same period. The state governments' fiscal deficit rose by about two percentage points and the combined fiscal deficit rose sharply from 4.3 per cent in 2007–8 to 10.0 per cent in 2009–10. The deficit to GDP ratio increased less dramatically, thanks to the growth momentum.

A calibrated exit from the expansionary stance of fiscal policy was announced by the end of February 2010 with partially rolling back of tax cuts and better expenditure management. The Union Budget 2010–11 has proposed to bring down revenue deficit and gross fiscal deficit during 2010–11 to 4.0 per cent and 5.5 of GDP, respectively. The reduction in deficits assumes several one-off receipts such a telecom licence fee and sale of some shares in public enterprises. The Medium Term Fiscal Policy Statement (MTFPS), laying down the fiscal consolidation path in terms of rolling targets, indicates that revenue deficit and gross fiscal deficit will be brought down to

2.7 per cent and 4.1 per cent of GDP in 2012–13, respectively. The government has also indicated in the MTFPS to reduce the debt to GDP ratio to 48.2 per cent by 2012–13.

EXTERNAL SECTOR AND THE EXIT

The improvement in fiscal position was accompanied by improvement in foreign exchange reserves from a level of US$ 76.1 billion, at end March 2003, to US$ 312.1 billion by end March 2008, while the external debt of the nation increased less dramatically to a level of US$ 224.57 billion. The level of external debt continued to be at modest levels (around 18 per cent of GDP) and short term components did not escalate significantly. The current account deficit was contained at around one per cent of GDP. Thus the external sector also had significant cushions to absorb shocks due to the crisis.

Moreover, the variety of instruments available for managing capital account, in particular controls over interest rates on foreign currency deposits of non-residents, external commercial borrowings and limits on foreign currency liabilities of banks, were used to moderate volatile and large capital inflows. Normalisation of these restrictions helped to some extent in enabling inflows and meeting concerns regarding adequacy of capital flows during the crisis. The extent to which each of the instruments that is in place is phased-out, also forms part of the exit policies.

SOME COMMON ISSUES ON THE EXIT STRATEGIES

Firstly, the existence of stimulus causes the standard indicators of monetary condition to be less reliable for assessing the evolving economic and financial conditions. The complexities in assessing the indicators are greater in respect of the developing economies that are undergoing structural transformation. In some countries there are some uncertainties regarding the sustainability of the recovery.

Secondly, there is a shift from managing convergence to managing divergence in the global economy. Management of the crisis could be coordinated at the global level, since there was serious threat of disruption in financial markets. There was a convergence of objectives among nations to avert the collapse of financial markets and depression, but that has now been replaced with divergence, since inflationary pressures have emerged in many economies while threat of deflation continues in several advanced economies.

Thirdly, the destination of exit is unclear. There is a need to exit from stimulus but it has to be towards a new normality that incorporates lessons from the crisis as well as management of the crisis. Some of the instruments used and unconventional measures taken during the crisis could form part of the permanent arsenal of monetary policy. In fact, the incorporation of financial stability as an objective of monetary policy is an example of the new normality. In other words, exit may not be in respect of all actions taken during the crisis. Further, exit may be partial or gradual, depending on the evolving circumstances.

Fourthly, the sequencing of exit in monetary policy will also depend on the progress in exit from related policies, especially in regulatory and fiscal policies. The state of financial market and its linkages with the real sector need to be assessed carefully. It is possible that the financial market and its indicators do not fully reflect the developments in the real economy due to the extraordinary situation.

Fifthly, the debate on exit strategies has to recognise the redistributive aspects as well as developmental aspects of exit policies. For example, the continued negative real interest rates for a prolonged period have adverse effect on savers and pensioners. The impact of inflation could be severe on vulnerable sections. At the same time, there is a widespread belief that inflation in the post-crisis period could be higher than what was during pre-crisis period, partly to provide policy flexibility to manage cycles and also to enable flexibility in management of huge public debt incurred during the crisis.

Sixthly, there are two sides to the exit from stimulus, namely, the response in terms of increase in aggregate demand from the private sector and correspondingly the withdrawal of the stimulus by public policy. The synchronisation between the two involves judgements on the part of both sides. However, there was convergence of interest in favour of easy monetary policy in managing the crisis which is now replaced by elements of divergence, since financial markets may be less enthusiastic for tightening of monetary policy in the short run. In such a situation, transparency and communication of monetary policies could pose issues. For example, there may be limits to spelling out in detail, in advance, the steps that are contemplated for exit due to the uncertainties and possible consequences of pre-commitment by policymakers. Explanation of actions after they are taken should, to some extent, make up for perceptions of lack of transparency in exit strategies. Further, some instruments could be discarded while others may continue to be in place but deactivated gradually, and communicating these in advance may constrain freedom of action for policy.

Seventh, in advanced economies where central banks have expanded the balance sheets significantly, the exit may involve contraction of the balance sheet. In the process, it is likely that the losses in the open market operations undertaken during the crisis would get crystallised. It may be necessary for central banks to communicate effectively the reasons for assuming the burdens of private sector under extraordinary circumstances.

Eighth, monetary policy may have to give greater weight to credit markets in assessing the restoration of normality. The banking system will, therefore, be critical to signal the conditions conducive to exit.

Finally, on a judgemental basis, it can be held that in managing the crisis, the government plays a more dominant role despite the monetary policy being the first line of defence. As the exit is designed, the disengagement between the government and central banks may be a process in which there may be conflicting considerations. In managing exit, the independence of central banks may be put to severe test since the short-term measures to avert a disaster result in burdens over medium term, and medium to long term is clearly the focus of central banks. Central banks may notice that stimulus can have elements of addiction, both for governments and financial markets.

CHALLENGES AHEAD FOR INDIA

There are challenges that are specific to policymakers in India, particularly to the RBI. Firstly, among some analysts, there is a perception that excessive stimulus was undertaken in the past. It is argued that the fiscal stimulus was more than necessary, and that it was partly driven by electoral compulsions. It is also noteworthy that most of the fiscal stimulus was in the form of additional expenditure, and mostly consisted of consumption in government. Similarly, it is argued that the monetary stimulus has been excessive. The amount of actual absorption of the refinancing facility was modest. Even in regard to the actual liquidity released, a large part was reabsorbed by the RBI under its Liquidity Adjustment Facility. It is also argued that some reduction in GDP that was observed soon after the crisis was partly on account of failure of agriculture and partly due to moderation in the growth of output that got synchronised with the global crisis as a result of the monetary policy actions taken earlier.

It is, however, possible to justify the extent of stimulus on two grounds, namely, the synchronisation of measures agreed through global initiatives, especially G-20 demanded such a stimulus by India; and it was better to be safe than sorry in a matter involving such a huge crisis. Overall, however, the early onset of inflationary pressures and the persisting liquidity do make the task of the monetary authorities significantly complex in withdrawing from the stimulus in place.

Secondly, there is a perception that exit has been delayed, and that policy actions for exit have been behind the curve. It is true that inflationary pressures were strong even as stimulus measures were being implemented, but the inflationary pressures were mainly attributed to the supply shocks in select commodities. It was only after a few months into the crisis that there was specific recognition about the presence of generalised demand pressures leading to underlying inflationary pressures. However, to the extent the inflationary expectations have started setting in, the task of exit becomes more challenging to the RBI.

Thirdly, external sector management is likely to be particularly difficult as exit is being managed. The current account deficit has accelerated significantly. The global conditions are uncertain and volatility in capital flows is not ruled out. While there is a widely shared feeling that India will attract strong capital inflows, it is necessary to recognise that among the major EMEs of Asia, India has persisting fiscal deficit and current account deficit which appears to be getting close to three per cent of GDP. Hence, a careful balance has to be kept in the management of capital account in terms of ensuring adequate flows to meet the current account deficits and, at the same time, avoiding excessive capital flows. This balancing is made even more complex by the predominance of portfolio flows (both in terms of stock and flow) to India relative to most other Asian economies, since admittedly portfolio flows are among the more volatile sources. The uncertainties in the global economy may add to the complexities.

Fourthly, the fiscal stimulus that has taken place was significantly over and above a structural fiscal deficit that already existed. Moreover, almost the whole of the stimulus was consumption expenditure, and more importantly, was in the nature of a recurring entitlement since most of them relate to salaries of public sector and rural employment programmes. In other words, there is limited scope for reduction in fiscal expenditure. However, withdrawal of tax concessions is possible, but is yet to take place. The higher growth will have to be the main stay for fiscal adjustments, rather than a deliberate significant exit from stimulus in view of the realities of political economy. Under the circumstances, a large burden of exit policy is likely to fall on monetary authorities. The regulatory policies have, in any case, reached normality, though it is too early to take a view on the possible excessive regulatory forbearance during the crisis that could impact the balance sheet of banks.

As against these unique challenges, India also has some unique strengths. Firstly, India has a large economy with impressive macro-economic balances. The upward trend in current account deficit observed recently is still modest. India's dependence on external trade is not very high and such trade is diversified. The innovative skills that India could command may help its export competitiveness. The investment and consumption demands are, by and large, balanced. In brief, India does not have significant macro-economic imbalances which need to be corrected as part of the post-crisis programme.

Secondly, the financial sector has exhibited strength and resilience. In particular, the banking sector is operating in a policy framework that is close to the regulatory reforms that are being considered globally. Hence, there is no serious regulatory rebalancing that is required as part of the post-exit scenarios, though there is need for reform of the financial sector to match the growing requirements of a developing economy.

Thirdly, several policy instruments that are in position provide ample scope to the RBI to calibrate them, depending on the evolving domestic and global situation. The balance sheet of the central bank has not expanded significantly, and hence does not require painful rebalancing.

Finally, the credibility of the RBI is considerable in its capacity to manage the crisis and maintain stability. India has been one of the earliest economies to initiate exit. It is, therefore, reasonable to expect that policymakers will successfully manage India's economy during challenges, when domestic compulsions may significantly diverge from global indications with regard to the policy direction.

Notes

1. *The Economist,* 17 November 2007, pp. 75–77.
2. Y. V. Reddy, "Some Comments on Macro-stability in the Indian Economy", 3 January 2008, BIS Review 4/2008, http://www.bis.org/review/r080114b.pdf, accessed 30 September 2010.

Index